Private Journal.

with the meteriology of each day, and thermometrical observations taken at 9 A. M. 12 M. and 4 P. M. — Fahrenheits' grade — and the instrument placed in a selected, shady place at the Office of the New Custom House N. Orleans.

T. K. Wharton
Camp, corner of Robin,
New Orleans
La.

QUEEN OF THE SOUTH
NEW ORLEANS, 1853-1862

THE JOURNAL OF THOMAS K. WHARTON

INTRODUCTION BY
SAMUEL WILSON, JR., F.A.I.A.

EDITED BY SAMUEL WILSON, JR., F.A.I.A.
PATRICIA BRADY AND LYNN D. ADAMS

REMEMBERING SAM WILSON
BY MARY LOUISE CHRISTOVICH

PUBLISHED BY
THE HISTORIC NEW ORLEANS COLLECTION
AND
THE NEW YORK PUBLIC LIBRARY

1999

The Historic New Orleans Collection is a museum, research center, and publisher dedicated to the study and preservation of the history and culture of New Orleans and the Gulf South. The Collection is operated by the Kemper and Leila Williams Foundation, a Louisiana nonprofit corporation.

Library of Congress Cataloging-in-Publication Data
Wharton, Thomas Kelah, 1814-1862.
    Queen of the South: New Orleans, 1853-1862: the journal of Thomas K. Wharton / introduction by Samuel Wilson, Jr. ; edited by Samuel Wilson, Jr., Patricia Brady, and Lynn D. Adams. — 1st ed.
        p. cm.
    "Remembering Sam Wilson by Mary Louise Christovich" — p.
    Includes index.
    ISBN 0-917860-43-8 (acid-free paper)
    1. Wharton, Thomas Kelah, 1814-1862 Diaries. 2. New Orleans (La.) — Social life and customs — 19th century. 3. New Orleans (La.) — Description and travel. 4. New Orleans (La.) Biography.
5. Architects — Louisiana — New Orleans Diaries. 6. Architecture — Louisiana — New Orleans — History — 19th century. 7. United States Customhouse (New Orleans, La.) — History. I. Wilson, Samuel, 1911- . II. Brady, Patricia, 1943- . III. Adams, Lynn D. IV. Historic New Orleans Collection. V. Title.
    F379.N55 W47 1999
    976.3505'092—dc21
    [B]
                                                                                99-44290
                                                                                CIP

© 1999 by the Historic New Orleans Collection
533 Royal Street
New Orleans, Louisiana 70130
Richard Koch Publication Fund
First edition. 2,500 copies
Printed in Canada

ACKNOWLEDGMENTS

The publication of *Queen of the South: New Orleans, 1853-1862, The Journal of Thomas K. Wharton* has been a collaborative effort calling for the cooperation and expertise of many people over a number of years. Richard Koch, a native New Orleanian, was one of the city's most prominent architects and preservationists; his firm renovated the complex of historic French Quarter buildings for General and Mrs. L. Kemper Williams now housing the galleries and administrative offices of the Historic New Orleans Collection. In a bequest to the Collection, Mr. Koch provided for the publication of original documents that illuminate the history of New Orleans, specifically indicating the Wharton journal's significance. This book is the latest of several volumes supported by the Koch Publication Fund, which was endowed with his gift.

Samuel Wilson, Jr., Mr. Koch's protégé and partner in the firm of Koch and Wilson, was both an active architect and the dean of architectural historians in the city. At his request, the journal, acquired by the New York Public Library from Thomas Wharton's widow, Emily Ladd Wharton, was photocopied and made available to researchers at the Collection. Mr. Wilson championed the publication of the journal, wrote the introduction to Wharton's life and career, and provided architectural annotation for this abridged edition, published jointly by the Historic New Orleans Collection and the New York Public Library.

Priscilla Lawrence, acting director of the Historic New Orleans Collection, and the board of directors of the Kemper and Leila Williams Foundation, which operates the Collection — Mrs. William K. Christovich, president, John E. Walker, Fred M. Smith, Charles A. Snyder, Meg Allan, and G. Henry Pierson, Jr., emeritus — have unstintingly supported the project through years of research, editing, and production.

Henry Krotzer, Jr., graciously read the entire manuscript and straightened out several knotty architectural attributions. He was a constant resource, willingly discussing problem footnotes on the spur of the moment, and contributed much to the accuracy of the book.

Louise C. Hoffman, the gifted editor of *The Historic New Orleans Collection Quarterly*, as well as other Collection publications, provided invaluable editorial assistance and eagle-eyed proofreading of each version of the manuscript. Gregory Osborn and Nancy Ruck worked assiduously on the enormous and seemingly endless task of annotation research. Mary C. Mees was indispensable in the final phases of copy editing, fact verification, and index checking, bringing precision, speed, and dependability to these and a myriad of other publications department tasks.

The journal was ably transcribed by Raimund Berchtold and Desirée Perrault. Linda Dawson of Koch and Wilson assisted Mr. Wilson in his editorial work. Roberta Frey and Jeanie Webb proofread the original transcription, and Linda Webster prepared the index. David W. Adams, Jason Wiese, and Siva M. Blake valiantly joined in the last weekend push of double- and triple-checking the index.

Special thanks are owed, as always, to the past and present staff of the Williams Research Center of the Collection and their extraordinary research expertise. Alfred E. Lemmon smoothed the path to publication at every turn, being particularly helpful in finding staff members for special tasks. Gerald Patout, Pamela D. Arceneaux, Mary Lou Eichhorn, Mark Cave, Sally Stassi, James Powell, Jessica Travis, and David Dibble of the research staff, as well as Warren Woods of registration, provided essential assistance.

The illustrations chosen to accompany Wharton's word pictures and sketches are an integral part of the book. John H. Lawrence generously devoted time to the selection of illustrations and gave informed advice on further searches, and John Magill shared his unerring knowledge of the New Orleans cityscape, reviewing all the illustrations for anachronisms and helping to avoid several errors.

David Dressing brought boundless enthusiasm to the task of picture research, going through the immense pictorial holdings of the Collection to assemble scores of possible illustrations.

Friends at other New Orleans institutions were most helpful in providing just the right image for a specific need: Kevin Williams of the Southeastern Architectural Archive, Tulane University Library; Jennifer Ickes of the New Orleans Museum of Art; James Sefcik, director of the Louisiana State Museum; and especially Claudia Kheel-Cox of the Louisiana State Museum, who interrupted her busy schedule to provide exceptional assistance. Sally Kittredge Reeves, archivist, and Maureen Reed Detweiler of the New Orleans Notarial Archives shared their gardening lore to identify trees and flowers mentioned in the journal.

The photography staff, under the able leadership of Jan White Brantley, incorporated the massive task of producing all of the transparencies for this book into their already hectic workload. Elizabeth Kellner was primarily responsible for this project, while Dustin Booksh and Chelsea Viles worked on a number of other publications. Ms. Brantley and her husband, photographer Robert S. Brantley, provided much-needed images of missing churches, taking time one weekend to capture St. Theresa of Avila. Chuck Patch provided computer expertise, and Steve Sweet and Terry Weldon contributed logistical support.

Moving this commission to the top of his long list of projects, well-known architectural artist Jim Blanchard researched and painted the map of Coliseum Place, graphically presenting Thomas Wharton's neighborhood. Not only a delight to the eye, the map will help the reader visualize the city as it was in the 1850s-1860s with its unpaved streets, open canals, and many empty lots.

Working with the staff of the New York Public Library was always enjoyable. Mimi Bowling, curator of manuscripts, has been the Collection's liaison for publication, solving problems and answering many queries on Wharton family genealogy and other necessary matters. Anthony Troncale provided excellent digital scans of Wharton's sketches on an impossible timetable, and

Benjamin Alexander coordinated photography and fielded endless questions. Richard Newman, former manager of publications, was always helpful during the initial phases of this project.

Heartfelt gratitude for the production of this book is due to two gifted individuals. Billie Cox brings an unerring sense of style to the art of typesetting, as well as a willingness to work ungodly hours. Artist and graphic designer Michael Ledet designed the first of his many books for the Collection more than twenty years ago; he always makes the extra effort to design publications as beautiful as they are useful, even taking his fax machine to the beach during the final stages of preparing this book for press.

Collaborating with all these talented people has made our work a pleasure.

EDITORIAL METHOD

Queen of the South: New Orleans, 1853-1862, The Journal of Thomas K. Wharton is an abridged edition of Thomas Wharton's journal, which comprises hundreds of loose manuscript pages (constituting one volume), six bound manuscript volumes, and a sketchbook. The original manuscript is in the manuscripts and archives division of the New York Public Library, which is co-publishing this volume with the Historic New Orleans Collection. Wharton wrote and sketched in ink, now much faded, on pale blue ruled paper. The bound volumes were rebound in brown cloth as a set by the library in 1937.

Thomas Wharton kept extensive notes on his early travels, but apparently did not begin keeping a journal until June 1853 when he was setting out on a five-month visit to Boston and New York. On loose pages (7¾ x 9½"), he began his "Notes of my Summer Tour of 1853," often accompanied by charming sketches, which he continued after his return to New Orleans in December. He also made drawings in a sketchbook (12 x 8¾").

Throughout the rest of his life, Wharton made entries in his journal almost every day. Still using the loose pages of the previous year, he began January 1, 1854, with a title page inscribed "Private Journal" and a declaration of his plan to record the temperature three times a day. During the succeeding years, he sometimes made sketches or wrote accounts of architectural projects on unused pages of earlier years; these entries have been placed in chronological order. In 1855 he began using larger bound books (varying from 11¾ x 8¾" to 11 x 9"), but with the same ruled blue paper.

Besides keeping his journal, in June 1854 Wharton wrote a lengthy account of his early life beginning with his family's journey from England to Ohio, continuing through his education and career in New York, and ending with his mother's death (1830-1834); the memoir was written in a small notebook (7¾ x 6¾"). Based on notes he made as a young man, it was used extensively in the introduction to this volume.

This published abridgment of Wharton's journal opens with the entry of December 8, 1853, on his return to New Orleans and closes with his last entry on May 7, 1862, shortly before his death. Because of the journal's great length and frequent repetitiveness, it has been abridged for publication. Slightly more than one-third of the journal is published here. Criteria for inclusion of entries included those with historical, social, intellectual, political, medical, or architectural interest, those that continued an ongoing story, and those with information on the development of the city. Generally, entries for an entire day were deleted; when only a portion of an entry was omitted, ellipses indicate that fact. At the Collection's Williams Research Center, an annotated transcription of the entire journal is available to researchers, as well as a photocopy of the original. All Wharton's journal sketches, but not his sketchbook, have been reproduced in this book.

In general, the transcription of the journal is literal. Spelling (including variants of names and places), capitalization, and punctuation have been retained as written with the following exceptions: each sentence begins with a capital letter and ends with a period; superscripts were brought down to the line with a period; dashes were changed to periods or commas when appropriate to meaning; temperatures were moved from the left margin to the first line of entries; and clearly accidental duplications were silently deleted.

Brackets, indicating editorial intervention, were used sparingly to clarify unrecognizable words, to expand abbreviations, or to supply illegible words.

Certain abbreviations common in the nineteenth century, now no longer in use, appear throughout the journal. "&c." is an abbreviation for "et cetera." In referring to the dates of letters, reports, and other documents, "ulto." is an abbreviation for "ultimo" (last month), "inst." for "instant" (the present month), and "proxo." for "proximo" (next month).

Every person or site mentioned in the journal is briefly identified in a note, except when no information could be found. In the index the descriptive note appears in bold for easy reference.

Illustrations were chosen to give the reader a visual tour of New Orleans in the 1850s-1860s. Contemporary depictions were preferred, but they could not always be found. When pictures from a later period were used, every effort was made to verify that the building or neighborhood still looked as much as possible as it did in Wharton's day. Unless otherwise indicated, all illustrations are from the holdings of the Historic New Orleans Collection; they are identified by an accession number.

The old St. Louis Cathedral and a corner of the Place d'Armes drawn by Thomas K. Wharton on his first visit to New Orleans, June 1845 (1974.25.14.169).

CONTENTS

In memory of Richard Koch

John H. Lawrence, photographer, ©1979

Much about Samuel Wilson, Jr., who has edited and annotated this nine-year diary, was as "Naturally N'Awlins" as any of its most ordinary citizens.[1] And therein lies the paradox of a complex man who quietly seemed as surprised as anyone that he would, within his eighty-two years, create his own legends and stir enough architectural scholarship to reach across continents.

To many, he wore the patriarchal mantle of historic preservation. To some, Sam Wilson was both teacher and spokesman for the city's preservation activists, having taught architectural history at Tulane University for nearly forty years. To all, he was a kind and willing resource.

The candle of local fame may burn brightly within a person's lifetime,

[1] Frank Davis's "Naturally N'Awlins," a popular television feature of WWL-TV, first went on the air in 1981.

REMEMBERING SAM WILSON

but the possibility of enduring recognition grows dimmer with each passing generation. This, too, could happen to Sam, despite his authorship of hundreds of articles and publications and his contributions to scores of building restorations throughout the Gulf South.

Taped interviews capture some of Sam's history, his dreams, and a hint of the tasks begging to be undertaken.[2] Within these tapes, Sam outlined his life and credited many individuals who led him from project to project. He neither stumbled nor traveled alone; however, his wisdom and personal discipline allowed him to expand many original possibilities, perhaps beyond his own aspirations.

In 1980 Sam mentioned three wishes: to go to Uxmal in the Yucatan (as a student, he had won an award for his Mayan design in Frans Blom's class at Tulane), to publish the New Orleans section of the Wharton diary, and to restore the Napoleon House (originally known as the Girod House, built in 1814, probably by Hyacinthe Laclotte, and considered the finest example of the continuing French architectural influence). It was only the latter wish that Sam, realist above all, knew to be an impossible dream. He finally did see Uxmal, and the edited Wharton diary — with copious illustrations that far exceed his ambitions — is now in hand.

Photographs of a young Sam show a tall, thin man whose dark hair contrasted with his large light-blue eyes. These images do not suggest the gravelly texture of his strong voice, rarely raised, but always heard to the last auditorium seat. A New Orleans pronunciation, neither southern nor inappropriately colloquial, identified him with the city. His laughter matched the tenor of his voice, polite rather than exuberant, while a smile often accompanied a natural detachment.

Years later, Sam's mannerism of combing his fingers down his thick, gray mustache would call attention to his large, graceful hands. He always walked quickly with a slight forward, almost anxious tilt, as if he wanted very much to move on, and then would hesitate sometimes to look around and back, always keen and observant. These gestures may provide insight into his personality.

2 Abbye A. Gorin, ed., *Conversations with Samuel Wilson, Jr., Dean of Architectural Preservation in New Orleans* (New Orleans, 1991).

The year of Sam's birth — 1911 — coincided with the founding of the Louisiana State Museum by the Louisiana Historical Society. The museum's beginnings, at Jackson Square in the heart of the French Quarter, would have attracted little attention in the Carrollton section of New Orleans where Sam spent all of his formative years. Yet, the French Quarter and the state museum, neither of which he visited until college, became the crucible in his formation as architect and writer.

Like most New Orleanians, Sam accepted his snug, well-conceived neighborhood, and it is reasonable to believe that he was unaware — as a child — that Albert Diettel, architect/builder, had designed his parents' cottage on Burthe Street. Henry Howard's monumental Greek Revival courthouse, converted into McDonogh 23 — his grammar school on Carrollton Avenue — would cause reflection only years later. To Sam the significance of Warren Easton High on Canal Street, named to honor a distinguished public school superintendent, lay not in architect E. A. Christy's excellent new design, but in the fact that it was the only public high school for boys at the time.

Sam confessed that he had no idea where his ambition to be an architect came from, only that it sprang from his earliest memories and his attraction to every new building being constructed in the Carrollton area. And perhaps he would see sophisticated structures changing Chicago's skyline when, some summers, he and his brother and sisters visited their maternal grandmother.

Trained in the Beaux Arts tradition, Nathaniel Cortlandt Curtis, dean of Tulane's School of Architecture, is credited along with Moise H. Goldstein with introducing students to modern architectural theories from Europe. In 1927, at sixteen, Sam fell under these influences, apprenticing in the Goldstein firm throughout college and working there as a draftsman for many years. Regardless of the emphasis on modern architecture, Curtis and Goldstein, together with Richard Koch — and led by such French Quarter residents as Elizabeth Werlein — became the vanguard in the movement for a French Quarter renaissance.

Propelled by the thrust of modernism, neither university leaders nor students had time to cultivate the art of historic restoration. They rushed forward, as did universities throughout the nation, toward the promotion of glass, steel, and the new age.

Meanwhile, the Great Depression brought many talented people together in projects of the Works Progress Administration. One of these was the Historic American Buildings Survey (HABS), and Sam, hired by Richard Koch, began his career as a major researcher. There he "not only perfected his art of measuring and drawing buildings, but he developed research and writing skills to unravel and tell the story of an old structure's life."[3]

Sam read French adequately, an essential for colonial title transfers in the New Orleans Notarial Archives, but often required help with those in Spanish. Shyness may have inhibited him in speaking French.

Whereas working on the HABS study pointed Sam toward his life's avocation, traveling on an American Institute of Architects scholarship to Europe in 1938 solidified his direction. Not only had he learned of the importance of architectural renderings and survey maps, he now discovered that many Louisiana historians had overlooked or had never seen some of the important visuals in Paris's Archives Nationale or the Ministère des Colonies. Within his four months there, Sam acquired all he could trace, photograph himself, or have photographed on glass negatives, forming a foundation for his study of early Louisiana architecture. The imminence of World War II impinged on his European sojourn and forced his return home.

Always an avid Boy Scout and Sea Scout, Sam tried to enlist in the Navy when the United States declared war. Underweight and with poor eyesight, he was not allowed to enlist but did secure a place in the Coast Guard where he served throughout the war. His brother, a West Point engineer, was later killed in Burma.

Immersed in architectural history, Sam also became fascinated with his own family history. He toyed with the possibility that a Samuel Wilson listed on an 1819 New Orleans passenger list was indeed his Irish great-grandfather, but with the honesty he applied to all research he could only provide his progenitor with a certain date of 1824. How he would have liked this early relative to have shared space and words with the famous Benjamin H. B. Latrobe, distinguished father of Greek Revival architecture in America and architect of the U.S. Capitol, also listed aboard.

Latrobe research was to be one of the driving passions of Sam's life, certainly leading to his introduction in 1950 to Ellen Elizabeth Latrobe — who became his wife in 1951. One can only imagine the joy of the day, in the Baltimore cathedral, when Sam waited under Benjamin Latrobe's blue and gold coffered dome as Betty walked the lengthy, vaulted nave to meet him at the altar. Within these interior spaces of flowing lines and incredible light, Betty's grandfather, Ferdinand Claiborne Latrobe, seven-time mayor of Baltimore, had often been a worshiper.

Although his father took Sam and his brother to hear Huey Long's harangues in the late 1920s, political connections in the Wilson family were few. Only an early friendship with A. O. King — interim governor of Louisiana until Long, before taking his U.S. Senate seat, manipulated to get O. K. Allen elected governor — produced a contract to design a house for King in Lake Charles. Sam never objected to others securing and including him on state or city jobs, but currying favor was simply not his style.

Sam did not discourage Betty's natural interest in politics when she helped found the Independent Women's Organization that successfully elected one of its members, Bland Bruns, to the state house of representatives. Betty also joined with friends July Waters, Pokey McIlhenny, and hundreds of college students in Chep Morrison's Broom Stick Parade. This successful ground swell helped rout the Old Regulars from City Hall. Betty, a true activist, coordinated her interests with those of her husband in a forty-year marriage, ended by her death in 1991.

Many historians of Louisiana painted florid, fanciful histories. Sam never did. Some might consider his style dry, but his fact-filled

3 Ibid., xix.

pages defy editing — disturb one line and you entertain the loss of an important thread. Every publication and lecture brought him closer to being identified as an architectural historian, an identity he did not relish over that of architect. Nevertheless, when post-war activities brought so-called "progress," his scholarship was in demand.

Mass demolitions of derelict mansions along rivers and bayous, on major and minor avenues, deep into old tree-lined neighborhoods, became the order of the day. Sam, who had accompanied an older Richard Koch on hundreds of photographic excursions to record plantations and thousands of individual architectural gems within the city, was shocked that the populace, in the main, had no idea of its heritage.

Down went the Olivier Plantation on lower Chartres Street — then the Delord-Sarpy house on Howard Avenue followed by more mansions, cottages, corner stores, row houses, warehouses, cemeteries.

Appalled by the loss of landmarks and futile attempts to save them, Sam and others, including Martha Robinson, Harnett Kane, Ray Samuel, and Leonard Huber founded the Louisiana Landmarks Society in 1950. Sam became its first president and remained so for the next six years. But he hated confrontation and was by nature not argumentative.

Sam thought himself first and foremost an active architect with a secret creative desire to build new structures, although his firm Richard Koch and Samuel Wilson, Jr., (formed in 1955 and renamed Koch and Wilson in 1970) was to be credited with no less than 1,500 renovations. He genuinely believed if you presented the facts concerning preservation that reasonable business and civic leaders would look and listen. But more often than not, they wouldn't. The concept of neighborhood ambience and architectural integrity seemed an emotional thing, inapplicable to individual structures when demolition provided space for new, albeit discordant buildings.

In one important instance, Sam broke with the bulk of the preservation community. Although he earnestly desired the removal of truck traffic from the riverfront neighborhoods — and participated in a study sponsored by the Bureau of Governmental Research — his ambivalence about the Riverfront Expressway (he thought a grade level roadway might work) caused consternation among preservationists.

And yet, the morning he died, October 22, 1993, he was scheduled to speak at City Hall against the demolition of an Eero Saarinen-style building, the Rivergate, designed by his good friend Buster Curtis — Nathaniel Cortlandt Curtis, Jr. This, despite the fact that the Jeanne d'Arc Plaza, a trim Koch and Wilson space connecting the Rivergate at the foot of Canal Street to the Edward Stone ITM building, had already been demolished.

To his family and early friends, he answered to Junior. He never seemed annoyed when called Sam by those much younger than he, but he did appreciate being revered as Mr. Wilson after many of his own mentors had died.

He should be revered and remembered. He lived simply, without ostentation, amassing and disseminating hard-gathered historic information, not a great monetary fortune. His published works, from which he received no remuneration, were all donated to the causes promoting the best for his beloved city and state.

— *Mary Louise Christovich*
President, Kemper and Leila Williams Foundation

Mrs. Christovich and Mr. Wilson worked together in the preservation movement in New Orleans for nearly forty years, beginning in 1952 as founding members of the Friends of the Cabildo. They were fellow members of the Louisiana State Museum Board, crusaded to bring the National Register of Historic Places to Louisiana, and served together on the board of Save Our Cemeteries, Inc.

THE LIFE OF THOMAS KELAH WHARTON

(April 17, 1814-May 24, 1862)

Daily life in mid-nineteenth century New Orleans is vividly portrayed in the detailed diary kept by the English-born architect Thomas Kelah Wharton from 1853 until shortly before his death in 1862. The diary was preserved by Wharton's widow, Emily Ladd Wharton, who sold it to the New York Public Library in 1919.

Thomas Wharton was born in Hull, England, on April 17, 1814. In 1829 his father immigrated to the United States, buying a farm at Piqua on the Miami River in west central Ohio. The next year Mrs. Wharton with their four sons and two daughters followed, sailing on May 3, 1830, and landing in New York City a month later. Although he was not yet keeping a diary, sixteen-year-old Thomas began making notes on the family's journey. Twenty-four years later he compiled these observations into a narrative about his early life in America.

The Whartons left New York July 1, going up the Hudson River to Albany where they boarded a boat on the Erie Canal, arriving in Buffalo a week later. Sailing west on Lake Erie, they landed at tiny Portland, Ohio, near Sandusky, where their father met them with a carriage and pair of horses to drive to the farm. They finally arrived at their new home on July 17.

Farming on the frontier did not suit the Whartons, however, and they sold the Piqua property and removed to Dayton in the fall of 1831, on to Springfield, and then to Columbus in the spring of 1832, looking for a new place to settle. Later that spring they decided on Zanesville, where they took a house. Mr. Wharton bought a large warehouse on the Muskingum River, establishing a general forwarding and commission business. During these Ohio years, young Thomas continued to record the family's peregrinations and to make a series of landscape sketches now in the New York Public Library.

True to their English heritage, the Whartons were Episcopalians. Wharton's strong religious bent, so apparent in the diary entries of the 1850s, was revealed early. He frequently recorded details of churches, ministers (or lack of them), and sermons in his notes and in his later autobiographical narrative.

In 1832, shortly after he turned eighteen, Wharton began looking for a career, weighing the opportunity to enter business or to study architecture with the firm of the extremely prominent New York architect Martin Euclid Thompson. Wharton had been much impressed with the Tuscan-style Episcopal church in Columbus, which Thompson had designed. The circumstances of the architect's offering him a place are unknown. Perhaps Wharton had written to Thompson or perhaps the two met when the family was in New York in 1830. In any case, Wharton accepted this offer and set off for New York, arriving May 8, 1832.

In Martin Thompson's office, Wharton began his architectural training, drawing the classical orders from Stuart and Revett's *Antiquities of Athens*, one of the standard design sources of the day. Such apprenticeships were typical of the manner in which young men studied for a number of professions, including architecture and the law. Wharton lived with the Thompson family at 24 Howard Street. He attended services at various churches, among them the classical Ascension Church (Episcopal) on Canal Street, designed by Thompson. Soon however, the architect fell ill and was unable to attend to his pupil.

That same summer of 1832 a world-wide epidemic of Asiatic cholera reached New York City, creating a state of panic. Wharton was invited to "seek refuge" at the Hyde Park home of Dr. and Mrs. David Hosack, a mansion on the Hudson River designed by Martin Thompson in the "enriched Italian" style. There he roamed the picturesque countryside, making numerous pencil sketches, watercolors, and crayon drawings, and enjoying the company of the large family.

Dr. Hosack took a fatherly interest in the young man, admiring his drawings and purchasing a large landscape. He strongly advised against pursuing an architectural career in New York City and suggested that Wharton consider other occupations. When the Hosacks set off on their travels, the doctor arranged for Wharton to stay with Colonel Sylvanus Thayer, superintendent of the U.S. Military Academy at West Point.

Wharton left Hyde Park on July 31 by steamboat and arrived at West Point that afternoon, eventually passing several months as the genial Thayer's guest. Thayer encouraged Wharton to continue his landscape painting and oversaw his studies of mathematics and descriptive geometry. The young man also profited from the company and conversation of a number of prominent neighbors and visitors, including Gouverneur Kemble, Joel Roberts Poinsett, and General Winfield Scott.

Kemble was the proprietor of a large ironworks across the Hudson River at Coldspring. Because many of his workers were Catholic, he had become friendly with their pastor, Father O'Reilly, who was a frequent dinner guest. Kemble decided to build a Catholic chapel on a rocky point jutting into the river and enlisted Wharton to help him with the design. The simple, Tuscan-style Chapel of Our Lady, which still stands, was identified by Wharton as "the very first architectural design I was engaged on."

Another of Thayer's dinner guests was William Augustus Muhlenberg, an Episcopal minister who directed a boys school at Flushing, Long Island. Muhlenberg invited the young man to take charge of the school's drawing department, which had an enrollment of about sixty students, giving him two months to prepare for the new position. On Thayer's advice, Wharton accepted the offer, remaining at West Point in the interim to further his studies in drawing and mathematics.

Wharton received encouragement and material assistance from his friends — money for drawing materials from Kemble and technical books and a generous check from Thayer. Late in November he left West Point with great regret, feeling as though he were "leaving a second home" to take up his new position.

His first year went well as he enjoyed his students (not very much younger than himself), the facilities and situation of the Flushing Institute, and his frequent visits to New York City for cultural events or calls on acquaintances such as Martin Thompson and Thomas Cole, a pioneer of the Hudson River School of romantic landscape painting. After the end of the school session, in August 1833, he returned to Ohio to visit the family in Zanesville, finding them ensconced in a larger house with the warehouse and store well established. His parents approving his plans, Wharton returned to his teaching position, spending a good deal of his leisure time in painting — "my favorite employment."

The following summer, he returned to the Kembles at Coldspring, where he had memorable encounters with cultural celebrities, including the author Washington Irving and the portraitist Thomas Sully. Back at school in the fall, he learned with great sorrow of his mother's death. His autobiography breaks off at this time, but other sources show that he remained at the Flushing Institute.

Sometime within the next four years, Wharton's father left Ohio and married Mrs. A. M. Reddie of New Haven, Connecticut, a well-to-do widow who had traveled in the East Indies. Her house in New Haven, called Bhurtpore Cottage, was fancifully designed to reflect the Indian architecture she had seen. This became the family home, and Wharton spent his vacations there. He made a sketch in 1837, from which he had an engraving made in 1839 and which he copied again in 1855, of the place he called "our last home at the north and linked with some of pleasantest recollections of our lives." Of Mrs. Reddie, he wrote that "I became very much attached [to her] and we all found her a most kind and considerate stepmother."

The Flushing Institute failed during the financial crisis of the Panic of 1837, and Wharton joined Dr. Muhlenberg the next year in a new venture, St. Paul's College at College Point on Long Island Sound. He served as professor of the arts of design and descriptive geometry for a couple of years before moving on to a new Episcopal school, St. Thomas's Hall in Flushing, founded by Dr. Francis Lister Hawks, former rector of St. Thomas's Church in New York City. Hawks launched the school with great fanfare, erecting beautiful Gothic buildings for the accommodation of 120 pupils. Unfortunately, by 1843 his debts far outstripped his revenues, and he was forced to abandon the school to his creditors.

But Hawks and Wharton did not give up the dream of a school. In the summer and autumn of 1843 they made a tour of exploration in the South and opened, in partnership, a "university" at Holly Springs, Mississippi. In November of the following year, however, Hawks accepted the rectorship of Christ Church, an Episcopal congregation in New Orleans, leaving Wharton in charge of the fledgling institution in Mississippi.

Before agreeing to come to Christ Church, Hawks had insisted that a new church be built for him in the Gothic style: he intensely disliked the existing temple-style church, designed in 1835 by James Gallier, Sr., one of the city's most prominent architects. At Hawks's request, Wharton made sketches for the new church. There is an elevation in the New York Public Library entitled "First rough sketch of a design for Christ's Church, N. Orleans, T. K. Wharton, Holly Springs, Miss., 1845."

Wharton first visited New Orleans in May 1845, probably bringing the design to Hawks, who was already there. He remained in the city through the early summer, sketching such sights as St. Louis Cathedral. During this visit, Hawks and Wharton decided to give up the Mississippi school. Their prospects in New Orleans seemed bright so Wharton returned to close the school and "to wind up our affairs at Holly Springs, which I did very favorably."

He remained in Holly Springs through the summer and fall. On October 19, 1845, he was married by Hawks to Maria Huling, the eldest daughter of Judge Frederick W. Huling. After the newlyweds moved to New Orleans in December, taking rooms in a Camp Street boarding house, Huling sold his cotton plantation in Mississippi and moved the family to a sugar plantation in Plaquemines Parish, downriver from the city. Wharton became a valued member of the close-knit Huling family.

In New Orleans, Wharton had a ready-made opportunity in architecture with the firm of James Gallier, Sr. Gallier's son, James, Jr., had been Wharton's student both in Long Island and Holly Springs. This long relationship no doubt influenced Gallier's offer of a position to Wharton. And Wharton's employment no doubt influenced the granting of the $56,000 contract for the construction of Christ Church to Gallier's firm. The contract for the new church, to be built at the corner of Canal and Dauphine Streets, was awarded April 21, 1846, and refers to four plans and drawings — Wharton's work — furnished by Hawks. In his new position, Wharton made detail drawings for his own first New Orleans design.

Some years later, in his 1864 autobiography, Gallier would claim that the design was his: "I had to make so many alterations in the plan, before it could be made practically fit to build from, as to make it amount to a new design." A comparison of Wharton's drawing with photographs of the church as built, however, reveals no noticeable alterations from his original design.

Besides his work on Christ Church, Wharton executed large drawings in perspective for Gallier, among them the architect's design for the new Municipal Hall (now Gallier Hall) opposite Lafayette Square, from which a lithograph was produced in London. Building activity in the 1840s, however, was sluggish and the Whartons moved to the Huling plantation. There Wharton pursued his studies in architecture and continued to make drawings for Gallier.

Wharton's involvement with the construction of the huge New Orleans Custom House, the work that would take up the rest of his career, began while he was still working with James Gallier, Sr. Gallier had been chosen in 1844 by William Barrett, collector of customs, to prepare a design for the proposed building. But collectorships were notorious political plums: when a new party took control in Washington, Barrett was superseded as collector, and Gallier lost the commission. The architect was furious, particularly because he had received no payment for the drawings, which were not returned to him for nearly two years.

The new collector, Denis Prieur, called for a competition in which several architects submitted plans, including Gallier. Although the original plans have been lost, it is clear that Wharton assisted Gallier in this second round of proposals. Among Gallier's drawings in the Southeastern Architectural Archive of Tulane University there is a "Plan shewing the position of the New Custom House, N. Orleans, on the proposed site, J. Gallier Architect. Drawn & adapted by T. K. Wharton, New Orleans 1847."

Despite Gallier's hopes, Alexander Thompson Wood, accused by a bitter Gallier of backstairs politics, was chosen as architect in November 1847. His plan was favored, at least according to one of the building's commissioners, because it covered the entire square, not wasting any of the allotted space, and because it was the least expensive of the proposals being "more free from unnecessary ornament."

Wharton would apparently have liked to continue working for Gallier, but needed steady employment. He moved back to New Orleans in December 1847, renting a house at Prytania and Erato, and accepted a position at the Custom House in January 1848. He worked there for the next fourteen years, until federal occupation during the Civil War brought construction to a halt.

On April 11, 1848, Wharton's wife died of pulmonary consumption, and he was granted a six-month leave to spend with his in-laws on their plantation. During these months, no actual construction was taking place at the Custom House. The old buildings on the lot were being cleared, bids taken, and building materials ordered and delivered to the site — a great trapezoidal block surrounded by Canal Street and today's Decatur, Iberville, and North Peters streets.

On October 23, the day workmen began digging trenches for the huge building's foundation, Wharton resumed his duties at the Custom House. On November 1, on the recommendation of Alexander T. Wood and Lt. Col. William Turnbull, chief superintendent of construction, he was named clerk and draftsman at a salary of $90 a month. When the cornerstone of the building was laid on Washington's birthday, February 22, 1849, among mementos placed in the stone were documents, medals, coins, newspapers, and a roll of parchment with a long list of names beginning with President James K. Polk and descending through state, city, and local officials to Wood, Turnbull, and "T. K. Wharton, draftsman."

In January 1850, Wood went to Washington to try to get an increased appropriation for the work. Not only did he fail to secure the funds, but Wood, a notable hothead who had served time in prison for killing another architect during an altercation, managed to quarrel with Secretary of the Treasury William Meredith, who notified the commissioners in New Orleans on May 4 that Wood had been discharged. For the next three years, the direction of the Custom House construction was in constant turmoil.

John Roy, one of Wood's assistants, served as acting architect during Wood's absence and in the months following his dismissal. Meanwhile, James H. Dakin, the architect who was just completing the Louisiana state capitol building in Baton Rouge, a Gothic castle on the Mississippi, requested Wood's position from his Mexican War acquaintance, President Zachary Taylor. In July 1850 Dakin received the appointment and took up his duties.

The new architect immediately proposed drastic changes to the plan, including moving the main business room to the Canal Street side of the building and creating an open court in its place in the center of the massive structure. His patron, however, had died; although the new president, Millard Fillmore, submitted Dakin's nomination to the Senate in March 1851, it was not confirmed. After Dakin's rebuff, Fillmore nominated James Gallier as architect, but Gallier had retired and left the city. In September 1851 Dakin finally resigned and was succeeded by Lewis E. Reynolds, a respected New Orleans architect.

Meanwhile, Wood, who naturally opposed all Dakin's proposed alterations, managed to muster sufficient political support for his own appointment as a sort of oversight superintendent to ensure that the construction continued according to his own design. He and Reynolds battled until Reynolds finally gave up and resigned. While the leadership of the Custom House constantly changed, Wharton continued gamely in his position, which must have been filled with stress and insecurity.

Throughout these turbulent early years of Custom House construction, Wharton was a widower living alone in a rented house uptown. Then, in his late thirties, he met a young graduate of the city's public high school for girls. Sixteen-year-old Emily Ladd was born in New Orleans, the daughter of a New Hampshire couple. Her parents had separated; her father, a commission merchant, moved to Boston while her mother remained in New Orleans with Emily and her eight-year-old sister, Ellen.

In anticipation of his marriage, Wharton rented a house on Coliseum Square, a desirable residential neighborhood where a number of new houses were being built. This area was much closer to the Custom House than his previous home. Wharton, who was a prodigious walker, now had a convenient stroll to and from work on good days, with omnibuses available for foul weather.

The new frame cottage that Wharton rented was on Camp Street, one lot from the corner of Robin (now Euterpe) Street. It had three rooms with a fireplace in the living room; all the rooms opened onto a hall running the length of the left side of the house. Galleries shaded both front and rear. The yard, with a side alley leading to the backyard, was enclosed by the white picket fence typical of uptown residences. In the back were a cistern, privy, and a service building, containing the kitchen with its hearth, as well as servants' rooms.

It was to this snug little house that Wharton brought his bride, whom he married December 18, 1851, a few months before her seventeenth birthday. The new household included Emily Wharton's little sister and their mother, Emily Prescott Ladd, who was only four years older than the groom. In September 1852 Thomas Prescott Wharton, the Wharton's only child, was born and became the center of the family. There was also an Irish cook/maid who lived in the rear building, as well as a nursemaid for the first two years of little Tommy's life.

Although small, this house became Wharton's heart's delight. He took immense pride in the neatness of the family's domestic and housekeeping arrangements. He and the cook regularly shopped at open-air markets in the neighborhood, and he enjoyed gardening in the tiny front yard, cultivating the Lamarck [Lamarque] rose he so much admired, a white climber with abundant and fragrant blooms. When the house was sold early in their marriage, Wharton attempted to buy it because of his wife's attachment, but he was outbid at the auction. Nonetheless, they remained as tenants throughout their marriage.

During all the architectural controversies at the Custom House, Wharton had maintained the confidence of the various collectors and of the commission appointed to oversee the timely construction of the building. He became acting architect pro tem on matters relating to construction in September 1852, and then on November 16, he was promoted to general superintendent of the construction work, taking orders from the commissioners, while they searched for a permanent solution to their management problems.

Finally, in May 1853 Major Pierre Gustave Toutant Beauregard of the U.S. Army Engineers and a member of a prominent Louisiana Creole family assumed the post of superintendent, and the commission was dissolved. Beauregard proved an efficient superintendent and work on the building proceeded at a steady pace for the next nine years until it was halted by the Civil War. Wharton and his friend John Roy continued working diligently at the construction site; they were Beauregard's immediate assistants, as well as rivals for approval and promotion.

Shortly after Beauregard took command of the construction site, Wharton asked for a leave of absence to visit the North. The reason, he wrote, was "my increasing debility . . . my present prostration arises from my constant and unremitting attention to the duties of the office, ever since the commencement of the work, say for 5 years, summer and winter in this enfeebling climate."

His request was granted, and on June 25, 1853, he and his family boarded the steamboat *Aleck Scott* for St. Louis. Included in the party were Wharton and his wife, her mother and sister, their nine-month-old son, and the child's nursemaid. They joined a group of friends on the boat, including Alexander Dunn, a former steamboat captain, and Dr. John Wright, a pharmacist. Other friends on board included William Alfred Freret, the son of William Freret, former mayor of New Orleans who now served as collector of customs. Just beginning his career, the younger Freret was an architect with whom Wharton frequently discussed building projects in the city.

At the end of their river journey, the Wharton party continued overland, arriving in Boston on July 8, where they lodged in a boarding house. Ellen and Mrs. Ladd moved in with her parents, the Prescotts, "a fine hearty couple" in their seventies. The Whartons visited with many members of the Prescott family, Emily's maternal relations, including grandparents, cousins, and her uncle, George W. Prescott, with whom Wharton maintained a lifelong correspondence. They also spent time with her father, Darius Ladd. Besides enjoying the city, they made driving excursions and called on relatives throughout "the suburb villages" and countryside surrounding Boston.

Wharton also continued his professional endeavors while on leave. In Boston, he met with the architect Gridley J. F. Bryant, who had been appointed in 1848 to oversee the stonework for the Custom House, making sure that it was done according to plan. Wharton and Bryant had corresponded for some years and together they visited the granite quarries at Quincy, Massachusetts. Here Wharton made several sketches of granite being quarried for the Custom House. He also called on Bryant's future partner, the prominent Boston architect Arthur Delavan Gilman.

Throughout their stay, Wharton visited the Merchants' Exchange, where he could find the latest edition of the New Orleans *Picayune*. A piece of news of special interest to him was the marriage of Alexander T. Wood, the architect who had designed the Custom House.

The Whartons left Boston for New York in November. There Wharton called on his old friend Martin Thompson, with whom he had begun the study of architecture. The family returned home by steamboat, stopping at Cincinnati to visit one of Wharton's sisters. They arrived in New Orleans on December 7, 1853, after an absence of more than five months.

The Whartons could not have chosen a better year to leave the city. During their absence, New Orleans had been struck by the worst epidemic of yellow fever in its history. Almost 9,000 people had died of the scourge during that summer and fall. On their return, the Whartons discovered that many of their friends and acquaintances had died and that the city was full of empty houses and stores.

Wharton was back in his office the day after their arrival, arranging the documents and accounts that had accumulated during his absence. Emily Wharton and her mother spent the day cleaning and straightening their cottage so that when he arrived home in the afternoon, the house had resumed its "former pleasant and domestic look." That evening, he began a diary, selected portions of which are published in this book.

During the ensuing years, Wharton recorded significant events of his daily life in his diary, carefully reporting each day the temperature at 9:00 A.M., noon, and 4:00 P.M., as recorded by "the instrument placed in a selected shady place at the office of the New Custom House." He noted professional and social events, local elections, national and international affairs, church attendance and sermons, and illness in the family. He frequently mentioned the happiness he had found in family life, expressing his devotion to his wife and son.

Wharton and his wife enjoyed an active social life, often entertaining or being entertained at tea or dinner by friends. They attended the theater, concerts, exhibitions, and balls. They also visited the outdoor gardens of Carrollton and the shores of Lake Pontchartrain.

Wharton was quite religious, reading and pondering over theological matters and recording sermons that struck him as particularly effective. The Episcopal church was the church of his youth, and for the first four years of their marriage the Whartons attended the Church of the Annunciation, an Episcopal church on Annunciation Square, five blocks from their home. But Emily and her mother never really took to the liturgy and order of worship of the Episcopalians, and Wharton eventually found the church "altogether too far off."

The new Coliseum Place Baptist Church, built in 1854, was only a block down Camp Street, and they purchased a pew there in 1855. The minister, W. C. Duncan, became a close family friend, and Wharton served as architect for the completion of the church tower and for some interior work. For several years, Wharton was content with the Baptist church and its doctrines. Later, perhaps influenced by his friendship with Episcopal bishop Leonidas Polk, he reverted to his original beliefs. For the last few years of his life, he seldom attended any church although the ladies continued to worship regularly at Coliseum Place.

In addition to his position at the Custom House, Wharton maintained an active architectural practice. A good deal of his work was done for the Episcopal Church, beginning with his design for the original Christ Church. He designed a college in Austin, Texas, for his brother-in-law Charles Gillette, an Episcopal priest. At the request of Bishop Polk, he submitted a design for the University of the South in Sewanee. He designed new doors and an organ loft for St. Paul's Episcopal Church and a pulpit for Christ Church, made in New York by John Gallier, the architect's brother.

Other notable architectural projects included the Methodist Steele Chapel, the Seamen's Home, a Baptist church, several warehouses, a cotton press, and the splendid residences of A. W. Bosworth and Paul Cook. The Bosworth house, which is still standing at 1126 Washington Avenue, is the most architecturally important of Wharton's designs. The elegant two-story center hall house, designed in 1859, has an unusual bowed front gallery. The Cook residence on St. Charles Avenue between Joseph and Arabella, completed in December 1861, was his last project and his largest. The mansion and all outbuildings were of brick and included such modern conveniences as gas and running water. The extensive lot was enclosed by an iron palisade.

Wharton frequently walked uptown to Lafayette, in the area today known as the Garden District, to observe the mansions being built there. A keen architectural observer, he commented on notable buildings, often making sketches as well.

He was also active in community affairs. He joined the Academy of Sciences and served two terms on the school board for the first district. As a school board member, he was diligent, interviewing prospective teachers and principals, visiting schools to hear recitations, and arranging a lyceum series for the benefit of the schools. He was also appointed secretary of the Board of Commissioners for Leveeing, Draining, and Reclaiming Swamp Lands for the first district.

As the 1850s wore on and tension between North and South became more intense, Wharton began to comment often and passionately on political and sectional affairs. Although he was born in England and had spent his youth in the North, Wharton was a committed southern loyalist, defending states' rights and raging against the "demonic" actions of northerners. From the time of Lincoln's election in 1860, he supported the secessionist movement and felt Louisiana had no choice but to join the Confederacy.

In the interim between the presidential election and secession, Beauregard resigned as superintendent of the Custom House because he had been appointed superintendent of West Point. With the secession of Louisiana, he returned to New Orleans and accepted a command in the new Confederate army.

On January 15, 1861, Wharton succeeded Beauregard as superintendent of the Custom House, the appointment he had so long desired. But by the end of the month, he was no longer reporting to the secretary of the treasury of the United States, but to the new Confederate government. He was quite satisfied with the arrangement, finding that his requests for payments were met promptly; he continued resolutely with the building's construction as long as possible.

He acquired many new obligations, however, as the South began to prepare for war. The great store of supplies at the building site was a much sought-after prize, and he tried to make sure that the materials were properly distributed. He also was involved with war work, adapting much of the Custom House to the production of cannons and other weapons. In a pocket diary, John Roy commented on the mental and physical strain that Wharton was experiencing: "I believe he will go out of his mind in consequence of the mighty responsibility that rests upon his shoulders."

As the war progressed, fortifications were thrown up above and below the city, temporary encampments of troops were situated throughout the city, and the U.S. Navy blockaded the mouth of the Mississippi River. Although he frequently asserted his confidence in a Confederate victory, Wharton was becoming overwhelmed and agitated. He apparently began drinking heavily, although his diary gives no indication of a problem with alcohol. Roy wrote on April 2, 1861: "Mr. T. K. Wharton inquired whether I had said he went too often to the corner [that is, to a tavern]. Told him I had said so and was sorry that what I said was true. . . . after some talk, he began to think so himself."

The Federal fleet under the command of Flag Officer David G. Farragut broke the chain barrier, which was the Confederate defense of the Mississippi River downriver, and ran past Forts Jackson and St. Philip to capture New Orleans without a battle on April 25, 1862. Wharton was devastated. Federal troops soon occupied the Custom House, the largest government building in the city, and all construction work there ceased. On May 6, 1862, Wharton attended the regular monthly meeting of the draining commission. The next day he wrote the minutes of the meeting and sent notices for a meeting on May 10. Here the journal abruptly ends.

Apparently Wharton was lost without his regular routine at the Custom House. He was also unable to take up new architectural projects in an occupied city. According to Roy, Wharton's drinking was out of control, and his health, never robust, began to fail. He died May 24, 1862, and was buried in the Girod Street Cemetery the following day — a cold, rainy Sunday. Roy wrote of the funeral: "This is an awful end to a man possessing the finest intellect with commanding talents, industry, and a love for his family to an astonishing degree."

Emily Wharton continued to live in the cottage on Camp St. for some years with her mother, sister, and son. In looking for employment as a teacher, she was no doubt aided by Wharton's exemplary service as a school board member. She eventually became the principal of the Clio Boys and Girls School on Clio Street between Prytania and St. Charles. Her son, Thomas Prescott Wharton, became associated with the dry goods establishment of Isaac S. West, Jr., at Magazine and Canal. The family moved to another house in the same neighborhood and continued to attend the Coliseum Place Baptist Church. Ellen married Henry W. Clark, and Mrs. Ladd survived her son-in-law by twenty-seven years, dying in 1889.

Sometime after 1895, Emily Wharton and her son moved to New York City. There Thomas Wharton married Louisa Cameron; they had no children, and she predeceased him. The Whartons suffered considerable financial reverses, and Emily moved into St. Luke's Home in 1908, the beneficiary of an endowment. Thomas died two years later on May 13, 1910. Doubtless because of financial problems, the widow sold her husband's sketches in 1914 and his diary in 1919 to the New York Public Library. She outlived her family, dying June 4, 1932, at the age of ninety-seven.

But Emily Wharton never outlived her love and admiration for the husband with whom she had shared more than ten happy years. She described him as "a man of culture, refinement — & polished address — a fine conversationalist — a dear lover of Nature — a Christian gentleman of the highest type. A member of the Church of England & later of the American Protestant Episcopal Church. A devoted husband and father — a loyal friend — a man of rare ability & virtues. Fine face & figure — tall & well proportioned. . . . Gifted as an artist, in early life he painted in oils (landscapes) & also made many drawings & sketches in India Ink, Sepia and pencil & Water Colours — all of which were highly appreciated by competent judges."

She admired his "happy, cheerful disposition, well stored and cultivated mind," writing that "he had the tenderness and refinement of a woman, united to the strength and virility of a manly man."

— *Samuel Wilson, Jr., F.A.I.A.*

New Orleans in the 1850s

It was the golden age of New Orleans history. During the decade that Thomas Wharton kept his journal, the city was indisputably queen of the South. It was an age of fortunes made and multiplied, of doubling population, of civic beautification, of dizzying technological advances — while the future smilingly promised more good times ahead. International rather than provincial, this least southern of southern cities outshone its urban rivals in the South, challenging New York as the nation's greatest port. A sharp-eyed observer walking the streets of the city in the 1850s found much to set down in his journal.

As with all boom times, the glitter was a little edgy, a touch frenetic, but all the more exciting for it, momentary downturns merely dramatizing the new heights reached by the recoveries. In the fifty years since the Louisiana Purchase of 1803, New Orleans and the vast new western territory had enticed entrepreneurs and businessmen who saw unlimited opportunities waiting to be exploited. The American victory at the Battle of New Orleans in 1815, climaxing the War of 1812, sealed the city's place solidly, if exotically, within the United States. The years since had delivered handsomely on those early hopes.

The dark underside to this gilded splendor was slavery. The best of times for some, it was the worst of times for the slaves upon whose labor the plantation economy rested so heavily. The cotton boom of the 1850s seemed to hold out the lure of boundless prosperity, but the era was destined to end abruptly and forever. New Orleans would never again be so rich or important.

The source of the city's great wealth — indeed the only reason for New Orleans to exist — was its commanding location on the Mississippi River. From the days when a few swashbuckling Frenchmen had come from Canada to extend the French colonial empire along the Gulf and up the Mississippi, the new city had been destined for international trade. As part of an expansive American nation, New Orleans was located in the right place — at the terminus of the vast Mississippi Valley watershed, the middle third of the United States — at what became the right time.

Down the river and its tributaries poured uncountable shiploads of cotton, sugar, wheat, corn, lumber, lead, liquor, building materials, and all the other commodities of a burgeoning nation. East-west roads were nonexistent or horrible: it was cheaper and faster to ship downriver. At the port of New Orleans goods were loaded onto sailing ships, their deep holds crammed with cargo for the markets of the Northeast or Europe.

From the colonial period, produce had been floated down the Mississippi to market, but the river's powerful current made serving the needs of the growing cities, towns, and farmlands upriver virtually impossible from New Orleans. The advent in 1811 of steamboats on the western waters — miraculously, the aptly named *New Orleans* survived the New Madrid earthquake, when the river ran backward and entire towns and a flotilla of boats disappeared — powered the commercial boom that followed.

By the 1850s river steamboats were almost as impressive as their legends. They were huge and fast, as ornate as wedding cakes, and capable of carrying immense loads of freight and passengers. In some ways the boats coddled their passengers, stuffing them like Strasbourg geese and providing grand salons for their social pleasures, but they were essentially cargo boats.

Freight, especially cotton, paid the bills on the big steamers, and passengers came a distant second. Captains and owners loaded boats to the groaning point, not in the hold (precluded by their shallow draft), but outside on the decks and guards. At some seasons, passengers were imprisoned inside giant walls of cotton bales — an inconvenience certainly, but also a fire hazard. Cotton bales were so flammable that any spark could send a wildfire sweeping through the boat.

Woodpiles to fuel the boats' furnaces, conveniently at hand for the stokers, also easily caught fire. The gravest danger, however, came from the huge steam-filled boilers driving the paddlewheels. As captains piled on heads of steam to outdistance their rivals, overstrained boilers could explode, blowing up or scalding passengers and crew with superheated steam and setting the boat afire. Spectacular explosions often claimed hundreds of casualties, particularly when boats were near the dock. Sensible men like Wharton argued for separate passenger and freight boats, but economic realities prevailed.

The river was the true main street of New Orleans: the city hugged the banks of the Mississippi's sweeping crescent, lined with the smokestacks of steamboats and the masts of ships, as thick as floating forests. All the important businesses, attorneys offices, warehouses, cotton presses, and retail stores were within a few blocks of the river. There clustered the factors, brokers, and wholesalers, the middlemen for the flood of trade, as well as the bankers who provided loans, currency, letters of credit, and all the intricate financial apparatus of trade.

The levee along the river was a broad, open esplanade stacked with the goods of the world, where New Orleanians went to do business, to shop, to meet friends, to get the latest news from arriving boats, to gossip and stare, to promenade and perhaps catch a bit of breeze off the river. The levee stretched for many miles up and down the river to protect the low-lying, swampy land from flooding.

In the spring when the river was at its highest, it sometimes flowed over the top of the levee for a few days. As long as the levee held, river water quickly ran off into the gutters and drainage canals that emptied into the swamps at the back of town. Overflowing held no terror compared to a break in the levee.

The Mississippi rushing downstream exerted immense pressure on the levee. When a weakened section collapsed, the powerful current boiled through, opening a gaping passage through which the river poured, flooding many square miles. Known as crevasses, these breaks in the levee could not be repaired until the level of the river dropped. Even after a crevasse was closed, floodwaters might remain trapped behind the levee for months. These disasters attracted fascinated sightseers, a few of whom inevitably slipped and were sucked to their deaths in the flood. Crevasses warned of the levee's fragility and the city's vulnerability to the river it depended on.

But the river's promise, not its danger, drew the thousands upon thousands who flocked to the city. Besides successful American (and some European) businessmen who came with capital to start at the top, there were many others with get-rich-quick schemes, professionals seeking wider clienteles, and countless ambitious young men eager to work their way up, starting as clerks and office assistants.

Driven by more basic needs were the Irish, German, and other impoverished immigrants seeking a better life. Many kept right on moving after landing in the port of New Orleans, seeking fairer prospects in St. Louis and points north and west. But the Irish in particular stayed to compete for jobs as manual laborers or servants. There were also the most transitory inhabitants: despondent blacks from the old plantations of the eastern seaboard sold "down the river" at the city's slave auctions to endure lives ever more onerous on raw new plantations in the Deep South.

The city expanded immensely to take in this flood of new inhabitants. Times couldn't have been better for architects, builders, and the construction business in general. Expansion, however, was strictly dictated by the geographical facts of life: most of New Orleans was below sea level, and all of it was below the level of the river. Firm ground lay in a relatively narrow strip along the river, bounded in the rear by miles of gloomy swamps, called by the French "drowned woods." Wharton vividly described "the heavy growth of Cypress, and the tangled underwood & vines which mantle over the slime."

The colonial city had consisted of a few square blocks (what is today called the French Quarter) with its main square facing the river. Of necessity, new faubourgs, or suburbs, had to be situated at either end of the old town. By the 1850s the old city was a very mixed proposition; changes had occurred almost house by house, rather than block by block. Free people of color tended to live here and in the downriver suburbs. Many wealthy old Creole families maintained elegant townhouses next door to what had become slum tenements for immigrants; others had built new mansions on Esplanade Avenue. Major P. G. T. Beauregard, the superintendent of the Custom House and Wharton's admired chief, was very representative of his heritage. As a widower, he lived in the old town; when he remarried — the lady also a member of the Creole elite — they lived in a grand house on Esplanade.

Most parts of town were filled with boarding houses, occupied by winter visitors, couples who hadn't yet set up housekeeping, and the several thousand single men who resided in the city, as well as the many transients — ship captains, entertainers, gamblers, painters, writers, adventurers, exiles, salesmen, and all other manner of travelers. New Yorker A. Oakey Hall wrote superciliously that New Orleans was called "the boarding house of these United States," estimating that every tenth house rented furnished rooms.

Examination of censuses, city directories, and sacramental records has disproved the old myth of Canal Street as an impassable barrier between implacably hostile Creoles and Americans: intermarriage was always common, and a mixture of ethnic groups lived in every neighborhood of the city. Nonetheless, wealthy American businessmen tended to gravitate to the uptown suburbs, where spacious lots were inexpensive and readily available.

The most popular of these areas was the independent city of Lafayette, which was incorporated into New Orleans in 1852 as its fourth district. In the area of Lafayette today known as the Garden District, many of the city's wealthiest businessmen built mansions in an eclectic variety of styles. As an architect, Wharton followed this building activity closely, and he frequently walked around the area, observing, commenting on, and sometimes sketching the grand new houses.

Immigrants clustered in tenements in the older parts of town, along the wharves with their stench and refuse, or at the back of town where the city dissolved into quagmires. Past Rampart Street, the old city boundary, plank roads pushed into the swamp, wooden gunwales framing gutters filled with "green stagnant ooze." Wharton described an area littered with trash, old clothes, slinking dogs, and screaming children. He noted: "From within the yards, alleys, open doors and windows issued fragmentary specimens of every language spoken under the canopy of heaven."

The city could expand so far beyond its original boundaries because modern public transportation had arrived. In the past, people who didn't own horses or carriages had to hire them from a livery stable or walk. Now horse-drawn coaches called omnibuses (picture a stage coach with a door at the rear) followed regular routes through the city, and the age of the railroad had arrived. Street railroads with passenger cars, pulled first by mules and then by small steam engines, reached out to the shores of Lake Pontchartrain. Wharton grumbled at their popularity: "an intensified nuisance rather than a convenience, for at the cheap rate of 5 Cents they are overwhelmed with all the 'Oi polloi' of the City and environs." In the 1850s railroads also began to run from New Orleans to Louisiana and Mississippi cities not accessible by the river, a great convenience for travelers.

Public and quasi-public buildings, too, were becoming a matter of civic pride. The new City Hall on Lafayette Square, today called Gallier Hall in honor of its architect, James Gallier, was a fine example of Greek Revival architecture. St. Louis Cathedral, the Cabildo, and the Presbytere were rebuilt or remodeled, and Jackson Square was renamed and redesigned. A grand new opera house celebrated high culture, and the city dedicated impressive statues to its heroes — Andrew Jackson, the victor of the Battle of New Orleans, and Henry Clay, political leader and patron saint of businessmen.

The federal government recognized the importance of New Orleans to the nation's economy in the usual manner of the day — a grandiose building program. A branch of the U.S. Mint on Esplanade Avenue supplied the South's hunger for currency, and a new marine hospital was begun in 1857 to care for the thousands of sailors who landed at the port in the course of a year.

But the most ambitious of the government's projects was a huge new custom house, reflecting the immense volume (and value) of commerce that passed through the port. The New Orleans Custom House, which provided Wharton employment for the last fourteen years of his life, was the largest federal building in the nation at the time, larger even than the U.S. Capitol. Overseeing its construction was certainly no sinecure, given that all the essential building materials — iron, bricks, granite, marble — had to be shipped in and that the city's soil was very unstable, shifting and subsiding, causing buildings much smaller than this to settle unevenly and crack. But the challenges were successfully met, and the massive granite structure is today a feature of Canal Street.

The romantic life of antebellum New Orleans, false or exaggerated in almost every particular, has been a staple of film and fiction. Wharton's journal is an antidote to such mythology because it presents a realistic view of middle-class life. He was a professional man, an architect proud of his ability to earn a decent salary, for most of his career somewhat less than $2,000 annually. On that salary, he could support a family comfortably and enjoy a standard of living that he found very agreeable.

When Wharton married in 1851, he brought his wife home to a small cottage without further ado; wedding trips were only for the wealthy. Emily Wharton's mother and little sister moved in with them, a common arrangement for extended families. Within a year, the Whartons' only son was born. By today's standards the home was quite small for so many inhabitants, but to the family it was snugly filled with every comfort and quite a few luxuries.

The cottage had three rooms, the back room partitioned into two tiny bedrooms. There was only one fireplace — in the parlor — so the chilly bedrooms would have encouraged quick dressing in the winter. With such limited space, rooms had multiple uses. The dining area, at different times, was in the parlor or the front bedroom. Although grand mansions had indoor plumbing, chamber pots and a backyard privy served the Whartons' needs. A large wooden cistern behind the house collected rainwater for drinking. The three adults and two children lived cozily in rooms lit by coal oil lamps and candles (modern gaslight was not installed until 1861), finding plenty of space for their daily activities and the entertainment of guests.

Wharton's garden was also small — his lot measured only 31' x 127' overall. He loved roses and chose for his front gallery a profusely blooming white climber called the Lamarque, first propagated in France twenty years before. He always spelled it Lamarck, however, suggesting that he might have purchased his roses from a German nurseryman. In front of the house were china trees (chinaberries), ubiquitous throughout the urban South. Basking in the mellow southern heat, they were quick growing and hardy, with lovely purplish blooms in the spring and yellow berries in the fall. True they shed at every season, but with unpaved streets and open gutters, their debris wasn't much of a problem.

The nineteenth century was disgustingly malodorous. After all, vehicles were horse- or mule-drawn, regular bathing was uncommon, open gutters clogged with sewage lined the streets, and garbage was frequently left to fester. No wonder sweet-smelling plants — sweet olives, jasmine, gardenias, roses — were planted at the entrances to homes, not just for their beauty, but to counteract the pungent smells of the street.

Anyone in New Orleans with even a toehold in the middle class expected to employ live-in servants. At the Whartons', a tiny servant's room adjoined the kitchen in a small detached building in the backyard. Although Creoles had black servants, slave or free, Americans generally found white immigrants more comfortable as domestics. From the time of their marriage, the Whartons employed a series of Irish cooks, who were also maids of all work. When the baby was born, they also hired a German nursemaid who remained with them for two years. These untrained, uneducated young women fresh from the countryside were willing workers, but they knew little of middle-class mores.

Wharton was frequently incensed at Irish servants and workmen, waxing sarcastic about their ignorance of asparagus or boiled puddings, attempted compliments ("blarney"), impudent demands for raises, and religion. Like most Protestants of the time, he was anti-Catholic to the bone. Originally an Episcopalian, he attended the neighborhood Baptist church to please his wife, endorsing a sermon comparing New Orleans to Jerusalem in the days of its approaching doom, a city "full of wickedness."

American Protestants, definitely including Wharton, were strongly sabbatarian, which meant they refrained not only from work, but also from pleasure or travel on Sunday. In their eyes, New Orleans Catholics were regularly guilty of desecrating the Sabbath. Attendance at morning mass was of course mandated (a duty more frequently observed by women than men), but then the rest of the day was regarded by Catholics as a day of rest and amusement. Their Sunday activities included visiting, games, sports, dancing, hunting, parties, the theater, and even gambling: to Catholics, innocent pastimes; to Protestants, deep-dyed sin.

The Whartons' social life was simple — rambles around the city, downtown shopping excursions topped off with sodas and ice cream, streetcar or carriage rides to river and lakefront resorts, visits with friends, concerts, lectures, the occasional free ticket to the opera. For the children, there were parties, circuses, and such rare treats as a hippopotamus. To the delight of art lovers like Wharton, famous paintings were taken on tour by entrepreneurs and exhibited around the country; locally they were shown in large halls because of the crowds who flocked to see them.

Many of the family's entertainments were meant to capture faraway places in both time and space. Panoramas did both, sometimes picturing foreign scenes, sometimes dramatizing the Bible or moral tales. At home, the stereoscope, a viewing device which gave a three-dimensional effect to photographic cards, seemed to Wharton "apparently real, real." Who needed to travel, he wondered, "with such an instrument as this at home, and such scenes imprinted as you would desire to visit."

Public celebrations were generally patriotic or civic in nature, such as the Fourth of July or Washington's birthday, marked by concerts, military reviews, parades, and speeches. The unveiling and dedication of the statues of Andrew Jackson in the renamed Jackson Square and of Henry Clay on Canal Street at Royal were vast civic events with hundreds of people gathering for the ceremonies. Companies of volunteer firemen, with their quasi-public status, annually entertained the city with their parade. Wharton particularly enjoyed inviting his family and friends to climb to the top of the Custom House walls for a bird's-eye view of these festivities.

Thanksgiving was not a national holiday with a fixed date in the 1850s; rather each state's governor declared — or didn't — a day of thanksgiving sometime before Christmas. The traditional feast of turkey, however, was generally respected. Christmas was celebrated quietly within the family with the exchange of a few gifts purchased on Christmas Eve. The parlor was decked with branches of myrtle, arbor vitae, and wild orange, their fruit serving as decoration. German innovations were being introduced in the city in the 1850s — evergreen wreaths and Christmas trees were both mentioned by Wharton for their novelty.

The custom on New Year's Eve, Wharton noted, was "to keep up a continual firing of guns, pistols and crackers all night long on the demise of the old year." The observance of New Year's Day itself was much more to his taste. It was a day of formal calls ruled by fixed conventions, their exactly graded levels of civility worthy of Chinese mandarins. He was immensely proud of his young wife receiving callers at home while he bustled about the city calling on acquaintances at homes and hotels, exchanging greetings with other men bent on the same errand, and preening himself on the number of calls he made.

The carnival season preceding Lent, a longtime tradition among New Orleans Catholics, was gradually adopted by American Protestants (the celebration, not Lent). Grand balls at the St. Charles and St. Louis hotels were crowded and popular affairs. The Whartons occasionally were invited to these balls and danced away the night with pleasure. But Wharton censured the ladies' excessive décolletage and such modish dances as the galloping polka and the sensuous waltz with its "intimate wreathings and intertwinings of the sexes." He warned himself: "Regular, legitimate, successful business operations harmonize but ill with the nightly orgies of our badly contrived fashionable assemblies."

Mardi Gras or Fat Tuesday, the last day of carnival hedonism before Lenten strictures began, was celebrated in the streets by the rougher elements of the population with public revelry and drunkenness. A much-applauded innovation of 1857 was a torchlit parade of decorated floats put together by the Krewe of Comus, a group of young American businessmen costumed and masked for the occasion.

Among his many interests as a scientifically inclined man, Wharton included the weather. Like George Washington, he recorded daily temperatures and commented, sometimes at length, on general weather conditions. Hurricanes in particular struck without warning and inflicted tremendous damage. He was also devoted to the city's public schools, which had been inaugurated in the early years of the 1840s. His wife was a graduate of the girls high school, and he served untiringly on the school board for their district, declaring the schools among the finest in the city.

But nothing gave Wharton quite so much pleasure as the upper reaches of the city. His own neighborhood, Coliseum Place, seemed quite bucolic with its streets "so neat and quiet and spacious, and so many trees, and so much green grass, and then the gardens, that it is as good as the country." In the summer cocoa grass grew in the unpaved streets. At first "the grassy streets in the upper part of town gave it an air of desertion and loneliness," but he soon grew to prefer the more secluded thoroughfares for his walks. He didn't even complain when "the rich soil of the streets" was converted into deep mire by heavy rains.

Despite all the charms of the cooler North, Wharton declared, "There is something about the genial South which after all charms and rivets our love." Luxuriant plant life was among the delights to him of this semi-tropical paradise. On his long walks, Wharton always observed flowers, shrubs, and trees. Colonial cities had been pretty thoroughly stripped of native trees when they were built. In the early urban ethos, trees represented the wildwood and cities, civilization. But by the nineteenth century the idea of a greener city with countrified suburbs had taken hold, and trees were planted along streets and in parks like Coliseum Place. Besides his favorite china trees, he noted weeping willows, live oaks, orange trees, mulberries, arbor vitae, bananas with their "rich purple pendants," and many evergreens.

And the flowers provided an amazing riot of color. The city was filled with roses of every shade from white to deepest scarlet. He admired yellow jasmine, "white bell flowered" yucca, the brilliant spikes of salvias, oleanders, double scarlet hibiscus, chrysanthemums of every shade, blue larkspurs, sweet peas, nasturtiums, gardenias, bachelor buttons, gladiolus, verbenas, and more. The beauty of the city struck him afresh each time he ran across a splendid new garden in bloom.

The skies themselves contributed to Wharton's pleasure. Spectacular sunsets colored the watery, shimmering atmosphere of New Orleans. In his eyes, "No climate can surpass ours in the beauty of its sky painting." The deeply black night sky of the nineteenth century (before modern lighting) was one of his simple joys with its panoply of stars, the wonder of a comet, and the beauty of moonlight — with the mellow strains of a brass band in the neighborhood sometimes wafting through the calm night air. Strolling back from an evening party, he enjoyed "moonlight, and sweet odors of orange bloom in going home."

Summer highlighted the class differences between the well-to-do "go aways" and all those who remained permanently in the city. The wealthy almost always left the city in the summer because of its heavily oppressive heat and danger of yellow fever. They stayed at family plantations, summer homes in the pine woods north of the lake and on the Gulf coast, or traveled on to northeastern resorts.

With the exception of a leave of absence when his first wife died, Wharton worked year-round at the Custom House for his entire career. In a lucky happenstance, he was granted another long leave to visit the Northeast in the summer of 1853. That year saw the most devastating yellow fever epidemic in Louisiana history — almost 9,000 people died in New Orleans alone. Yellow fever was the city's particular plague, terrifying in its unpredictable, but frequent recurrence.

Death and despair hung over New Orleans like a miasma that summer. Longtime residents had acquired some degrees of immunity from the fever, but the sword of pestilence cut down unsuspecting natives and attacked areas of the countryside formerly believed safe from infection. Unacclimated newcomers contracted the disease and died by the thousands. Apparently perfectly well one day, victims would suddenly be struck with fever, jaundice, black vomit, and delirium, dying the following day. Others would linger for several days, unexplainably dying or surviving. Whole families died here, children there, and parents elsewhere. So many children lost parents in 1853 that orphanages were opened to care for them.

Unburied bodies stacked up for lack of tombs, and gravediggers worked through the night by torchlight. Cemeteries filled up, and new ones opened. Because of their numbers, immigrants were hurriedly buried in mass graves. Mourning crepe was nailed to doors all over town, and funeral notices fluttered dismally from lampposts, banners of death's unchallenged rule.

The dominant medical theory of the day traced most illnesses to an imbalance of the body's humors (fluids). Enduring the sufferings demanded by the era's heroic medicine, patients were bled, blistered, sweated, purged, and generally depleted of bodily fluids. Fortunately, many were strong enough to survive the drastic treatment, as well as the illness. One of Wharton's sovereign remedies for any little indisposition, for example, was a dose of blue mass, a powerful laxative. More pleasantly, travel was also considered an effective medicine for those who could afford it.

Improved sanitation was one of the few useful theories suggested to fight yellow fever. New Orleans was undeniably filthy; perhaps, some thought, clean streets, gutters, and privies would be an improvement. No doubt about that, but aside from the esthetic and general health benefits, clean-up efforts also cut down on the unsuspected carriers of yellow fever — mosquitoes. Thousands of swarming and biting mosquitoes were another of the city's plagues, causing the bedeviled residents to cower under mosquito netting. But it was not until the twentieth century that their role in the cycle of yellow fever infection was discovered, and the disease was finally banished.

Wharton's diary begins with the aftermath of the terrible epidemic of 1853. On his return from the Northeast, he found empty houses and stores; many of his acquaintances were dead. Of a neighboring family missing from their church pew, Wharton noted solemnly, "now they are all but three swept away and the place when I went by this morning looked closed up and very desolate."

Although he had lived through earlier epidemics, after 1853 he began recording death statistics from Charity Hospital and compulsively watching for any sign of an outbreak. During the years he kept his diary, there were three more severe fever years. He worried about his family and congratulated himself on his own good health. Noting the arrival in 1854 of 2,000 foreigners in two days, he gloomily foresaw thousands of fatalities: "The Lord help the unacclimated stranger, and the citizen too, whom business ties here for the summer."

It also might seem that Wharton was obsessed with fires, jumping up in the night to observe many a blaze. But until 1860 the loudly tolling bells of St. Patrick's were the city's central fire alarm system, making it a little hard for neighbors to sleep through the din. New Orleans was plagued by fires in the 1850s because of its many large warehouses and cotton presses filled with combustible goods. Once one of these buildings caught fire, the combination of open spaces (speeding the flames) and party walls (spreading them to adjoining buildings) made fires practically impossible to control. Volunteer fire companies — twenty-four engines, four hook and ladder, and several hose companies — did their best, not least because of the rewards offered by insurance companies tired of expensive losses. The hand-operated pumps which drew water for the hoses were simply too slow to quench large fires. The arrival in 1855 of *Young America*, a fire engine with a large steam-powered pump, was cause for rejoicing, but it proved too heavy and hard to maneuver in narrow streets. It was soon replaced by an engine built in New Orleans that continued in service for several years; its steam pump delivered great quantities of water quickly and considerably improved firefighters' efficiency.

Quite as dangerous as its fires, the violently partisan politics of the 1850s reflected the city's growing pains and the clash of its contending cultures. In 1836 the city had actually split into three separate municipalities; in 1852 those sections were reunified with the addition of a fourth district, the former suburb of Lafayette. With all the power and patronage available in a large city, the stakes of political control were high.

The long-standing opponents of the nineteenth century were the Democrats and the Whigs, but the Whig party had fallen apart in the late 1840s. The Democrats in New Orleans were led by the old families, often Creoles, and they habitually enrolled Catholic immigrants fresh off the boat as voters for their party. Generally speaking, the Whigs had been the party of business; when their party dissolved, American businessmen looked for a successor and found an unworthy one in the new American or Native American Party. More popularly known as the Know Nothings, members refused to disclose the party's tenets to outsiders.

The Know Nothings were pro-business, but also anti-immigrant and anti-Catholic. Members pledged to block the employment and political participation of immigrants and Catholics in favor of "native Americans," that is, Anglo-Americans. New Orleans was once again an anomaly in that its ruling natives were French Catholics. The party first entered New Orleans politics in the early 1850s as an "independent" reform party with a fiscal-responsibility, anti-crime platform.

Supported by the uptown business community, the Know Nothings came to dominate city politics throughout the decade. Their party machinery was very effective in winning elections, especially the employment of gangs of thugs to prevent immigrants and other suspect Democrats from voting. Election violence, fueled by the whiskey ladled out freely by both sides, grew into riots as the Irish fought back.

Finally, reformers convinced P. G. T. Beauregard to run for mayor. His supporters formed a Vigilance Committee to prevent electoral intimidation and general thuggery. Their methods, however, were violent. They seized the state arsenal, armed themselves, and threw up barricades around Jackson Square. Their opponents also took up arms and assembled in Lafayette Square for lengthy and indignant speeches. Federal troops moved in; the election went peacefully for a change, but Beauregard lost by a hair. By the time city elections began again after the war, the Know Nothing party had fallen apart. It was an odd chapter: the nation's largest Catholic city ruled by an anti-Catholic party in the name of reform.

Attitudes about race hardened as the nation staggered toward civil war, and the situation for African Americans in New Orleans took a sharp downward turn. The city had been unique in the South for its large, highly visible class of free people of color. Many were well-educated and well-to-do, large property owners with successful businesses; others were skilled craftsmen and merchants, composers, artists, and writers. For slaves, the city had also offered latitude unusual in the South. Manumission and self-purchase had been often-used paths to freedom.

As abolitionists fought to end slavery and slaves sought their freedom by flight or violence, southern defense of the plantation system hardened. Its apologists justified enslavement by the supposed inferiority of the black race. Laws controlling slaves grew more severe, punishments more draconian, and manumission was forbidden. Because successful free people of color were a living rebuttal to racist ideology, their very existence a rebuke, their rights were progressively curtailed and their lot worsened across the South.

In this time of racial controversy, Wharton seldom mentioned blacks in his journal, except in passing, even though he frequently indulged in anti-Irish diatribes. His views may be inferred, however, by his references to "fanatics in Massachusetts" and "the canting, hypocritical, 'Black Republican' party." Common sense, he suggested, was opposed to anti-slavery agitation. He eventually stopped going to church because he blamed "the immaculate and supremely pious!! Puritans of New England" and their ministers for the "troubles" afflicting the country.

The economic and social chasm dividing the North and the South had widened steadily throughout the nineteenth century. In the end, though, secession and civil war came as suddenly as a clap of summer thunder. Less than three months after Abraham Lincoln was elected president, South Carolina seceded and six other southern states, including Louisiana, followed her fiery lead. The news from South Carolina had been celebrated in New Orleans with hours of jubilant gunfire. Some businessmen hoped that the city would remain in the Union or perhaps adopt a neutral status, but pro-secessionists prevailed. A period of intense suspense followed, in which elation and fear mingled.

During this interlude, federal buildings such as the Custom House were taken over by seceding state governments. Wharton, like other converts more royalist than the king or more Catholic than the Pope, became an ardent southern patriot, even though he was English by birth, a New Yorker by education, early career, and many friendships, and a New Englander by marriage. A dedicated federal bureaucrat with no financial stake in the plantation system, he fiercely defended secession and southern independence.

Like many Americans, he didn't believe that war would follow secession. Fort Sumter and its aftermath proved them wrong. As the conflict ground on, he raged against the "savage and demonic war" waged by "the imbecile but arrogant Northern foe, whom I have learned to contemn more intensely than the meanest reptile that crawls on earth's surface." He habitually referred to northerners as barbarians, vandals, and madmen.

Most New Orleanians, including Wharton, trusted the strength of the city's defenses. More seriously, the new Confederate government disastrously underestimated the danger of a Union attack. The compass of the Confederacy had swung far to the east, and Louisiana's best troops were routinely ordered to the Virginia theater of war, depleting the city's defenses. Mistake compounded miscalculation as ancient or bumbling officers were given command; army, navy, and civilian officials labored under divided authority; and the government stubbornly maintained that any attack on the city would come from upriver.

For defense the city had its "mosquito fleet," a hodge-podge of ships recently adapted for naval service. Wharton's pride was the iron-clad ram *Manassas*; his workshop at the Custom House had fabricated her plating. Downriver stood Forts Jackson and St. Philip, recently strengthened and reinforced, situated on opposite banks of the river to create a murderous crossfire. Stretched across the river, a chain barrier connected to a series of hulks blocked upriver access.

While the Confederate government discounted the possibility of an attack on New Orleans, United States authorities were absolutely convinced of the strategic importance of the city, blockading the mouths of the Mississippi as soon as practicable. A year into the war, the fleet of Flag Officer David G. Farragut moved into the river to mount an attack. Mortar boats bombarded the defending forts for days, and then in the very early morning of April 24, 1862, Union ships broke the chain barrier, ran the gauntlet of the forts in the darkness, and disabled Confederate ships upriver. It was a short, fierce encounter, but once past the forts, there were no further defenses of importance.

Wharton shared the disbelief of his fellow citizens. That day he wrote in his journal: "Great excitement in town on the news of some Federal gunboats having passed the Forts. Silly nonsense!" Not silly nonsense at all, as they learned when the warships sailed around the bend in the river. Since the fleet could easily reduce the city to rubble by bombardment, Confederate forces evacuated, leaving the mayor to surrender. Furious crowds of citizens obstructed the proceedings until Union troops took effective control of the city, imposing a sullen calm. At first people couldn't comprehend just what military occupation meant. Wharton went down to the Custom House as usual, to find it taken over by the enemy; he returned home lost without his customary occupation.

New Orleans remained under Union control throughout the remainder of the war. The Queen had been swept from the board, and although no one knew it yet, the war would play out slowly to checkmate at Appomattox. Without the port of New Orleans, the South could not prevail. And during the long years of wartime and Reconstruction, national and world trade patterns definitively altered. New Orleans would never regain the commanding position of the 1850s. The capture of the city marked the end of its golden era.

—Patricia Brady
The Historic New Orleans Collection

Front Elevation on Camp Street.

Wharton cottage, Plan book 43, Folio 31, February 16, 1854, New Orleans Notarial Archives.

New Orleans, December 8, 1853.[1]

Heavy rains in the night with change of wind to North West. Fine bracing air this morning, cold high wind, and alternate clouds and bright sunshine.

At the Office until 3 P.M. arranging the Documents, accounts, &c. that have accumulated during my absence, then returned home to dinner and passed the evening until 10 P.M. amongst my accounts.

December 9

Lovely weather with clear bracing air, but not quite cold enough to form ice, or even wilt the vines.

We all had a profound night's rest and have already quite got over the fatigue of the journey.

Emily & Mrs. Ladd have been on the wing all the time, and things are quickly reassuming their former pleasant and domestic look.[2] I like my comfortable cottage better than ever and its locality is unrivaled.[3]...

Floor plan of Wharton cottage.

[1] For health reasons, Wharton obtained leave from his position as general superintendent of the new Custom House; he and his family left New Orleans for Boston on June 25, 1853, and returned December 7, 1853.

[2] Emily Ladd (1835-1932) became Thomas K. Wharton's second wife on December 18, 1851. She was the daughter of Darius Ladd and Emily Prescott Ladd of New Hampshire, who had moved to New Orleans in the early 1830s. After 1838 Darius Ladd removed permanently to Boston. Emily Prescott Ladd (ca. 1810-1889), Wharton's mother-in-law, remained in New Orleans with her daughter's family until her death. Marriage license file, New Orleans Public Library (hereafter NOPL); *Daily Picayune*, Apr. 8, 1889.

[3] Thomas K. Wharton rented a one-story frame house at 424 Camp Street between Robin (now Euterpe) and Terpsichore from James Dunn, the proprietor of the Western Verandah Hotel. Wharton's residence (no longer standing) was on a lot 31' by 127'. It was described as a three-room cottage with hall, a gallery front and rear, and a one-story frame kitchen with three rooms and a cistern in the rear. New Orleans Notarial Archives (hereafter NONA), William Monaghan, Nov. 11, 1853, Mar. 18, 1854; Second District Court, Inventory of James Dunn, docket 6906, NOPL.

1853

Children carrying coffins during the yellow fever epidemic of 1853, from History of the Yellow Fever *(Philadelphia, 1854) (1974.25.11.130).*

December 11

Sunday. Sunny and genial like the month of May, but as we need a good rest we did not go to church (except Mrs. Ladd) and I went no where in the morning except to market in Magazine Street, which I found greatly improved since last year.[4] The stalls clean and the whole house well arranged, and supply abundant, and of excellent quality, plenty of game, venison, wild ducks and teal, very fine beef and vegetables, tomatoes, green peas and okra, &c. &c. and prices moderate. I took our new cook with me and was pleased to find that she understood the choice of meats, &c. which is an important quality and difficult to find among the Irish. My little boy and his nurse came a square or two to meet me.[5] The streets around here are so neat and quiet and spacious, and so many trees, and so much green grass, and then the gardens, that it is as good as the country for him, and he really seems to enjoy it.

I spent the morning in reading and reviewing early papers &c.

The epidemic of the summer has made a marked difference in the appearance of the city, even the business streets are not by any means so thronged and noisy as is usual at this season of the year, and in my neighborhood, and towards the suburbs it is positively village-like, which the increased stringency of the sanitary and other municipal regulations, growing out of the late mortality has given an air of superior neatness and cleanliness which contrasts very favorably with the appearances of the city in former years.[6] A good deal, too, has been accomplished in building, both public and private, so that the general aspect of things is far more inviting than I have ever known it. There are certain spots, however, which tho' beautiful in themselves, from their connection with the appalling fatality of the summer, cannot be passed without depressing and painful feelings amongst the rest. The sweet, pretty place which belonged to the large family of the "Groves" a square above me. I remember seeing them all out in the garden one fine evening last June watering and trimming their beautiful plants, and now they are all but three swept away and the place when I went by this morning looked closed up and very desolate.[7]

At noon William Freret called and sat awhile giving me a sketch of his summer tour after we left him at Niagara. He and his father's family got back in October.[8] After dinner I was again immersed in papers, and looking thro' the records of years long since past until surprised by the falling shadows. Nothing could exceed the beauty of the moonlight which followed, and the mellow strains of a brass band in the neighborhood were wafted thro' the calm night air.

[4] The Magazine Market occupied the triangle formed by Sophie Wright Place, St. Mary, and Magazine.

[5] Thomas Prescott Wharton (1852-1910), the Whartons' only child, was born September 23, 1852, in New Orleans. He was associated for a number of years with Isaac S. West, Jr., a dry goods merchant on Magazine Street. After moving to New York City, Wharton married Louisa P. Cameron. He died in New York and is buried in Woodlawn Cemetery. Genealogy of the family of Wharton, Miscellaneous Papers in the Manuscripts and Archives Division, New York Public Library.

[6] The yellow fever epidemic of 1853 was one of the most virulent ever to attack New Orleans. Nearly 9,000 people in the city died of the fever between May and October 1853. John Duffy, *Sword of Pestilence: The New Orleans Yellow Fever Epidemic of 1853* (Baton Rouge, 1966).

[7] John B. Groves, a merchant from Tennessee, and his family lived on Camp Street at the corner of Race. Four daughters died between August 13 and August 28, 1853, and Groves died September 1, all of yellow fever. *Daily Picayune*, Sept. 3, 1853.

[8] William Alfred Freret (1833-1911), the son of New Orleans Mayor William Freret (1804-1864) and Fanny Salkeld Freret, was trained in engineering and architecture in England. He designed several major buildings in New Orleans in the late 1850s. After the Civil War, Freret designed the reconstruction of the old state capitol in Baton Rouge and numerous public schools, courthouses, post offices, and federal buildings. *Dictionary of Louisiana Biography*, ed. Glenn R. Conrad (Lafayette, 1988) (hereafter *DLB*).

William Freret, 1856 (1994.83.3), gift of Suzanne Wynne Friedrichs; St. Ann[a]'s Asylum, ca. 1873–1874 (1951.41.38).

December 17

After soaking rains in the night the wind changed to North West and today we have a sharp bracing air and bright sun. The cold increased and the wind rose considerably after dark.

The change in the weather has made me feel quite well and elastic again, so that I got along rapidly with my classification and entry of back accounts and records at the Office. By the end of another week I hope to have all fully written up, and attend to the current business besides. Today I remained at my desk until near 4 P.M. Emily and Mrs. Ladd who had been shopping called at the Office for me and we rode up together to dinner. Towards evening I took a brisk walk thro' the principal streets in my neighborhood and part of Lafayette, and found but little change except the completion of some buildings commenced before I left.[9] The re-painting and general beautification of others, and some few structures in brick begun during the summer and now in progress, of which the most conspicuous is the fine large building intended for the Widows "Home" on the corner of Prytania and St. Mary Streets.[10] The principal improvements of the summer have been confined to the business parts of town. The increase in the number of dwelling houses appears to be but trifling, desirable ones

[9] The City of Lafayette, the area of New Orleans in Jefferson Parish from Felicity Street to Toledano, was incorporated in 1833; Lafayette was the seat of the parish government until 1852 when it was annexed to the City of New Orleans as the Fourth District. It included the area of New Orleans now known as the Garden District.

[10] St. Anna's Asylum for the Relief of Destitute Females and Their Helpless Children of All Religious Denominations was erected in 1853 by Little and Middlemiss, builders. Located at 1823 Prytania Street, it still serves as a home for the elderly.

scarce, and rents proportionably high. Mine is raised from $420 to $480. Flour and some other articles of domestic consumption are high owing to the scant water in the Western Rivers, and fuel exorbitant for New Orleans. Coal I am buying at $1.25 per Barrel, (Pittsburg) and wood $7.50 per Cord, against 75¢ and $5.50 last year. Provisions for the table, however, in general are reasonable, very plentiful, and choice in quality, so that as to living we are at no loss for a good dinner, and an excellent cook to prepare it withal.

December 18

Sunday. Frost sprinkled over every thing this morning and a pure, bracing air from the north west. Bright sky and genial sunshine as lovely a Sabbath as ever dawned upon the world.

We have been married two years today, two pleasant, very, very pleasant years, a little abatement only from occasional ill-health, but even that has passed away and every thing looks bright and smiling both without and within, and our dear little treasure of a boy is animated with unusual glee, running and dancing around the room, and performing a variety of intricate evolutions to the infinite delight of his admiring parents.

We went to church in the morning, and I was glad at heart to sit in our old pew again, and sincerely thankful when I recollected that the last time I occupied it I was taken so unwell that I had to leave in the middle of the service. This was early in the spring, and now I am so strong and well, and so thoroughly restored, that the contrast filled me with gratitude, and Mr. Preston's plain discourse on "The peace of God which passeth all understanding" fell pleasantly on my heart, and I felt how deeply I was indebted to that God for unnumbered sources of happiness which have flowed in upon me since I was last within these walls, and for our exemption, too, from that terrible fatality, of which we were forcibly reminded by the deep mourning which appeared in different parts of the church, and especially in a pew very near us, which contained all that are left of the once numerous family of the "Groves", but most of the familiar faces were still in place, so that livelier thoughts were on the ascendant, and the church itself had been so thoroughly repaired, painted and re-furnished during the summer that it looked quite pleasant and cheerful.[11]

In the afternoon I took a wider circuit thro' Lafayette than yesterday, and in broad daylight, enabling me to judge more correctly of the suburban improvements of the summer. Indeed I find several very handsome new private residences, especially on Nayades Street [now St. Charles Avenue] and between it and Magazine, and the gardens in this neighbourhood are still very beautiful, the leaves cling lovingly to the deciduous trees, and some, as the Weeping Willows &c., are in full foliage, while numerous Live Oaks, and abundance of glossy evergreen shrubs, give richness and mass to the general verdure, and the rose trees are covered with splendid blooms from the purest white, to the rich damask scarlet. Indeed but for the keen racy air, there is nothing here to remind one of Winter, blossoms, green leaves and sunshine every where.

Mr. Young spent the evening with us, and after he left, Emily and I sat awhile by a bright fireside before retiring, just as we did on our wedding night, and looking round saw no change except for the better, increased comforts, increased health, very much the same sort of night too, the keen, biting air outside giving an additional charm to the ruddy, blazing hearth, and well lighted parlour.[12] It was nearly 11 when we went to our chamber.

December 22

Thanksgiving day, by appointment of Govr. Hebert.[13]

Works at the New Custom House suspended. I got up before daylight and went with my cook to market, animated with the customary ambition of honoring the day with a carefully selected dinner.

Several housekeepers of my acquaintance were already there, some of them politicians, who rarely neglect the opportunity of dropping a few insinuating remarks to the sturdy voters of the "Stalls" while laying in their supply. This latter end was easily attained, every thing good and abundant....

There was no going out so we spent a real pleasant domestic day at home. Drawing, reading, talking, the Piano, and the "infant phenomenon" all contributed to our entertainment, and all in full

---

[11] The Episcopal Church of the Annunciation was built in 1845 at the corner of Orange and Pacanier (now Chippewa). It burned in 1858. Nathaniel Ogden Preston (d. 1866), the first rector, lived at the corner of Race and Constance streets. Herbert Cope Duncan, *The Diocese of Louisiana: Some of Its History, 1838-1888* (New Orleans, 1888), 129.

[12] George B. Young, Jr., (ca.1805-1879) of Cook, Young & Co., publisher of the *Price Current*. His residence was on St. Charles Avenue near Tivoli Circle. NOCD 1853, 1857; *Daily Picayune*, Aug. 6, 1879.

[13] Paul O. Hébert (1818-1880) was governor of Louisiana from 1853 to 1856. On November 16, 1853, he proclaimed the celebration of Thanksgiving Day for the state. A national Thanksgiving, with a consistent date, was not declared until 1863. *Daily Picayune*, Dec. 8, 1853.

health and spirits, with a Thousand Things to be thankful for, the pleasantest Thanksgiving day I ever spent.

December 23

…A good deal of firing and other demonstrations today in honor of the engagement of Decr. 23, 1814 about 6 miles below New Orleans, which saved the city and paved the way for the decisive action of January 8th. 1815.[14]

December 24

Cold and gloomy, raw air from North East to North West, dripping rains set in at 2 P.M. with therm. down to 50°.

Our usual visit to the brilliantly lighted and decorated stores of Royal & Chartres Street on Christmas Eve was out of the Question (large Q!) in such dreary weather, so I strayed away from the Office for a short time in the morning and made my Christmas purchases, and carried the parcels home, when I returned to dinner, under my capacious cloak, so that no one suspected I had anything for them until towards dark when I incidentally, as it were, produced them one by one. Nothing could exceed the rapture with which the little boy fastened on a box of ninepins which I had intended for Ellen but he seemed resolved to appropriate them, and spent the rest of the evening in arranging and rearranging them with untiring delight.[15] His tactics are most unmistakably boyish, and he very quietly passed over to Ellen a gaily decked Persian tambourine player which I meant for him. He already enunciates some short words very distinctly, such as "house, box, Papa, horse &c.", and clearly understands their meaning.…

December 25

Sunday and Christmas day —

So raw damp and chilly and such an "eager air" from the North East that we thought it best not to go to church but spend our Christmas quietly at home. The tendencies were decidedly towards the fireside, and as to outdoors, I contented myself with an early walk to market to choose the Christmas turkey, and then a promenade with the little boy before dinner to bring the colour to his cheeks, and air his new cloak of mazarin blue of which he is not a little proud.

December 29

White frost in the night. Beautiful, sunny day mild air from North West to South East. Therm[omete]r. at even 57°.

The Commissioners received today specific and minute instructions from the Honorable Secretary of the Treasury for the future conduct of the work at the New Custom House, in its business details, forms, and duties of employees etc.[16] They differ in some particulars from those heretofore observed by the introduction of certain features from the regulations which govern the works under the control of the Engineer Department, but the general distribution of duties, and plan of operations, will remain unaltered.

After dinner finished my gardening operations and put every thing, round the house, in nice order. The rest were availing themselves of the lovely evening to do some shopping &c., so that we all sat down to a good hot supper with a keen relish, indeed, it tastes even better than usual as Emily had received her New Year's present of Silver from the jeweller's where it had been left to be marked, and was used this evening for the first time.

[16] James Gutherie (1792-1869) of Kentucky was appointed secretary of the treasury in 1853 by President Franklin Pierce; he retired in 1857. *Dictionary of American Biography* (hereafter *DAB*).

[14] Before the news of the end of the War of 1812 reached America, British troops under the command of Gen. Edward Pakenham attempted to take New Orleans. The first engagement occurred on December 23, 1814, on the plantation of Jacques Philippe Villeré, below New Orleans.

[15] Ellen Ladd (b. 1845), Emily Ladd Wharton's sister, lived with her mother and the Whartons; she later married Henry W. Clark. *Daily Picayune*, Apr. 8, 1889.

North side of Canal Street, 400-600 blocks, showing the Custom House under construction, surrounded by scaffolding, Jay Dearborn Edwards, photographer, between 1857 and 1860 (1982.32.2).

Private Journal

*with the meteorology of each day, and
thermometrical observations taken at 9 A.M.
12 M. and 4 P.M. Fahrenheit's grade — and the
instrument placed in a selected, shady place at
the office of the New Custom House N. Orleans*

January 1   45° 49° 55°

Sunday. White frost in the night and as lovely a day as ever shone — pure and cloudless with a mild, pleasant air from the north west changing to South west in the afternoon.

Emily and Mrs. Ladd went to church without me this morning, for altho' I have but a slight cold, I fear the damp air of a church which has been closed up all the week, they warm and ventilate their churches badly here, which is a serious fault in so humid a climate, and a fruitful source of catarrhs and intermittents. Emily had made all her preparations to receive her callers tomorrow, as we took it for granted that the usual New Year's visiting would be done on Monday.[1] Several gentlemen, however, came in during the afternoon and I find that there is a good deal of calling today, as the Banks will be open tomorrow and prevent men of business from taking the usual rounds. The calls today, however, are quite informal as most families have postponed their regular preparations and tomorrow will be <u>the</u> "Jubilee". The offices and works at the New Custom House will be open, so that I expect to go to my business as usual, and make a few calls in the afternoon. The New Year's observances are too pleasant, and too social to be abandoned, on the contrary, they ought to be carefully cherished, and I am only sorry that when the 1st. falls on Sunday our business assignments are such as to prevent its celebration on the first week day.

[1] New Year's was the traditional day in New Orleans for gentlemen to make formal calls on friends while ladies stayed at home to receive callers.

1854

January 2   46° 55° 57°

Another white frost in the night followed by a day of unparalleled beauty for mid-winter a soft west wind and glowing sunshine.

I was quite busy at the office until 2 P.M. and then commenced my calls. The visiting by this time was becoming quite general, and one gentleman after another appeared on the field, as they could manage to tear themselves away from the tyranny of commercial routine. I made some nine or ten calls while Mrs. Ladd and Emily were receiving friends at home. It was a gay and joyous afternoon and evening....

January 3   48° 50° 54°

Very mild and sunny, North west wind, changing to East in the afternoon.

Paid off all outstanding accounts, so that I commence the New Year entirely free from debt. Completed the Reports and other Documents connected with the works for the month of December, and opened the Records for the New Year. Our trunks &c. sent by sea from Boston per ship "Clarissa Currier" were delivered at home today all in good order....

January 4   53° 62° 64°

Charming weather, warm sun and mild air from the East.

Every thing as usual at the Office, the progress of the works this fine weather is very rapid. 417.775 Bricks laid during December in the second tier of Ground Arches and adjacent walls....

January 8   43° 42° 43°

Sunday. The day was ushered in with the usual cannonading in honor of the Victory of Chalmette. (1815)[2] Bitter cold, dull damp looking sky, searching North wind. Severe weather for the poor with Coal now at $2.25 and wood at $11. Cold as it is I noticed in going to market a fine Lamarck [Lamarque] Rose climbing over a two story gallery front, its leaves quite green and fresh, and covered every where with large, full blown, white Roses, and innumerable beautiful buds ready to take their place, and just as Fragrant as in summer-tide. In other gardens I saw noble crimson roses, Solfâtres, Heliotropes &

[2] The anniversary of Andrew Jackson's victory over the British invading forces led by Pakenham at the Battle of New Orleans on January 8, 1815, is celebrated annually in New Orleans.

P. G. T. Beauregard, Harper's, *April 27, 1861 (1974.25.27.27).*

Arabian jessamines in full blow. It was too raw and uncomfortable for Emily to go to church, so I contented myself with a walk before dinner, reading &c....

January 10   53° 56° 58°

Mild air from the North East to East. Clouds & light showers with bursts of sunshine, warm sunny evening. Wet, clammy condensation of moisture on the sidewalk and brick work generally.

Short visit today at the office from Capt. Bowman of the Engineer Corps, lately appointed Superintendent General of Custom Houses and other Public Buildings now in progress under the Treasury Department.[3] A. B. Young of Boston is retained in the Bureau as consulting architect.[4] Major Beauregard showed him the works &c.[5] He spoke in very flattering terms of the returns, reports, &c. transmitted from our offices to the Department in Washington, their accuracy, promptness, and complete attention to detail &c. The General Supervising Bureau of Public Buildings under the Treasury Department, is now fully organized in Washington with Capt. Bowman at its head, so that our relations with him hereafter will be quite intimate, and our plan of operations more than ever assimilated in detail to that of the Corps of Engineers.

January 22   40° 44° 45°

Sunday. Keen frost in the night, bright, sparkling morning. North wind and not a cloud. I took sheets of ice off the water tubs in the yard, as thick as common window glass, with a beautiful florescence of leaves depending from the under surface, all perfectly formed, and delicately pinnated like the rock Maple and Weeping Birch. The Frost-Angel is the most exquisite artist in the world, none weaves

such elegant and magical structures, and in such an incredibly short time — but like every thing that is most beautiful, they are most evanescent.

Judge Huling called and sat awhile on his way to the Boat.[6] Emily and I went to Church, it was lovely in walking there but raw and wintry when we returned. Mr. Preston preached from that passage in the Romans beginning "and now I am ready to be offered and the time of my departure is at hand."...

January 23   43° 44° 47°

Raw, cold and cloudy, with bursts of vivid sunshine, North East wind, very penetrating. Three days ago the thermometer was at 78°. Now in the forties.

Major Beauregard returned this morning. Major Chase spent sometime at the office.[7] And as lively and dashing as usual. Alexr. Dunn also called.[8] Our large 40 foot arches have settled materially. We have been obliged to shore them up. This construction is as perfect as it was possible to make it, and the settlement is in no respect due to the workmanship, and seems to be inevitable to their position in the building. The foundations, however, have been severely tried during the period of comparative inaction, and the "Original Plan" has hardly had a fair chance.[9]

[3] Alexander H. Bowman (d. 1865) of Pennsylvania was the engineer in charge of the Office of Construction under the Treasury Department. Francis B. Heitman, *Historical Register and Dictionary of the United States Army* (Washington, D.C., 1903).

[4] Ammi Burnham Young (1798-1874), appointed first supervising architect of the Office of Construction of the Treasury Department in 1852, designed numerous federal buildings. Adolphe K. Placzek, ed., *The Macmillan Encyclopedia of Architects*, 4 vols. (New York, 1982).

[5] Major Pierre Gustave Toutant Beauregard (1818-1893) was appointed superintendent for the construction of the New Orleans Custom House in September 1852, assuming his duties on May 4, 1853. During the Civil War, as a general in the Confederate army, he fired the first shot of the war in 1861 at Fort Sumter. Beauregard's first wife was Marie Laure Villeré (1823-1850), whose father, Jules Villeré, owned (Upper) Magnolia Plantation, about fourteen miles below New Orleans at English Turn. *DLB*; NONA, James Fahey, June 9, 1880.

[6] Judge Frederick Watts Huling (ca. 1792-1861), a native of Pennsylvania and a cotton planter of Holly Springs, Mississippi, and Sara Huling (ca. 1794-1859) were the parents of Wharton's first wife, Maria Huling (ca. early 1820s-1848); the Whartons married in 1845, and she died three years later. The Hulings moved to Plaquemines Parish in 1846 and purchased a sugar plantation on the left bank of the Mississippi, some fifty miles below New Orleans. The Hulings were neighbors of the Villeré family, in-laws of Major P. G. T. Beauregard, Wharton's supervisor at the Custom House. Although Wharton had remarried, he remained on friendly terms with his former in-laws. NONA, Philip Lacoste, Oct. 2, 1846; *Daily Delta*, Apr. 12, 1848, June 23, 1861; *Daily Picayune*, Mar. 11, 1859; U.S. Census, La., Plaquemines Parish, 1850, 1860.

[7] Major William H. Chase (1798-1870), a U.S. Army engineer, had served on the board convened by the Treasury Department to settle the dispute over the design of the Custom House in 1851. He later served as a brigadier general in the Confederate army. James Patrick, *Architecture in Tennessee, 1768-1897* (Knoxville, 1981), 146; *DLB*.

[8] Alexander Dunn (d. 1863), a New Jersey native, was a retired steamboat captain who accompanied Wharton on the trip north in June 1853. *Daily Picayune*, Oct. 7, 1863; Thomas K. Wharton Diary, New York Public Library.

[9] Some of the original plans of the New Orleans Custom House are in the Notarial Archives. A. T. Wood's plans had the main business room in the center of the building, as opposed to the plans proposed by James H. Dakin to place this great room on the Canal Street front. Arthur Scully, Jr., *James Dakin, Architect: His Career in New York and the South* (Baton Rouge, 1973), 183; Bates Lowry, *Building a National Image: Architectural Drawings for the American Democracy* (New York, 1985), 214.

January 27   67° 63° 66°

Sudden dashes of heavy rain which moderated the oppressive sultriness of the air. By 8 O'clock the Canal opposite was filled, so that the City has had a thorough washing.[10]…

In a conversation with Dr. Barton he told me that he was still busily engaged on the "Sanitary Board of Commission" and from the thorough way in which they are pursuing their investigations he thinks they will hit upon some plan that will be of practical benefit to the health of New Orleans.[11]

January 31   50° 57° 60°

Light frost in the night. Brilliant sky, pleasant air from North East.

Very closely engaged. Calculations of work performed during the month, monthly papers &c. &c. to transmit to the Department. Emily has begun today to wean little Prescott. It seems a sad and painful task to withdraw him from his long accustomed delights, but he submits with a good grace, and takes refuge in "book, book" — 'C'est le premier pas qui coûte."[12]

February 3   46° 47° 53°

Wind changed to north in the night and blew hard, dispersing the clouds and heavy stagnant atmosphere of the city, today is bracing & pure with a sunny sky.

Friends called at the office to go over the building with me. They, as usual, had no idea of its vast extent and admirable arrangement until they saw the interior and its exterior and imposing system of groining. The Exterior work has been so long "in suspense", so encumbered with heavy scaffolding, and unchanged in elevation, say 40 odd feet high, that it now fails to strike the passers by, and it is only when they see the busy life within and ascend to the top of the second tier of groins that they realize the true magnitude and intricacy of the work. The city and Levee views, too, from the top of the walls add a new and interesting feature. A communication from the Granite contractors was received today praying for relief.[13] But still the same answer, as it will be impossible to resume stone setting until the interior brickwork is brought up to the level of the exterior, and consequently notice for shipments must not be delayed. 410.896 Bricks laid last month.…

February 4   46° 56° 58°

Light frost in the night, buoyant air, north East to East. Fine in the extreme.

I was quite ill all the morning but attended to my business as usual, and endeavoured to drive it off by going up at intervals to the top of the second tier of granite arches, which, by the bye, commanded a view of the scene of last night's disaster. The destruction by fire of 6 steamboats and half a million of property. Some 30 negroes perished, and the brother of Capt. T. P. Leathers [Captain John Leathers] and some deck hands, and this, too, at the wharf. The fire originated on the fine Nashville Packet Chas. Belcher which arrived in the night with 500 bales of cotton &c. and among the steamers destroyed were the superb Natchez with some 2.500 bales of cotton and the "Saxon" which was our companion for some distance in coming down the river. This terrible calamity, and the destruction of the Georgia, loaded also with cotton, at the railroad wharf on Lake Pontchartrain — but a week ago — confirms all my prejudices against cotton carrying steamers. Many lives were lost on both occasions and yet the shore was within a few yards. When will they establish lines exclusively for passengers, and others for freight, here, as on all other great watercourses?

February 21   54° 57° 63°

Very beautiful morning. Mild air from the North West.

Got up early feeling much better but still weak, took a short brisk walk before breakfast. Dr. Hamilton came after breakfast & kindly walked down with me to the office.[14] The beautiful weather, the exercise, and pleasant talk improved me vastly.…

---

10 An open drainage canal ran along Camp Street from Felicity and drained into the Melpomene Street canal. Later covered, they are still part of the city's drainage system.

11 Dr. Edward H. Barton (d. 1857) lived at 304 Camp Street. One of the most prominent physicians in New Orleans, he served as president of the Louisiana State Medical Society (1851-1854). In September 1853, the Board of Health appointed five physicians as a Sanitary Commission to study all aspects of the raging yellow fever epidemic. Barton chaired the commission, wrote much of the report, and was particularly charged with making suggestions for improving sanitary conditions in the city. John Duffy, ed., *The Rudolph Matas History of Medicine in Louisiana*, 2 vols. (Baton Rouge, 1958-62), 2:78; *DLB*; NOCD 1856; Duffy, *Sword of Pestilence*, 130, 137.

12 Trans.: It is the first step that is painful.

13 Granite for the exterior of the New Orleans Custom House was furnished from the quarries at Quincy, Massachusetts.

14 Dr. Charles Hamilton, a physician, lived at Calliope corner of Prytania. His 36-year-old wife, Sarah G. Hamilton, had died of yellow fever August 7. NOCD 1853; *Daily Picayune*, Aug. 10, 1853.

Scaffolding around the Custom House, Jay Dearborn Edwards, photographer, ca. 1858 (1974.25.8.94).

The burning of the steamer John Swasey *at New Orleans, March 19, 1853, shows graphically the spread of fire in the crowded port (1958.43.14).*

The Henry Frank *at the New Orleans levee, dangerously overloaded with cotton bales (1974.25.32.525). Captains boasted about the number of bales their boats carried, as shown in the banner flying from the flagstaff.*

The news today is positive as to the commencement of a general war in Europe and the withdrawal of the English, French & Russian ministers from their respective courts.[15]

February 22   50° 62° 70°

The booming of cannon at an early hour announced the birthday of Washington, admiration and reverence both spring into life at the bare mention of his name, for he is the only chieftain whose character exhibits in union the three loftiest elements of greatness, statesmanship, military prowess, and pure moral worth.[16] The works are suspended, as usual, at the New Custom House, indeed the day is a general festival not only in this city but in every part of the Republic — and wherever Americans are to be found, the world over, and so may it continue to be until time itself shall be no longer....

At 11 Emily & Mrs. Ladd & I walked down to Canal Street, made purchases & saw the military procession &c. & returned in the omnibus at 1. The sun being now too hot for walking. Then while the rest went out again to make a call before dinner, I amused myself with reading, & playing with Prescott &c. He can already pronounce every letter in the alphabet distinctly, besides quite a fund of short words, clearly articulated, and with a most entire & palpable knowledge of their specification, smart child, that! I never have been in the habit of noticing such very young children much, so he appears to me the most perfect and intelligent little creature that ever existed. That, of course, is impossible, but it is a pleasant hallucination notwithstanding.

February 25   58° 62° 64°

Violent storm of wind and rain all night. When we looked out this morning the Canal had overflowed its banks and the whole of Camp Street and Coliseum Place presented a uniform surface of water, lying to the depth of nearly 2 inches on the high banquette [sidewalk] at my gate.[17] It had been much higher and was then falling fast so that by 9 the water had returned to its accustomed channels. The rain, however, still continued, with a light wind from the Eastward.

Stone's Infirmary (1977.232);
Dr. Warren Stone (1974.25.27.416).

I did not think it advisable to leave the house, as I am by no means well this morning. Dr. Hamilton called about 10 and still attributes it all to bile, but he agrees with us all that it would be well to consult with Dr. Stone who is the highest medical authority here, and has promised to see him and make an engagement to meet here some morning soon.[18] Very dark at noon, torrents of rain, thunder and lightening, and the canal rising again rapidly. At 2 O'clock still darker

[15] The newspapers of the day were filled with accounts of the imminent outbreak of the Crimean War; France, England, and their allies were opposed to Russia for strategic control of Turkey.

[16] Washington's birthday was celebrated with salutes fired from the principal public squares and a military parade on Canal Street. *Daily Picayune*, Feb. 23, 1854.

[17] Coliseum Place was a part of Barthélémy Lafon's 1806 plan for the Faubourg Annunciation. A triangular park between Camp, Coliseum, and Race streets, opposite Wharton's Camp Street residence, it was the centerpiece of the neighborhood that has since become known as the Lower Garden District. The park was also called Coliseum Square, the name by which it is now commonly known.

[18] Dr. Warren Stone (d. 1872), Louisiana's greatest antebellum surgeon, was one of the first to use ether as an anesthetic. Stone's Infirmary, or Maison de Santé, at Canal and Claiborne, was designed by James Dakin in 1838. Duffy, *Matas History of Medicine*, 2:11, 386; Scully, *James Dakin*, 85.

Concert on Canal Street commemorating Washington's birthday, C. E. H. Bonwill, delineator, 1864 (1959.159.5), gift of Harold Schilke and Boyd Cruise. The Custom House, lacking the iron cornice that would eventually top the building, is shown at left with spectators on the upper walls, the vantage point where Wharton frequently took friends and family to observe public celebrations.

Orleans Theatre, Vieux Carré Survey, Historic New Orleans Collection.

and darker, the windows of heaven wide open, and such a deluge! A perfect sea again opposite the front windows, and trees and fences, by mistake, as it were, implanted in the water. And every now and then a heavy thunder peal, with startling loudness, followed instantly on the flash. Every thing, however, is pleasant and comfortable indoors, and the bright ruddy fires offer a lively contrast to the desolate scenes without — and I never saw little Prescott in a merrier mood. Towards sunset the clouds parted and the light gleamed thro' and the "waters were abated from off the face of the ground." But the banquettes were left in a deplorable condition, and the thick slimy sediment told of the large proportion of earthy matter held in solution.

February 26   56° 58° 59°

Sunday. A sort of clearing up day. The cool West wind driving heavy masses of vapor across the sky, and the sun making quite an effort to dry up the moist puddly deposit of yesterday's rains. We all remained at home in hopes of better times....

Dr. Stone arrived, punctual, as usual, to the moment. He and Dr. H. remained with me a full hour, and Dr. Stone made a careful examination, and enquired closely into all my symptoms, &c. The whole resulting in a decided opinion corresponding with that already given by Dr. Hamilton, says that there is no organic disease, the lungs are perfect, but the liver <u>may</u> be slightly enlarged, and that the annoying symptoms all proceed from a slight irritability of the stomach & duodenum, impressed as they are by the irregularity of the secretions from the liver. He says positively that the derangement is in no respect serious, and advises a continuance of Dr. Hamilton's treatment with blue mass [laxative], attention to diet, exercise &c....

February 27   54° 59° 63°

The day opened without a cloud, & the breeze blew gently from the north — lovely day throughout.

Went to the office as usual but suffered severely from head-ache &c. Got thro' my business, however, about 3. Received letter from Geo. W. Prescott, and Major Heiman.[19] A very serious accident happened last night at the "Orleans," part of the upper galleries gave way — killing, it is stated, at least 5 persons, and injuring quite a large number. This fact pleads eloquently against the desecration of the Sabbath by the wretched custom here of keeping the theatres open. It also speaks loudly against the detestable parsimony which directs the construction of buildings designed for the reception of an enthusiastic and often overflowing audience.[20]

[19] George Watson Prescott (b. 1820) of Boston was Emily Prescott Ladd's brother. With his father he had obtained a patent for a machine to make wood shavings (excelsior). William Prescott, *The Prescott Memorial* (Boston, 1870), 84, 116. Adolphus Heiman (1809-1862), a Prussian stonecutter, immigrated to the U.S. in 1834, spending time in New York and New Orleans before settling in Nashville. One of Tennessee's most important architects, he served with P. G. T. Beauregard, William H. Chase, Lewis E. Reynolds, and Ammi B. Young on the board convened by the Treasury Department to settle the dispute concerning the New Orleans Custom House. Heiman is said to have produced the design and probably made drawings for modifications to the building as recommended by the board, perhaps working with T. K. Wharton. Patrick, *Architecture in Tennessee*, 146.

[20] The Orleans Theatre was originally designed in 1806 by architect Hyacinthe Laclotte; construction was delayed by financial problems until 1810 when Laclotte and his partner, Arsène Lacarrière Latour continued it. Part of the building was completed by 1813, but the first performance in the theater was not staged until October 1815. The theater burned in September 1816; it was rebuilt to somewhat the same design and reopened in November 1819. The interior of the theater was later redesigned with wrought iron rods supporting the galleries. When one of the rods broke and the upper gallery fell, killing two people and injuring about forty, the renovation architect, Jacques N. B. de Pouilly, and the ironwork contractors, the Pelanne Brothers, were blamed. Within two weeks, the theater had been restored by Gallier, Turpin & Co., architects and builders. Henry Kmen, *Music in New Orleans: The Formative Years, 1791-1841* (Baton Rouge, 1966), 63, 75-80, 88-90; Benjamin Henry Latrobe, *Impressions Respecting New Orleans*, ed. Samuel Wilson, Jr. (New York, 1951), 34, 41; *Bee*, Feb. 28, 1854. Like most American Protestants, Wharton was a sabbatarian who strongly disapproved of the Sunday amusements enjoyed by Catholics in New Orleans.

Spent part of the evening in computing the Brickwork for the month at the New Custom House. It only amounts to 11.697.5 cubic feet, equal to 233.948 Bricks. This is mainly owing to the failure of the contractor to supply brick fast enough and partly to bad weather. Part of the mason's force had to be suspended for several days, but the contractor is confident that such a contingency must not be apprehended hereafter.

March 7   60° 75° 72°

Humid air from S. East. Vapory clouds. Heavy showers at noon and hot sunshine afterwards.

Every day from the lofty parapet of the new Custom House I see the swelling green of the trees on the far bank of the River, and not unfrequently long for the freedom and spicy freshness of the northern groves. After a busy morning at the office and a hot walk home I was glad to sit down to a nice quiet dinner. But walked down to Canal Street again before tea. And strange to say I have been entirely free all day from those distressing sensations in the head which have so long been my bane. I could not help, however, looking out for them as usual, but they came not. This, together with my daily increasing physical vigour induces me to hope that the pleasant prophecies of my physician are likely soon to be realized, which makes me very thankful.

March 10   69° 70° 65°

...This property is to be sold tomorrow on account of the succession of James Dunn deceased, and I would gladly purchase, as Emily has set her heart upon it but I fear my competitors are prepared to give more for it than I am able to offer....

March 11   54° 58° 64°

Cloudless sky, cold, rigid, penetrating north wind, decidedly aguish weather. However I got along very well....

I went to the sale and bid up to $3510.00 which is full $500 more than its actual value, but another party was bent upon having it so I stopped and he got it for $3525. So that business is settled, much to my chagrin, as I wished especially to gratify Emily by the purchase. Nor should I have stopped where I did, had not my opponent shown conclusively that he was resolved to have it even at an extravagant price — why — I can't imagine....

View of the levee and the Mississippi River with Algiers and the countryside in the background, Jay Dearborn Edwards, photographer, between 1857 and 1860 (1982.167.3).

March 12   57° 60° 67°

Sunday. A morning of incomparable loveliness. Every object sparkling with lucid sunshine and the gentle South west wind just strong enough to spread the flags which deck the forest of masts along the Levee on Sundays....

Emily and Mrs. Ladd went to church but I had to remain at home as I took Blue mass again last night. This time it acted more kindly than ever, and I am every way so much better that although Dr. Stone & Dr. Hamilton both called by appointment this morning yet their professional inquiries were dispatched in a few minutes, and we then entered upon an animated conversation on general subjects for full two hours....

March 13   62° 67¹/₂° 69°

Mild & pleasant, thin veil of shady clouds, South East wind....

This evening we are going to Madame Sontag's concert at Odd Fellow's hall.[21] Before sunset the sky looked threatening but it subsided into a lovely moonlight, so we walked down, Emily, Mrs. Ladd and I. The room was full (say 1500) but the temperature very pleasant. Our position excellent tho' somewhat too near, as it brought us within range of the muscular rigidities in the difficult <u>strains</u>. Madame Sontag shows somewhat of these, which at times mar her otherwise sweet and polished features. Her voice, however, is still rich and flexible, and her manner unexceptionable, but Devries surpassed her in vocalization, and was so palpably the favorite, that the other fair dame must have felt more <u>dame</u>-like than lamb-like as the bouquets fell in showers and the plaudits re-echoed around her rival of the evening. None feel the stings of envy with such pungency as your public singers....

It was a brilliant affair, however, and the audience appeared to great advantage under the splendid lusters suspended from the ceiling. Familiar faces appeared every where. But one thing I more and more antipathize, and that is, the concert dress, or rather undress

Odd Fellows Hall, John T. Hammond, lithographer, ca. 1858 (1954.9.6); Creole family at the opera, Alfred R. Waud, delineator, July 15, 1871 (1951.74 iii).

---

[21] Henriette Sontag (1806-1854) was a celebrated German soprano. She gave her first New Orleans concert at Odd Fellows Hall on February 14, 1854, and made subsequent appearances in Mobile and New Orleans. *Daily Picayune*, Mar. 13, 1854; *Daily Delta*, June 26, 1854; Stanley Sadie, ed., *The New Grove Dictionary of Music and Musicians*, 20 vols. (London, 1980). Odd Fellows Hall was built in 1852 on the corner of Camp and Lafayette, opposite Lafayette Square. George Purves was the architect. The site is now occupied by the John Minor Wisdom United States Court of Appeals Building (Fifth Circuit). *Daily Picayune*, Oct. 5, 1852.

of some of our showiest young belles, perfect "aphrodites" rising from a sea of silks, head and shoulders out, and more, too. I feel tempted to apply to them the quaint old reprimand of King James.

"Fie, fie for shame "Forsooth! ye be to blame."…

March 15   73° 78° 82°

Hot, very hot. Broad sunshine. Broad shadows. South west wind, and summerlike in every particular.

I had to take the omnibus today (in returning to dinner) for the first time. It was far too hot to walk. After dinner I went up to Mr. Hathaway's in Lafayette, and took a long walk with him on a tour of inspection to look at sundry properties in his neighbourhood, but found nothing to suit.[22] There is very little <u>improved</u> property in market now, that would answer my purpose, but I have the whole summer before me, so that I need not decide in haste. It was nearly dark when I got home.

March 16   73° 77½° 81°

Blazing hot sunshine, with shady clouds in the morning but an open summer sky in the afternoon, and a pleasant South West wind.

Mr. Hathaway called at breakfast time to report a very pretty place near him for sale at $6000. I heard the fire bells in the night but had no idea of the extent of the conflagration until I went down this morning, no less than 12 large and valuable stores at and near the corner of Magazine and Natchez. The ruins completely surround the Canal Bank, which now stands alone, and strange to say but slightly injured.[23]…

The vapour from the smouldering wreck filled the air to a great distance in the direction of the New Custom House the whole day, and threw a complete Indian Summer veil over every thing. The news from Europe today is very exciting, the embarkation of troops from England, and warlike preparations on a grand scale every where.…

Canal Bank, R. W. Fishbourne, delineator, William Greene, lithographer, between 1833 and 1838 (1957.73.3 iii).

March 19   65° 68° 70°

Sunday. Mild & rather cooler, very dusty and thick smoky atmosphere. The air at night was so stagnant and so laden with the odors of orange & locust blooms, night & yellow jasmine &c. that it was oppressive beyond conception. Superfluous and overpowering fragrance is like "killing with kindness."

We were all inexpressibly lazy today, the sultry, sleepy air acted like an anodyne, we did not go to church, did not go out anywhere, but spent the day in reading and talking, and amusing or being amused by little Prescott.…

At about 9 P.M. we were roused from our quiescence by the alarm bell and springing of rattles &c. and from the front gallery saw the commencement of a fire at no great distance, in 20 minutes time it became quite formidable, and the whole western hemisphere was lit up with a ruddy glow. It had attained its acme, however, and sank down by degrees until 10 when all was dark again.

March 20   65° 70° 75°

Pleasant air from the N. East, thin shady vapours.

The fire last night, as appears by this morning's Delta, destroyed four handsome frame houses on the corner of Dryades and Euterpe Streets. Dense smoke from the windows, and thick dust from the streets all day.

---

[22] William H. Hathaway of Rice & Hathaway, commission merchants, lived on Chestnut St., near Second. NOCD 1854.

[23] This disastrous fire resulted in the death of one fireman and additional deaths a day later because of the collapse of a wall. The temple-style building on Natchez Street occupied by the Canal Bank was built in 1832-1833 as the Commercial Bank, designed by the architect George Clarkson.

March 27   53° 60° 62°

Lovely weather, but still cold & shivery from the North East. A bright sun, however, & lucid sky.

Emily's birthday. She is 19. Our German nurse had a beautiful wreath of flowers and evergreens, ready when she came in before breakfast. It was selected and arranged with great taste and showed a refinement & feeling not often met with in domestics, entirely self-suggested, too....

Got thro' my business at the Office rather earlier than usual and returned to dinner at 3. Went to the polls, however, first. Swarms of patriots around, but all quiet. The election is for the municipal offices, and a strong effort has been made to detach them from all connection with federal policy. With what success tomorrow will show. The Reform Ticket has not been formed with judgement. There are names on it which are too closely associated with the arena of party strife to offer much prospect of improvement, and one prominent nominee is especially objectionable on the ground of personal dishonesty. Reformers, of all others ought to be "unsuspect". Not a passing breath to dim the mirror of their fair fame.[24]...

March 28   58½° 64° 67°

Very beautiful weather, light North East wind, genial sunshine. And my own health & spirits as buoyant and elastic as the day is pleasant....

The "Procession" in honor of the arrival of Ex-President Fillmore passed the office at noon, Mr. Fillmore was in an open carriage with the Mayor and two Recorders.[25] He has an unusually fine head, with a hale, wholesome complexion, and a genial sunny smile. The social and intellectual in well mingled harmony....

The Election yesterday was marked by unusual excitement, especially at the 7th. Precinct, and some bloodshed. Two men are known to have been killed and several wounded. Tomorrow we shall have the particulars in a reliable shape, together with the complete returns of the ballot box.

[24] John Lawson Lewis of Lexington, Kentucky, a Democrat, was elected mayor of New Orleans over James W. Breedlove, the independent Reform candidate. *Daily Delta*, Mar. 29, 1854.

[25] Former president Millard Fillmore was enthusiastically received in New Orleans with a trip on the river, salvos of artillery, and a parade on Canal Street, Chartres, St. Ann, Royal and St. Charles to City Hall. *Daily Delta*, Mar. 27, 1854; *Daily Picayune*, Mar. 29, 1854.

March 29   62° 70° 75°

Mild air from the East to South, very dry and sunny in the morning. Overcast towards evening with sprinkling rain.

Busier than usual at the Office. One account alone of nearly a year's standing cost me 5 hours of close uninterrupted calculation to examine it for payment. It amounted to over $8500 all in small items requiring to be closely looked into and classified. I found a brisk walk home quite refreshing, and sat down to dinner at 4 with an inordinate appetite. The election returns show a majority of 4 in the council in favor of the Reformers, out of 40....

We may now hope for an energetic and efficient Police, and a more faithful and judicious appropriation of the Municipal resources to the interests of the city, and no longer diverted, as they are said to have been, to the selfish purposes of corrupt and unscrupulous partisans.

March 30   65° 65° 73°

Bland spring morning, tepid dews, South wind. At 8 it became suddenly very dark, and for half an hour rained and blew with violence, some thunder & lightning too. The rain continued with much abatement, however, until near noon with change of wind to the north. At 1 the sun beamed out full again with warm South west wind.

A letter from Mr. Guthrie this morning dated the 23rd. authorizes the increase of my Salary to $1800 from the 1st. of February last. The application was only sent to Washington the 16th. Inst. so that the reply has been very prompt. Only 14 days there and back. After this, and the handsome manner in which my application for a leave of absence and continuance of salary for the time was responded to by the Honorable Secretary, I may well unite in the praises bestowed upon him by Capt. Bowman, and, in fact, by all who know him best....

March 31   67° 68° 67°

At sunrise the air was filled with a lurid yellow haze and clouds on the horizon of intense blackness. In a few minutes a heavy storm burst upon us. Rain in torrents, loud thunder peals, and fierce winds from the North west. It was all over by 8 but the sky continued very unsettled, with change of wind to the West. And in the afternoon to the South East and cold wintry showers.

Very busy at the office preparing the monthly papers for Washington, closing up the Quarter's accounts &c. &c. Our brickwork for the past month measures well, say 14.893 cubic feet containing 297.860 Bricks nearly all of which consists of the finest & most difficult operations of groin-cutting & construction of semi-elliptical groined arches. We expect to complete the second Tier next month....

Great complaint is made of the slow progress of the building, but only by those who are profoundly ignorant in such matters and know nothing of the difficulty of getting together materials for such a stupendous construction, especially in a place like New Orleans where every thing has to be transported from a great distance, involving not only enhanced cost but also great irregularity in the supply. To give an idea of the quantity of materials required I give the following figures up to this date.

Lake Bricks for wall & Piers.		8.918.219	
Square Pressed Bricks for arches		1.704.410	
Wedge etc. etc. etc.		264.313	
		10.886.942	

Granite	6.813	3/13	Tons
Lumber	3.875.721	1/6	Feet
Lime	9.646		Barrels
Cement (Hydraulic)	14.370		"
Sand	52.619		"
Shells	18.818	3/4	"
Cast Iron Caps for Piers 2	99.511		Pounds
Iron Tiers for Anchors	1.056.381		"

April 1   57° 58° 62°

Cold, & clear, sharp north wind changing to North West. Quite wintry again.

We all dined at Mr. R. Dolbear's and returned home early as the night air would have been rather too severe for Prescott, who was of the party.[26] Mr. Dolbear is one of the newly elected Council, and on the Reform Ticket, and it is worthy of remark that his election was accomplished without the expenditure of a single drop of "whiskey" or the exercise of any sinister influence whatever on his part. He feels sanguine as to the prospects of abolishing the "grog shops" in New Orleans altogether....

[26] Rufus Dolbear and his brother had a writing and bookkeeping academy, founded in 1832. His wife, Clotilde Dolbear, died at Covington, La., on Sept. 27, 1855. NOCD 1854; *Bee*, Sept. 27, 1855.

April 2   49° 55° 63°

Sunday, A brilliant day. Pure air from the North, life and health in every breath.

Emily and I went to church in the morning....

After dinner took a long walk, thro' the Fourth District. The beautiful gardens of which are in the full flush of spring-time all radiant with flowers and fresh green leafing. The sunshine was perfectly dazzling and not a speck of vapour on the pure blue, but the air sharp and cutting from the realm of frost. And, of course, far fewer promenaders than usual on Sunday afternoon. The people of New Orleans are singularly sensitive to cold, and shrink from the north wind as the Sicilian from the Sirocco....

April 6   66° 70° 73°

Mild spring weather, threatening clouds, but no rain. South East wind to East.

When I got home to dinner I found the men busy at work putting up a new cistern, which has long been a desideratum; this and the tinner-work connected with it, is the first step of my new landlord towards the improvement of the purchase, and a most important one.[27] Good water and plenty of it, in all climates, but especially here. Air, light, and water, lie at the very basis of all domestic health and comfort in these languid, stagnant latitudes. Emily, too, had been very busy in the flower borders, and brought the rank growth within the limits of neatness and good training.

April 8   68½° 74° 77°

Very mild and sunny with passing clouds, and light breeze from the Eastward.

Quite busy all the morning at the office. Returned home to dinner at 4. Then went to work and completed my gardening operations a little before dark. Every thing around looks neat and orderly, and in good spring-tide condition. And we are all in most excellent health, for which we cannot be too thankful. We have, and have had much, very much to be thankful for. Awakened at midnight by a pleasant band of music in honor of our opposite neighbour, the "Recorder elect." The rich poetry of moonlight and music charmed

[27] Rainwater collected in circular wooden cisterns on brick foundations was the principal drinking water in nineteenth-century New Orleans.

for a moment, and then sunk into flat prose, and harsh huzzas, and loud outcries for "Summers," followed, most probably, by the usual "friends and fellow citizens" from the balcony of the "hero."[28]

April 12   70° 72° 74°

Cloudy and threatening rain. South East wind.

The medicine I took last night compelled me to stay at home today.

Read an Extract from the proceedings of the Charleston City Council, of Dec. 20th. 1853, demonstrating beyond a doubt the value of a strict Quarantine in excluding "yellow fever." It is an able, sound and intelligent document and presents a strong contrast to the crude and aimless views expressed by members of our own city "faculty" and is a bitter reproach to the inaction and besotted stupidity of the "authorities" in Louisiana. With the terrible realities of last summer before their eyes, and after all the parade of "Committees" and "Investigations" they have done absolutely nothing at all. Another summer is just at hand, and if we escape, our safety will be due to the kindness of an all-disposing Providence, and in no respect to the judicious and intelligent decisions of our "deliberative bodies." Rain set in towards noon, a quiet spring rain, and "down with the dust" at last. My thirsty cistern which has been parching and seasoning in the hot suns of the past week is filling up fast. And we shall soon have plenty of good, pure water....

April 18   56° 61° 65°

Brilliant sky in the morning with keen North East wind. Cloudy & threatening in the afternoon.

War is at last declared by the allies against Russia. Each steamer will now be looked for with anxious interest.

April 19   60° 67° 72°

Keen unwholesome north wind with a blazing hot sun, very dry, too, and dusty. Bad weather for invalids.

Emily, Mrs. Ladd and Ellen came to the office at 11 and I went

[28] Henry M. Summers (ca.1813-1865), a cotton and tobacco factor, lived on Terpsichore, corner Coliseum. NOCD 1859; WPA, *Administrations of the Mayors of New Orleans* (New Orleans, 1940), 101.

Wooden cistern common throughout nineteenth-century New Orleans, Plan book 46, Folio 53, New Orleans Notarial Archives.

with them to see Rossiter's Paintings on exhibition at the Armory Hall.[29] "The Captive Israelites" is a fine piece of colouring the atmosphere full of golden light, all the glow and flush and purity of an oriental evening. The shadows, even, radiant with lucid particles. The figures well grouped and full of interest, and altho' not unattended with serious defects yet upon the whole better conceived and rendered than is usual with our historical painters. Whilst we were there the poor little orphans of the 4th. District Asylum, came to see the pictures.[30] They numbered some 50 or 60, with but one attendant. Neat, orderly, and cheerful looking, and to all appearances well cared for and healthy.

April 20   65° 70° 74°

Warm sun, light gathering clouds. North East wind. Had to keep good fires at the office.

When I returned to dinner I found Emily and the nurse full of business, all the domestic particularities having suddenly devolved upon them. Our cook who has proved an admirable servant up to this week is also a very rigid Catholic and kept Lent with a degree of abstemiousness truly surprising in one of her bulk. But alas in an evil hour Emily gave her permission to spend last Sunday evening amongst her "people," and Lent being over they must have had a "compensating" time of it for she came home most unmistakably drunk, and the poison once in she has continued more or less so ever since, so that this morning we were obliged to send her away until she is herself again. She makes very fair promises &c....

April 22   69° 77° 80°

Very beautiful seasonable weather. South East wind.

---

[29] Thomas Prichard Rossiter (1818-1871), a well-known New York painter, exhibited his historical paintings at the Armory Hall. George C. Groce and David H. Wallace, *The New-York Historical Society's Dictionary of Artists in America, 1564-1860* (New Haven, 1957); *Daily Picayune*, Mar. 21, 1854. Armory Hall, the armory of the Washington Artillery Battalion on Camp Street, opposite Natchez Alley, was frequently used for exhibitions. The hall was built with the bricks of the old Camp Street Theatre (1822-1823). B. M. Norman, *Norman's New Orleans and Environs* (New Orleans, 1845).

[30] The fourth district orphan asylum was located at Live Oak (now Constance) and Seventh streets. Established as the Protestant Orphans Home in 1853, a large brick addition designed by architect Thomas Sully was built facing Magazine Street in 1883. It became the Protestant Children's Home in 1956 and closed in 1972. The Sully building, used for mixed residential and commercial purposes, still stands.

Got up early and went to market. A great improvement since the close of the Catholic absurdities of Lent. What are they but a system of excesses, excess of starvation at one time, excess of surfeit at another. As a religious observation more than useless, as a physical influence dangerous, as a weapon of priestcraft, no doubt advantageous, or it would long ago have been consigned to oblivion. The vote of yesterday gave an overwhelming majority in favor of the new railroad ordinance.[31]

April 23   74° 77° 80°

Sunday. Thin veily clouds. South wind.

Emily cannot go to church today. She has too much on her hands at home, her cook having left for good. She came yesterday afternoon to say that her <u>cousin</u> had arrived and offered to take her to Louisville, so that we are out at sea again in that item. The dreamy summer air indisposed me for any exertion, even reading and writing were too much labor....

April 24   75½° 80° 82°

A scorching hot summer day and very dusty; a fine breeze, however, from the South East.

The second tier of groined arches was completed on Saturday; having been commenced on the 17th. of November last, say in all 5 months and 5 days. The Foreman of Brickwork began today to lay off the walls for the third story. The arches just finished contain 55030.9 cubic feet of masonry, inclusive of backing up, equal to <u>1.100.615 Bricks</u>. The arches of the first story were commenced August 10. 1852 and finished June 15. 1853. They contain 91.737 cubic feet, including backing, say in all <u>1.834.740 Bricks</u>. This embraces the great 40 feet arches of the central portion and the contiguous railroad passages all round of 15 to __ feet wide. Arches of the 1st. story 6 feet rise. 2nd. story 4'6" rise and one brick, say 9 in. thick, haunches backed solid.

---

[31] The railroad ordinance approved by the Common Council of New Orleans provided for the subscription by the city to the capital stock of the New Orleans, Jackson and Great Northern Railroad and the New Orleans, Opelousas and Great Western Railroad companies. *Daily Delta*, Apr. 22, 1854.

Carrollton Gardens, 1889 (1974.25.29.61).

April 25
75° 77° 82°

Gathering clouds, hot sun, high wind from the north East. The city half concealed in dust.

Upwards of 2000 passengers from foreign ports have arrived within 2 days, and thousands are said to be waiting on the other side for some friendly Charon to ferry them over. And a fatal ferry boat it promises to be to many of them during the fervid months of the coming summer, with no Quarantine laws, no sanitary arrangements worth a straw, a feeble city government, an inefficient police, and an embarrassed city finance. The Lord help the unacclimated stranger, and the citizen too, whom business ties here for the summer....

May 2
66° 72° 71°

Still dry, cloudless and north wind, the air full of dust and glare.

Very busy all the morning with the monthly papers, estimates &c. and some important outdoor business affecting the progress of the work. The brickwork for April measures well under the circumstances, say 12.565.9 cubic feet containing 257.315 Bricks. The walls of the third story are now fairly under way, and the interior masonry will soon be sufficiently well advanced to resume and complete the exterior Granite work. The heavy scaffolding for that purpose is now undergoing thorough repairs, and will soon be ready.

It was funny to hear an Irishman caught tripping in his blarney last evening at Hamilton's. The man was laying concrete on the walks. As we approached he touched his hat to me "and how do ye do Mr. Wharton, an sure now an if ye were a bad man ye would be in the New Custom House at this day." Ah! Pat you missed it this time.

I must be the worst man there, for I was there at the first and have been there ever since. He had been at some time or other a laborer on the works but I did not recollect his face. Had the poor man been posted up his compliment would have been just the other way, as it was, he held his peace. Why <u>do</u> they make such blunders? Even the quickest witted among them. Now my cook is excellent in her way and yet, what was my astonishment at dinner today to find that she had cut off the rich, juicy tender tops of the asparagus, and served up at table the stringy stumps.

After dinner I took Emily & Ellen and little Prescott to Carrollton. The trip was delightful and the cool fresh breeze on the river bank quite invigorating after the heat and dust of a day in town. We met pleasant friends in the gardens and found every thing much changed, if not improved, since last May.[32]

The abrasions of the River have made a new Levee, far within the old one, absolutely necessary. Obliterating entirely one of the beautiful and far-famed gardens. The shady lane, too, of lofty oleander which last year was covered at this time with a perfect waste of blossoms. The pleasant walk on the river bank arched over with China trees. The lovely alleys of Cape jessamines, and the white bell flowered Yucca, from which years ago I derived my first impressions of the exuberance of southern vegetation, all, all, have vanished and in their place nothing but a long, bald, earthy, embankment, a wide dusty road, immense piles of cord wood (for supplying the steamboats), with rail tracks in every direction to facilitate their transmission from point to point. Stagnant pools of muddy water between the old Levee and the new. In short, deformity for beauty, utility for poetry, but the grand river still redeems it all, and the fresh green woods on the distant bank, and the fresh pure air blowing across its restless current. My little boy was charmed with the noble steamers five of which passed during the short time we stood on the bank. At the garden his nurse put him in the swing and gave two or three passes, but he did not take kindly to it. We returned home just before dark.

[32] The town of Carrollton was developed from the sugar plantation of Barthélémy Macarty above New Orleans which was acquired by Bernard Marigny, Samuel Kohn, John Slidell, and Laurent Millaudon in 1831. The town plan, drawn by Charles F. Zimpel, surveyor, appears on his *Topographical Map of New Orleans and its Vicinity*, published in 1834. Carrollton, now part of uptown New Orleans, was the seat of Jefferson Parish from 1854 until it was incorporated into New Orleans in 1874. It was the terminus of the New Orleans and Carrollton Railroad, now the St. Charles Avenue streetcar line. Carrollton Gardens, a popular resort with a hotel and gardens, was built by the New Orleans and Carrollton Railroad Co. near the terminus.

May 13   79° 83° 85°

High wind from the South East, hot sun, moist air....

Major Beauregard left today for Memphis to be absent until the 1st. Proximo. Before going he and Mr. Penn entered into agreement for the delivery of a million of Lake Brick, so that we shall soon have a supply and resume active operations upon the walls of the third story.[33]...

May 18   75° 79° 82°

Hot sunshine, bracing dry air from North West. Thin film of cloud in the afternoon giving a delightful temperature.

We expected to resume brickwork today, but the first cargo of 55.000 Bricks under the new order is reported sunk at the mouth of the Tchefuncta River, so that it will be the beginning of the week before we can put the masons at work again.[34]

May 23   79° 83° 84°

Cloudy & threatening in the morning with fine breeze from the South East. Showers and bursts of hot sunshine in the afternoon.

Mr. Penn returned today a short time before I left the office for dinner. It was quite late when I got home and nearly 5 when we left the dinner table. Happening to be in the French Quarter this morning I was struck with the extreme beauty of the shrubbery and flowers that embellished the Square opposite the Cathedral. Every thing is kept in the most complete order, and I observe the hand of improvement busy in the rear of the Cathedral as well as in front.[35] That neighborhood has changed more than any other part of the city since I first knew it in June 1845, and the alterations are generally for the better, and of a substantial & enduring character. The breeze blows fresh from the river over a garden of lovely plants in place of the parched sterile square of former years. But the modernized exterior of the church of St. Louis, and its skeleton spire of perforated Iron work are but an indifferent substitute for the venerable, weather stained, picturesque turrets of the "olden time."[36]

The Pontalba buildings, on the contrary, occupy the place of a poor delapidated shattered cluster of old cabarets and eating houses which used to throw a dingy gloom over either side of this beautiful Square.[37]

May 25   75° 80° 83°

Heavy showers, thunder and lightening set in at daybreak. Got quite wet in returning from Market but the rain is very refreshing after the sultry air of yesterday. Showers until 11 when it cleared off, and the breeze blowing over the upper arches of the Custom House was perfectly delightful, fresh from the river and but little tainted with the impurities of the city.

Went to see Powell's picture of the discovery of the Mississippi by De Soto.[38] After exhibition in the different cities of the Union it is intended to fill the vacant panel in the Rotunda at Washington. It is very rich in carefully painted detail but the general effect of the

[33] P. G. T. Beauregard and Alfred G. Penn, a federal dispersing agent, were put in charge of the construction of the new Custom House in 1853 when the previous commission was dissolved.

[34] The Tchefuncte River flows into Lake Pontchartrain on the north side of the lake. Bricks are still produced from St. Tammany Parish clay.

[35] The public square in front of St. Louis Cathedral was renamed Jackson Square in January 1851 in honor of Andrew Jackson, hero of the Battle of New Orleans. The iron fence around St. Anthony Square in the rear of the cathedral, designed by Louis H. Pilié, was erected by Pelanne Bros. in 1853. NONA, William Monaghan, July 13, 1853; Leonard V. Huber, *Jackson Square Through the Years* (New Orleans, 1982).

[36] Except for the lower part of the front wall, including the bases of the two hexagonal towers, St. Louis Cathedral was entirely rebuilt in 1849-1850. The architect was Jacques Nicolas Bussière de Pouilly, a Frenchman who had come to New Orleans about 1834. One of the unusual features of his design was a spire above the central tower that appeared to be of cast iron, but was actually of timber with ornamental inserts of decorative wrought iron. In 1859 this open-work spire was covered with its present-day sheathing and slate roof. Leonard V. Huber and Samuel Wilson, Jr., *The Basilica on Jackson Sqaure* (New Orleans, 1965).

[37] The properties on St. Ann and St. Peter streets flanking Jackson Square were acquired by Andres Almonester y Roxas beginning in 1777. Several rental properties were built between then and 1811 when his widow, Louise de la Ronde, built a fine house at the corner of St. Peter and Decatur. In 1849-1850, their daughter Micaela, Baroness de Pontalba, had the deteriorating buildings demolished and the present Pontalba buildings erected by Samuel Stewart, builder. When she came to New Orleans, the baroness brought a set of plans for the buildings by an unknown architect. Later plans and specifications, perhaps based on those drawings, were executed by James Gallier and Henry Howard. In later years, Gallier did not claim credit for the final design; Henry Howard did. The definitive answer is still unknown. The St. Ann Street building now belongs to the Louisiana State Museum, and the St. Peter Street row is owned by the City of New Orleans. Leonard V. Huber and Samuel Wilson, Jr., *Baroness Pontalba's Buildings* (New Orleans, 1964), 35-40; Christina Vella, *Intimate Enemies: The Two Worlds of the Baroness de Pontalba* (Baton Rouge, 1997), 277-82, 278-79.

[38] William Henry Powell's painting *DeSoto's Discovery of the Mississippi* was exhibited at Armory Hall for one week in May 1854. *Daily True Delta*, May 17, 1854.

The Cabildo, new St. Louis Cathedral, and the Presbytere, Louis Xavier Magny, lithographer, 1850 (1940.3).

Old St. Louis Cathedral, before 1849, Vieux Carré Survey, Historic New Orleans Collection.

Upper Pontalba building, Vieux Carré Survey, Historic New Orleans Collection.

Trinity Church
Lafayette from "our cottage".   T.K.W.

Steel Chapel
Felicity Road New Orleans   T.K.W. May 28. 1854

grouping and the atmospheric tone of the whole suffer somewhat from the prominence and decision given equally to every object which compose it. It is all action and the eye roams in vain over the whole in search of some spot which it can repose upon. It is a fine picture, however, and full of interest, in the drawing & colouring of the figures, costumes, armory &c....

May 27   79° 83° 83°

Very hot steamy air, clear hot sunshine in the morning. Dense clouds in the afternoon. South East wind. Showers between 4 & 5 P.M.

Wrote to Mr. Bryant of Boston in answer to his of 22nd. Ulto. enclosing drawings of arches, Iron caps &c. of New Custom House.[39] It has been a busy time yesterday and today at home, taking up carpets and putting down matting, and a general renovation, cleaning and <u>rightning up</u> for summer.[40]

Every thing about the house looks sweet and fresh, and well arranged this evening, and in harmony with the charming May atmosphere after the shower, as the last yellow rays shot thro' the front windows and gave fresh luster to the pictures and ornaments....

May 28

Steel chapel...was erected by the Methodist Society A.D. 1850 from original designs by T. K. Wharton Architect, and under the superintendence of Rupert C. Foster, a young archt. of much promise (since deceased) who modified the ornamentation of the tower by introducing the brackets in place of a pediment in the original.[41]

---

[39] Gridley J. F. Bryant (1816-1899) was a prominent Boston architect. Among his major works was the Massachusetts State House extension. Placzek, *Macmillan Encyclopedia.*

[40] Spring housecleaning was an annual custom in New Orleans — replacing carpets with grass matting, removing curtains, and covering furniture with light slipcovers in preparation for the summer heat.

[41] The Steele Chapel at the corner of Felicity and Chestnut streets was named in honor of the Reverend Elijah Steele (ca. 1811-1841), a native of Mississippi who died of yellow fever and was buried in Cypress Grove Cemetery. At first called the Elijah Steele Methodist Episcopal Church, it became the Felicity Church in 1858 and was destroyed by fire in 1887. The present Felicity United Methodist Church was built in 1889. Rupert C. Foster (ca. 1818-1853) designed a house on Baronne Street for Abraham Haber and the synagogue of the Congregation Shennaria Hassad on Rampart, between St. Louis and Conti streets. NONA, Theodore Guyol, May 13, 1850, Hilary B. Cenas, July 5, 1850; *Daily Picayune*, Dec. 14, 1853.

Its length is 101 feet by 48 wide and 40 high, with basement of 10 feet 8. for school and classrooms and pews in nave and gallery for 1000 persons. Whole height, to top of the spire 110 feet 8. It is built of brick covered with warm coloured stucco, and is a pleasant comfortable little church, but chiefly conspicuous for the extreme beauty of its position, near the head of Camp Street with its long avenues of China trees, wax berry Myrtle and other rich foliage, and in the immediate vicinity of Coliseum Place, the largest and, when fully laid out, the most beautiful open park in the city....

The chapel derived its name from the Rev. Mr. Steele, a much beloved pastor of the Methodist Church who died some years ago. The building cost $20.000 and the ground about $4000, which sums were raised by voluntary subscription of the Society throughout the city and state, forming part of a gross amount having for its object the extinction of all outstanding indebtedness of the Methodist Church in this city, and the erection of the present edifice....

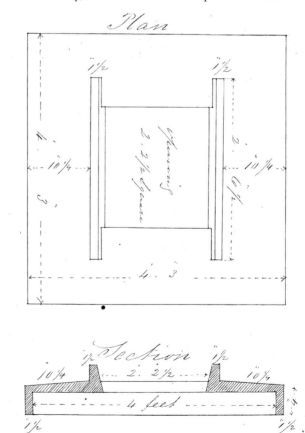

Iron caps used as skewbacks to the ground arches in the New Custom House New Orleans. They are laid in Cement on the top of the Piers, and the arches which spring from them are backed up with solid brickwork at the haunches, and levelled to the crown with concrete, ready to receive a floor of marble tiles. The Caps were cast at the Iron works of Messrs. Knap and Wade, Pittsburg.[42]

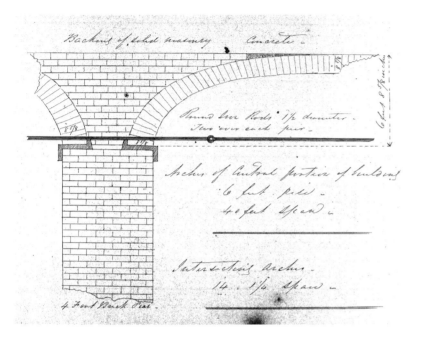

The ground arches of the First story of the New Custom House are of various spans from 9.6 to 40 feet. They are constructed of Lake pressed Brick furnished by J. A. Blanc (the Contractor) of the following dimensions viz. $8^{5/8}$ inches x $4^{1/4}$ x $2^{1/2}$.[43]

These bricks are laid in Cement. The Backing up of the haunches and the brickwork of the Piers are of the Common Lake Brick furnished by Messrs. Bobb. Kendall & Co. and laid in Cement with a certain proportion of Lime.[44] In the Central Compartment of the Building the anchors employed consist of Iron Rods (as shewn in the sketch), $1^{1/2}$ inch diameter. Two over each pier, secured by strong nuts and washers at each end, and 96.6 inches in length, with Joints as shewn opposite. The anchors in other parts of the building are flat Bars, 3" x $^{1/2}$" with key joints, passing thro' from street to street. Two Bars to a course and at intervals of four to six feet vertical, and in addition to these anchors, a large quantity of band-iron, 3" by 3/16 has been built into the walls. The same system of anchoring is pressed in the walls and ground arches of the upper stories, except as regards the round $1^{1/2}$ inch Iron which is used only in the Central Compartment of the First Tier of Ground arches.

Section of the Ground arch in Central Compartment of the New Custom House, showing the Iron Cap in the top of the Pier. The Iron rods used as anchors. The brick backing, concrete &c.

The arches of the second and third stories differ in proportion and the Caps are modified according to the different piers which they surmount.

T.K.W. June 1, 1854

May 30   81° 84° 86°

Large floating clouds, fierce heat at times, steamy air. East to South East wind. Showers at noon.

Went out to the Lake after dinner, but left the little boy behind as his teeth have troubled him a good deal today and he is quite restless. The progress of improvement at the Lake end of the road is slow but regular, and many conveniences, such as bath houses &c. have been erected since we were there last year (April 16th.) and they are pushing out the works into the Lake so as to create eventually a firm solid mole, which will be in every respect as good a steamboat landing as that at the terminus of the old railroad.[45]...

June 3   72° 76° 78°

Pleasant, sunny day, north east wind but far too cool for June....

I have been in the United States 24 years today. On the 3rd. of June 1830, at sunrise, the woody hills of Neversink and Staten Island lay within a few miles of us, all glowing with lustruous sunshine. I well remember the day, it was one of intense and beautiful excitement. As we passed the narrows and sailed up to the City of

[42] The ironwork for the Custom House was furnished by the Pittsburg iron foundry of Knap, Wade & Co. The proprietor was Charles Knap.

[43] Probably Jules Arnaud Blanc (1819-1904), a dealer in bricks and lumber, at 9 Julia Street landing. *Daily Picayune*, June 16, 1904.

[44] Bobb, Kendall & Co. had furnished bricks for the Custom House since April 27, 1848, when they contracted to supply 18,000,000 bricks. On February 3, 1852, they transferred this contract to Sam F. Butterworth of New York. NONA, F. N. Haralson, Feb. 3, 1852.

[45] West End was a popular resort on Lake Pontchartrain at the terminus of the New Basin Canal. A shell road for carriages ran along the canal.

New York thro' that unrivalled Bay, every object was new to us, every thing awakened a separate interest, and over all breathed an atmosphere of untainted purity, and lucid as a sapphire. It seems long, long, ago, and I recollect it now as a lovely dream. I am tempted to take a hasty review of the changes since that day. After a delightful rest of a month in N. York at Mr. T. Slocum's in Beekman Street, we proceeded westward by the Hudson, Erie Canal, and Lake, and reached our new home at Piqua, Ohio on the 17th. of July. My Father had purchased an excellent farm on the Miami, a mile from the town, it contained about 250 acres of fine land under culture, besides woodland and two luxuriant sugar groves, a comfortable frame homestead, convenient outbuildings, and very large orchards of the choicest peaches and apples, a garden, too, in which my Father took great pride. We had no lack of society, as the neighborhood from its fertility and healthiness had attracted many agreeable and estimable families. But the two years we spent there were by no means happy ones. My poor mother's health was very delicate and we were all ill-fitted for the deprivations of the backwoods. My Father sold the place and early in 1832 we removed to Zanesville [Ohio] where he purchased a large warehouse on the Muskingum [River] and established himself in general forwarding & Commission business. In April of that year I left my dear family for the first time, and threw myself into the busy world. I went to New York and entered the office of Mr. Martin E. Thompson, Architect, and had just got fairly thro' the mysteries of the classic orders &c., when the Cholera broke out in the city and I received an invitation from Dr. Hosack to take refuge for awhile at his charming retreat on the Hudson at Hyde Park.[46] A month of uninterrupted pleasure soon slipped away, when one day amongst the frequent guests at the Doctor's sumptuous table were Col. Thayer and Mr. Go[u]verneur Kemble of West Point.[47] They both urged me to visit them before I returned to the city. Col. Thayer was at that time Superintendent of West Point and living alone, and Mr. Kemble at Coldspring opposite. When I got to the Colonel's he kindly told me that he should not think of letting me go until all

danger was over in the city. So that I was soon fully domiciliated with him, and remained for more than five months, during all which time the Colonel was constantly devising means to promote my improvement and happiness. He assisted me thro' a course of mathematical study and Descriptive Geometry. He encouraged me to indulge my fondness for landscape painting by rambling with me among the scenes of enchantment around, and searching out their choicest and more latent beauties. He introduced me to men of taste, refinement and distinction who flocked to West Point that summer, and added luster to the elegant dinner parties at the Colonel's and Mr. Kemble's amongst whom I may enumerate Mr. Paulding, Washington Irving, General Scott, Major Leslie and Mr. Poinsett.[48] In short it was a period of rare enjoyment and rare advantages, it has thrown a happy influence over the whole of my subsequent life, and I never can think of Col. Thayer without the liveliest emotions of pleasure and gratitude. Among visitors of the summer was the Rev. Dr. Muhlenberg, Principal of the Institute at Flushing, whose educational views quite won the Colonel, and prepared him to think highly of an offer I received from Dr. Muhlenberg in November to join his establishment.[49] Accordingly in December I left my kind friend and went to Flushing, Long Island. During the vacation of 1833, in August and September, I crossed the mountains and revisited my family at Zanesville. My mother was in better health and we spent some happy days together. The autumn came, and I parted with her for the last time. It was midnight, dark and gloomy, and I tore myself away, and the night dews fell chillingly upon me as I hurried to the stage in waiting. One year after my poor mother died. I was spending the vacation of 1834 at Flushing when the sad tidings reached me, and I immediately went up the North River to Fishkill near the mountains and spent a month by myself in that quiet and secluded village. None but those who knew her could tell how deeply I felt the loss. I was many years at Flushing, occupying the Professorship of the Arts of Design & Descriptive Geometry at the "Institute" and studying the classics, divinity and general "belles lettres." In the meantime my Father was married again to Mrs. A. M. Reddie, to whom I became very much attached and we all found her a

[46] Martin Euclid Thompson (1787-1877), a carpenter and self-taught architect, was in partnership with Ithiel Town from 1826 to 1828. He designed many important buildings in the Greek Revival style, including the New York Merchants Exchange (1825-1827) and the Brooklyn Naval Hospital (1833-1841). Placzek, *Macmillan Encyclopedia*, 4:207.

[47] Colonel Sylvanus Thayer (1785-1872) was superintendent of the U.S. Military Academy at West Point from 1817 to 1833, after which he served as an army engineer in New England. *DAB*. Gouverneur Kemble (1786-1875) built a factory known as the West Point Foundry Association at Coldspring, New York, where he lived, across the Hudson River from West Point. He served as U.S. congressman from 1837 to 1841. *DAB*.

[48] James Kirke Paulding (1778-1860), author; Washington Irving (1783-1859), essayist, novelist, and historian; Winfield Scott (1786-1866), general; Major Charles Robert Leslie (1795-1859), painter and author; Joel Roberts Poinsett (1779-1851), South Carolina congressman, who later served a controversial term as American minister to Mexico. *DAB*.

[49] William Augustus Muhlenberg (1796-1877), an Episcopal clergyman, was rector of St. George's Church in Flushing, Long Island. *DAB*.

most kind and considerate step mother. Her accomplishments, too, made her society delightful. I used to spend my vacations with her at New Haven, her place was very beautiful, surrounded by spacious gardens and ample grounds, all of which she had laid out herself with great taste, and always kept in fine order. The house, too, was her own design. Doric with canopies over the upper windows in Hindostan[ee?] fashion. Conservatory on the South side with the drawing room windows opening into it, and rich clusters of grapes hanging from the glazing. What happy evenings we used to pass. My mother was a thorough musician, the piano on week days, the organ on Sundays, and my sisters were there, too, so that we had no difficulty in filling up the parts, and to my fancy our anthems were not deficient in harmony. Bhurtpore Cottage (for so she called it to perpetuate her recollections of the East Indies) was endeared to us by a thousand pleasant incidents, but it is all changed now. Poor Henry and Charles [Wharton], too, are both gone, and my Father! In 1838 Dr. Muhlenberg purchased a fine body of land on the Sound 3 miles from Flushing called it College Point and commenced the establishment of St. Paul's College. Here I spent about 2 years when the Revd. Francis L. Hawks commenced the cognate Institution of St. Thomas' Hall at the Village of Flushing and I was induced to join him.[50] It enjoyed an unprecedented reputation for awhile, and the Doctor's educational abilities shone out in all their strength, but his financial talents were at fault and in April 1843 the whole concern was in the hands of his assigners, and all my savings were absorbed in the failure. Fortunately, however, the education of my two sisters which for some time past had devolved wholly upon me, was now just completed at the Seminary of the Revd. J. Brown at Astoria. So that the casualty was less disastrous than it would otherwise have been. Dr. Hawks still retained the Rectorship of St. Thomas Church in New York, and after the failure at Flushing took a house for his family in Brooklyn Heights where I joined them in May 1843. Dr. Hawks' impulsive nature was chafed and fretted by his pecuniary difficulties at Flushing, and in his despondency he longed for the South. Accordingly in the summer and autumn of 1843 he and I made a tour of exploration which resulted in our commencing in partnership an University at Holly Springs Mississippi. On the 2nd. October 1843 we returned to Brooklyn from our Southern journey and then made arrangements for entering upon our new undertaking. I withdrew my sisters from Astoria and crossed the mountains with them, leaving them in the care of my brother Robert John at Cincinnati and then proceeded Southward and joined Dr. Hawks & family at Holly Springs on the 1st January 1844.[51] Our project went on bravely. The Doctor's peculiar talents again found a field for successful action. But unfortunately he must needs let himself be proposed for the Bishoprick of Mississippi, which gave rise to new difficulties as he met with determined and successful opposition in convention on the ground of his former financial embarrassments, tho' I who knew the circumstances best have no doubt that they spring from a want of judgement and in no respect from dishonest purpose. This new vexation made the Doctor uneasy again, and he became languid in his efforts at Holly Springs. In the summer of 1844 I went to Cincinnati to make purchases &c. for our Institute and see my sisters, and early in 1845 Dr. Hawks was induced to visit New Orleans with an offer of the rectorship of Christ's Church in that city, and an opportunity of founding an University that would make ample amends for the position we resigned in Mississippi. So he impressed me, and in May I paid a short visit to New Orleans where his family had already arrived and he had entered upon his new charge. The prospects seemed favorable enough and I returned to wind up our affairs at Holly Springs, which I did very favorably. Spent the summer there, and on the 19th. Octr. was married by Dr. Hawks to the eldest daughter of Judge Huling of Holly Springs. In December I went with my wife to New Orleans and took rooms for the winter at Mrs. Cornell's in Camp Street.[52] In the meantime Judge Huling sold his Cotton Plantation, and purchased a sugar estate in the Parish of Plaquemines 52 miles below the City of New Orleans, to which he removed that winter. Dr. Hawks' University scheme all fell to the ground, and he confined himself in a very short time to his rectory which he resigned again with his usual facility in a couple of years and went back to New York. In the meantime I gradually reverted back to the occupation in which I commenced life, architecture, which I was again led into from having made the designs for Christ's Church New Orleans during the last summer I spent in Holly Springs, and being engaged in making the detail drawings during the spring of 1846 with Mr. Gallier who

---

[50] The Rev. Francis Lister Hawks (1798-1866), a prominent Episcopal clergyman, was rector of Christ Church in New Orleans from 1845 to 1849 and then became the first president of the University of Louisiana (later Tulane). Hodding Carter and Betty Werlein Carter, *So Great A Good* (Sewanee, Tenn., 1955), 74.

[51] Robert John Wharton was married to Jane Brooks Wharton. He died of cholera July 3, 1854.

[52] Mrs. M. F. R. L. Cornelle operated a boarding house at 215 Camp Street. NOCD 1846.

Design for Christ Church by Thomas K. Wharton, 1845, New York Public Library; Canal Street – North Side, including Christ Church, Marie Adrien Persac, delineator, 1873 (1958.78.1.8).

superintended the erection of the building.[53] I made an engagement with Mr. Gallier to go into effect in the winter of 46-47 but the depressed state of architectural operations at that time prevented our carrying it out and I passed the greater part of the time during the summer and winter of '46 and the ensuing spring & summer on the Plantation pursuing closely my studies in architecture and executing some large drawings in perspective for Mr. Gallier.[54] In Decr. 1847 I took a house in Prytania Street New Orleans and commenced house-keeping and in January 1848 received the appointment at the New Custom House which I have held ever since. On the 11 April 1848 my wife fell a victim to the most fatal form of pulmonary consumption — abscess of the lungs — and I left town not long after and spent the summer on the plantation. Oct 23 I resumed my duties at the New Custom House and pursued them steadily until I was compelled by ill-health to take my northern tour last summer. August 1, 1849 I removed to a house on Apollo Street [now Carondelet], and Oct. 1, 1851 to the house I now occupy. Decr. 18 of that year I was married to Emily and Sept 23, 1852 my little boy was born. Last summer we all enjoyed ourselves abroad at the north. This summer we hope to enjoy ourselves at home. All well and happy around us, every comfort that we could desire, few wishes ungratified and fewer drawbacks than fall to the lot of most persons. And in closing this hasty retrospect I cannot doubt that my experience is not dissimilar from that of almost every one who will chose to reflect. Sorrows there have been, bitter sorrows, but the hours of happiness have far outweighed the hours of pain & grief. And even those latter might have been lessened by a better temper of mind, and a more steadfast reliance on the great anchor "Hope."

[53] The first sketch of a design for Christ Church at the corner of Canal and Dauphine was made by T. K. Wharton at Holly Springs, Miss., in 1845. In 1846, Christ Church contracted with James Gallier for $56,000 to build a Gothic-style church at the corner of Canal and Dauphine streets in accordance with "four plans and drawings furnished by the Rev'd Francis L. Hawks." In his autobiography, James Gallier mentions that the drawing master at Hawks's school had made a sketch design for the new church, but that he had to make so many alterations in the plan that it amounted to a new design. Photographs and prints of the now demolished church, however, show that it was built substantially in accordance with Wharton's design. NONA, William Christy, Apr. 21, 1846; James Gallier, *Autobiography of James Gallier, Architect* (1864; reprint, New York, 1973), 40.

[54] A lithograph, *Municipal Hall, Lafayette Square, New Orleans* (Gallier Hall) was made by F. Bedford, London, from a drawing by Thomas K. Wharton (1935.1).

June 12   81° 87° 89°

Cool north wind, hot sun. Large passing clouds....

After dinner I walked out to the Rail Road Depot at the corner of Clio and Solis [now South Robertson] Streets. It is quite in the swamp, on the last street opened in that direction, and no less than 18 squares, or $1\frac{1}{2}$ mile back from the river. The great Northern road starts from it about parallel with the Shell road & New Canal which is here only a Square or two distant. At a few hundred feet from the Depot the rails cross the wide draining Canal over a construction of wood work. The rails are of very heavy iron and apparently of excellent quality, but the springy soil beneath them seems to yield greatly and with much irregularity to the pressure of the Engine. One of "Baldwin's" large locomotives passed over the Track while I was there. The Depot is but a temporary construction of wood but answers its present purpose very well. Two very neat cars were there finished and ready for use, a third under the hands of the workmen. Standing on the Canal bridge the track curves out of view, and is lost in the heavy growth of Cypress, and the tangled underwood & vines which mantle over the slime on either side. The Streets as far as the Depot are all opened and the building lots filling up rapidly, but after you pass Hercules Street [now South Rampart Street] the improvements are of the cheapest character, altogether for the poorer sorts of people. Plank roads at intervals are pushed far into the swamp, but the banquettes cease and wooden gunwales and planks take their place. The gutters filled with green stagnant ooze, and the tenements jostle each other and are graced with innumerable stores of empty barrels, dilapidated wash tubs, remnants of ancient costume, and old and new garments flaunting from the clothes' lines. Children and dogs without stint clustered around the gateways and from within the yards, alleys, open doors and windows issued fragmentary specimens of every language spoken under the canopy of heaven.

June 19   84° 86½° 87°

Fierce sunshine, floating clouds, and light air from South West....

People are going out every day, and peaches are coming in. The "go aways" are going fast, and the "stay at homes" are settling down into a state of summer quietude.

Jackson Railroad yard, Jay Dearborn Edwards, photographer, between 1857 and 1860 (1982.32.6).

Cotton press, after E. H. Newton, Jr., photographer, 1860 (1959.159.6), gift of Harold Schilke and Boyd Cruise.

June 21   84° 88° 91°

Fine air from the West. Shady clouds, but hotter than ever in the middle of the day....

The stonesetting on the exterior of the New Custom House was resumed on the 12th. Inst. and today we forwarded a requisition for part of the Granite lying at the Quincy Quarries, we shall probably call for the whole of it at the beginning of next month.

June 24   84° 88° 89°

Very sultry, clouds & sunshine; high winds from the East during the middle of the day....

Towards evening I took a long walk down Race Street to the River Bank where the breeze blew freshly over the water, then by the Reservoir home. The Levee at this point was unusually quiet and summerish, few drays, few seamen, and but few ships loading. At most but one at a pier and wide gaps between, thro' which the green trees of the other bank contrasted cheerfully with the bricks and mortar of the town. There appeared to be some little activity within the long ranges of "Cotton presses" & "pickeries" which occupy block after block in this section of the city. But the streets between were very quiet and the cocoa grass is already taking possession of the sidewalks. When I first came to New Orleans, the grassy streets in the upper part of town gave it an air of desertion and loneliness that was almost painful, but I am used to it now and take the more secluded thoroughfares from choice....

June 25   84° 87° 89°

Pleasant, shady day, quite warm enough, but a light air from the East and thin veil of clouds prevents it from being oppressive.

What a contrast to the stifling pernicious air of the same day last year. The "yellow fever" too had then already made rapid strides, but this year it is widely different. Hitherto I have not heard of a case, and judging from "the Hospital" report of the last week, the general health must be extremely good, notwithstanding the intense heat of the noon day sun and the hitherto sultry, breezeless nights.[55]

During the week there were but 23 deaths in that vast Institution (the barometer of public health) and only 444 remaining under treatment in its wards....

I well remember the depression of spirits not unmixed with gloomy forebodings with which we left our cottage for the north just a year ago this evening. How providential it was that we did so! And yet so weak and thoroughly worn out was I that it would have taken but very little to have prevented the journey altogether. The least thing would have turned the scale against it, and all its countless advantages been irretrievably lost. "There is a providence that shapes our ends, Rough hew them as we may."

June 28   88° 93° 97°

Hottest day yet. South West wind. Thermo. stood at 97° when I left for dinner, and the open sunshine was unrelieved by the usual breeze. Many deaths today from sunstroke and in most places the thermo. reached 99° in the shade. My thermo. is in one of the coolest situations in town.

The sudden death of "Sontag" by cholera in the city of Mexico is the chief theme now in musical circles, while all who ever saw and heard her receive the tidings with heartfelt sorrow. Apart from her unrivalled powers as an "artiste" she was the most winning and elegant woman that perhaps ever appeared before the public.

---

[55] Statistics on the cases of yellow fever at Charity Hospital were regularly published in the local newspapers.

New Orleans Waterworks.
Corner Richard and Religious Streets

J.K.W. 1854

July 1   85° 89° 93°

A sudden and very copious rain fell in the night, and every thing looks fresh and pleasant this morning with a pleasant temperature. Pleasant breeze from the S. East, and pleasant sky overhead.

The "Delta" gives a list of 12 deaths from the heat on Thursday, in addition to 8 reported the day before. Our men, fortunately, have escaped, and in the whole 165 hands now on the works I have not heard of a single case of serious illness from the heat. But we keep them well protected with awnings &c. in the exposed parts of the work. The Brickmasons have laid 243.000 Bricks in third story walls &c. during the month of June, and the exterior Granite work was recommenced on the 12th. since when there have been 100 pieces set on Old Levee Front, consisting of Column and Antae stones & intervening Ashlar. Very busy today in closing up accounts for the month of June and for the Fiscal year ending yesterday, and in preparing the monthly, quarterly and annual papers for transmission to the Treasury Department....

July 8   85° 87° 91°

Thin clouds in the morning and fierce sunshine. Light, cool air from N. West, the wind having changed a little after midnight with a sudden storm of rain, thunder and lightening.

After dinner took a long walk towards the river and by the Waterworks, making a light sketch of the latter at the intersection of Richard and Religious Streets.[56]...The Building to the left is the end of one of the long ranges of Cotton Presses which have almost undisputed possession of this part of town.

[56] The waterworks was established in 1833 by the Commercial Bank of New Orleans. The reservoir occupied the entire square bounded by Market, Religious, St. Thomas, and Richard streets. The work was completed during 1834-1835. Norman, *Norman's New Orleans*, 146.

St. Paul's Church, James Wells Champney, delineator, Scribner's Monthly, *December 1873 (1974.25.7.90); Coliseum Place Baptist Church, Smith W. Bennett, delineator, from James Curtis Waldo,* Illustrated Visitors' Guide to New Orleans *(New Orleans, 1879) (1974.25.7.16).*

July 15

Pleasant day. N. East wind.

The work of improvement is going on rapidly in Camp Street. The gas works have been extended beyond my Cottage up to Felicity road. Two large brick churches, Episcopal & Baptist, are in progress, besides McStay's handsome mansion, a fine block on the corner of De Lord St. The Bible-house opposite St. Patricks and some large stores at the corner of Natchez Str. while private dwellings already occupied are undergoing various embellishments in the form of

elegant iron Fronts, galleries &c.[57] But that abomination the American Theatre, and its musty precincts, and the still viler shanties near the intersection of Girod Street still disgrace the most progressive street in the city.[58]

July 21

Beautiful weather, shady clouds. Cool north east wind. Distant thunder. Altogether a "model" summer atmosphere. Shower in the evening.

Having occasion to go to court this morning I was quite surprised and pleased at the cleanly, orderly appearance of every thing in the heart of the French quarter, so different from its condition in former years. The beautiful [Jackson] Square opposite the Cathedral is kept with scrupulous attention. I walked thro' it after finishing my business at court.[59] The flower beds are in excellent order and stocked with choice varieties. The grassy circle in the center, which is used in the evening as a play ground for little children and their nurses, is surrounded with a hedge of orange trees, well clipped, and of the liveliest green. The streets around and in fact all Royal,

[57] The building contract for St. Paul's Episcopal Church at the corner of Camp and Bartholomew (now Gaiennie) was signed on May 7, 1853. The builders were Theodore E. Giraud and Thomas Lewis; John Barnett was the architect and superintendent. The cost of construction was $35,500. The first service was held on Christmas Eve 1854. The church was destroyed by fire in 1891. NONA, H. B. Cenas, May 7, 1853. The Coliseum Place Baptist Church still stands at the corner of Camp and Terpsichore streets, although its spire was destroyed by Hurricane Betsy in 1965. John Barnett was the architect, with later modifications by Wharton. Nelson McStea of J. Burnside & Co. lived at 257-261 Camp Street, between Delord (now Howard Avenue) and Poeyfarre. NOCD 1856. John Barnett was the architect for the building (now 725 Camp Street) that was built for the South Western Bible Society at a cost of $9,940. The builders were Little and Middlemiss. NONA, H. B. Cenas, Apr. 19, 1854. St. Patrick's Church on Camp Street between Girod and Julia was designed and begun by James Dakin in 1838, and completed by James Gallier in 1839-1840. Its square Gothic tower was, until the 1920s, the tallest structure in New Orleans. Scully, *James Dakin*, 88.

[58] The American Theatre on Poydras Street near Camp, which backed on Lafayette Square, burned in July 1842; it was rebuilt the same year at a cost of $28,000. Norman, *Norman's New Orleans*, 180.

[59] The courts sat in the Presbytere, designed by architect Gilberto Guillemard after the fire of 1788 destroyed the parish church and its adjacent rectory. Intended to be the new rectory, the building was left unfinished at the death of the donor, Don Andres Almonester y Roxas, in 1798. It remained a one-story structure, rented as shops, until 1818 when a second story was added; Gurlie and Guillot were the builders. The Presbytere was purchased by the state in 1853 and became part of the Louisiana State Museum in 1911. Leonard V. Huber and Samuel Wilson, Jr., *The Presbytère on Jackson Square* (New Orleans, 1981).

Chartres & Levee Streets paved with Square granite blocks, and the delapidated relics of ancient times giving place to substantial modern constructions.

July 22   82° 84° 84°

Pleasant temperature. Air from the S. West. Floating clouds, shading the glare of the summer sun.

We finished moving into the new offices lately erected within the building in the large apartment designed for the United States Court room, in the second story.[60] The offices are much larger and more commodious than the old ones. Will be retired from the noise and excessive dust of the streets below, and in fact every way more agreeable. The temporary buildings which we occupied on the neutral ground will be sold at Auction on Monday and removed, but we still retain the privilege of the ground for the deposit of heavy materials &c.

July 23   82° 83° 83°

Sunday. Very pleasant westerly breeze. Thin shady clouds which now & then let the sunshine thro' but never oppressive....

The Charity hospital report for the week still shows a very healthy condition of the city. The deaths were 21. One of those, however, of yellow fever. It has raged so long in Cuba that with our total disregard of Quarantine regulations it would be next to a miracle if we escaped it....

July 24   82° 87° 90°

Sunshine & clouds in the morning, blazing sunshine the rest of the day. North East wind.

The shell of our old offices & carpenter's shop on the Neutral ground was sold this morning at Auction and brought the unexpected sum of $675, which is largely over the actual value. But the bidding was quite spirited. This amount will go a good way towards paying for our new and very superior accommodations inside the building....

---

[60] The United States courtroom, along the Decatur Street side of the Custom House, extended through the second and third stories and except for the Marble Hall, the great central business room, was the largest room in the building. Later floored over at the third floor level and cut up into offices, it was partially returned to its original proportions during a 1978-1980 restoration.

Family death scene during the yellow fever epidemic of 1853, from History of the Yellow Fever *(Philadelphia, 1854) (1974.25.11.126).*

July 29   83° 88½° 87°

Hot sun, large passing clouds, East wind. Showers in the after part of the day.

Wrote a long article in reply to one that appeared in yesterday's Delta full of mis-statements as to the progress &c. of the New Custom House. It is to appear in tomorrow's Picayune in the form of a communication from the Commissioners.[61]

July 30   83° 82° 84°

Mild & cloudy. Scarcely a breath of air. S. East wind.

The Charity hospital report for the week, instead of increasing its figures with the season (as usual) shows, on the contrary, a remarkable diminution, only 18 deaths. Our article in the Picayune is very well inserted....

---

[61] Wharton wrote an article, signed by Beauregard and Penn, explaining the apparent slowness in the construction of the Custom House. *Daily Picayune*, July 30, 1854.

August 1   84° 89° 88°

Very hot sunshine. North East wind.

Pleasant walk into town after dinner and delicious ices at "Vincent's" far more refreshing this hot weather than heating stimulants.[62]…

Mr. Simon Tracey spent the evening with us.[63] He told us how the Howard association first came into existence.[64] In the epidemic summer of 1833, he and Ricardo and J. P. Freret with quite a large party of gentlemen were playing ten pins late at night in the alley next to Freret's Cotton Press when a message was sent to them by a "fever" patient in the neighborhood that the noise was a serious annoyance, when some of the party made a half jocular proposition that they should give up play and turn to waiting upon the sick.[65] The hint, however, was followed up in earnest, and the foundation laid of a society that has done more to mitigate the sufferings produced by "yellow fever" than all the municipal and individual efforts put together.

August 4   87° 93° 89°

Hot night and hot, very hot, until near evening when clouds began to gather and the pleasant North West wind made itself felt.

Towards sunset I take a walk down to Canal Street and round by Carondelet almost every evening, and in that way meet with acquaintances that I might not see in months during business hours. In addition to the pleasure of the walk, for New Orleans <u>is</u> pleasant on a summer's evening, it helps to keep up connections. Then there are the most delicious ices at Vincent's and the most refreshing Soda at Sanderson's to allay the feverishness of noon day, and always

[62] J. Vincent had a confectionary "saloon," where he sold ice cream, sherbets, coffee, and chocolate, on Canal Street at the corner of Carondelet. NOCD 1856.

[63] Simon (Simeon) Tracey (ca. 1814-1854) was a brother of General Elisha B. Tracey. He died of cholera on December 1, 1854. His funeral took place from General Tracey's residence at St. Charles and Girod streets. *Daily Delta*, Dec. 2, 1854.

[64] Wharton apparently misunderstood the year. The Howard Association, organized by a number of young men during the 1837 yellow fever epidemic, was incorporated to care for victims of the nearly annual epidemics. Flora B. Hildreth, "The Howard Association of New Orleans, 1837-1878" (Ph.D. diss., University of California, Los Angeles, 1975), 48-49; *Daily Picayune*, Aug. 10, 1853.

[65] Daniel I. Ricardo (ca. 1810-1863) was a prominent notary whose records run from 1844 to 1856. He was secretary of the Howard Association for many years. *Daily Picayune*, Feb. 21, 1863. James Peter Freret (1800-1869) and his brother William (1804-1864) operated a cotton press in the early nineteenth century. *DLB*; Mrs. Thomas N. C. Bruns, comp., *Louisiana Portraits* (New Orleans, 1975).

something good to take home for the little boy. The people are not "all gone" and Camp and Canal Street about 6 O'clock in the evening are as full of life and animation as in the busier season.

August 5   87° 93° 95°

Hotter than ever and scarcely a cloud. South West wind. My thermo. got up to 95° but I noticed one in a very shady position on Canal Street at 3 P.M. up to 98°.…

A terrible fire raged all the morning in the very best part of Tchoupitoulas and Magazine Street just above Poydras. Whole blocks of the best class stores were in flames from about 9 O'clock, and such was the intense heat of the sun and scarcity of water that little could be done to arrest this progress. I went up to the top of the "walls" from time to time during the middle of the day, and still the pitchy smoke and fierce flames rose high into the air, even at 3 O'clock when I went up to dinner I saw from the windows of the omnibus more than one large warehouse with the fire streaming from every opening.…

August 8   84° 91° 94°

Hot & dry. South west wind.…

Took a long evening walk into town and all over the ground of the late disaster and should have made a sketch on the spot but for innumerable peering eyes of uncouth lawyers who invariably haunt the purlieus of a great city fire. The total loss is variously estimated at little short of a million, and the amount insured, as far as stated by the city offices, about half that sum. Still more, however, is no doubt effected in Northern Policies.…

August 27   83° 86° 87°

Sunday. Hot sunshine and alternate showers, very copious in the afternoon from the Eastward.

Went nowhere but to market before breakfast. Our cook has been such an excellent servant, and already so long with us that we thought we were safe for some time to come, especially as she is somewhat in years. But, as is invariably the case with Irish servants, the "easy time" has to come to a sudden pause. Her month is up today, and even before breakfast this morning, without any previous note of warning, she came in to Emily and begged "she would excuse her" but she was going off immediately "to get married."

Fire at the New Orleans Cotton Press, between 1843 and 1849, typical of the uncontrollable fires that raged through large presses and warehouses (1955.35).

August 31   79° 82° 82°

Variable weather and showers, very heavy at noon with wind and vivid lightning. South East wind.

Very busy, as usual, at the end of the month in preparing the papers &c. for Washington and closing up the current monthly bills &c. computing the brickwork and other details. The brick measurement exhibits a very fair amount of work, considering the difficulty of keeping up a regular supply of brick, bad weather &c. It amounts to 14.479.4 cubic feet containing 289.586 Bricks....

September 1   78° 80½° 79°

Very heavy showers with gleams of hot sunshine raw cold wind from the East.

The Front of Mr. Florence's Stores, corner of Natchez and Camp, is nearly finished.[66] The iron is all put together, and it is <u>all</u> iron.

Very fine castings. These fronts are a great improvement in store building, but I fear will give rise to an incalculable amount of false ornamentation. The facility with which ornaments are executed in such a plastic material is a temptation too strong, to introduce them every where until the great principle in architecture is soon lost sight of that construction is but a means to an end, and that ornament is something superadded to beautify the construction, but where the <u>end</u> is not palpable the <u>ornament</u> becomes contemptible. As, for instance, in the front above alluded to. The principle feature in the embellishment is a range of lofty pilasters surmounted by rich Corinthian capitals, projecting strongly from the face. Those, one would naturally suppose, would have to support <u>something</u>, but no! Nothing appears above but a light semicircular system of lead mouldings over the top line of arched openings, and even those not resting on the abacus of the capitals, but finished in a foliated corbel of their own a little above them, so that these elaborate antae actually support no detail whatever.

[66] Cast-iron fronts were in vogue in the 1850s and 1860s. Benjamin Florance's buildings at 48 Camp Street are no longer standing.

September 2   81½° 83½° 79°

Steamy air and sunny in the morning. Copious rains and heavy thunder in the middle of the day. After a shower of unusual violence at 2 the thermo. fell to 78¼°. South East wind.

Completed my monthly papers &c. for transmission to the Department. The order has at length gone forward today to the Granite contractor to proceed with the shipment of all the stone which was lying ready at the Quarries when I was there last year. It completes the third requisition, and will carry the walls up to the Entablature, thus embracing the ponderous Capitals of the Columns, 16 in all. 4 on each front. Thus —

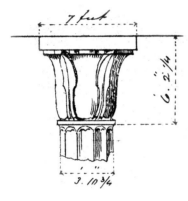

The antae Caps, also, 34 in number, 10 being on Canal Street front and 8 on each of the other fronts. Thus —

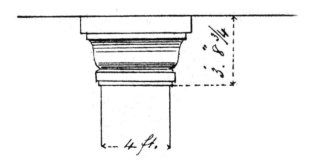

The large new hoisting Crane weighing 44 tons was moved on its wheels to the wharf yesterday, and every thing will soon be in readiness to discharge the Granite & Marble ships when they arrive.

Omnibus, detail, The St. Charles Hotel, Frederick J. Pilliner, delineator, 1853 (1959.27.2).

September 8   84½° 90° 93°

Blazing sky without a cloud and cool north west wind. Yesterday the thermo. rose to 94° at 2 P.M. and today to 93° at the same hour.

Yesterday morning one of our laborers, A. Gibson, was taken ill and left the works, he died at night, together with another man in the same house after a few hours' illness. The physician pronounced the cases "yellow fever" but attended with strong indications of "Cholera."

In the evening Emily and I took little Prescott in the Magazine Street omnibus as far as the end of the plank road.[67] It is quite a long ride (full four miles) and thro' the pleasantest part of the suburbs. Fine groves of live oak. Grassy fields and commons on one hand, and on the other the enclosures of the different places along the bank of the river, adorned with pretty groups of Pecan trees, willows, and other foliage, with glimpses of the city, and its churches in the distance. And far fewer instances of suburban poverty and neglect than are found in every other direction around New Orleans.

[67] The plank road (now Carrollton Avenue) ran from the river to the New Basin Canal.

It was nearly dark when we got home, having been out nearly two hours, little Prescott was very loathe to leave the omnibus, which is a mode of conveyance that has taken a strong hold on his simple republican fancy.

September 9   83½° 90° 93°

Scorching hot after a close sultry night. N. West wind.

A recent letter from Mr. Guthrie furnished me with information necessary to complete a set of statements such as are required by the engineer Department. The letter in question gave us the exact balance in the Treasury to the credit of the N.C.H. [New Custom House] on the 30th. June 1854. This enabled me to complete the papers and they were signed and dispatched today, as follows, viz.

"Full Quarterly Returns of Second Quarter 1854"

"Statement of Funds expended to the 30th. June 1854"

"Statement of Estimates, Appropriations &c. to the 30th. June 1854".

These documents are very full and explicit and compose an entire financial history of the works in a Tabular Form from the very commencement. The same Department letter announces officially the late appropriation of $395.000, so that the Amount available for the works during the Fiscal year commencing the 1st. day of July last stands as follows, viz.

Balance in Treasury	$138.410.94
" " Hands of Disbursing agt.	11.580.15
Late appropriation of Congress	395.000.00
Total available	$544.991.09

This is certainly a large provision for one year's expenditure, but we expect to receive heavy requisitions of Granite, and white Marble, which are extremely costly, and will swell the disbursements considerably beyond the figures of any previous year.

September 12   83° 87° 86°

Hot and sunny in the morning. Cloudy in the afternoon, wind South to West....

A good deal of disturbance has been going on since Sunday in the densely peopled purlieus of St. Mary's Market and some lives sacrificed, as if the pestilence were not sufficient but human violence must be added to its horrors.[68] In this neighborhood, however, it has been as usual perfectly quiet.

September 13   83° 87½° 88°

Very hot. Light shower 3 P.M. S. West wind.

It seems that in a melee the night before last, 3 Irishmen were killed, one dangerously wounded and their leader, a Dr. Meighan, locked up in jail to await examination.[69] Last night the military were out in force and order preserved.

September 15   81½° 87° 85°

Cleared off in the night and today we have a bracing north wind, and hot sun, with clouds and a shower early in the afternoon.

The musquitoes have been worse this summer than I have known them in the city for years, and especially since the first of the present month, day and night both, ants, too, and other domestic plagues in proportion.

September 16   80° 87° 86°

Cold north wind. Changing to East with very hot sun in the middle of the day. Very dangerous weather for those suffering with "yellow fever."

Further disturbances last night have drawn out a "Proclamation" from the Mayor inviting citizens to come forward and enroll themselves as a "Special Police."[70]

[68] St. Mary's Market was located on the median between North and South Diamond streets, running from South Peters to Tchoupitoulas. It was built in 1822 and extended in 1830 and 1836. NOCD 1838. The city of New Orleans, divided into three separate municipalities in 1836, was reunited in 1852 with the addition of the suburb of Lafayette. Partisan politics dominated elections, particularly after the rise of the Know Nothings, an anti-immigrant, anti-Catholic party led by American businessmen. Violence, stolen ballots, and street fighting were common throughout the 1850s. Leon Cyprian Soulé, *The Know Nothing Party in New Orleans: A Reappraisal* (Baton Rouge, 1961), 47-60.

[69] Dr. John Meighan, an Irish leader living at 10 Annunciation near St. Mary's Market, was arrested beside St. Patrick's Church and charged with murder, leading a riot, and carrying a concealed weapon. Riots between the Irish and the Know Nothings erupted when a rumor was spread that the latter intended to burn St. Patrick's Church. Charles L. Dufour, ed., *St. Patrick's of New Orleans* (New Orleans, 1958), 72; *Daily Picayune*, Sept. 12, 1854.

[70] As a result of the riots, Mayor John L. Lewis issued a proclamation on September 16 calling on good citizens to enroll as special police for the protection of life and property. *Daily Delta*, Sept. 17, 1854.

St. Mary's Market by Ellsworth Woodward, 1887 (1974.25.20.85).

September 20
81° 84° 84°

Warm air from the Gulf. Repeated showers and intervals of hot sunshine. High wind in the afternoon from South East....

Took a walk thro' Lafayette. Every thing looks rank and overgrown, buried under a pall of the darkest shadowy green. The rich soil of the streets, except when planked, has been converted by the rains into deep mire. The brick banquettes are thickly grassed over, with a narrow path "for one" worn thro' the middle. The unfilled lots are overgrown with a dense jungle of weeds, as tall as a man, thro' which gleam the pools that have collected during the wet weather. In short the whole faubourg compares unfavorably with its bright and cheerful looks in spring and early summer. At this time of the year, the heart of the city, or the wide open country, are preferable even to the most ornamental suburbs. [Art?] carries on the war but feebly against the sturdy growth of this summer climate, and weeds take possession of the gardens and thoroughfares.

September 21
79° 77° 77°

...Major Beauregard's brother, Armand Toutant, has taken the "yellow fever" but is doing well.[71] This is considered among the old residents one of the bad "epidemic years" yet coming after the frightful pestilence of last summer it seems to excite but little attention. Such is the power of "contrast."

[71] Armand Toutant (1827-1881), who did not use the name Beauregard. Frances Parkinson Keyes, *Madame Castel's Lodger* (New York, 1962), 26.

September 26   80° 85° 81°

Strong South East wind. Large masses of cloud sweeping across the sky, hot sunshine in the intervals. Shower in the morning.

Major Beauregard's brother is quite out of danger, but the victims of the epidemic are still numerous judging from the white and black crape hanging from the doors of dwelling houses, and closed stores and the white printed notices fluttering from the lamp posts at the street corners, still the city in general looks as cheerful and busy as usual at this season.[72] And I have not heard of anyone I know dying from fever. The general temperature, especially at night, is changing fast, and with the advance of the cold season we may hope for a rapid decrease in all diseases depending upon a vitiated atmosphere.

September 27   80° 80° 81°

Warm air from the South. Heavy rains.

Every thing damp, clammy and blighted with mold & mildew. No wonder the epidemic continues so bad. One of our Foremen and the Engineer are lying sick of "yellow fever".…

The Carpenters commenced the repairs of our Cottage preparatory to painting &c. for the winter. The weather is very unfavourable and their progress necessarily slow. I have resumed my claret at dinner and feel much the better for it. The wet, unwholesome air requires a bracer to keep it in check.…

October 1   76° 79° 76°

Sunday. October is ushered in by a violent rain storm from the East. It began to drip as I was returning from market and soon after poured down in torrents.

I cannot but rejoice that we are all safely thro' the sickly month of September and have no doubt that the rapidly declining suns and reduced temperature of the present month will have a marked effect in restoring the general health of the city. By ten O'clock Coliseum Square opposite formed a miniature lake, with divers grassy islands at intervals, and dark green china trees growing out of the water. Waterfalls at different times thro' the day came thundering down from the heavens. During one of these the kitchen chimney took fire from the over heated zeal of the cook who unhappily flew off to the opposite

---

Example of funeral notice posted in New Orleans (1957.124.20), gift of Harold Schilke.

extreme and served up a fine leg of mutton very much "under-done." The fire, however, could not have happened at a luckier moment, as the falling torrents precluded all danger, and in ten or fifteen minutes not a particle of soot remained in the Flue. It was a perfect "chef d'oeuvre" of Chimney sweeping. The sun peeped out for a few moments over the "moist, unpleasant" earth before he retired for the night.

October 2   76° 81° 85°

Fine clear sky. Wind N. East to South East.

I signed a new lease of my house today for another year at $480. The repairs are going on and are done remarkably well. The report of interments up to last Sunday at 6 A.M. shows a marked decrease.

of yellow fever	269
other diseases	154
Total	423

Our Foreman of Labourers returned to the works today very weak, however. The Engineer is recovering, but the Receiver of materials is dangerously ill. Amongst the hands three have died of yellow fever and three are now lying sick. Several others are off the works sick but it is not yet known how many of them have the fever. There is a good deal of it yet in different parts of the city.…

---

[72] Funeral notices were posted on lamp posts to announce funeral arrangements.

October 4   73½° 73° 73°

A change came at last in the night and today is very fine with a cold wind from the North N. East to North West.

The city council reassembled the other evening after their summer recess. The Mayor in his message uses language which tallies well with my predictions in spring — "in referring to the health of the city His Honor deprecates the entire absence of any board of Health or Sanitary commission during the prevalence of the epidemic which has carried off 1805 of our citizens during the last ten weeks. And states that he is unable, for this reason, to lay before the Board any information in regard to the disease, further than that, in type and malignity, he had been informed it was similar to the awful calamity of the previous year."

Owing to the lamentable inefficiency of our city government, as at present organized, things have in a great measure to take their course, and run themselves out. Epidemics, riots, crimes, abuses of all sorts, receive but feeble checks from the "constituted authorities" in spite of a taxation to sustain those authorities unexampled in republican experience. But the ever patient, enduring public have had enough of it. A change must come, and that soon.

October 10   74° 78° 78°

Warm air from the North East. Hot sunshine. Showers in the middle of the day.

Our architect Mr. A. T. Wood died last evening and what makes the event the more distressing is the absence of his wife at Ocean Springs.[73] It is less than a year since they were married. The works are suspended for the day, and the Government Flag at half mast. He had no equal in this city in the profession. He was a thoroughly practical architect, confident and self-reliant, bold and daring in construction, of which abundant evidence remains in the grand edifice which he leaves incomplete, but which will stand as an imperishable monument to his talents and architectural genius.

I met Judge [J. B.] Robertson in the omnibus. He is out for the second time, and says that he regains strength so imperceptibly that he is almost discouraged. His attack of yellow fever was extremely violent. However, the disease is said to be generally more unmanageable this year than ever. The Judge tells me that Mr. Moise the Attorney General is dying of a relapse.[74] He says he saw a very distressed family this morning, seven children of Mr. Christian's in Jackson Street, Lafayette. The father died of yellow fever a short time ago, the mother last evening and two of the children are now sick with it.[75] I see for the first time today the death of J. H. Whitney by "fever" on the 17th. Ulto. He was a most worthy man, for years a member of Mr. Preston's choir, and selected by him to conduct the church services during his summer's absence. At 4 O'clock I walked thro' the silent streets of Lafayette to attend Mr. Wood's funeral. The house was full of people and a long line of carriages was drawn up before the gate. I noticed that the furniture was removed from the principal room, and workmen's tressels in its place. A very beautiful border in fresco was in progress on the ceiling. It was one of the deceased architect's favorite implements to beautify and add to the conveniences of his home. Dr. Scott performed the obsequies very impressively and the procession then formed and moved towards the cemetery on the Metairie ridge.[76] I walked along with it in company with several friends to the end of Apollo Street and then returned home. Mr. Wood was married to his present wife on the 8th. of Novr. 1853. He leaves a little boy by his former wife, about 5 years old, now an orphan.

October 11   76° 77° 76°

Dull and very rainy. East wind....

Mr. Penn called me to his room early yesterday morning and in a

---

[73] Alexander Thompson Wood (1799-1854) was an architect who practiced in London before opening an architectural academy in New York in 1831. He was at work in New Orleans by 1833; in July 1835, Wood killed architect George Clarkson, a former employee, in a fight and spent five years in the state prison at Baton Rouge for manslaughter. Wood was appointed architect for the Custom House in 1848, but was dismissed two years later. He returned to the Custom House in 1851 to ensure that his original plans were followed. He had resumed his duties as architect at the time of his death. Wood's first wife, Sarah Strong Mallory of Woodbury, Connecticut, died in July 1853, leaving an infant son, Thompson Mallory Wood. Later that year, he married Elizabeth J. Wallace. Among Wood's designs is Tezcuco plantation. *Courier*, July 28, 1835; Samuel Wilson, Jr., *A History of the U.S. Customhouse in New Orleans* ([New Orleans, 1984]), 25; Gallier, *Autobiography*, 39; NONA, Joseph Cuvillier, Nov. 14, 1848, James Graham, July 29, 1853; *Daily Picayune*, Nov. 10, 1853.

[74] E. Warren Moise was attorney general of Louisiana from 1855 to 1859. *Louisiana Almanac, 1995-96*, ed. Milburn Calhoun (Gretna, La., 1995), 474.

[75] John T. Christian (ca. 1816-1854), an accountant from Tuscumbia, Alabama, was married to Ann Cooper. NOCD 1854; *Daily Delta*, Sept. 27, Oct. 10, 1854.

[76] The Rev. William A. Scott was pastor of the First Presbyterian Church on Lafayette Square from 1843 to 1854. NOCD 1854. A. T. Wood was buried in Cypress Grove Cemetery which is located at the end of Canal Street. Cypress Grove was founded in 1840 by the Firemen's Charitable and Benevolent Association. *New Orleans Architecture*, vol. 3, Mary Louise Christovich, Leonard V. Huber, and Peggy McDowell, *The Cemeteries* (Gretna, La., 1997), 27.

long conversation told me that <u>his plan</u> was to write to the Department immediately not to hurry the appointment and then to have me made Mr. Wood's successor. Having been on the building from the first and closely engaged with Mr. Wood in the preparation and perfecting of all the plans as they at present exist. I know more about the building than any one else can know, and more, too, about Mr. Wood's ulterior intentions as to completion, so far as he had developed and disclosed them....

October 28   71° 72½° 74°

North East wind and dense clouds. Rain set in at last at 8 A.M. and fell in heavy showers during the day with change of wind to South....

The dry weather continues long enough to finish my roof and give time for the mortar of the capping to set, and it proves perfectly tight. The inside painting is also finished today and looks very well indeed.

October 29   69° 70½° 72°

Sunday. Bright & sunny, tho' the sky was obscured by passing mists when I went to market at sunrise. The North west wind, however, soon cleared every vestige of cloud, and left the air much cooler than yesterday but not cool enough for health.

We all stayed at home today and spent it in reading, writing &c. Having noticed the fire bells at about 4 this morning, and heard during the day that Dr. Scott's church was destroyed by fire. I walked down with Ellen to Lafayette Square towards evening, and found that it was so indeed, nothing remained but a mere shell filled with smoking ruins.[77] It was the oldest Protestant church in the city having been created in 1835, and had just undergone repairs painting &c. to the amount of $10.000. Gen. Tracey and staff were mustering their troops on the Square, the minute gun firing, and quite a crowd assembled in and around the enclosure to witness the pageant. I learned afterwards that they were preparing to form part of the

[77] Construction of the First Presbyterian Church on Lafayette Square began in 1834. Its design is attributed to George Clarkson, a young Scottish carpenter-architect who had come to New Orleans in 1833 under contract with A. T. Wood to work on buildings for the New Orleans Architects Company. Samuel Wilson, Jr., *The First Presbyterian Church of New Orleans* (New Orleans, 1988). Lafayette Square, originally known as Place Gravier, was the public square included in Carlos Trudeau's 1788 plan for Ville Gravier, later Faubourg St. Mary. The name of the square was changed after General Lafayette's visit to New Orleans in 1825.

First Presbyterian Church, 1843 (1985.253), gift of Samuel Wilson, Jr.

funeral cortege of Lieut. Governor W. W. Farmer who died of "yellow fever" at 7 O'clock this morning.[78] The disease is still very malignant. The report of the week to 6 this morning shows

of yellow fever	107
other diseases	136
Total	243

November 1   68° 71½° 74°

The month comes in with bright sunny skies, gentle West wind and the thermometer still ranging in the Seventies at mid-day.

No indications of cold weather yet, and the musquitoes as cruel as ever. They are nature's homeopathic "cuppers and bleeders", provided to reduce that redundancy of blood which in a hot climate might take a febrile direction....

This is "All Saints" day and the Catholic population are engaged in solemnizing their accustomed funeral rites at the different cemeteries. A continuous stream of well dressed men and women has been setting in that direction all day so that they must be very crowded.

[78] W. W. Farmer (ca. 1812-1854) was elected lieutenant governor in 1852. *Daily Delta*, Oct. 30, 1854.

Decorating tombs at St. Louis Cemetery No. 2 on All Saints Day, John Jurkin, engraver, 1885 (1974.25.6.644).

Surviving relatives adorn the marbles with wreaths & festoons of artificial flowers, black & white, and "les fleurs immortelles" and the priests are in attendance chanting the formulas suited to the time.[79] The idea is a very solemn and touching one, a whole people uniting in a tribute of memory to the departed. But in execution it must be greatly marred by its assimilation to a general holiday, and the presence of so many who are drawn there by pure curiosity....

November 4 $69^{1}/_{2}°$ 71° 70°

Soft & humid air, indicating rain. Wind from the North.

When I returned at 3 to dinner I found some new furniture sent up which did not work as well as it should, so after dining I had to post all the way down again, tired as I was, a mile and a half, to bring up a man from the Store to remedy the evil. It is next to impossible at this time of the year to have any thing well done. Every body wants every thing, and nobody gets exactly the thing wanted. The fall months in New Orleans are all bustle and confusion to prepare for the short lived winter, and the early spring is consumed in preparing to get away for the summer. The restless, driving class are a numerous and highly respectable body, and moreover wield a mighty element of power, the percentage (ad libitum)[80] of profit in traffic. The less ambitious and more permanent residents who would gladly avoid the vortex, are drawn in, much against their will, and if not engulfed, rarely escape uninjured from the abrasion....

November 6   63° 65° 66°

...The epidemic is declining fast....

This is very favorable, especially as we have had nothing yet even approaching a frost, and the musquitoes still very tormenting. The "yellow fever" seems to act quite independently of all meteorological conditions of the atmosphere, and the subtle influences that govern its rise and decline continue to elude the most searching investigation.[81] This year it has been marked by extraordinary

fatality and the epidemic just closing is pronounced the worst that has ever existed in New Orleans except those of 1847 and 1853. In the former year the mortality was 2.600. In the latter upwards of 8.000. This year up to last Sunday (yesterday) 2.407.

November 11 $68^{1}/_{2}°$ $69^{1}/_{2}°$ 68°

Cloudy and threatening; high wind from South East and blinding dust from the Levee.

We were disappointed, however, in our hopes of rain, only a few drops fell in the middle of the day. The temperature, tho' cool at night, is still quite oppressive during the day. We can scarcely be said even to have had autumn weather yet. If the frost holds off much longer we shall soon breathe a living atmosphere of musquitoes. To say nothing of the novel scents eliminated from the unwashed streets.

Answered Mr. Bryant's letter in full. Armand Toutant, the Major's brother, called at the office today, looking better than I ever saw him, after his severe attack of yellow fever, from which he has entirely recovered. Camp Street was startled the other day by the failure of Horace Bean's private Banking Concern. And today by the stoppage of Matthew's and Finley, also private bankers.[82] These houses professed to be "Savings Banks" but they have turned out sad "losing concerns" to many a poor depositor who entrusted with them their little "all," attracted by the 5%. And considering it the safest way of employing their small means so as to realize a little from it, secure from the fluctuations of active trade.

The "money editor" of the Delta takes a proper view of this subject. He says, "We are constrained to believe that it is due to friends, the public, and country at large, that all exchange and banking houses incapable at this moment of showing assets to the amount of one hundred cents on the dollar, should go into immediate liquidation. This attempting to do business on other people's money, in capital borrowed at call, will never succeed in this city. Here we have in the short space of ten days, two failures, in the face of the most plentiful supply of money, which is recorded in the financial history of our city."

---

[79] Placed on New Orleans tombs, immortelles were permanent memorials to the dead. Such memorials included bead or metal wreaths and metal disks with stenciled glass fronts.

[80] Trans.: in accordance with one's wishes

[81] The connection between the mosquito and the spread of yellow fever was not discovered until 1904 by William Crawford Gorgas in Panama at the time of the building of the canal.

[82] The Money Market column reported the suspension of payment by the banking and exchange houses of Matthews Finley & Co. and Horace Bean & Co. *Daily Delta*, Nov. 11, 1854.

November 12   57° 57° 56°

Sunday. Great change in the weather. Rain enough in the night to quench the dust. And today, wild, stormy looking clouds, and a cold gusty wind from the North West.

In the afternoon the clouds parted and I took a long walk thro' Lafayette. The sun shed a broad glare of light but no warmth, and the keen wind swept thro' the street. People buttoned up their thick coats and walked very fast. But the gardens are more beautiful than during the rank redundance of summer, and the lawns and flower borders in high order, fine perfect roses, splendid Salvias and the double flowering Scarlet Hibiscus sparkle among the sober greens, while, as at the north at this season, the starry chrysanthemums of every dye are in the ascendant. Other varieties again define our latitude more clearly and lofty bananas fling open their rich purple pendants and reveal the fruit clusters in heavy bunches. This plant groups charmingly with the more compact shrubbery, and fine examples of its introduction occur on the grounds of Mr. Briggs, whose place, by the by, is to my fancy the most tasteful in the entire suburb.[83] Mr. Robb, however, is destined to take the lead of all competitors. His noble mansion is rapidly hastening to completion. And the entire square on which it stands is already graded and pulverized preparatory to laying out the gardens and ornamental terraces around it.[84]

November 13   46½° 48° 52°

Bitter cold, with a pure bright sky, and wind from the North West.

The change, tho' very sudden, is charming. Health and spirits rise as the temperature descends, and life regains its full value. Still we are not at freezing point yet. But the epidemic is nearly over without it, as was the case last year also. Contrary to the usual New Orleans

Charles Briggs residence, Tina Freeman, photographer, 1982 (Mss 98-9-L).

prejudice that it requires a frost to extinguish the "fever." The advent of the one <u>may</u> occur simultaneously with the disappearance of the other — and that — often — without furnishing sufficient grounds to trace a connection between them. But there is no more common error than to infer causation between two facts that are found in contiguity simply from the event of their nearness....

November 15   59° 63° 67°

High wind from the West to South West. Sky without a cloud....

The Superintendent of Stonework has raised his mast in the centre of the building auxiliary to his large derrick for setting marble in the "general business Room." This mast is full 160 feet high, with horizontal strips about 1 foot apart nailed to it all the way up for steps. Three or four of our riggers were running up and down it all day as nimbly as squirrels, fixing the blocks and cordage &c. to raise the other pieces. When I first looked up I saw one of these active fellows standing on the very top of the spar fixing a block to it, and apparently as much at his ease at that giddy height as if he were at work on the floor below. These riggers, however, are thorough bred sailors — real "salts" — and are indispensable around our lofty scaffolding, cranes, and hoisting apparatus.

---

[83] The house of Charles Briggs at 2605 Prytania Street, at the corner of Third, was built in the Gothic Revival style in 1849-1850. James Gallier was the architect. NONA, P. Lacoste, Apr. 10, 1850.

[84] James Robb (1814-1881) was a wealthy banker and entrepreneur. The original plans for his mansion on Washington Avenue between Camp and Chestnut streets were drawn by R. Morris Smith of Philadelphia in 1853 and are in the Southeastern Architectural Archive at Tulane University. The house, in a much modified form, was built by James Gallier, Jr. In 1890, it became the home of H. Sophie Newcomb Memorial College of Tulane University and a second story was added. It subsequently housed the Baptist Bible Institute, which became the New Orleans Baptist Theological Seminary, and was demolished in 1954.

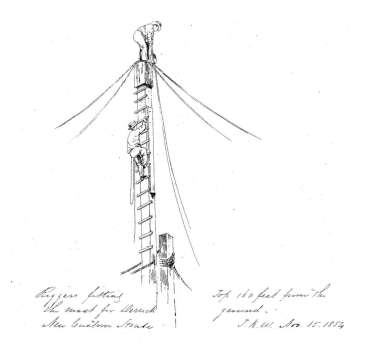

Riggers fitting
the mast for Derrick
New Custom House

Top 160 feet from the
ground.
J.K.W. Nov. 15. 1854

November 16   59° 60° 62°

Very beautiful weather, not a cloud, but very dry and dusty. Light air from N. East to N. West....

The vertical Post of the large Derrick for setting Marble was fitted complete today and the American Flag waved on the top of it by noon. It measures to the Iron Strap 155 feet from the ground line. It is held in place by 6 strong guys of 7" Italian Hemp rope made fast to the outer works of the building....

I may remark that the 6 guy ropes which secure the derrick, together with 6 of common 5 inch rope further down, are only temporary. To be replaced by firm wire rope when the instrument is all put together. We have just received 3000 lbs. of No. 4 Wire rope from New York for that purpose. The Vertical post is further secured by a strong frame across the circular opening thro' which it penetrates the 1st. tier of groined arches at 25 feet from the ground. Three small shipments of Marble for the great "centre room" have already arrived, consisting of 46 pieces. Some column & antae bases, and some ashlar.

November 18   57° 58° 60°

Dry piercing north wind. Very cold, with clear sunny sky.

The long drought has at length seared the grass and robbed it of its usual bright green for the first time this year. Every object is powdered over with dust, so fine and impalpable, that it penetrates the closest joints of the window and door openings and keeps the polished furniture within constantly dim in spite of the best housekeeping. Cistern water is becoming scarce, but the most serious effect of the unusually dry season is to keep down the water of the upper rivers at so low a point that the trade of the great West is virtually excluded from our city. The stock on hand of western produce is becoming lamentably scanty and prices proportionally enhanced, making more than ever apparent the necessity of an extensive system of railroad connection, which would at once render us independent of water courses which are too frequently least available at the very season when most needed. The Jackson road, now finished to the Mississippi line is already elucidating this truth in the large amount of Cotton and country produce which it brings in daily.[85]

November 21   56° 62° 64°

Moist air from the North East. Sunny sky but clouds gathering towards noon and evening.

The prettiest theatre in town "Placide's Varietes" was destroyed by fire at two this morning.[86] It is quite a loss to the pleasure seeking public. The St. Charles is a badly contrived damp, unpleasant structure.[87] The "American" execrable, and the Orleans too small, and too far from the usual resorts of strangers. Then the opera is less attractive than the usual stage productions, except to the few who know how to relish the highest range of musical composition.

[85] The New Orleans, Jackson, and Great Northern Railroad ran from New Orleans to Osyka, Mississippi. The depot was on Solis (now South Robertson) between Clio and Calliope streets.

[86] Placide's Varieties Theatre on Gravier between St. Charles and Carondelet was built in 1849. Mr. Ellsworth was the architect and superintendent. A new Varieties Theatre designed by Benjamin Morgan Harrod was built on Canal Street in 1871. It was demolished when the Maison Blanche building was erected in 1906.

[87] The original St. Charles Theatre, located on St. Charles between Commercial Place and Poydras, was built in 1835; Antoine Mondelli was the architect. It burned in 1842 and was rebuilt.

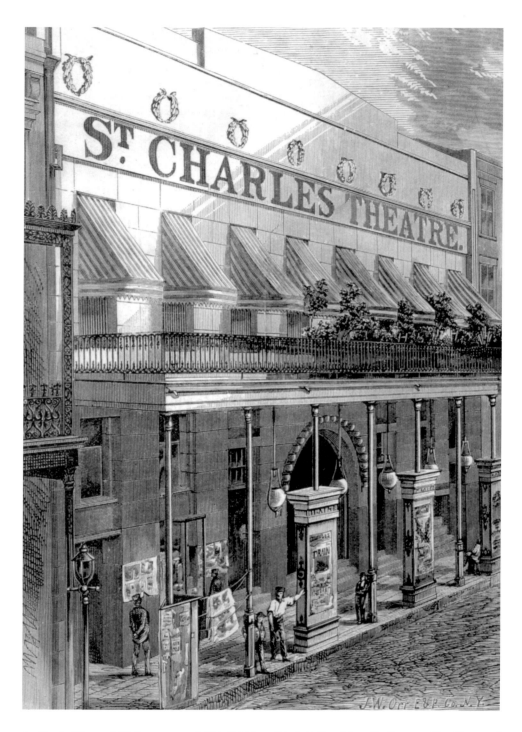

St. Charles Theatre, J. W. Orr, engraver (1951.41.9) from Edwin L. Jewell, Jewell's Crescent City Illustrated *(New Orleans, 1873).*

November 26   51° 52° 54°

Sunday. Not a cloud. Bright and cold.

The high North West wind sweeps away the leaves from the China trees, and mulberries. But in this part of town we scarcely miss them as there is so great a predominance of fine large evergreen trees, that the avenues of bright verdure remain almost without noticeable interruption. The city is filling up fast, and the streets today were well thronged with church-goers. Emily & Mrs. Ladd heard a good sermon at the new Baptist Church on the next Square. Ellen and I remained at home with little Tommy.

December 7   43° 46½° 51°

Frost in the night. Brilliant sky today with a pure bracing air from North West.

It is a year today since we got home from the north. And having stood by New Orleans so faithfully this summer I live in hopes of revisiting it again next summer. That is, the North….

December 8   46½° 50° 52°

Frost in the night. Fine pleasant weather, light clouds in the afternoon. East wind.

Five commercial houses have gone to protest since yesterday morning, and the fine Coast Steamer "Gipsy" burned to the water's edge with a loss of 8 lives.[88] The former casualties attributable to the depression of trade arising from the low waters of the upper rivers. The latter, (the loss of the steamer) to the wretched practice which prevails on the Western boats of stacking up the wood in close contact with the furnaces, no screen to prevent accident, and so little space that it is always matter of surprise to me that the dry sticks don't take fire oftener. In this case the flames broke out in the starboard wood pile just under the office and spread with such rapidity that those who saved their lives could save nothing else.

December 10   58° 60° 61°

Sunday. Air saturated with moisture. Soft and spring like. Scudding clouds flying across the sky from the South East which gathered into compact gloom about midday. Dull rains in the afternoon.

Stayed at home today. Read, amongst other things, Mr. Pierce's Message.[89] A plain unpretending paper. Pacific in its general tone, but presenting sensible and patriotic recommendations for the increase of the Army and Navy, both in Force and Efficiency. Relates in full the cause which led to the bombardment of San Juan de Nicaragua. And exhibits a general sketch of the Financial condition of the country which is to say the least highly flattering.…

December 11   55° 54° 53°

Raw and cold. Dull leaden clouds. North west wind growing sharper and more penetrant every hour.…

The mortuary returns for the week report no yellow fever, but the aggregate is so large (294) that in the absence of a specific classification of disease this unusual mortality for the season must be attributed to cholera which, tho' not noticed by the press, seems to have prevailed here for sometime past. Mr. Tracey and the wife of John D. Bein both died of it, and many other cases have for some weeks been named to me.[90] One of our carpenters died of it on Saturday. Sad to have it follow immediately on an epidemic summer.

But it is not surprising when we know that no less than 12.000 passengers have arrived in New Orleans since the 1st October, most of them from foreign ports, and of the usual destitute class which composes the bulk of emigration.

December 14   51° 54° 56°

Mild and sunny. Cloudy in the morning but very pleasant in the afternoon. North West wind.

This cheerful and pleasant street was made mournful in the afternoon by the unusual spectacle of a military funeral, on the next square. The deputy coroner of the city who is said to have died suddenly of cholera. The cries of the widow were so loud that they were audible as long as the cortege remained in sight.[91]

---

[88] A protest is a sworn declaration that payment of a note or bill has been refused and that all responsible signers or debtors are liable for resulting loss or damage.

[89] Franklin Pierce (1804-1869) served as president from 1853 until 1857. His message to Congress was reported at length in the *Daily Picayune*. The country is described as peaceful and prosperous, and the president mentions the policy of avoiding entangling alliances. *DAB*; *Daily Picayune*, Dec. 5, 1854.

[90] John D. Bein of the hardware firm of Priestly and Bein lived on Camp, above Julia. NOCD 1854.

[91] William C. Terrell died on December 14, 1854. *Daily Delta*, Dec. 15, 1854.

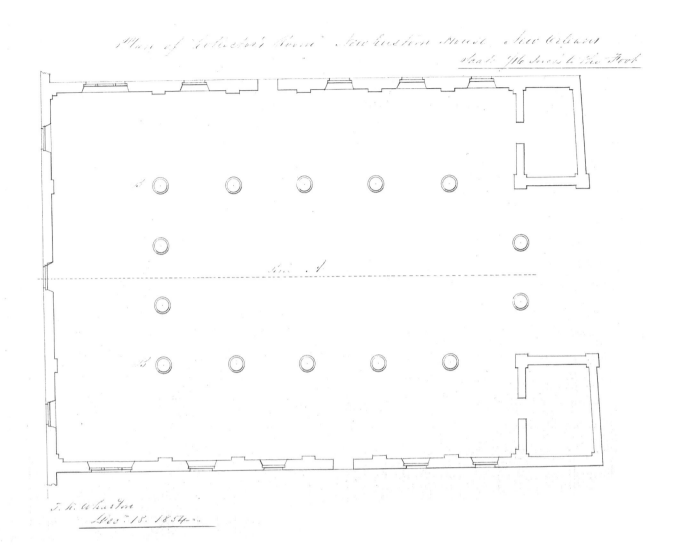

Plan of Collector's Room New Custom House New Orleans
Scale 3/16 Inch to the Foot

Line A

J. H. Wharton
Decr. 18. 1854

December 16

Very lovely weather. Light air from the West to North West, and the purest sunshine.

The streets at midday were <u>almost</u> crowded, and as gaudy as a flower garden. So many strangers from the interior, ladies who make a short winter visit to the "great city" and straightway invest all their spare funds in the showiest and most expensive costumes. Which, however depleting to the domestic resources certainly add much to the gaiety and display of our winter thoroughfares.

December 18

The annexed Plan and Elevation shew the effect of a change in the Collector's Room at the New Custom House N. O. proposed by Major Beauregard and sanctioned by the Department. It consists in substituting full columns in the place of square Pilasters at B. B. which the architect had introduced with a view to overcome certain irregularities in the distribution of the room; but which seemed to involve the greater defect of disturbing the symmetry and beauty of the whole colonnade, which being of white Marble and from the rich

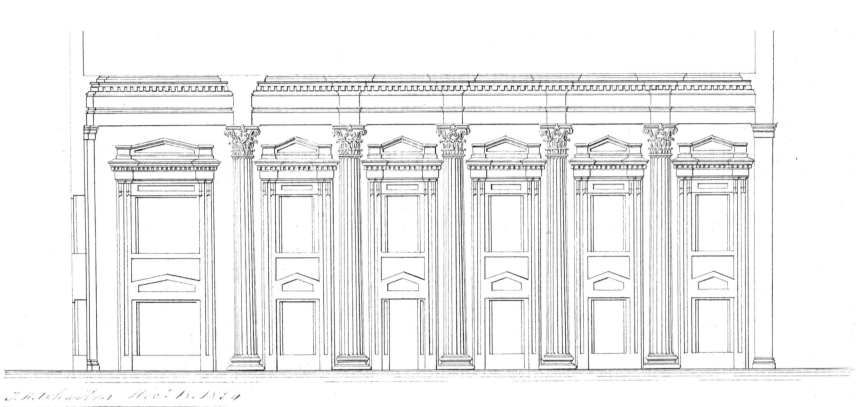

J. R. Richardson Dec. 18. 1854

example of the "Monument of Lysicrates" will form the principal feature in the apartment. The Columns are fourteen in number and the room 116' 10¹/₄" by 89' 8⁷/₁₆".

December 20   39° 41° 42°

Severe wind from the north West all night. Sky today without a cloud, dry piercing air from North East.

After dinner went down to Judge Walker's "sanctum" with some sketches I made when at Barataria which he desires to introduce into his paper in the form of wood cuts to illustrate a series of articles on the early history of New Orleans which he commenced last Sunday. The engraver was there, and after a little talk to the Judge, I went over with the former to his rooms where he showed me some quite pretty specimens of his pencilling and some good "proofs" from his blocks. His name is "Goater" a very young man but apparently full of

enthusiasm in his art, and draws with freedom and taste.[92] On my way down I met Dr. Barton driving home. He called to me to step into his office on my return. I did so and he presented me with a copy of the work we have looked for so long. The Report of the Sanitary commission on the epidemic of 1853, with numerous tables and facts illustrative of the sanitary condition of New Orleans for many years past, existing causes of disease, and theory of the

[92] Alexander Walker (1818-1893), a city court judge (1846-1850) and journalist, wrote for the *Daily Delta* (1846-1860) and was later editor of the *Times*, the *Herald*, and the *Picayune*. His articles for the *Daily Delta* on the early history of New Orleans were illustrated with woodcuts signed by J. H. Goater, an engraver and commercial artist active in New Orleans from 1854 to 1856. Walker was the author of *Jackson and New Orleans* (New York, 1856) and *The Life of Andrew Jackson* (Philadelphia, 1860). *Daily Picayune*, Jan. 25, 1893; *DLB*; *Encyclopaedia of New Orleans Artists, 1718-1918*, eds. John A. Mahé, Rosanne McCaffrey, and Patricia Brady Schmit (New Orleans, 1987) (hereafter *ENOA*).

origin of yellow fever and other malignant disorders incidental to the locality.[93]…

December 22   46° 52° 53°

Sharp frost in the night. Bright sunny day. South East wind.

Emily, Ellen, little Tommy and his nurse all came down to the office, and first went over the whole building, from the shadowy arches of the basement to the topmost course of stonework, which, by the by, now commands a noble view of the whole city being already higher than the average height of stores and public buildings around us. After delighting little Tommy with the details of the carpenters' and blacksmiths' shops, we went down thro' Chartres and Royal Streets to see the stores all decked out with their splendid display of novelties for "Christmas" and "New Year's" made some purchases and brought up at the tempting confectionary near the Cathedral of St. Louis. Then after due refreshment, threaded our way slowly back thro' the gay groups on Royal Street to the omnibus on Canal and so home to a late dinner. This was Thanksgiving's day last year but the Governor has determined to dispense with the observance this year, on the ground, I am told, that so many holidays coming about the same time offer too serious an interruption to the tenor of business. Judging from the complaints of the merchants that "there is absolutely no business doing worth speaking of" I should think his Excellency's scruples rather uncalled for.

December 23   58° 60° 63°

Mild air from the East and South East. Clammy and humid. The Granite of the New Custom House reeking with moisture. Thick grey clouds & misty rain at intervals.

Went down again after dinner to buy Christmas presents. Caught in the rain. The evening having set in wet and sloppy much to the disappointment of many who have put off visiting the shops and laying in their Christmas stores until the last day of the week. At best, however, the Christmas observances in this tepid atmosphere are but a languid, spiritless affair, after the buoyant hilarity of the season in more rigorous latitudes. A thermometer ranging from zero to 30° is a wonderful quickener of the pulses of life in countries where winter is "winter."…

93 *Report of the Sanitary Commission of New Orleans on the Epidemic Yellow Fever of 1853* (New Orleans, 1854) (60-69-L.3).

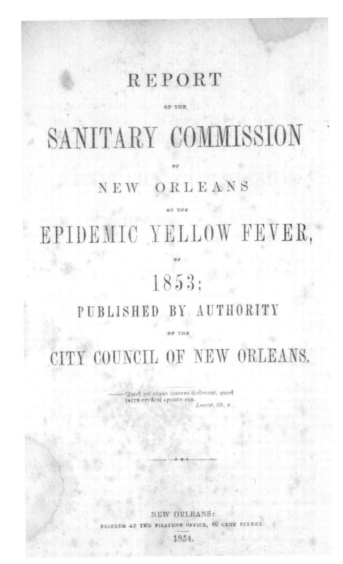

REPORT

OF THE

SANITARY COMMISSION

OF

NEW ORLEANS

ON THE

EPIDEMIC YELLOW FEVER,

OF

1853;

PUBLISHED BY AUTHORITY

OF THE

CITY COUNCIL OF NEW ORLEANS.

NEW ORLEANS:
PRINTED AT THE PICAYUNE OFFICE, 66 CAMP STREET.
1854.

December 24   63° 66° 65°

Sunday. The sun struggled hard this morning for the supremacy, but the transient radiance was quenched in vapory mists, and the air swept by from the south east laden with dank moisture, and feeling like escape steam.

I am reading with great interest Dr. E. H. Barton's "report on the Sanitary condition of New Orleans." He sets forth his facts with all the boldness and vigor of absolute certainty, and reasons from them with great perspicuity and clearness, fortifying his positions with tables and statistical observations which exhibit the close and garnered labors of years and throw a flood of light upon a subject hitherto shrouded in the mists of conflicting theories, and undigested opinions. He brings forward uncontrovertible evidence to prove a simple but most unpalatable truth that "New Orleans is one of the dirtiest, and with other conjoint causes, is consequently the sickliest city in the Union, and scarcely anything has been done to remedy it." But he also assures us that this state of things "is remedial" and proceeds to exhibit the means by which the evil may be greatly lessened, if not wholly obliterated....

December 25   64° 67° 66°

Christmas day. Dripping rains in the night. Moist and clammy this morning, dull grey sky, warm air, and when I went to market at an early hour, every thing looked wet and comfortless, except the jolly butchers, and the brawny vegetable women, who were evidently chuckling over the great and unusual prices they were exacting from eager housekeepers. Showers all day which confined us to the house.

Prescott and Ellen kept up a lively uproar from morning till night with their Christmas Toys and fire crackers. I spent the morning on a pen and ink drawing of Fort Warren and Boston Harbor, then answered Col. Thayer's last letter of Novr. 30 and enclosed the sketch to him as a Christmas token. There is a warmth and vitality about the friendships of our early youth which do not often characterize the connections formed in later life.

December 26   56° 60° 62°

Cleared off in the night and today is quite radiant again, with a light air from the South West.

The city, too, has returned to its normal condition of health again, as appears by the returns published this morning. 144 deaths of all diseases. Cholera and yellow fever both seem to be extinct. All we who have passed thro' both, secure and unharmed, have more than usual to be grateful for, and never would a general Thanksgiving-day have been more appropriate than now, but "gubernatorial" wisdom has decided otherwise. Just after dark the Fire alarm called us to the front gallery. The flames looked so formidable that I followed the concourse setting in that direction and on reaching Canal Street found that it was the handsome Hall of the Mechanics' Society of New Orleans, making the third large Public building which has been

destroyed by fire in the last two months.[94] The crowd around the square was very great but I was able to penetrate near enough to get a fine view of the billows of flames as they swept thro' the different stories of the building, and gathered one by one to the smouldering heap of ruin beneath.

December 29   47½° 50° 53°

Yesterday in the Tropics, today in Maine. A difference of full 20 degrees since last evening at 4, and the keen blasts from the North and North West whistling thro' the streets. But the air is pure and inspiring and the cheerful sun shines out with unwonted brilliance.

Major Beauregard proposes further changes in the architectural features of the "Collector's Room" and has addressed the Department and Marble Contractors on the subject today. The late "Bill" procured from Congress enables us to substitute an Iron for a Marble Roof.

December 30   49½° 52½° 58°

Very keen frost in the night. Every thing powdered over at sunrise. Brilliant sunshine today, with a pleasant air from the South West.

The business of the month, monthly papers, estimates &c. have kept me unusually busy at the office for some days past. All are now completed, and the business brought up regularly so as to make a fair start for the New Year. Major Beauregard went down the river this morning on a visit of inspection to the Forts so that I had the office almost wholly to myself and kept the pen racing over my paper at a rapid rate until 3 O'clock.[95]

December 31   54° 57° 58°

The year closes with a delightful atmosphere pure and elastic. It was very cold in the night and somewhat too raw and chilly when I went to market, but after a late breakfast the sun shone out in his might and tempered down the sharp edge of the morning air, and the South-west wind blew lightly.

[94] The Mechanics Institute, a handsome structure in the Gothic Revival style, was designed by R. P. Rice, architect. Construction began in 1851. In 1856 it was rebuilt in the classical style by James Gallier, Jr. The building later became part of the adjacent University of Louisiana (Tulane). The site on University Place is now occupied by the Fairmont Hotel. The other two public buildings that had burned recently were the First Presbyterian Church and Placide's Varieties Theatre.
[95] Forts Jackson (1822) and St. Philip (1787) are on opposite sides of the Mississippi River in Plaquemines Parish.

It is pleasant to end the year with a Sabbath. It furnishes not only a motive but an "aid to reflection." Passing by the church of St. Theresa on our way from St. Mary's market, all Ireland seemed to be streaming from its portals.[96] It is astonishing how large an element they form in our resident population, that is, the Irish. A stranger from Dublin or Londonderry might fancy himself quite at home again in our streets, especially about the time of "matins" and "vespers." Mr. Walker's third article on the "early history of New Orleans" appears in the Delta this morning, and presents the character of the freebooter Lafitte in an altogether new and very favourable light. He treats his subject with great apparent fairness, and with a bold and eloquent pen. The article is illustrated by a wood engraving from one of my sketches of "Barataria." The young artist has touched it with truth and spirit. But the quality of the paper is adverse to a clear and perfect impression. I expect, however, the proofs will show it to advantage....

After dinner I took a long walk thro' Lafayette, and was struck with the air of stillness, quiescence, almost absolute stagnation that prevails every where in that attractive suburb. Every thing looks as it did a year ago, few improvements, if any. Indeed the same note may apply to the city generally, indicating that the last has been anything but a prosperous year. At any rate that capital has found more remunerative sources of employment than the enlargement and increased elegance and comfort of this pleasant city. Various elements of depression have been at work. Much fatal sickness and that for two successive seasons has disturbed the public confidence in the "future" of New Orleans. Commercial credit has received some severe shocks. Our connection with the rich teeming West almost severed by the insufficiency of water in the upper rivers, and the general derangement and distrust in foreign relations springing from the troubled condition of the European Continent. All in a greater or less degree combine to retard the prosperity of our city. But these, we trust, are only transient checks, not permanent evils....

It is the custom here to keep up a continual firing of guns, pistols and crackers all night long on the demise of the old year. Long after we retired shot after shot echoed thro' the still moonlight, and our dreams were strangely intermingled with visions of the Crimea, and the distant shock of armies on the heights of Sebastopol. Long may we be unused to ought save the mimicry of War, and its stern realities for ever averted from this eminently peaceful Soil.

St. Theresa of Avila Catholic Church, Robert S. Brantley and Jan White Brantley, photographers, ©1999.

---

[96] St. Theresa of Avila was built in 1847 at the corner of Camp and Erato streets. T. E. Giraud was the architect.

January 1 54° 60° 63°

The first flash of dawn came cheerily into our bed room windows, dappled with rosy light, and promising us a charming day. Little Prescott was soon awake and dressed, and wished us all round a happy New Year with as much earnestness as if he understood all about it. The morning paper opens the year with pleasant tidings of the gush of waters from the upper rivers, tidings which will convey gladness to the hearts of thousands. At 12 the "home squadron" were all "drawn up in line" in the parlour to receive the "Salutes" of the New Year, and I left them to their "receptions" and entered upon my own tour marked out for the day.

So many had been disappointed last year by the calls of business (the "first" having fallen on the Sunday) that they seemed resolved today to indemnify themselves for the loss....

Every where I found people in the highest spirits, and every house full of smiles and hilarity, except in two instances where bereavement has thrown a shadow over their annual festival. Emily and I sat up until near midnight, talking over her visitors and my visits &c. &c. and but very slightly tired by the unwonted exercise of the day, and so ended a truly "happy New Year."

January 2 58¹⁄₂° 64° 65°

Sunlight glancing amid fleecy vapors, and the air from the South East moist and tepid....

The engraver sent me a handsome "proof" of the little "wood cut" of Barataria. It looks remarkably well and gives the character of the scenery with great fidelity and effect. It is a great pity that it could not appear as well in the "Journal" for which it was executed, but the quality of the paper employed by the principal press here is ill adapted to receive the lines of a finely touched plate, or spirited wood cut.

January 3 63° 66° 65°

Sultry air from the North East, and East. Sunshine, thin clouds, and light shower in the afternoon.

They have begun to take down two buildings which disfigure the public grounds opposite to us, preparatory to enclosing the whole with a handsome fence, and making other ornamental improvements....

1855

January 5   65° 70° 68°

Air very damp and saturated with steamy vapor from the Gulf, inclining to rain in the afternoon, with rising wind from the South East and sea birds wheeling their flight in shore.

Wrote to Judge A. Walker relative to his "pioneer effort" to introduce "illustrations" into the periodical press here, and enclosed him some notes I made when at Barataria, descriptive of loca[li]ties which figure conspicuously in his series in the "Delta" on the early history of the State....

January 6   67° 70° 70°

High, gusty wind from the South East. Clouds threatening rain....

Received a Telegraphic Dispatch from the Department requiring the Superintendent to suspend the construction of the third tier groined arches. This order seems to imply the substitution of Iron Girders.

January 8   55° 58° 60°

Anniversary of the Battle of New Orleans. Works at the New Custom House suspended. Weather moist and cheerless but not enough so to damp the ardour of patriotism. The keen air from the North East did not deter the ladies from sharing the general holiday. I took Ellen down to see the display, calling first at the office for a short time and mounting to the top of the arches. We then took a position on Canal Street, which gave us an unobstructed view, and clear of the crowd. Soon after the military were in motion and all the different companies filed past us in admirable order, and attended by good bands. The dense and admiring concourse sweeping by on either side of the soldiery in long compact masses, and, as usual here, all quiet and well-behaved. I never saw a popular gathering in New Orleans otherwise....

January 11   55½° 60° 62°

Thick fog, warm South wind. Cleared off in the forenoon with North East wind....

I have closed accounts for the 4th. Quarter of 1854 and find the Total expenditures of the New Custom House to Decr. 31. 1854 amt. to $1.383.406.07.

January 12   56° 63½° 66°

Cloudy, warm and damp with gleams of hot sunshine.

The Rivers in the interior are every where rising, and with them the spirits of our merchants, and housekeepers are looking with some hope to a corresponding depression in prices.

January 15   48° 53° 54°

Clouds and warm sunshine, after a sharp frost in the night. North East wind.

Beauregard is again confined to his house by inflammation of the eye, and sent for me. A long walk in the French parts of town is really a pleasant change. So many remains of an earlier period, so much that wears the stamp of a different people, of different habits, and different modes of life from those which surround us in the upper districts of the city....

January 18   54½° 59° 59°

Calm, clear and spring like. Light air from the North....

Clouds and gloom envelope the commercial interest every where. Important failures are now of daily occurrence, and all operations based upon "credit" are undergoing a severe and most scrutinizing ordeal.

January 20   64° 67° 69°

Warm saturated air. Clouds and sunshine. South wind. Quite high in the middle of the day and prospect of rain.

In reply to Mr. Bryant's enquiries relative to the Secretary of the Treasury's Report on the Foundations of the New Custom House, I write as follows,

"The inequality of pressure on the foundations, whether due to inadequate calculation on the part of the Architect, or to the progress of the exterior so much in advance of the central compartment, has shewn itself in the failure of the large 40 foot arches under the Collector's Room and in contiguous ranges, in a line running from the centre of New Levee to the centre of Old Levee fronts. Practically, however, this evil will, in all probability, only involve the removal of the arches in question, and the substitution of Iron Girders similar to those which will be employed in place of the third Tier of Groined Arches.

The actual maximum subsidence of the foundations of the exterior walls from Decr. 6 1851 to Decr. 22. 1854 is .797 of a foot, say a little over 9½ inches. This occurs on Custom House Street [now Iberville] front (the entire height of the walls being at this time about 54 feet above the Plinth all round) The minimum .382, attended likewise with a slight outward tendency of said walls. It is confidently hoped, however, that the great additional weight of the Collector's Room will when added to the present pressure on the inner foundations have a tendency to arrest, if not entirely overcome, the irregularities which have been thus far noted.

Major Beauregard hopes to restore the equilibrium of the building without having recourse to any measures for extending or strengthening the foundations but I cannot help thinking that a system of "sheet piling" might be introduced with advantages all round, to prevent the immense pressure of the building from forcing out the yielding soil laterally. Tho' as far as this mode of construction is concerned it would have been far better had it been employed when the foundations were first put in. It will be a difficult and costly operation to meddle with them now.

January 21 58° 61° 60°

Sunday. Dark rolling clouds and showers early in the morning. Sudden change of wind to North West, blowing very fresh and cold, and sweeping away every vestige of vapour, driving back the scowling clouds to the Gulf from whence they came. By church time a genuine "norther" had replaced the late stagnant atmosphere and the sun shone with unclouded brightness. This is another example of those rapid depressions of temperature which are so trying to the thin blood of the South. The feeble arm of "winter" is no longer able to restrain the impatient vigor of our vegetation. The "morus multicaulis" the "althea" and others are bursting into foliage, and the "Lamarck rose" which hangs over my front gallery is dotted over with plump flower buds. This weather will set them back for a short time....

The wind rose to a gale at noon and blew hard all the afternoon and all night and severely cold, with an atmosphere of intense purity. Just as we sat down to tea the alarm bells pealed out and drew us to the front gallery. The flames were towering above the houses in the direction of St. Mary's market in Lafayette about 5 squares off and with the raging gusts from the North West threatened to become a serious affair, but in spite of the high wind the firemen managed to confine its ravages to the Square in which it originated....

January 31 36° 38° 44°

More severe than ever....

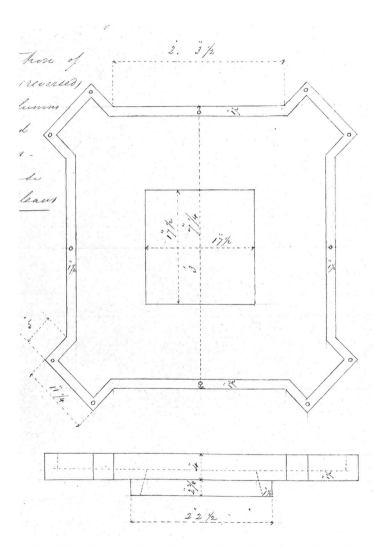

Plan and elevation of cast iron cap (reversed) for the brick columns of vestibule and U.S. Court Room.

February 1 40° 42° 44°

Weather moderating. No frost last night. Light clouds today. Raw air from North East to West.

The Ball last night was a very brilliant affair.[1] I ordered the carriage pretty early but owing to the imperious claims of the toilet and little Tommy we did not reach the scene of action until after 9 O'clock. A little pleasant chat in the apartment of our friends and then we all "proceeded in state" to the dancing saloons. Three rooms of large size and opening into each other. But they were soon filled to such an extent that it became a task of no little difficulty to pass from point to point without infringing somewhat upon the "rights of man" and woman, too; there must have been upwards of a thousand persons in and around the rooms. And at supper, which by the way was an admirable one; we could not be put down at less than 6 or 700 and still many were unprovided with places. The dancing was spirited and well varied, the music heavy and cumbersome, too great a preponderance of "brass." But the great charm of the evening lay in the fact that so many of our friends were there. We spent in consequence a delightful evening and I confess I saw the rooms "thinning out" at 2 O'clock with regret. Emily and Mrs. Ladd enjoyed it exceedingly. Altogether it was the pleasantest "soiree" I ever attended in New Orleans....

The Major is worse today. Confined to his bed. His absence from the office is, however, less felt at this time, as our operations are much retarded by want of marble and the delays consequent upon the change in the third story from groined arches to Iron girders. This and the proposed Iron roof will have the effect of diminishing materially the weight of the upper portion of the structure, and will also furnish a very large and profitable order to our friend Charles Knap the contractor.

February 2 43° 46° 48°

Weather much milder but excessively dry. Light clouds, smoky air. Wind South West to North West. Money and water are becoming equally scarce. The drought is without a precedent.

[1] Balls were held during the annual carnival season at the city's leading hotels. Mardi Gras, the climax of the season, was on February 20 in 1855.

February 3 44° 48° 51°

White frost in the night with ice. Very dry and cloudless. Air filled with dust. Wind South East....

Dined sumptuously at John's Restaurant, and then walked down to the New York Steamer lying opposite to the Cathedral of St. Louis.[2] The bells were chiming for vespers. They are musical but inexpressibly plaintive. The fine shrubbery of the Square is powdered over with thick dust from the Levee.

The dark front and spires of the church. The heavy French style of the Court buildings on either side. The vast piles of brick ranging on the north and south side of the Square forming the Pontalba blocks. And the sombre colours of the evergreens within the enclosure. All presented stern and rigid features, and partook rather of gloom than solemnity as the shadows deepened into twilight. I always miss the fine old trees that in old times decorated the Square, and set off to such advantage the moss grown Spanish Turrets of the former Cathedral.[3]

February 5 59° 63° 64°

Mild and springlike. Gleams of sunshine and clouds threatening rain. Brisk south wind to West laden with vapors from the gulf. The granite walls of the New Custom House reeking with moisture.

Note from Major Beauregard; still unable to leave his house.

The mist cleared away in the evening, and the Stars shone out with unwonted lustre after nightfall. At about 9 the carriage was at the door, and whirled us off to the St. Louis, Emily, Mrs. Ladd & I.[4] The dancing fairly commenced at a much later hour. The music very fine. In all its appointments it was universally conceded that this was one of the most superb invitation Balls ever given in New Orleans....

One thing, however, I never can reconcile myself to those excessively benevolent, warm-hearted Polkas. The opening quadrilles were elegant, but the following dances I will not characterize. If

[2] John's Restaurant, owned by John Strenna, was at 9 Carondelet St. NOCD 1856.
[3] In 1808 the city council ordered three rows of trees to be planted in alleys on each side of the square. The trees were still standing when Wharton sketched the scene in 1845, but were removed about 1851 when the square was redesigned as a French garden. Vieux Carré Survey, Historic New Orleans Collection.
[4] The St. Louis Hotel and City Exchange occupied an entire block on St. Louis Street between Chartres and Royal. Designed in 1835 by the architect Jacques N. B. de Pouilly, it burned in 1840 and was rebuilt by the same architect. The hotel was demolished in 1916; the Omni Royal Orleans Hotel now occupies the site.

Byron spurned the waltz of his day what would he have thought of the Polka and Schottische of ours. These intimate wreathings and intertwinings of the sexes greatly disfigure our modern assemblies but as they exist every where and are due to the prevailing taste and not to individual indelicacy, why I suppose they will have to be tolerated until the times are mended, and the whole thing put to the blush by the introduction of better and purer modes. The party began to subside about 2 and we took to the carriage somewhat before the concluding dances. We have two invitations for Thursday next but "it is a beautiful thing to know where to stop." Not too often, is the great secret of enjoyment.

February 6   56° 59° 62°

Dry, clear and dusty again as ever. Light air from West to South East.

Dr. Barton called at the office to tell me that I was last night unanimously elected a member of the N.O. Society of Arts and Sciences.[5] I had not the slightest idea that he intended me the courtesy to propose me. The mild air tempted Major Beauregard down to the office, but he looks much enfeebled. His brother, Armand, on the contrary, came in from his place below, the picture of rugged, robust health, town versus country.

February 7   59° 65° 66°

Dark gathering clouds, high wind from the gulf, very warm, South East. Light rain at 9....

Just before the evening meeting at the Baptist Church on the next Square I stepped in for a few moments and chose a pew for the year. I have given up mine at Dr. Preston's Church, and Emily, & Mrs. Ladd seem decidedly to prefer our neighbour to any other in town. Dr. Preston's was altogether too far off. Our cook is a good willing woman and prepares her dishes very nicely, but sometimes loses her self-possession sadly when we have friends. Today, for example, after removing oyster-soup what was my amazement when she placed before me a huge cannon ball of a pudding which would have been in very good time half or three quarters of an hour later. But the excellence of the regular dishes when they appeared made amends for her error.

[5] The New Orleans Academy of Sciences was founded in 1853 as a men's intellectual organization. Duffy, *Matas History of Medicine*, 2:298.

February 11   48° 51° 55°

Sunday. Keen white frost in the night. Still air and sparkling sky. Rain as far off apparently as ever. My cistern holds out and I am still able to supply a neighbour with drinking water, but I have already taken the precaution of a hogshead of river water to help out. This can be filled from a neighbouring Hydrant as fast as it is emptied, thus economizing the cistern water for the Table....

We all went to church. Mr. Duncan's subject was the same as the last two Sundays from a different point of view.[6] I think I shall soon get to like the church very much, and we are decidedly fortunate in the selection of a pew. I am glad, too, to gratify Emily who has found it difficult to accustom herself to the ritual of the Church in which I was brought up.

February 12   54¼° 63° 64°

Mild temperature, high wind from the South East filling the whole city with dust from the Levee. Gathering clouds and intervals of hot sunshine. Light sprinkle of rain in the afternoon.

After tea in company with Dr. Barton I attended a meeting at the City Hall of the "Academy of Sciences" of which I was recently elected a "Fellow."[7]...

This evening there were some twenty to twenty five members present. Men of talent and information, several of them personally known to me. Dr. Barton in the chair, the deliberations were conducted with admirable ease and courtesy, and strict attention to parliamentary usages. The subjects discussed of great interest and touched with ability. The whole, however, did not occupy more than a couple of hours as there was no scientific paper before the society this evening....

February 14   52° 54° 56°

Very beautiful weather. Dry and searching air from the North West. The rain has not done much for us. In the suburbs river water is actually selling for one dollar a cask. The cisterns being in most cases quite exhausted and the hydrants not extending to the Fourth District.

[6] The Rev. William Cecil Duncan (1824-1864) was pastor of the Coliseum Place Baptist Church. He lived at the corner of Annunciation and Basin (now Terpsichore). *DLB*, NOCD 1856.

[7] The third floor of the city hall contained a large, handsome auditorium known as the Lyceum Hall where lectures and meetings were held. Plans of this room, designed by James Gallier in 1850, are in the Southeastern Architectural Archive at the Tulane University Library. The room was cut up into offices in the 1860s.

City Hall with police station at left, Jay Dearborn Edwards, photographer, between 1857 and 1860 (1982.167.7).

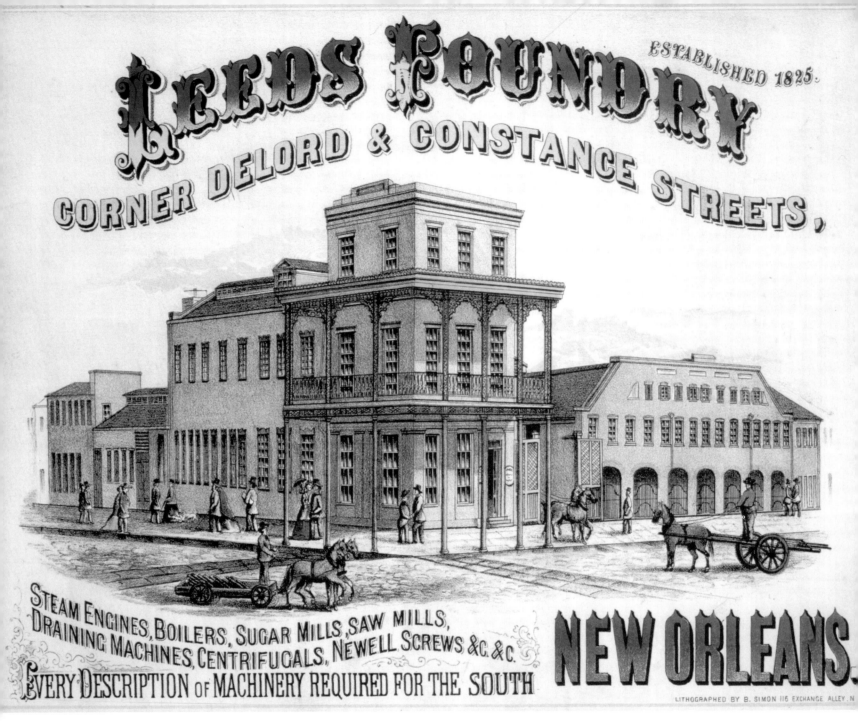

Leeds Foundry, Benedict Simon, lithographer, between 1872 and 1878 (1949.1.10).

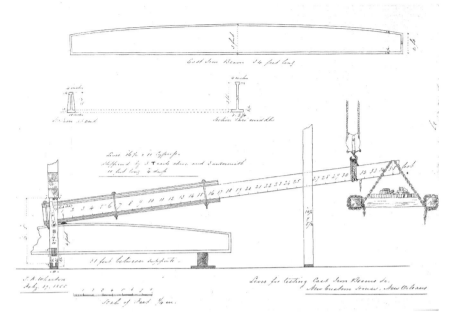

February 18   50° 51° 53°

Sunday. Rain in the night. Cloudy and mild this morning. Harsh air from the North East. Rain set in seriously about 5 P.M. and came down in a steady stream replenishing the empty cisterns, and filling up to overflowing the pores of the thirsty earth....

Mr. Preston happened to be at my house yesterday when Mr. Gillett first called, and they will be together at Mrs. Carter's which will make it very pleasant for Mr. G.[8] I regret that I have not a spare room to offer him, but he will be quite near and his principle object in coming to New Orleans now is to mature his plans for the College in Austin, so that we shall have to be very much together. He has already secured a subscription of $25.000 which is $10.000 more than when he last advised me.

February 19   48° 48³/₄° 51°

Rained nearly all night. Cold north wind today, cloudy but cleared up in the afternoon.

Took a severe cold yesterday so that I did not stay long at the office but returned home to a warm fire at 12.

[8] The Rev. Charles Gillette, rector of Christ Church, Houston, married Wharton's sister Marianne in 1847. He organized a diocesan school, St. Paul's College, in 1852 and served as its principal until 1856. DuBose Murphy, *A Short History of the Protestant Episcopal Church in Texas* (Dallas, 1935), 34.

Mr. Gillet and I spent an hour this morning in discussing Plans for St. Paul's College at Austin. He joined us again just after dinner and stayed the rest of the evening, receiving clerical friends, &c. &c. Revd. N. O. Preston &c. I give a sketch...of the mode of testing Cast Iron Beams and girders at the New Custom House, with a drawing of 4 Beams cast by Messrs. Leeds & Co. to carry the inner wall of staircase entrances on Custom House & New Levee Streets, 2nd. story, 2 in each, acting as bressummers and built into the thickness of the wall, with the regular ventilating Flue passing between them.[9] These beams weigh about 5 1/5 tons each, say, 11.633 lbs. The pressure is applied to the middle of the beam, and exactly under the 1 foot mark on the Lever, being one foot from the fulcrum (or point on which it works) the load at the other end (say at the 35 foot mark)

is 204 Bricks, or	1017.143	Pounds
to which add weight of Instrument &c.	1840.	"
in all	2857.143	Pounds

multiplying by 35 feet gives a pressure of 100.000 Pounds on the Beam at the point of application. The Beams subjected to this pressure did not deflect more than ³/₄ inch. The whole length of each being 34 feet.

[9] Leeds & Co., founded in 1824, was one of the principal iron foundries in New Orleans. It was located at the corner of Delord (now Howard Avenue) and Foucher (now Constance Street). *DLB*; NOCD 1859.

February 24   50° 49° 50°

Rain in the night. Raw and very cold today. Cloudy with North East wind....

Emily and Ellen came to the office for me at 3 after shopping. I took them up to the top of the third tier of arches and on one of the cars on the scaffolding, and gave them a fine view of the city and neighborhood. It is their last chance to get as high for some time as we have commenced tearing down the centering already executed for that tier of arches, in order to substitute Iron beams, girders and segmental arches as per order of the Treasury Department....

February 28   35½° 37° 41°

Severely cold wind from North East to North West. Very fresh. Even the horses show the effects of this rigorous weather. Their sleek coats are become rough and shaggy and each particular hair stands on end as dry and crisp as in the streets of Boston.

At the Custom House we have to suspend the masonry and that which has been executed during the past week is much injured. The mortar has flaked off or crumbled out of the joints, so that part will have to be rebuilt and the rest repointed. The air, however, is perfectly delightful, pure and elastic and the brightest sunshine floods the hemisphere. Emily and I, Mrs. Ladd & Ellen spent the evening at Mr. R. Sumner's.[10] It was little Clara's annual party, but several adults were also invited informally, going early and returning at about midnight after a very handsome supper. The children appeared like a rich bouquet suddenly induced with locomotion, and their dancing very graceful & correct....

There were about 25 ladies and gentlemen and 30 juveniles or upward, every thing in good taste, the rooms spacious & elegant, every one at their ease. In short far pleasanter altogether than those densely crowded, close packed gatherings on <u>great occasions</u>, of which we have every winter more than enough. Indeed the whole system of fashionable parties needs revision sadly. One half the invitations, and one half the expenditure on female costume, and that more generally distributed over the arms and shoulders, earlier commencement, and earlier departure, but, above all, the total and unqualified abolition of the Waltz

and all its voluptuous progeny. The present modes may do well enough amongst a class who have little or nothing to do, and rolling in wealth. But we have no such class in this country, and God forbid we ever should have. Every body here has, or ought to have, work enough to do. And parties with us ought to be made an agreeable relief from graver engagements, and not a serious hindrance to them. Regular, legitimate, successful business operations harmonize but ill with the nightly orgies of our badly contrived fashionable assemblies. On the score of health the present arrangements are even still more reprehensible.

March 2   40° 48° 51°

White frost in the night. Weather moderating, light clouds, checkered sunshine. South East wind.

Conversation in the afternoon on the use of Kyanized wood at Fort Jackson, has already stood the test of 14 years. This information from the mechanic who did the work, whom I met at Lafayette Square during my evening walk....

March 4   49° 56° 57°

Sunday. Mild and cloudy, but no rain. Light air from the north east. Turned out very fine and warm in the afternoon.

All went to church in the morning. Mr. Duncan preached well from 1 Peter 1.8, "Whom having not see ye love." The services were occasionally diverted by the distant Music of the "Firemen's procession". The 4th. is their annual celebration day.[11] But that is no good cause for the desecration of the Sabbath. It deserves and will receive severe reprehension. Such sunday displays are becoming more and more opposed to public sentiment, as American views

---

[10] Richard Bartlett Sumner (ca.1817-1868) of J. P. Whitney & Co. had purchased the Belleville Iron Works at a sheriff's sale in 1849; he and his wife, Harriet Johnson Sumner (ca. 1820-1904), were the parents of Clara (b. ca. 1847), Hattie (b. ca. 1853), and [L.?] (b. ca. 1859). U.S. Census, La., Orleans Parish, 1860; *Daily Picayune*, Mar. 26, 1868, Mar. 22, 1904; NONA, A. C. Ainsworth, Oct. 19, 1849; NOCD 1854.

[11] The fire companies met at their engine houses to celebrate the anniversary of the founding of the fire department with a procession on Canal, Carondelet, and Camp streets. *Daily Delta*, Mar. 3, 1855.

Annual parade of the fire department, Charles Upham, delineator, Frank Leslie's Illustrated Newspaper, *March 17, 1883 (1974.25.2.144).*

Touro Synagogue, after Louis E. Cormier, photographer, ca. 1910, showing a later temple rebuilt to the original plan (1974.25.7.97).

more and more prevail, but in so mixed a population as we still have around us there must still also be a large number in their favor. Especially as the opinions of continental Europe on this subject are held by a large proportion of our citizens…

March 14   70° 75° 76°

Hot and cloudy, high wind from South West. Winter is fast retreating to his native Pole. The sun shines on a waste of bloom and bursting leaf buds. Superb roses are in the ascendant. The yellow jessamines fill the air with fragrance and spring birds the neighbouring gardens with melody.…

Commenced a sketch for a new Synagogue at the request of Mr. William Florance.[12]…

March 16   75° 79° 78° 80° at 2 P.M.

Very sultry. High wind from South East. Vapory clouds.

Letter from Mr. Guthrie to Major Beauregard announces a new appropriation for our work of $275.000 for the year commencing next July 1st. instead of $60.000 as stated by Mr. Slidell to Mr.Penn.[13] After dinner at Baptist Church with Mr. Low.[14]

Close drawing after dark until bedtime. Front design made.

March 17   76° 72° 70°

Hot, damp, and oppressive. Floating clouds. South East wind.

Mailed the set of Plans for St. Paul's Col. to Mr. Gillett with a letter. Showers set in at 11, with change of wind to North West, and sudden reduction of temperature. At the New Custom House we commenced setting the Marble of the "Collector's Room." The marble is from the Quarries of East Chester. Fine drove at the yard in N. York, and tho' strongly laminated in texture, and clouded in many places with blue veins, will generally have a fine effect. The rubbed surface would, to my fancy, have been preferable but the Department has expressed a strong opinion in favour of fine droving.…

March 20   58° 62°

Very charming spring weather. North East wind.

Peaches & other fruit trees, Accacias and Roses innumerable in full bloom.

I give…a sketch shewing the brickwork of Columns in the Principal Vestibule and Court room of N. Custom House. The brick is "Baltimore Brick." 4" x 8³/₈" x 2¹/₂".

The Vestibule of the Collector's Room N. Custom House, on Canal Street is enriched with six of those Columns.…The United States Court Room on Old Levee front with Four Columns. The Capital is designed for Cast Iron, of the Composite order with very ornate foliation. The Iron Cap shewn in the drawing being provided with proper rivet holes to bolt in the Iron faces of said Capital. A Base and Pedestal of Marble is intended to encase the lower part of the Column, and the Shaft is Panelled, and to be finished carefully

---

[12] The Congregation Dispersed of Judah (later Touro Synagogue) was organized in 1845 and was given the old building of Christ Church at Canal and Bourbon by Judah Touro. A new synagogue was built on Carondelet Street between Julia and St. Joseph in 1856, for which William A. Freret was the architect and Little and Middlemiss the builders. William E. Florance (ca.1810-1864) lived on Religious corner Richard. *Daily Picayune*, Aug. 24, 1864; NOCD 1855.

[13] John Slidell (1793-1871) was a key political figure in Louisiana state politics in the 1850s. He served in the U.S. Senate from 1853 to 1861 and represented the Confederacy in France throughout the Civil War. *DLB.*

[14] James H. Low (1817-1890) was a cotton factor. *Daily Picayune*, Mar. 10, 1889, June 5, 1890.

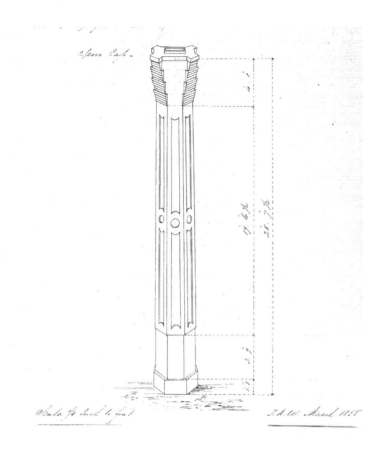

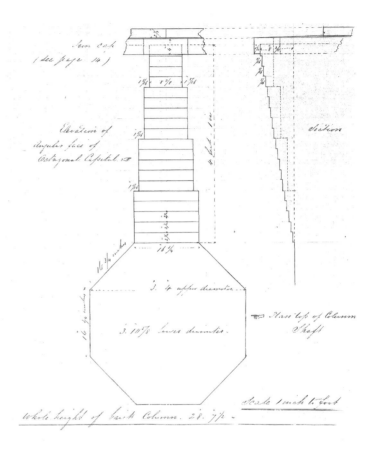

with firm Stucco, or such covering as shall be selected for its durability and perfection of surface.

The change from brick to Iron in the Third Floor will probably demand a corresponding change in the design of these columns, indeed drawings have already been made in the Architect's office to change to proportions of those in the Canal Street Vestibule and substitute the Capital from the Tower of Andronicus Cyrrhestes for the Composite contemplated by Mr. A. T. Wood.[15]

---

[15] Andronicus Cyrrhestes, an astronomer, built an octagonal, marble tower to the eight winds in Athens. Now known as the Tower of the Winds, the structure functioned as a water clock, as well as a sun dial. *Harper's Dictionary of Classical Literature*, ed. Harry T. Peck (New York, 1923).

March 21   54° 56½° 56°

Light clouds. Harsh air from the North East. Cold rains at night....

March 22   49° 52° 55°

Very beautiful weather. Bracing air from the North East....

By working every night this week until quite late I have finished a general Design for a New Synagogue on St. Charles Street (with buildings accessory thereto) which, if approved will furnish the basis of a complete Set of Plans for said proposed structures.

Bird's-eye view of New Orleans with the First Congregational Unitarian Church in the foreground, Theodore J. Lilienthal, photographer, ca. 1870 (1988.134.2 i,ii).

March 23 48³/₄° 52° 55°

Bright & sunny, cold air from North East to South West.

Detained by business until late. Presented my sketch of Synagogue for consideration. After dinner went to see the works in progress at the new church, corner of St. Charles and Julia, and <u>our</u> church on the next square.[16]

March 24 52¹/₂° 58° 62°

Clear and cold. Raw air from North West to South West.

After tea Emily and I went down to the Armory Hall to see the much vaunted Panorama of "Bunyan's Pilgrim's Progress."[17] Attendance, as usual, good, but the work possessing not a single feature of artistic merit, merely coarse "Scene painting." The descriptive comments of the proprietor, however, as the canvas

[16] The First Congregational Unitarian Church on St. Charles between Julia and Girod was erected in 1853 (Theodore Eugene Giraud and Thomas Lewis, master builders; John Barnett, architect). The handsome, octagonal Gothic church cost $54,000. The Rev. Theodore Clapp, the noted preacher, was the minister. NONA, William Shannon, July 8, 1853.

[17] First patented in London in 1787, panoramas were large circular paintings that were lit from above and behind. Spectators, who stood on a central platform, found the effect startlingly realistic. John F. McDermott, *The Lost Panoramas of the Mississippi* (Chicago, 1958); Karin H. McGinnis, "Moving Right Along: Nineteenth Century Panorama Painting in the United States" (Ph.D. diss., University of Minnesota, 1983).

slowly unrolled gave it some interest, tho' intoned at times in diverting mimicry of the sublime. The main fault of such exhibitions is to create and maintain a low standard of public taste in "Art" especially as they are presented with numerous credentials from the press, claiming to be the productions of the highest artistic talent in the country.

March 26 59° 65° 67°

Fine & clear. Mild air from the South West. Very hot sun in the middle of the day.

Messrs. Low and [Jeudon?] of the <u>new church</u> came in after tea, and the Revd. Mr. Duncan (the Pastor) joined them during the evening. Time passed rapidly in very animated and agreeable conversation and it was near 11 when they left. I like what I have seen of our new church friends very much. There is infinitely more fraternity and warm <u>individual</u> interest among them than is usual among Episcopalians in this country. With them the fact of your being a member of the same church or a pew holder therein seems to create not the slightest evidence of a new social interest, or the most distant desire for social intercourse. This, as far as I have seen, is characteristic of the practical working of Episcopalianism in America, and hence one cause of its slow progress among a people who are eminently social in their tendencies, and its general want of success as a system when in contrast with the practice of so many other denominations, where the "esprit de corps" is dominant.

March 27 51° 53¹/₂° 56°

Winter still lingers in the lap of Spring. Hot yesterday harsh and piercing today, with high wind from the North West and blinding dust.

The municipal elections yesterday resulted in a complete triumph of the "Reformers," and a large majority in favour of our worthy friend Judge Bright for Recorder against "Winter" a man of no character at all.[18] There is some hope for New Orleans yet....

[18] In the election of March 25, 1855, the American or Know Nothing party obtained a complete victory over the Democrats, thereby gaining control of the legislative branch of city government. One of the promises of the Know Nothings was to solve the city's financial problems for which they blamed the incumbent Democratic administration. George Young Bright (1800-1877) was editor of the *Price Current* (1829-1834) and at various times served as recorder for the first, second, and third districts. J. L. Winter served as chief of police of the second municipality for several years and as recorder for the first district. *Daily Delta*, Aug. 26, 1849, Mar. 26, 1855; *Daily Picayune*, Apr. 4, 1877; NOCD 1854; Soulé, *The Know Nothing Party*, 61-65.

Canal Street on election day, probably 1872 (1978.200).

Marble cutting at the
New Custom House New Orleans   *J.K.16*
                                                 1855

March 30   48° 51° 52°

Still harsh and cloudy. North East wind, cold and damp.
Tendency to rain in the afternoon and actual rain after nightfall.

Studied the principles of Gothic Vaulting and the equilibration of arches after an early tea.

April 3   67½° 72° 74°

Hot sunshine. Air saturated with moisture. South wind.

Call from Judge Huling at the office. Took tea with us.

Major Beauregard returned from a visit of inspection to Proctor's Landing to select a site for the proposed Fort.[19] He and his brother in law J. R. Proctor, narrowly escaped with their lives yesterday from an unprovoked attack by a large party of drunken Spanish fisherman who had been engaged during the day in "election" Saturnalia, and

were armed with long knives &c.[20] The Major & Proctor being unarmed, and they had unfortunately forgotten that it was an "election day." The Parishes of Plaquemines & St. Bernard have not yet learned to do <u>those things</u> quietly.

April 4   69° 72° 75°

Very mild and seasonable. South East wind. Signs of rain.

The number of Government Works of which Major Beauregard has more or less the oversight is so great that our office is a perfect rendezvous of people thro' the business hours. Some on affairs of great moment, the majority, however, might almost as well stay away, as they interfere in a most irritating manner with the Major's intricate business details, and interrupt generally the regular current of our office work. Some are Americans, but the French predominate, and the difference between them appears to be that the former have a little to say about everything, the latter a great deal to say about nothing at all.

April 10   67° 69° 70°

Hot sunshine floating clouds, South East wind.

On striking the centre of the elliptical arch which carries one side of the Octagon or Tower of the Baptist Church the arch failed and thrust out the north East Buttress forming a dangerous fracture. It is a serious misfortune and indicates very deficient calculation on the part of the Architect.

April 14   70° 73° 75°

Hot sunshine. Fine southerly breeze. Floating clouds.

Fine strawberries at the Verandah for the first time this year.[21] Musquitoes slowly reviving. The town literally swarms with people attracted by the "Races" from all parts of the Interior.[22]

---

19 Fort Proctor, a masonry fort near the south shore of Lake Borgne, east of New Orleans in St. Bernard Parish, was named for Colonel Thomas Proctor, an American Revolutionary War officer who received a Spanish land grant. It was placed on the National Register of Historic Places in 1978. *States-Item*, July 22, 1977.

20 J. Richard Proctor (ca. 1816-1882) was married to Beauregard's sister Elodie. Keyes, *Madame Castel's Lodger*, 26. Isleños, the descendants of Canary Islanders, were brought to south Louisiana under the Spanish colonial regime.

21 The six-story Verandah Hotel at the corner of St. Charles and Common streets, diagonally opposite the St. Charles Hotel, was designed by Charles B. and James H. Dakin and erected in 1837. It was distinguished by the two-story iron galleries built over the sidewalks on the two street facades. The Verandah burned July 19, 1855.

22 The Metairie Race Course, built in 1838 where Metairie Cemetery now stands, was the South's leading racetrack. After the Civil War it became known as the Metairie Jockey Club. *Daily Delta*, Apr. 14, 1855; Henri A. Gandolfo, *Metairie Cemetery, An Historical Memoir* (New Orleans, 1981), 12-15.

April 15   70° 73° 76°

Sunday. Fine sunny day, fresh breeze from S. East....

Mr. Day called in the afternoon and after chatting awhile, proposed I should go round with him to Mr. Slark's to see a drawing of his New Mansion at Stonington in Connecticut.[23] On the way we went into the Baptist church, and examined the construction of the tower, causes of failure &c. Mr. Day's building is a fine Gothic composition, 52 feet front 106 feet flank, 3 stories high, and furnished within with every elegance and convenience, surrounding [sic] with rich native forest, and commanding a sweet water prospect. Altogether a charming retreat after a winter of driving business in N. Orleans. He and family leave tomorrow week.

April 16   71½° 75° 76°

Hot sunshine. Fresh Breeze. South to North East.

Went over Mr. Clapp's new church in the afternoon, now near completion. The stained glass window, as usual now, very strong and positive both in design and color....

April 19   73° 77° 83°

Foggy morning, very hot, dry & dusty after 10 A.M....

Before tea went over the new church with Mr. Low and the Revd. Mr. Duncan, and spent the evening at Mr. Low's house, where I expressed my views pretty freely on the errors of construction which have shown themselves in the tower of the church, condemned most unhesitatingly certain <u>perforated</u> Iron girders which are intended to be introduced to give support, and suggested what I conceive to be the proper mode of proceeding in the present critical stage of the works.

April 20   73° 77° 82°

Very hot and very dusty. Dry air from N. West to South West.

Last night that "ancient nuisance," & perpetual eye-sore "the American Theatre" was effectually annihilated. At 2 O'clock A.M. I was aroused by the fire bells, and was induced by the uncommon brilliance of the flames, to dress and walk down to the scene of action. When I reached Lafayette Square the Theatre and the entire block on which it stands were wrapt in sheets of fire. The splendid illumination of the tower of St. Patrick's was of itself sufficient compensation for the walk....

April 22   77° 80° 83°

Sunday. Blazing hot with the faintest possible breath of air from the West. Every object powdered over with the finest dust. And worst of all the dreaded musquitoes have suddenly sprung into existence. The unusual severity of the winter has for some months past protected us from them but our day of immunity is past....

Long walk in the afternoon amid the beautiful residences of the Fourth District. The air loaded with perfume, and comparatively free from the dust of the City. Mr. Robb's grand square mansion rapidly approaching completion, and the grounds around, comprising the entire square, already laid out in sweeping walks, and grass plots, parterres and groups of planting and embellished at suitable points with statues, and rich vases. A wide parapet, carefully sodded and faced with a high breast wall of solid masonry surrounds the house, and gives it an imposing effect.

April 26   72° 76½° 79°

Intensely hot, very dry. South East wind....

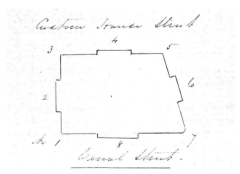

[23] James Ingersoll Day (1812-1895) of Slark, Day, Stauffer & Co., a hardware firm, was married to Sarah Armitage (1816-1896), sister of Mrs. Robert Slark. He returned to his native Connecticut prior to the Civil War. *Daily Picayune*, Sept. 23, 29, 1895; Edwin L. Jewell, ed., *Jewell's Crescent City Illustrated: The Commercial, Social, Political and General History of New Orleans* (New Orleans, 1873), 123. Robert Slark (1796-1868) of the same hardware firm and his wife, Abigail L. Armitage, lived on Annunciation St. between Melpomene and Thalia in a house believed to have been designed by James Dakin. *Daily Picayune*, Mar. 5, 1868; *New Orleans Architecture*, vol. 1, eds. Samuel Wilson, Jr., and Bernard Lemann, *The Lower Garden District* (Gretna, La., 1971), 22; Scully, *James Dakin*, 116.

Spring meeting at the Metairie Race Course, Frank Leslie's Illustrated Newspaper, *May 4, 1872 (1974.25.2.159).*

James Robb residence, photoprint courtesy Samuel Wilson, Jr. (Mss 98-9-L).

April 27   74° 79° 80°

Intensely hot in the sun. Dry S. West wind....

Closeted until 3 O'clock with Messrs. Penn, Beauregard and Capt. Bowman, on the Iron, Marble & Brick contracts &c. &c. One result of the conference was to call upon Mr. Knap for propositions in regard to certain varieties of Iron which will be required for our building under the changes sanctioned by Congress, and which do not appear to have been contemplated by his contract. He presented his terms and they were fully approved of and referred to the Hone. Secretary of the Treasury for his decision....

April 30   76° 80° 81°

Wondrous hot and the fine breeze from the South East only seemed to fill the city with dust.

At half past four went to the Baptist church to meet by appointment Messrs. Esterbrook, Reynolds and Ferguson, Architects, and Mr. Low to consult as to the causes of failure in the Tower, and the proper remedy.[24] We examined the work carefully, and will meet again tomorrow to conclude the enquiry. Two grave errors at least are apparent in the Design. These added to much vicious construction make one strongly in favour of rejecting the intended spire, and after proper measures to secure stability in the lower part of the Tower, to finish the whole with Square Lantern and Pinnacles of some enriched Design.

Fig. 1 Beam 12 feet long, 10 inches deep, area 20 inches. Strength with safety 24.604 lbs. weight to a foot of Floor 17 lbs. area to be covered 75.463 feet, weight 1:282.871

[24] Richard Esterbrook (1813-1906) of Cornwall, England, worked in New York before moving to New Orleans in 1837. He was associated with James Gallier, Sr., as a stair builder and after Gallier's retirement in 1850 became a partner with James Gallier, Jr., and John Turpin in the firm Gallier, Turpin & Co. Upon the dissolution of that partnership in 1858, the firm of Gallier and Esterbrook was created. Esterbrook's building career ended in 1868 with the death of Gallier, Jr. Gallier, *Autobiography*, 26, 46; *Daily Delta*, Mar. 4, 1858; *Times Democrat*, Oct. 15, 1906. Lewis E. Reynolds (1816-1879), a native of Norwich, New York, was one of the most prominent New Orleans architects of the 1850s. After studying under architects in Louisville and New York, Reynolds came to New Orleans in 1843. His major extant buildings include the Henry S. Buckner house at Jackson Avenue and Coliseum (1856), the William M. Perkins house at 1411 Jackson Avenue (ca. 1851), and Factors Row on Perdido at Carondelet (1857). Jewell, *Jewell's Crescent City*, 152. In 1851, Charles Ferguson is listed as an architect, corner Magazine and Washington in Lafayette. NOCD 1851.

Pounds. Girder including Tier 23 lbs. to a foot of floor, breaking weight 97 727/1000 Tons or 276½ lbs. to a foot of floor with safety, area to be covered 69.127 Feet.

Weight	1.589.921	Pounds
add weight of Beams	1.282.871	"
Total weight of Floor	2.872.792	"

Fig. 2 This girder is about the same as above. 69.127 feet
The Beams as above but only in corridors 6.336 "
Segmental arches between girders 75.463 feet

Fig. 3 This floor is supposed to contain the same Amount of Material as the last, and to be one third stronger, much easier of construction, and distributes its weight more uniformly over the walls.

Recapitulation

Girder and Beams	2.872.792	Pounds
Girder and Corridor Beams only	1.697.633	"
diffe.	1.175.159	"

N. B. Constant multiplier for Tubular Girder (wrot. iron) 21.5 Tons.

May 4   76° 80° 82°

Fine air from South West, but intensely hot sunshine.

Wrote to Danl. Dodd, Newark, New Jersey enclosing Bill of Lading of Box from Emily, to Mr. Knap. The Commissioners have today sent on a recommendation to the Secretary of the Treasury to raise my Salary from $150 to $180 per month. The language employed very gratifying. My landlord called with Lease of this house until Novr. 1. 1856 which I signed.

May 5   75° 78½° 80°

Intensely hot in the sun, fine air from the Northeast.

Emily came to the office for me at 2 and brought Ellen & Tommy. Went and had a fine daguerreotype taken of the two on the same plate. It became too late to have Em's taken today so we deferred it until next week and returned home to a late dinner. In the evening we all went to the church to see the effect of the room by gas light, it is to be used for service tomorrow for the first time and the Basement room heretofore used for that purpose, now

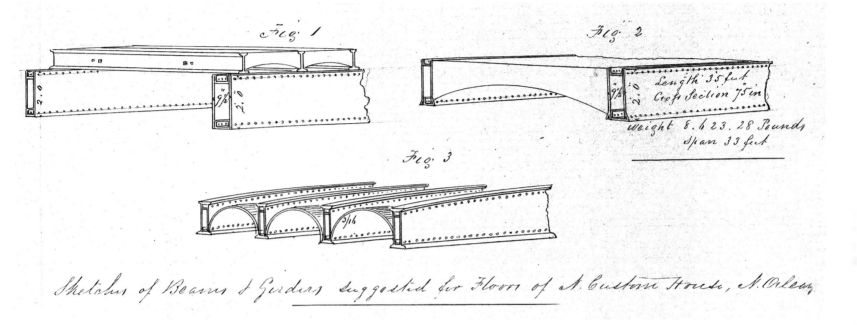

Fig. 1

Fig. 2

Length 35 feet
Cross Section 75 in
Weight 8.623.28 Pounds
Span 33 feet

Fig. 3

Sketches of Beams & Girders suggested for Floors of N. Custom House, N. Orleans

becomes the lecture room &c. The church has a fine, airy effect and the pews very comfortable and well arranged. The choir were practicing and I went over a few pieces with them. Mr. Duncan and friends among the congregation were there too, drawn by the same motives as ourselves.

May 10   71° 73° 75°

Cold wind from North East. Light clouds.

...I give a sketch from the Bank of the River about 4 miles above New Orleans. I made it the other evening when we all went out together to get a mouthful of fresh air. It shows one of those old Plantation houses which are fast disappearing, but some of which still remain to link us with the time when the now populous region lying between the city and Carrollton was laid out wholly in quiet

farms and rich Plantations.[25] Many a splendid group of foliage and fine grazing tract still exist. But the corn and sugar fields are all gone.

May 12   74° 78° 78°

Very <u>very</u> dry. Fine large clouds float overhead, reminding one that a shower is just a bare possibility, but that is all. In the meantime the sun blazes out with summer splendor and the East wind whirls the dust thro' the scorching streets.

I made a little sketch last evening. A distant glimpse of one of our most conspicuous buildings [St. Patrick's]...our suburbs tho' flat affords some very pretty artistic combinations.

[25] This was not an old plantation house, but a suburban residence erected in 1832 by Cornelius Hurst in his new subdivision, Hurstville. The house stood on Tchoupitoulas Street at Nashville Avenue. It was dismantled in the 1920s and reconstructed on Garden Lane in Metairie, a suburb of New Orleans, for I. H. Stauffer (Armstrong & Koch, architects).

Mississippi River —
4 miles above New Orleans . May 3. 1855

Lavillebeuvre's

Old Plantation House on the

River 4 miles above N. Orleans.

Th. Wharton

May. 3. 1853.

May 17   77° 79° 81°

Very hot in the sun. Wind variable from E. to N. East.

All eyes turn Eastward in expectation of exciting tidings by the next steamer, and all tongues are parched with drought, while the thirsty earth gapes wide for the long delayed boon. The city is looking with some impatience to the action of the Quarantine Board, and the Governor's proclamation on this head as the yellow fever has already appeared in Havana, and one of the members of the Board told me some days ago that a case of "black vomit" had occurred in this city in the neighbourhood of the shipping.[26]

May 24   81° 85° 87°

Last night was another example of unmitigated heat, without a breath of air to create a circulation thro' our rooms. Today, too, is as bright & glaring as ever with a gentle breeze from N. East.

I give…a copy of a sketch which I sent to cousin Fanny [Frances Merritt]. In one of her letters she wished me to give some idea of New Orleans and I intend this as one of a set of sketches for that purpose. The following descriptive notes accompany it.

"It exhibits in one view four of the ten churches that stand on or near the line of Camp Street. The open square is carpeted with close smooth grass, and planted with luxuriant trees. It is more than one fourth mile long, and four or five hundred feet wide, surrounded with beautiful houses, and gardens filled with the choicest flowers, roses blooming all the year round, and at this particular season the air is almost oppressive with the luscious fragrance of the orange bloom and the different species of Jessamine, especially the "Grand Duke" and "Arabian." Then at night we are entertained by the song of the "Southern nightingale" among the beautiful trees at Judge Slidell's, whose grounds are a few yards from our house. All the children of the neighbourhood with their nurses &c. and some of larger growth, too, gather on the Square in the evenings, and form the liveliest and prettiest groups imaginable, playing at different games, jumping the rope, and chasing one another among the sweet clover blooms. You may guess how Tommy enjoys it. My sketch looks longitudinally over the Square, consequently does not embrace the fine mansions which lie along its sides. Nor does it even include our house which lies concealed behind the China trees on the right of the picture. From the front gallery, however, we have a full view of the entire Square, which you could not fail to admire from its rich contribution of foliage with tasteful and elegant architecture. Of the Churches that to the left is "Swedenborgian"[27] (the Christian Chapel, founded in 1850). The next (St. Theresa, Roman Catholic) belonging to the celebrated Female Orphan Asylum. The top of whose roof appears beyond, and the Rectory in front of it. Next, and in the distance, is the fine Tower of St. Patrick's Cathedral (Roman Catholic) and then the unfinished tower of St. Paul's (Episcopal) this church is fully completed in the interior, and occupied. But the exterior is still in progress. The tower will be crowned by a perforated spire, and two other towers or turrets not seen in the view, are intended to carry spires. The new Baptist Church stands on the next Square to us, and would be seen in the sketch but for the trees on the right. It is all finished now but the tower, and is a very fine structure both for music and speaking, and the general purposes of public worship. The Interior 60 x 100, Gothic, open truss roof, and general appearance light, airy and comfortable."…

May 28   83° 86° 90°

Very hot enfeebling weather, tantalizing vapors sweeping across the sky, but they soon passed off and the sun almost scorched us to death. Light air from North West.…

The mortuary returns of last week are startling. No less than 385 deaths, 204 of Cholera, exclusive of Bouligny where the disease has been most destructive.[28] 150 to 170 is the usual range for this time of year. But such heat, drought and scarcity of wholesome food, all combined cannot fail to affect such a mixed and careless population as ours.…

[26] One of the characteristic symptoms of yellow fever is "black vomit," vomit composed of dark-colored, broken-down blood.

[27] Wharton's footnote: This ought to be "Campbellite." The teachings of Swedish religious visionary Emanuel Swedenborg (1688-1772) were the inspiration for the Church of the New Jerusalem, which reached the U.S. in the late eighteenth century. Alexander Campbell (1788-1866) advocated a return to the simple practices of early Christianity; his followers grew into one of the first indigenous American churches, known as the Disciples of Christ or the Christian Church.

[28] Originally the Cottage plantation, Faubourg Bouligny was subdivided in 1834. It centered on Napoleon Avenue and extended from General Taylor Street to Upperline, and from the river to Clara Street. *New Orleans Architecture*, vol. 7, comps. and eds. Dorothy G. Schlesinger, Robert J. Cangelosi, Jr., and Sally Kittredge Reeves, *Jefferson City* (Gretna, La., 1989), 46.

St. Patrick's Cathedral   J. W. W.

New Orleans from the River Bank 4 miles above-   May 11. 1855

Coliseum Place
New Orleans

T. K. Wharton
May 24. 1855

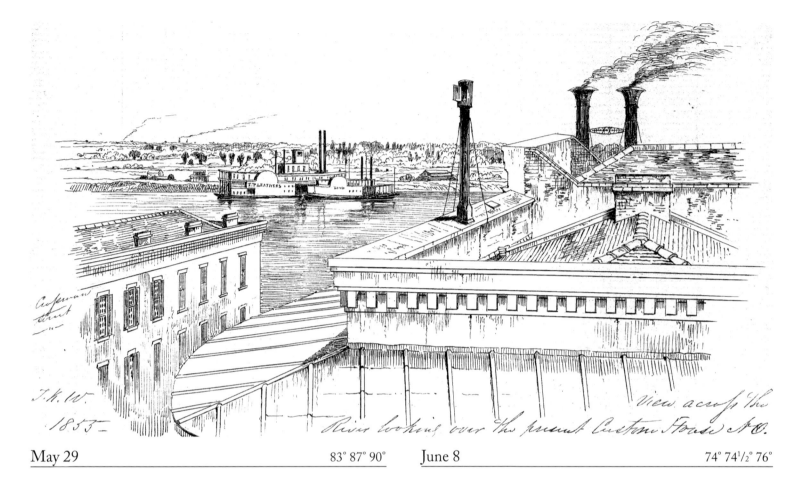

T.K.W. 1853 — View across the River looking over the present Custom House N.O.

May 29   83° 87° 90°

Still very hot and dry. South West wind....

When I got to the Custom House I found a letter on my desk from R. C. Morgan of the Treasury Department, advising me that the recommendation for the increase of my salary was successful. This was very kind of him as the illness and absence of the Secretary of the Treasury had delayed official action. I replied by mail.

June 5   78° 81° 82°

Very hot and dry, and again dusty. South East wind....

The whole house in commotion, taking up carpets and putting down matting, and otherwise purifying and preparing for summer.

June 8   74° 74¹/₂° 76°

Light rains thro' the night and again this morning, and the sky dense with stormy clouds. Copious showers and North East wind. Partially cleared in the afternoon.

For three or four days domestic affairs have been in the most active movement, and things are now brought to a complete state of summer neatness and perfect order. The accumulated dust of the winter has disappeared from the apartments, carpets removed, and bright, clean new matting taken their place. The change is pleasing to the eye as well as indispensable to health.

June 11   76° 79° 83°

Brilliant weather, change of wind to north. Fresh and cool. An atmosphere of intense purity and quite cloudless....

There have been 1270 Interments in the city within the last three weeks, but it would seem that the mortality is greatly on the decrease. And it seems, as usual, to have been confined chiefly to the improvident and reckless, and those, too, who were most exposed to the deprivations of the late serious drought. Young children have suffered severely and many unacclimated strangers have been carried off. "Yellow fever" is not the only enemy that the newly arrived has to battle against in this mephitic climate. Water, meats, fish, fruits and vegetables are all different from those he leaves behind, and hence may become elements of disease, while the fierce sun overhead relaxes his system, rendering it open to morbific influence; while at times and especially during the night the stagnation and often saturated condition of the air generates positive poison from the neighbouring marshes, and pours the subtle venom thro' his veins....

June 15   80° 81½° 83°

Clouds threatening rain. South East wind....

A card of invitation from Mrs. Renshaw to the exhibition and distribution of prizes of Miss Hull's school.[29] We were in good time to seat ourselves to advantage but the great room of the City Hall filled up fast and when the exercises commenced many were unable to find sitting room. The whole thing was done with great taste and elegance, and the musical performances admirable. Miss Mary Renshaw's fine vocalism and Miss Cora Hennen's instrumentation were beyond praise.[30] Either the race must be improving fast or New Orleans has more than her share of female loveliness....

[29] Henry Renshaw (b. ca. 1812) of the firm Turner & Renshaw was a tobacco merchant on Camp Street and a neighbor of Wharton's. He and his wife, Elizabeth A. R. White Renshaw (1820-1901), were the parents of Mary Louisa (1838-1856), Medora (b. ca. 1840), H.[enry?] Alla (b. ca. 1844), James (b. ca. 1847), and William (b. ca. 1849). NOCD 1856; U.S. Census, La., Orleans Parish, 1850, 1860; *Daily Picayune*, Aug. 7, 1856, Mar. 1, 1901. Sarah Hull's school, located on St. Joseph Street, had been established by 1822 by her father, Rev. James Hull, rector of Christ Church, and was continued by her until her death after the Civil War. Duncan, *Diocese of Louisiana*, 53.

[30] Cora Hennen (b. ca. 1839) was the daughter of the attorney Alfred Hennen and Ann Maria Davison Hennen; they lived on Royal St. U.S. Census, La., Orleans Parish, 1850.

June 19   81° 82½° 85°

Clouds and sunshine, North West wind.

Walked down to the office with Mr. Low and had a conversation about the tower of the Church, and called at his office again on the same subject. They have adopted our report and wish me now to carry it out, but my time will not admit of it. So I have proposed to Mr. Low the plan that occurs to me as best to get good drawings for the changes and completion we recommended, and to have the whole carefully executed.

June 21   78° 81½° 81°

Light clouds, cool air North West to South. Fine showers in the afternoon, and high wind.

Mr. Duncan informs me that the Trustees of the church still clamor loudly for the spire which I reported against. They would nearly as soon give up the church itself, as give up the "Spire." I am sorry for it, but I cannot recede a single step from the position I have taken.

June 30   80° 82½° 83°

Heavy clouds and alternate sunshine. South East wind.

Time has passed away and the city continues healthy. The Quarantine is in full operation but how far it will be salutary, or how judiciously it will be administered remains yet to be seen. In the meantime certain physicians maintain that there have already been some cases of yellow fever in the Charity Hospital, traced to the shipping. It is not unlikely that the confined hold of a vessel lying at the Levee might generate the disease during the summer months of this latitude even without communication with a sickly tropical port. Still a rigid quarantine would be of immense value to this city by excluding a vast amount of morbific influence which every summer flows freely into it, and aggravates the danger of a naturally unwholesome atmosphere.

July 1   78° 78° 79°

July opens with fertilizing showers, and a cool pleasant air. Heavy clouds rolling up from the Eastward, and the squares & gardens around buried in the richest verdure, and vocal with summer birds. The stillness of Sunday and summer-tide reigns in the streets. The migratory families have nearly all left.

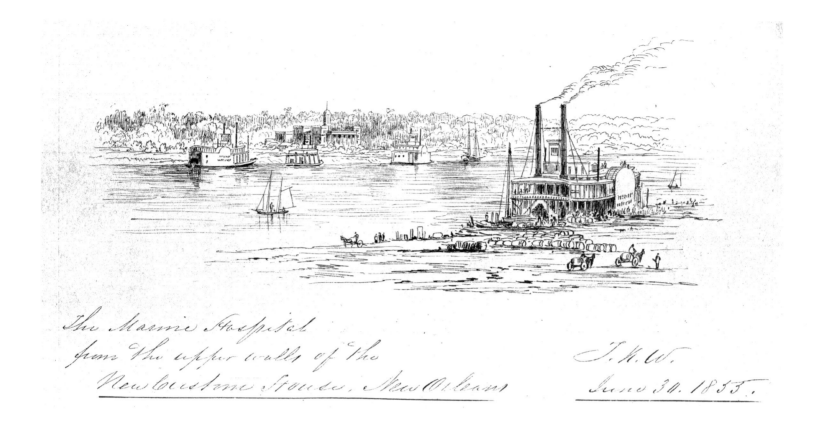

The Marine Hospital
from the upper walls of the
New Custom House, New Orleans

J.H.W.

June 30. 1853.

It looked very threatening as we were preparing for church and no sooner were we within the walls and the opening anthem commenced than the sluices of the firmament were opened and the deafening roar on the metal roof effectually drowned the choir, and bid defiance to any attempt to continue the service. The congregation was quite large for the time of year, and after waiting a reasonable time without any prospect of abatement, I suggested that we had better retire to the basement lecture room. Mr. Duncan immediately gave the notice and we were soon assembled below where the war of elements scarcely reached us, and the service went on, Mr. D. preaching an eloquent sermon from the text "being sanctified by faith." In the meantime the floods descended without intermission, and when the service was over at one P.M. the deluge without effectually barred all egress from the church. After a short pause the Communion was administered upstairs, but that concluded the pitiless flood around still cut off all retreat.

The rain had ceased and the waters began slowly to ebb away....

3 O'clock arrived and several omnibusses, hacks and carriages drove up in succession, and gradually took off the people by means of heavy scantling projected from the entrance to the middle of the street. I waited until near 4 so as to give time for the water to retire sufficiently from the banquette in front of my house, which, by the bye, is on the very next square from the church. I then took the first carriage that came, and we all got in Emily & myself, Mrs. Ladd & Ellen, and drove round by Magazine Street, which being on a ridge, was quite out of the water. When we got to the front of the house, Mary & little Tommy were on the lookout for us. The water still stood deep on the Banquette, tho' dry within the gate, so I told Mary to bring a light ladder, and by that bridge we were landed easily and without wetting a thread....

Stereographic view of Canal St., shell road to lake, ca. 1870 (1988.134.24 i,ii).

July 3   78° 79° 80°

Threatening clouds and intervals of warm sunshine. North West wind....

Drove down to the Lake by the Bienville Street shell road, and rambled about for an hour on the beautiful grassy pier, watching the splendid changes of the sunset reflected from the calm Lake.[31] Pres. [Tommy] took a special interest in the Schooners gliding quietly out from the embouchure of the Canal by the Lighthouse...the gigs & equipages, too, driving up in succession to the Hotel.[32]...

[31] Bienville Street led to Metairie Road and the Metairie racecourse and continued along the old shell road to the lake at West End. The Bienville Street shell road was completed and opened April 24, 1853. *Daily Crescent*, Apr. 25, 1853. Shell roads, an improvement over dirt roads, were made from oyster shells dredged from Lake Pontchartrain and surrounding areas.

[32] This octagonal lighthouse was on the east bank of the New Basin Canal at the lake, near the location of the present lighthouse. It was built in 1838 by Francis Dean Gott for the U.S. government. David L. Cipra, *Lighthouses and Lightships of the Northern Gulf of Mexico* ([Washington?], 1976), 29.

July 11   82° 85° 87°

Charming day. Clear sunshine. Cool air from N. West.

Letter from George Prescott to Mrs. Ladd, expresses a hope that Massachusetts may eventually rid herself of her fanatics and that common sense and common honesty may at least have a voice in the management of her domestic polity....

July 18   82° 82½° 81°

Clouds & hot sunshine, showers, distant thunder, and fine breeze from the North East....

The population is greatly reduced, and the musquitoes are greatly multiplied, but we have as an offset to these and the summer malaria, fine breezes. Cooling and frequent showers. Luscious figs, peaches and melons, and many other sweets mingled with the inevitable cup that must be drained to the dregs of a long summer, and a long tedious autumn, before we feel again the sharp and bounding breezes of the icy north.

Lighthouse on Lake Pontchartrain
Entrance of the New Canal.

J. W. Wharton July 3. 1855

Steam-powered fire engine, Girod Street, Jay Dearborn Edwards, photographer, between 1857 and 1860 (1982.167.12).

Verandah Hotel, 1838 (1950.10.3ii).

July 19   81° 79° 79°

Clouds & sunshine. S. East wind. Heavy tropical rains at 11 and again at 1 with distant thunder.

I was aroused last night by the unusual clangour of the fire bells, and saw a fierce blaze at the foot of Camp Str. It turns out to be the Verandah Hotel which is entirely reduced to ashes, at a loss of about $150.000. The new Steam Fire Engine was on the ground at a late stage of the proceedings, and did wonders.[33]

July 23   81° 81° 81°

Clouds & sunshine. Distant muttering thunder. Heavy rains passed around us in the afternoon with dense piles of vapour along the horizon, but very little rain fell in the city. South East wind....

Went down after dinner to see the trial of the new steam fire engine at the corner of Canal and Camp. Very large concourse of people, streets lined, galleries and balconies crowded. The engine

threw two columns of water over from one to two hundred feet of the neutral ground with volume and force enough, one would think, to drown the fiercest flame in a few minutes. The nozzles were occasionally directed against the trees and the stream cut off the leaves and smaller twigs with the precision of sharp shears....

July 25   80° 82° 79°

Day opened with clouds & bursts of hot sunshine. South East wind. Heavy rain at noon, with muttering thunder and a fall of 2 degrees in the thermometer during its continuance. Again at 2 O'clock, and between 4 and 5 a perfect deluge of rain with loud thunder, wind, and vivid lightening.

Little Tommy quite feverish today, and his usual boisterous merriment sobered down to a quiet languid inaction. But a little light medicine will soon reinstate him.

I give...an exterior window sill and part of jamb, of Granite, on New Levee [now Decatur] side N. C. H. showing the rough stock entering the wall, brick backing, Iron ties, portion of external scaffolding &c. &c. River bank in the distance. Store of R. W. Adams Grocer &c. &c. on the Levee.[34]

---

[33] Developed in 1852, the first steam fire engine in New Orleans was the "Young America," which arrived from Cincinnati in 1855. Crushingly heavy and awkward to maneuver through the city's badly kept streets, it was abandoned later that same year and replaced by improved models. Exhibition brochure, *Ready at First Sound: The New Orleans Fire Department* (Historic New Orleans Collection, 1991).

[34] Robert W. Adams (1823-1892) of Kentucky had a wholesale grocery business on Common, corner Front and Fulton. *Daily Picayune*, Aug. 25, 1892; NOCD 1855, 1856.

J. H. Wharton
July 25. 1855

Window opening on
New Levee front. N. Custom Ho.
New Orleans
Shewing the Granite work. Brick backing and
Iron anchors - Scaffolding &c

St. Alphonsus Church, Robert S. Brantley and Jan White Brantley, photographers, ©1992.

July 26

80° 83° 80°

Clouds and hot sunshine. South East wind. Copious showers in the afternoon with distant thunder....

Walking out with Ellen after dinner I met W. Freret who asked me to walk round with him to Live Oak street between Josephine and St. Andrews and see the commencement of a new Catholic church which he had just discovered.[35] There I found in connection with the noble buildings the Romanists have already erected on that and the opposite Square, the walls (already considerably advanced) of

one of the largest and finest churches in the city, best Lake brick, cement mortar, Iron bases to Pilasters, Piers projecting nine inches from main wall, workmanship very superior and the design, so far, solid, massive and finely proportioned. This is the first either William or I had seen or even heard of it. "That Church" certainly challenges admiration for the magnitude and superior excellence of its edifices, and the noiseless but unwearied energy with which it pushes them forward. "That Church", as regards its machinery, is a sublime organism. Unity of purpose, vigour and efficiency of action, and completeness in the management and distribution of all its details, as fully characterize it now as they did three centuries ago. And while Protestant Christendom presents the mortifying spectacle of a church divided into a hundred fragmentary elements, each struggling to maintain an independent existence, convulsed with intestine dissensions, and useless controversies, the Romanists still

[35] The Church of St. Alphonsus was designed by Louis Long, a Baltimore architect, who had designed the similar Jesuit church of St. Ignatius there. The cornerstone of St. Alphonsus was laid on June 10, 1855, and the church was dedicated on August 2, 1857.

T. W. Wharton
Augt. 7. 1855

Lake Terminus of the Shell Road
from the Pier of the Jefferson and
Pontchartrain Railroad

pursue the same even course, under an unbroken system of organization, and accomplish with apparent ease what we with all our strength and business-like bustle dare not even aspire to. I allude more particularly to the construction of churches and the establishment of grand institutions for benevolent purposes. With great exertion we protestants occasionally manage to rear a half finished and ill-built ecclesiastical structure or asylum, while the Catholics are filling the city with costly and admirably designed structures, and that without any visible effort, or any parade of subscriptions, contributions, fairs, entertainments, and other questionable means that are habitually resorted to by protestant sects for the erection of church buildings, and the extinguishment of church debts. If we employed half the energy and judgement in the defence of truth, that they do in the propagation of error, the face of Christendom as far as protestantism is concerned would wear a much healthier and more cheerful complexion....

August 6   78° 79³/₄° 82°

Dark and threatening sky. Cool wind from the North West. No rain during the day but showers at night.

Wrote to Major Beauregard, enclosing Papers from U.S. Dist. Attorney relative to the Government purchase at Proctorville, 3 N. Papers & T. Dispatch.

The week's mortality is as follows,

Yellow fever	222
other diseases	114
Total	336

The epidemic seems to pursue its usual course shewing a gradual increase every week until it attains its culminating point. The constant moisture, and chill, stagnant atmosphere at night add greatly to the danger, but the reduced population very much diminishes the numerical fatality. Unacclimated people are getting to look upon "yellow fever" now as a fixed fact and all, who can, get away before it sets in to any extent. The Quarantine regulations, as far as this disease is concerned, have signally failed during the present season.

August 7   78° 80° 81°

Turbid clouds, menacing looks from every quarter of the sky. South West wind quite fresh. Rain set in between 8 and 9. Showers until noon....

After dinner Emily and I, Ellen and Prescott took the cars for the Lake and spent a delightful evening.[36] The wind blew from the water, and was exquisitely fresh and exhilarating. The sun went down behind the waste of water in great splendour and the sky was dashed with threads of lucid gold. The long pier at the end of the railroad, and the galleries of the Hotel were enlivened with families, who, like ourselves, were in quest of the pure air and pleasant scenes of the water side. Numbers of small boats were drawn up near by, their wells filled with beautiful red-fish, croakers and perch, which the fishermen were selling to the visitors at very moderate rates. Unfortunately I had forgotten the Basket, and missed the chance. The track is in excellent order, and cars comfortable. Left at 7¹/₂ and at home to tea at near 9. I made a little sketch from the Pier.... It shows the Hotel &c. at the end of the shell road near the Canal which is about a quarter of a mile from the Hotel at the terminus of our railroad. A smooth shore road connects the two, gigs and carriages all the time passing to & fro.

August 9   81¹/₂° 85° 87°

Clouds and sunshine. Wind South to South East.

Letter from Mr. D. Ladd in Boston.

Took a long walk after dinner thro' Lafayette and sketched the fine mansion of Mr. Jas. Robb, now nearly completed.... The building and surrounding gardens cover nearly the whole square. The principal entrance being from Washington Avenue. The house rises from broad, and elevated terraces, beautifully turfed and adorned with vases and statues. The grounds laid out with great taste and embellished with shrubbery and rare plants such as only this genial latitude can produce. Altogether it promises to be the most sumptuous and tasteful residence in this charming suburb.

August 10   82° 85° 86°

Hot sunshine, gathering clouds, wind South to S. West....

After dinner walked up to Mr. Robb's to get a few details of sketch omitted yesterday. Returning met Revd. Mr. & Mrs. Duncan. They insisted on my calling with them on the family of Mr. E. C. Payne, First and Live Oak.[37] They have a charming place, and amongst other fine plants in the gardens Miss Payne pointed out to me

---

[36] This was probably the Pontchartrain Railroad that ran on Elysian Fields Avenue from the river to Milneburg on Lake Pontchartrain. Established in 1831, it was the first railroad west of the Alleghenies. *The WPA Guide to New Orleans* (New York, 1983), 296.

[37] Edward C. Payne (1809-1863), a native of Kentucky, was a partner in Payne, Steele & Co. D. D. Kingsbury was the builder for his house, which cost $13,000. NONA, T. O. Stark, June 19, 1851; *Daily Picayune*, Jan. 16, 1863.

T. K. Wharton Augt. 9. 1855

Residence of Jas. Robb Esqr.
Washington Avenue New Orleans

Samuel J. Peters, Jules Lion, lithographer, 1838 (1970.11.140); St. John the Baptist Church with school at left, Centennial: St. John the Baptist Parochial School, 1955 (96-196-RL).

several bushes of the "green rose," which is one of the greatest botanical curiosities I have seen for some time past. The flowers are very numerous and luxuriant, and just like the common rose except that instead of the usual petals the calyx is filled with innumerable little green leaves which are simply a repetition of the pointed leaf which encloses the bud of the ordinary rose. It is a modest and unobtrusive production and so exactly is the colour of the foliage repeated in the flowers, that its peculiarities might remain unnoticed if not specially indicated….

August 12 83° 85° 87°

Sunday. Very hot and almost cloudless. Light air from the South West.…

The death of Saml. J. Peters Esqr. yesterday is a public grief.[38] To him the first District chiefly owes its present importance, and to his genius and energy as the guiding spirit of the City Council are we indebted for the noblest structure that adorns the city "the Municipal (now City) Hall." And individually I have received from him many marks of consideration and kindness especially during the latter part of his Commissionership at the New Custom House. His disease was cardiac,

and for months past has been gradually wearing him down to the grave. He was a just man, and of financial capacity unequalled in New Orleans.

August 18 81° 83° 83°

Hot atmosphere. Clouds. Sunshine and showers. North East wind.

After dinner, walking round with Emily, to a store on Dryades Street I took the opportunity to examine the improvements that have been achieved in that neighbourhood since I was last thro' the street, which is some years ago. Amongst other buildings I noticed particularly a very large three story, brick building, nearly finished, and of excellent masonry. It stands on the same lot with a neat Church whose short spire is surmounted with a "cross." It was an unnecessary question, but I did ask, and found as I expected that it was another school for the Roman Catholics.[39] What a contrast to the slight wooden buildings erected on a neighbouring Square by the City Council for "the use of the Public Schools" and glorified by the names of "Jefferson" and "Webster."[40]

Drawing after tea until quite late.

[38] Samuel Jarvis Peters (1801-1855), a native of Toronto, arrived in New Orleans in 1821 and soon formed Peters & Millard, a wholesale grocery firm. He was on the city council (1829-1831) and the council of the second municipality (1837-1850) before serving with George C. Lawrason as commissioner for the Custom House. A successful business leader and developer, Peters is credited with founding the New Orleans public school system. *Daily Picayune*, Aug. 13, 1855; *DLB*.

[39] This was probably the school for St. John the Baptist Catholic Church on Dryades and Calliope streets. The first church was erected in 1851 by Giraud and Lewis, architects and builders, at a cost of $7,145.

[40] The Jefferson School for boys and the Webster School for girls were located at the corner of Dryades and Erato.

This drawing of the interior of the Custom House, Canal Street side, with St. Patrick's and the dome of Odd Fellows Hall in the distance, was probably submitted by Wharton to Harper's. *Vieux Carré Survey, Historic New Orleans Collection.*

September 4   82° 85° 84°

Hot and sunny. Dashing rain from 12 to 1. Loud thunder. South East wind.

In the evening finished an interior drawing of the New Custom House, showing several mechanical details, formation of groined arches &c. &c.

September 7   82° 85° 87°

Hot and dry. Fine air from the South East.

Wrote an article to go with my drawing of the interior of the New Custom House, and view from Coliseum Place to "Harper's Magazine." Read that part of it referring to the N. C. H. to Mr. Penn who was highly pleased with it and kindly offered to send a note with the parcel to the "Harper's."…

September 12   82° 84½° 85°

Sultry air. Fine breeze from the South East. Clouds & hot sunshine.…

The railroad track of the Second Tier of Scaffolding at the New Custom House is completed and forms a charming promenade of 1200 feet round the entire building at the height of 63 feet above the ground.

Drawing until late.

PLATE 1. *Notebooks in which Thomas K. Wharton kept his private journal. The books have been rebound, but the open volume shows the original pale blue ruled paper with his observations and one of his many ink sketches. Thomas Kelah Wharton Diaries and Sketchbook, 1830–1862, Manuscripts and Archives Division, New York Public Library.*

PLATE 2. *New Orleans from St. Patrick's Church, John William Hill, delineator, Benjamin Franklin Smith, Jr., delineator, lithographer, 1852 (1954.3). In the center is Camp Street, the street down which Wharton walked to work when the weather was bearable. Many of the landmarks mentioned in his journal are shown*

here, counter-clockwise from the right of Camp Street: a portion of the roof of St. Patrick's, the dome of Odd Fellows Hall, the first St. Charles Hotel with its landmark dome, the steeple of the Wharton-designed Christ Church, City (Gallier) Hall, and the original First Presbyterian Church, as well as Lafayette Square.

PLATE 3. *Wharton cottage, Plan book 43, Folio 31, February 16, 1854, New Orleans Notarial Archives (1979.227.43.31), a watercolor made in connection with the sale of the property at auction. The white picket fence was typical of the period; iron fences became fashionable later. With their fragrant purplish flowers and yellow berries, the china trees (chinaberries) in front of the house were a popular feature of the New Orleans streetscape; they were the predominant ornamental tree throughout the cities of the antebellum South.*

PLATE 4. *Interior of the* Princess *by Marie Adrien Persac, 1861, Louisiana State University Art Museum, reproduction (1974.25.34.71). This very rare antebellum view of the interior of a luxury steamboat, similar to those in which the Whartons traveled up and down the Mississippi River, shows such details as the lavish service at the men's dinner seating, tables for top hats, and the ubiquitous American spittoons.*

PLATE 5. *View of Jackson Square, J. Dürler, delineator, 1855 (1948.3). The new look of the Place d'Armes: In 1849–1850 St. Louis Cathedral had been rebuilt, the elegant Pontalba buildings flanking the square built, and the gardens redesigned. In 1851 the square was renamed in honor of the hero of the Battle of New Orleans, and in February 1856 the large equestrian statue of Jackson by Clark Mills was unveiled. The levee is in the foreground.*

PLATE 6. De Soto's Discovery of the Mississippi *by William H. Powell, Kurz & Allison, lithographers, between 1880 and 1921 (1982.247). This painting was exhibited in a number of American cities; Wharton saw it at the Armory Hall in New Orleans on May 25, 1854.*

leaves. Speaking of Rachel, whom he has seen every night she has played since his arrival, he says that in "Camille" she looks like "une statue antique descendue de son piédestal et animée par Dieu lui-même et que cette vie factice doit cesser avec la pièce."[49]...

October 31   67° 73° 72°

Very hot sunshine. Dry & dusty. Wind East to North....

The apartments which we have been engaged in preparing for the Appraisers since the 10th are now ready and will be turned over to them tomorrow. They afford the amplest facilities for their business tho' the arrangement is but a hasty and temporary one. They shew also what may be expected from the entire structure, when completed, as to light, space, dryness and purity of the air. This partial experiment is in the highest degree satisfactory.

November 5   74° 78° 79°

Warm steamy air. Heavy clouds and high wind from the East & South East....

Indian summer is upon us with its untimely heat and mischievous musquitoes. Far more cruel & vindictive than at Midsummer. The weekly returns of mortality, however, show an extraordinary degree of Public Health. Only 82 deaths altogether of which 6 from yellow fever....

November 7   64° 64° 63°

Dark clouds, drizzling showers. Cold north wind.

The floods of yesterday have given the city a most thorough cleansing bath, which it much needed after the accumulated deposits of a long and pestilential summer. The streets still reek with moisture, but every thing looks fresh and clean and the reduced temperature prevents the formation of mephitic exhalations from the wet earth. The deluge has happened most opportunely for the public health during the coming winter months.

November 8   59½° 62½° 63°

Cold raw wind from the North East. Light misty showers. Positively disagreeable.

The "American Party" were eminently successful in the city in the general election of Monday. But the returns as they came in from country Parishes are more hopeful for the Democrats.[50]

November 12   66° 69° 70°

Close damp & cloudy early in the day, cleared off at noon with North wind to North West and hot sun.

The long files of shipping up and down the River flung out their canvass to the sunny air to dry out the damp mildew of the past week. The view of the Levee from the top of our building for miles either way was unusually cheerful and animated after the protracted "wet spell." Wrote to Major Beauregard. The "summer cloud" has passed away. The weekly record gives assurance of re-established health. The deaths are only 72, the smallest report I ever recollect to have seen and no "yellow fever."

November 14   71° 74° 73°

...The Major writes that the question of Iron Beams and Girders is now definitely settled, and he will send me the details by and by. So far good! But the great "Malakoff" (the marble controversy) is not attacked yet.[51] This is the turning point in our northern war, and its issue becomes the more doubtful from the increased extravagance of the value put upon their work by the contractors, for instance, the 14 Column Caps at $8.830 each when less than half the money would leave them a large profit. The terms of the contract are so vague, having been drawn up by politicians in Washington some 6 or 7 years ago, that the Contractors have an advantage in the contest. This contest never could have arisen had the contract been made by the Commissioners here, about the time when the materials were

---

[49] Rachel (Elisa Felix, 1820-1858), usually considered the greatest of the French tragediennes, made her American debut in 1855 as Camille in Corneille's *Horace*. Gerald Bordman, *The Oxford Companion to the American Theatre* (New York, 1984). Trans.: An antique statue brought down from its pedestal and animated by God himself and that this fictitious life must stop with the play.

[50] The Native American or Know Nothing Party, formed about 1853 as the Whig Party was disintegrating, was both antiforeigner and anti-Catholic. In New Orleans, it became the political vehicle of uptown American businessmen in opposition to the downtown Creole Democrats, who depended heavily on newly arrived immigrants for their support. Through superior organization and intimidation at the polls, the American Party's candidates for federal and state offices won sweepingly in the city, but lost the state by a margin of 3,000 votes. Soulé, *The Know Nothing Party*, 3, 71-72.

[51] Malakoff was one of the decisive battles of the Crimean War (1853-1856), the conflict that Wharton followed with keen interest.

PLATE 8. *New Orleans from Algiers, John Bachman, delineator, 1851, Thomas Muller, lithographer, between 1851 and 1860 (1939.1). This bird's-eye view emphasizes the importance of the port with its bustling levee, wharves lined with ocean-going sailing ships and river steamers, and busy river traffic.*

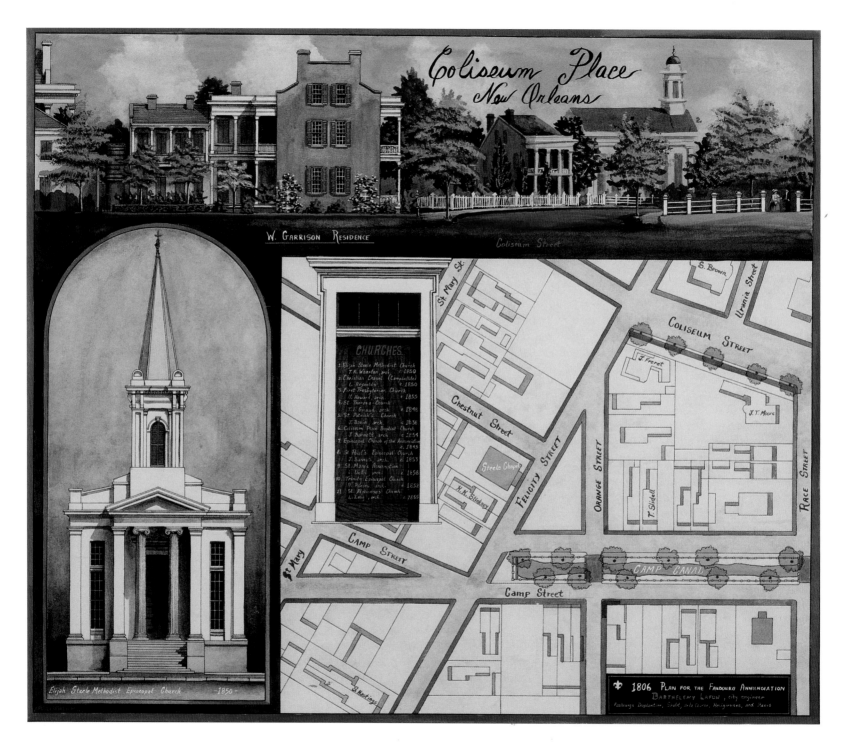

PLATE 9. *Coliseum Place in the 1850s by Jim Blanchard, 1999. The cross section at top shows, from left, the residences of William Garrison and James Wray; the Christian, First Presbyterian, St. Theresa of Avila, St. Patrick's and Coliseum Place Baptist Churches; and the Whartons' cottage with its Lamarque roses and chinaberry trees and the cistern and kitchen/servants quarters in the rear. Bottom left is the Wharton-designed Steele Methodist Church.*

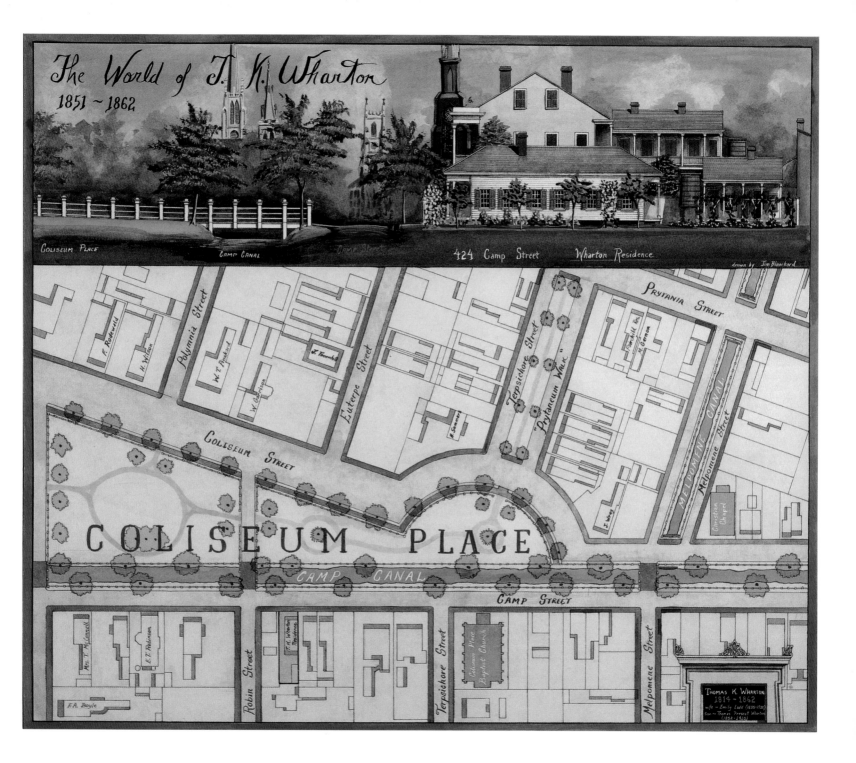

The World of T. K. Wharton
1851 ~ 1862

drawn by Jim Blanchard

COLISEUM PLACE   CAMP CANAL   Camp Street   424 Camp Street   Wharton Residence

COLISEUM PLACE

CAMP CANAL

CAMP STREET

Polymnia Street
Euterpe Street
Terpsichore Street
"Prytaneum Walk"
Prytania Street
Melpomene Street
MELPOMENE CANAL
Robin Street
Terpsichore Street
Melpomene Street

COLISEUM STREET

Christian Chapel

Coliseum Place
Baptist Church

Thomas K. Wharton
1814 ~ 1862
w/fe ~ Emily Ladd (1835-1732)
Son ~ Thomas Perrot Wharton
(1852-1910)

PLATE 10. *St. Charles Hotel in Flames by J. R. P., between 1851 and 1855 (1992.156).*
A center of the city's social life, the hotel was rebuilt almost immediately after it burned in

1851. Shown collapsing in the fire, its dome was a prominent feature of the New Orleans skyline, but it was not replaced in the new hotel.

PLATE 11. *James Robb, attributed to George Peter Alexander Healy, ca. 1845 (1988.43). Robb was the city's financial leader in the 1840s and 1850s, with major investments in banking, gaslights, and railroads. His mansion occupied a square block in the uptown neighborhood of Lafayette, and his was the only major art collection in New Orleans.*

Stereographic view of a swampy area at the edge of Lake Pontchartrain, Samuel T. Blessing, photographer, ca. 1877 (1979.221.19).

September 18   80¹/₂° 83° 84°

Pleasant and sunny. Light air from the South West.

The evening Papers give a most disastrous account of the gale on Saturday night. The Lake coast is left in a state of pitiable desolation attended with some loss of life. The son of our acquaintance G. W. Givens (aged 14) was killed at Mississippi City.[41]

September 21   82° 86° 88°

The equinoctial storm came in advance this year and today is all calm unmitigated sunshine.

L. E. Reynolds, the architect, tells me that he has just lost a niece of 17 by "yellow fever," and has six of his family still under treatment for it. The hot sun and cool north wind today are very unfavorable to patients. The air, however, from the top of the Custom House walls felt cheery and refreshing to me after being confined at home yesterday. As I went down to the office I ordered a carriage for 4 O'clock. We had a delightful ride down to the Lake by the winding shell road along the Bayou St. John. But the state of the road beyond the Mouth did not admit of our going on as far as the terminus of the Pontchartrain R. Road. We walked to the end of the Pier and enjoyed a fine Lake sunset. But landward at this Point the all pervading "Swamp" appears in its native deformity unrelieved by the gardens & improvements which embellish the Lake end of the other roads.[42]…

September 26   81° 84° 81°

Hot & dry. Clouds mustering from the South East for rains. It set in about 4 P.M. with cool air from the West and North West.

The movements on the Levee already show signs of an unusually early reanimation. And the long vistas of commercial streets and

[41] The storm, probably a hurricane, caused great loss of life and desolation on the Mississippi Gulf Coast from Mobile Point to Bay St. Louis. *Daily True Delta*, Sept. 19, 1855.

[42] The shell road along Bayou St. John ended at the lake at Spanish Fort. The terminus of the Pontchartrain Railroad was at Milneburg, a mile to the east.

ranges of wharves as seen from the top of the New Custom House are all astir with business and brisk moving figures. It is a pleasant change up there, now & then, from the confinement of the desk.

September 27   75° 79° 80°

Sunny sky. Cool fresh breeze from the North East.

Adolphus Hamilton called this morning, he is regaining his strength after his attack of yellow fever.[43] Mr. James Robb's daughter (16) died of the fever yesterday. She was one of the young ladies who graduated at Miss Hull's school with so much credit in June.[44]...

September 30   77° 78½° 79°

Warm steamy air from the South, floating clouds....

Mr. Tisdale spent the evening with us. The fever at Pass Christian determined him to bring his family at once back to the city.[45] The fever here continues to decline, for the week ending today it is

yellow fever	70
other diseases	111
Total	181

The mortality during the present epidemic already reaches 2500. But its worst feature is its general diffusion thro' this State and lower Mississippi. Formerly the timid found a safe retreat from the scourge of the city in the country towns and on the Plantations of the Coast. Now "the country is no longer safe." Since 1853 the whole southern portion of the United States seems to have become the home of "the fever" that is more particularly in strictly alluvial positions along the water courses and in the marshy Bays and inlets of the Sea and Gulf Coasts.

October 20   72° 75° 74°

Clouds & hot sunshine. Sultry air from the South East. Slight rain in the afternoon.

[43] Adolphus Hamilton was a commission merchant who lived on Washington Avenue at the corner of St. Charles. *Daily Picayune*, June 16, 1850; NOCD 1856.

[44] Louisa Robb was one of the five children of James and Louisa Robb. The family had remained in the city during the yellow fever season because Mrs. Robb was too ill (probably with cancer) to leave. Patricia Brady Schmit, "Robb Papers Discovered," *The Historic New Orleans Collection Newsletter* 4(Winter 1986):3.

[45] Pass Christian on the Mississippi Gulf Coast was incorporated in 1838. It became a summer resort for New Orleanians to escape oppressive New Orleans summers and yellow fever epidemics. Nola Nance Oliver, *The Gulf Coast of Mississippi* (New York, 1941), 19.

At 2 O'clock the "Black Warrior" appeared from our lofty parapets rounding the opposite Point of Algiers under full steam, and crowded with returning citizens who have been away all summer.[46] The city is filling up again and the shipping and "Boats" begin to thicken again along the vast curve of the Levee Front.

October 22   70° 73° 74°

Clouds and sunshine. Damp air from the North East.

Returns for the week are of yellow fever	15
other diseases	106
Total	121

A writer at the beginning of the century, Thomas Ashe, Esqr., speaking of New Orleans in 1806 says, "Accounts similar to this, perhaps higher coloured and still true, lead thousands into this country in search of a paradise, and they find a grave. The climate is horrid. On an average 9 strangers die out of 10 shortly after their arrival in the city, and those who survive are of shattered constitution and debilitated frame. The entire country, however, is not subject to malignant disease," its strongholds being "Orleans and the Natchez," where population and other circumstances incident to cities favor the development of malarious poison.[47]

New Orleans is bad enough but not quite so bad as this. The gradual improvement of the city and suburbs, and more settled habits of life, and superior medical skill, have greatly diminished and modified the forms of danger. And many like myself for instance, live on from year to year with regularity, indeed, and prudence, and never have the yellow fever at all. It may be called an "unsafe" not a "horrid" climate.

Pleasant ride in the afternoon with Emily, Tommy & Ellen to the Bayou St. John. The writer above referred to makes honorable mention of the "beautiful gardens and country seats on the Bayeau St. Jean" even in his day. They are beautiful still but the ancient bridge has been reduced to a few ragged posts protruding from the still water. And a new bridge has taken its place, thrown across further down stream, strong and tasteful in design....

October 26   52½° 59° 61°

White frost in the night, the first of the season. Ice formed at Vicksburg night before last one inch thick. Mild and bright today. East wind.

[46] The town of Algiers, now incorporated into New Orleans, is just across the Mississippi River from the French Quarter.

[47] Thomas Ashe, *Travels in America* (London, 1809), 304.

First Presbyterian Church, P. S. Duval & Sons, lithographer, after 1856 (1945.10).

The foundations of the new Presbyterian Church on Lafayette Square are nearly levelled up. They are put in with greater care than is usual here.

Strong grillage of Flat boat gunwales or 3 inch Plank (for the Tower) in a trench about 10 feet deep. The brick work well bedded in good cement mortar, and not more than 2 inch offsets. The Design is pointed Gothic with a lofty spire on the corner of St. Mary and South Str. A light harmonious and graceful composition by Henry Howard.[48] The general character, however, is derived from the Romanesque design of young [William] Freret, which was adopted and afterwards withdrawn by him for reasons which he deemed sufficient.

October 29   64° 69° 68°

Soft air from the South. Cloudy tending to rain....

The report of Interments for the week gives a very gratifying assurance of restored health, viz.

of yellow fever	11
other diseases	95
Total	106

Of the yellow fever deaths but 3 or 4 were in private practice so the disease may be considered at an end with the close of the month....

Thus we have had three epidemic summers in succession. It is to be observed, too, that they have resembled each other in both the malignity and duration of the Disease. This year and in 1853, it commenced very early and was all over in October. Last year it began very late and was not extinct until the first week in December sometime after the early frosts, giving color to the assumption that the yellow fever is pretty uniform in its rise, climax and decline. In the interior where it always begins late, frosts often seem to aggravate rather than check it, for awhile at least.

October 30   66° 67° 65°

Cloudy and threatening. Wind South East to East.

Letter from Major Beauregard dated the 20th Inst. in New York, does not expect to be in Washington until the 10th Proximo. His health is improving rapidly, and he is deep in the "Marble Controversy" hopes to settle everything satisfactorily before he

[48] Henry Howard (1818-1884), a native of Ireland, came to New Orleans in 1837 and began working as a carpenter, specializing in stair building. He was the architect of the First Presbyterian Church on Lafayette Square, built after the first church on the site burned in 1854, and numerous houses, public buildings, and plantation houses. *DLB*; NONA, Hilary B. Cenas, Aug. 21, 1855.

leaves. Speaking of Rachel, whom he has seen every night she has played since his arrival, he says that in "Camille" she looks like "une statue antique descendue de son piédestal et animée par Dieu lui-même et que cette vie factice doit cesser avec la pièce."[49]...

October 31   67° 73° 72°

Very hot sunshine. Dry & dusty. Wind East to North....

The apartments which we have been engaged in preparing for the Appraisers since the 10th are now ready and will be turned over to them tomorrow. They afford the amplest facilities for their business tho' the arrangement is but a hasty and temporary one. They shew also what may be expected from the entire structure, when completed, as to light, space, dryness and purity of the air. This partial experiment is in the highest degree satisfactory.

November 5   74° 78° 79°

Warm steamy air. Heavy clouds and high wind from the East & South East....

Indian summer is upon us with its untimely heat and mischievous musquitoes. Far more cruel & vindictive than at Midsummer. The weekly returns of mortality, however, show an extraordinary degree of Public Health. Only 82 deaths altogether of which 6 from yellow fever....

November 7   64° 64° 63°

Dark clouds, drizzling showers. Cold north wind.

The floods of yesterday have given the city a most thorough cleansing bath, which it much needed after the accumulated deposits of a long and pestilential summer. The streets still reek with moisture, but every thing looks fresh and clean and the reduced temperature prevents the formation of mephitic exhalations from the wet earth. The deluge has happened most opportunely for the public health during the coming winter months.

November 8   59½° 62½° 63°

Cold raw wind from the North East. Light misty showers. Positively disagreeable.

The "American Party" were eminently successful in the city in the general election of Monday. But the returns as they came in from country Parishes are more hopeful for the Democrats.[50]

November 12   66° 69° 70°

Close damp & cloudy early in the day, cleared off at noon with North wind to North West and hot sun.

The long files of shipping up and down the River flung out their canvass to the sunny air to dry out the damp mildew of the past week. The view of the Levee from the top of our building for miles either way was unusually cheerful and animated after the protracted "wet spell." Wrote to Major Beauregard. The "summer cloud" has passed away. The weekly record gives assurance of re-established health. The deaths are only 72, the smallest report I ever recollect to have seen and no "yellow fever."

November 14   71° 74° 73°

...The Major writes that the question of Iron Beams and Girders is now definitely settled, and he will send me the details by and by. So far good! But the great "Malakoff" (the marble controversy) is not attacked yet.[51] This is the turning point in our northern war, and its issue becomes the more doubtful from the increased extravagance of the value put upon their work by the contractors, for instance, the 14 Column Caps at $8.830 each when less than half the money would leave them a large profit. The terms of the contract are so vague, having been drawn up by politicians in Washington some 6 or 7 years ago, that the Contractors have an advantage in the contest. This contest never could have arisen had the contract been made by the Commissioners here, about the time when the materials were

[49] Rachel (Elisa Felix, 1820-1858), usually considered the greatest of the French tragediennes, made her American debut in 1855 as Camille in Corneille's *Horace*. Gerald Bordman, *The Oxford Companion to the American Theatre* (New York, 1984). Trans.: An antique statue brought down from its pedestal and animated by God himself and that this fictitious life must stop with the play.

[50] The Native American or Know Nothing Party, formed about 1853 as the Whig Party was disintegrating, was both antiforeigner and anti-Catholic. In New Orleans, it became the political vehicle of uptown American businessmen in opposition to the downtown Creole Democrats, who depended heavily on newly arrived immigrants for their support. Through superior organization and intimidation at the polls, the American Party's candidates for federal and state offices won sweepingly in the city, but lost the state by a margin of 3,000 votes. Soulé, *The Know Nothing Party*, 3, 71-72.

[51] Malakoff was one of the decisive battles of the Crimean War (1853-1856), the conflict that Wharton followed with keen interest.

U.S. Marine Hospital, Samuel S. Kilburn, Jr., delineator, July 24, 1858 (1959.159.38), gift of Harold Schilke and Boyd Cruise.

required instead of years beforehand. The Contractors, too, seem inclined to take every advantage. To adopt a very luminous passage in a letter from Mr. Roy on the subject "their conchences [consciences] are as hard as the material they deal in."[52]

November 20

58½° 67° 66½°

Charming weather. Fine air from North East.

Letter from the Secretary of the Treasury dated Novr. 13 requesting me to examine and report upon the Marine Hospital here with reference to certain proposals (copy enclosed) for the repairs of the same, so that the Department might have the proper date to decide upon their reasonableness.[53] I immediately went over the River and took Mr. Kerr with me.[54] Examined carefully the condition of the Building, and got back to my office at 1....

The air over at Algiers today was sweet and fresh. So different from the gaseous oppression of the city. New Orleans looks strange, very strange from the opposite shore. But for a few prominent and familiar objects, such as the Cathedral &c., its general aspect seemed

wondrously changed. The long lines of steamers and shipping were there and the long line of buildings shrinking away from the Riverfront but the combination seen for the <u>first</u> time from the other side struck me as something very different from what I had expected, and I may add totally different from the general view of any city I had ever seen or imagined. Had I been able to stay over longer I should have made free use of my pencil, but such is the extent of its sweep that one or even two sketches would not be sufficient to embrace the whole. It must be taken in sectors to convey it fully. The Levee foreground is bald and fragmentary, chiefly nautical in its accessories. The fine Live Oaks & noble trees that once clothed the shore have been removed from the immediate bank, but appear in all their native freshness and beauty at a little distance back from the river. A grove or two of oranges, and an occasional garden, with any quantity of vacant land of untold fertility tell plainly what a charming suburb this <u>might</u> be made, but the dread of the reckless torrent that dashes by deters improvement.

November 27

60° 60½° 60°

Damp, cold and cloudy, showers. Wind N. West to North East.

Answered sister Emily's letter of the 11th. Inst. with a pen and ink drawing of Bhurtpore Cottage, New Haven, from a sketch I made in 1839. She begged me to make one for her from recollection, but fortunately I had the one alluded to from nature....

[52] John Roy worked with Wharton as an architect for the Custom House. Later he was the architect for the Robert E. Lee monument at Lee Circle. Excerpts from his diary from 1860-1862 were published in the *Journal of the Society of Contractors of Federal Buildings* 13(June 1911):6; NONA, James Fahey, Dec. 18, 1877.

[53] The old Marine Hospital, designed in the Gothic Revival style by Mondelli and Reynolds and built at a cost of $33,000, was begun in 1835. It was located on the west bank of the Mississippi River at McDonoghville. The hospital was being used for the manufacture of gun powder for the Confederacy when it was blown up on December 29, 1861.

[54] Richard Hulton Kerr (1820-1906), a native of Nassau, Bahamas, was a member of the firm of Bennett, Kerr, & Co. *Daily Picayune*, Feb. 18, 21, 25, 1906; NOCD 1855.

Bhurtpore Cottage
Near New Haven in 1839. West Rock &c.
our last home at the North.

J. N. Wharton
Nov. 27. 1855

December 24   54° 54¹/₂° 53°

Dark gloomy weather. Raw searching air from the North East. Thick brooding fog hanging over the River....

As usual too disagreeable to take the children down to see stores decorated for "Christmas eve" however, they had a much pleasanter time at home. Emily astonished them with a tasteful "Christmas tree" all hung with Christmas presents and garnished around with fruits and a variety of pretty objects, and the presents all duly endorsed with the names of the recipients. Tommy was amazed and delighted beyond measure, and Ellen only wished that Christmas eve could be protracted to an indefinite duration.

December 31   41° 42° 43°

Severely cold, and gloomy rains. North wind.

The year ends with frowning skies but pleasant recollections. To me the crowning feature has been the recovery in a great measure of my original health and vigor, in spite of unwholesome damps and unlooked for changes, and a more than usually fatal epidemic. I have all the time felt my former self coming back to me steadily and perceptibly....

The year, too, has been one of health and comfort to all my family. Every thing has gone well with us. Every day has brought with it new enjoyments and but very few drawbacks....

1856

January 4   37° 40° 40°

Ice formed in the night on still water. Cold North East wind, sunshine & clouds.

Major Beauregard writes to Mr. Penn that the President and his lady insist upon his remaining with them at the "White House" until after the festivities of the "First" so we can hardly look for him until the middle of the month. Wrote to the Hulings.

January 9   41° 41½° 43°

Dull murky sky. Bitter cold and damp air from the North East....

I stayed at home and read the President's message. Admirable paragraphs on the subject of Northern interference with the domestic policy of the South. British aggression in Central America. State of the Treasury &c.

January 26   59° 61½° 55°

...Received from Messrs. Learned & Fisher per ship "Sultana" a large and exquisite Photograph of the Capital of Columns in our Chief business Room. The example of monument Lysicrates, highly enriched, with bust in place of honeysuckle on one side and some other innovations on the remaining three, executed in Vermont Statuary Marble.[1] The Photograph introduces a portrait of the Sculptor Otto, very pure in line & shadow, and altogether very beautiful. Sent a note of thanks by Mail.

February 4   28° 30° 33°

Intensely severe weather. A strong wind blowing from the north all night and ice formed 1⅛ inch thick.

A fire in Chartres Street at midnight endangered our external scaffolding but we escaped without injury.[2] Cloudless sky today, but freezing all the time. Went with Major Beauregard, Capt. Smith & Roy to examine and correct model in clay of full length figure of

[1] The marble capitals for the columns in the Marble Hall, the chief business room of the Custom House, are ornamented alternately with the sculptured heads of Mercury, Roman god of commerce, and Luna, Roman moon goddess, symbolizing the tie between trade and New Orleans, the Crescent City. Wilson, *The U.S. Customhouse in New Orleans*, 66. The monument of Lysicrates in Athens was built in 335 B.C.

[2] The fire on Chartres Street between Canal and Customhouse (now Iberville) destroyed Lloyds' dry goods establishment. *Daily Delta*, Feb. 4, 1856.

Capital of column in Marble Hall, Custom House, Louis T. Fritch, photographer, between 1911 and 1921 (1974.25.3.197); Marble Hall, Vieux Carré Survey, Historic New Orleans Collection.

"Bienville" life size by De Frasse.[3] It is to be done in Statuary Marble for our "principal business room" and promises to be a fine work. The head & lower extremities were excellent but the bust & shoulders especially need much alteration. On our way back stopped at the "Artesian boring" in Canal Street, examined the process, took a specimen of thick, fine grained, blue clay from a depth of 508 feet which is the present limit.[4]

February 7   53° 54° 52°

Hard rains in the night. Clouds & sunshine today. North West wind and turning cold again.

Call from Mr. Grimshaw relative to the new organ screen at Christ's Church which they propose putting up from my Design.[5]...

February 9   40° 43° 47°

Lovely day. Cheerful sunny sky. Cool North East wind.

Cannon at daybreak announced the fete of the inauguration of "Mill's" Statue (on Jackson Square) of the "famous old General."[6] Wrote my letters at the office then Ellen came down to see the "Procession &c." Emily and Mrs. Ladd did not feel curiosity enough to mingle in the crowd, and I feared it would be too fatiguing for little Tommy. I was very sorry afterwards for they all missed a far more superb "spectacle" than we any of us anticipated. First Ellen & I went up to the top scaffolding of the Custom House and saw the Procession forming on the Neutral Ground of Canal Street far below us, itself a grand scene. Then we threw ourselves into the vast human stream, and moved down Chartres Street to the "Cathedral Square" where we took up an advantageous position clear of the crowd and saw the long "cortege" as it filed past us into the Square with rich banners and excellent music. Then we passed rapidly from point to

point, taking different views, and finally went over thro' a quiet bye-street to the Levee opposite the Square, which at this point is quite elevated, and withdrawn from the dense multitude, commanding a noble view of the entire Square, the Cathedral & courts. The Pontalba Buildings, their long galleries filled with the richest costumes sparkling in full sunshine, and gay military uniforms, and gilded banners grouped around the "Monument" in the Centre, or glancing among the beautiful evergreens and foliage of the Square. We found several friends, too, who had wisely selected this spot in preference to the crowded avenues on the other three sides. When "Sigur" the orator of the day, mounted the platform, as we were too far off to hear, we left for awhile and went on board the Packet ship "Sultana" lying near by.[7] Capt. Barret was not on board but the first officer showed us every attention. Went over the cabins &c. then returned to the Square just in time to see the beautiful equestrian statue of "Jackson" uncovered, and its fine proportions and rich gilding thrown open to the sunshine. The vast human mass of at least 20.000 then began to disperse, and a salvo of 100 guns closed the splendid drama....

February 11   52° 53° 55°

Bright sunshine, pleasant air from North West.

William Freret made me a present of a pretty Photograph of his design for the new Presbyterian Church of Lafayette Square which was adopted....

February 16   58° 64° 67°

Warm spring day. Rich sunlight. Pleasant air from South West....

Emily, Mrs. Ladd, Ellen & Tommy came to the office at 11. Went over the Building with them, then took the omnibus to Jackson Square, to see the Monument. Went to the French market bought quantities of Bananas & other fruit, then back to the Armory Hall to attend the interesting Panorama of the Russian War. Fall of Sebastopol &c.[8]...

[3] A bas-relief figure of Jean Baptiste Le Moyne, sieur de Bienville, founder of New Orleans, by Auguste Defrasse (1820-1864) is part of a three-part sculptured panel above the entrance at the river end of the Marble Hall. A native of France, Defrasse was a well-known sculptor in the 1850s in New Orleans. *ENOA.*

[4] An artesian well was bored by the city government in 1854 in the neutral ground of Canal Street between Carondelet and Baronne. *Daily Picayune*, Sept. 1, 1884.

[5] James F. Grimshaw was a vestryman of Christ Church. Carter and Carter, *So Great A Good*, 77, 93.

[6] The statue of Andrew Jackson by Clark Mills erected in the center of Jackson Square was a replica of the Mills statue in Lafayette Square, Washington, D.C. Huber, *Jackson Square.*

[7] Laurent J. Sigur (b. ca. 1818), owner and editor of the *Delta* newspapers, was introduced by former mayor A. D. Crossman, president of the Jackson Monument Association. U.S. Census, La., Orleans Parish, 1850; *Daily Picayune*, Feb. 10, 1856.

[8] Hanington's dioramic panorama of the Crimean War opened at the Armory Hall on February 11, 1856. *Daily True Delta*, Feb. 13, 1856.

Procession in honor of the unveiling of the equestrian statue of Andrew Jackson in the renamed Jackson Square, formerly Place d'Armes, 1856 (1974.25.14.157). The crowds, flags, soldiers, and site of the celebration reflect the ceremony accurately, but other details are inaccurate. The new cathedral, as well as the lower Pontalba building, should have been pictured; this view of the old cathedral and shops is copied from an 1842 lithograph by Jules Lion (1971.32), bequest of Richard Koch. Statue of Andrew Jackson, December 1873 (1974.25.14.159).

February 19   51° 57° 59°

Threatening sky, cleared off at noon. South East wind & very dusty....

Visit from ex-mayor Crossman & Mr. Heyliger introducing Clark Mills Esqr. the Artist of the Jackson Statue.[9] Went over the Building with them. Mr. Mills had a beautiful miniature model of the horse in bronze which exhibits the mode in which the statue sustains itself on its hind legs on the simple principle of equipoise. That is, drawing a vertical line from the front of the hind hoofs upward, the amount of metal on one side of it is exactly equal to that on the other. He explained to me several of his processes in casting, finishing &c....

February 25   52° 54° 55°

North wind. Cloudy & damp.

Went in the evening to the "Academy of Sciences" City Hall, to hear the Annual address of the President Prof. Riddel.[10] It was a short but able paper on the progress of the leading Sciences during the past year preceded by a few brief remarks on the objects and present condition of the Association. I found many new members since I was there a year ago, and an increased interest in the proceedings and apparent efficiency of this learned body.

February 28   59° 66° 67°

Lovely spring weather, light air South West to North East. Leaves bursting & vegetation taking a start.

The City commenced today to grade, plant and fence Coliseum Square opposite; it will be a charming improvement....

H. Brown called at the office and invited me to take a drive after dinner and try a fine horse, a new purchase; we set out at half past 4 for the [Metairie] Ridge & Bayou St. John, and drove at a merry pace down Felicity Road.[11] But there our felicity ended. Just as we

[9] Abdil Crossman (1803-1859), a hatter who was a native of Maine, entered politics in 1839. He served as mayor for four consecutive terms (1846-1854). Under his administration Gallier Hall was built, levees were repaired and extended, some streets were paved with granite, and a new charter consolidated the city's former three municipalities. *DLB.* Louis Heyliger was assistant editor of the New Orleans *Bee.* NOCD 1856. The sculptor Clark Mills (1815-1883) was in New Orleans to supervise the erection of his statue and to speak at the installation ceremonies. *ENOA.*

[10] John L. Riddell (1807-1865), a physician, chemist, and botanist, was a chemistry professor at the Medical College of Louisiana (now Tulane University) from 1836 until his death. He served as postmaster of New Orleans from 1860 to 1863. *DLB.*

[11] Henry Brown (d. 1859) was Wharton's landlord.

Andrew Jackson by Clark Mills, 1855 (1983.142).

Felicity at Dryades, Jay Dearborn Edwards, photographer, between 1857 and 1860 (1982.32.14).

Parish Prison, A. Edmonds, delineator, 1873 (1974.25.3.244).

turned the Plank Road corner of Liberty & Thalia the horse took fright and reared in grand style, then dashed, gig and all, into the ditch on the road side. The gig turned over and Brown being on the upper side, leaped off and gained the opposite banquette unhurt. I being undermost, and the gig-cover up, had to watch the chances, and concluded to wait till the kicking & plunging was over, then slipped out, also unharmed, except the sudden jar from the first stroke at the bottom of the ditch. We soon succeeded in extricating the horse and gig, with the assistance of several men who immediately came to our aid. One of them observing that he never expected to see me come out alive. Mr. B. then made the best of his way to the stable, and I home on foot taking care to avoid the public eye as much as possible in my delapidated and bespattered condition, a matter of no small difficulty as the brilliant sky had invited every one especially the ladies into the sunshiny streets. My unlooked for reappearance at home startled them all not a little. I can hardly see yet how so formidable an accident could have passed off so quietly, and with no more injury to the person or even nerves of the parties than if we had just turned back of our own accord.

March 3   49° 53° 53°

Cold and raw. East wind. Gleams of sunshine.

The exciting topic today is the defalcation, flight, and capture at the Balize, of Wm. H. Garland, the City Treasurer. He now lies in the Parish Prison awaiting examination.[12]…

March 10   57° 59° 58°

Cloudy & threatening. North East wind.

Mr. A. Dunn brought a dozen ladies & gentlemen to go over the Building. I showed them every thing worth inspection and the noble views from the top, &c., with which they were both surprised and delighted. Few even of those who live close by know how much there is of interest within the two acres covered by our great work. I had one of the superb Marble Capitals unboxed to show them.

The afternoon raw and dreary nevertheless I walked till near dark thro' the upper part of the city to the river at Washington Avenue, sketched the "Haunted House" &c. &c.[13]

[12] William H. Garland was the president of the Louisiana Savings Bank and city treasurer. *Daily Delta*, Mar. 4, 1856.

[13] The Haunted House was the old Livaudais plantation house at Washington Avenue and the river. It was abandoned after Marie Celeste Marigny divorced Jacques François Enoul Livaudais and moved to Paris.

March 26   67° 71° 74°

Hot sunshine. Floating clouds, high wind from the West, and very dusty....

The Revd. Mr. Keener called to get a design for the front of a new Methodist Church on Dryades Street.[14] I gave him a sketch....

March 28   56° 59½° 62°

Cold North E. wind. Clear, dry and very dusty....

Went with Major Beauregard to "Jacobs' Daguerrotype Establishment."[15] Mr. Jacobs kindly initiated us into all the mysteries of the Photograph, explained the details of his simple laboratory &c. The Major had his photograph taken with great success. We spent a couple of hours in his rooms, and work shop in the rear, and were made familiar with the intricate and beautiful processes of his profession. Tho' our object in going was simply to get the Photographic likeness "aforesaid."...

April 3   71° 72° 73°

Cloudy, threatening and very warm, debilitating weather.

Very busy with monthly and Quarterly papers &c. at the office. Major Beauregard asked Stevens to accompany us to Jacobs' Salon at 1.[16] The Major's Photographs were completed to satisfaction. Lieut. Stevens and I then went thro' the process. Ours will be ready in a few days. I had to go thro' the manipulations twice as Mr. Jacobs was not perfectly satisfied with the outline of the hair in the first picture....

April 7   65° 68° 70°

Hot, dry and dusty. North wind....

Mr. Low called at a late hour in the evening, just from the meeting of the Seamen's Home Committee.[17] He brought with him the Plans and Specifications for the Building, and said they had appointed me Superintendent. I am to meet the gentlemen on the ground on Wednesday evening.

I had just finished another drawing for the stairway of the Baptist Church, which seems to meet all requirements. We talked it over together, and various other matters connected with both buildings.

April 9   66° 70° 73°

Very hot, very dry, very dusty. N. East wind....

Met by appointment at 5 the Building Committee of the Seamen's Home at the Building. After a long discussion and the discovery that no two gentlemen thought alike, & that all the plans now before them were liable to objection, it was proposed that I should consider the whole subject, make a sketch of my views, and meet the Committee on Saturday evening at 5 at J. W. Stanton's office, to make a decision.[18]

April 18   72° 75° 76°

Bright and fresh after the rain. Pleasant sunshine. Wind North East to South East. Vegetation refreshed and the gardens decked in their beautiful summer robes.

After dinner finished Plans for the "Home" to present to Trustees tomorrow. Then walked for an hour with Tommy. After tea finished report from Records in the case of "Cronan versus U.S."[19] It sums up $12.438.99 amount of hauling done by other parties than Cronan, which he claims to be a breach of his Contract, which plainly gives him the hauling of "all the material" to be used in the work.

April 19   72° 75° 76°

Very fine and clear. Hot sun. North wind....

Fine view from the top of the Building of the destruction by fire of Steamer "Trabue" at 3 O'clock, on the opposite side of the River. ½ an hour completed the work of demolition....

[14] The Reverend John Christian Keener (1819-1906) was bishop of the Methodist Church South. *Daily Picayune*, Jan. 20, 1906. The Dryades Church (German Methodist) was located on Dryades near Felicity.

[15] Edward Jacobs's daguerreotype and photography "saloon" was located at 93 Camp Street, below Poydras. *Daily Picayune*, Jan. 2, 1851.

[16] Perhaps Isaac Ingalls Stevens (1818-1862), a soldier and senator, served with Beauregard in the Mexican War and was appointed governor of Mexico by General Winfield Scott. T. Harry Williams, ed., *With Beauregard in Mexico: The Mexican War Reminiscences of P. G. T. Beauregard* (Baton Rouge, 1956), 9; *DAB*.

[17] The Seamen's Home was organized in 1851 as a temperance boarding house with a reading room. Located at the corner of Suzette (now Erato) and New Levee, it was built at a cost of about $27,000 and could accommodate 250 sailors. NOCD 1856, 1857; *Daily Delta*, Oct. 25, 1857.

[18] J. W. Stanton, the president of the board of the Seamen's Home, was a commission merchant with offices at 91 Camp Street. NOCD 1856.

[19] The case of Denis Cronan vs. Samuel J. Peters, et al., was appealed to the Louisiana Supreme Court from the Second District Court. The case concerned a contract made by Cronan, a subcontractor for the Custom House, with the federal government for the hauling of building materials for the Custom House. The decision was published in the *Reports of Cases Argued and Determined in the Supreme Court of Louisiana, Volume IX for the Year 1854...* (New Orleans, 1855).

Bas reliefs in Marble Hall, Louis T. Fritch, photographer, between 1911 and 1921 (1974.25.3.194).

April 22   69° 74° 79°

Very high wind from the West. Dry and very dusty. Hot sun. Call at the office from Judge Huling....

Engaged Mr. Jacobs to Photograph the casts of proposed colossal medallions, or bas reliefs, of Bienville, Jackson & arms of Louisiana, which are to be cut in Carrera Marble for Panels of Business Room. They are now placid [sic] in position for the Photograph and have a fine effect, doing great credit to the moulder and designer, Mr. Defrasse. I also went to see the editorial dignitaries of the Delta, True Delta, Picayune, and Courier, and invited them to come and take a look....

All went down after tea to the Fair for the Orphan Asylum at "Odd Fellows' Hall" very crowded.[20] Spent an hour or two very pleasantly amongst friends &c. &c. and returned home before midnight. The Asylum is the offspring of the scourge of 1853.

[20] The three-day benefit for the orphans home was held at the Odd Fellows Hall, opposite Lafayette Square, April 22, 23, and 24.

April 23   72° 72° 72°

Mild & cloudy after light rain in the night. South West wind. Rain, thunder & lightening set in at noon. Cleared off at 2 P.M....

I then went to Mr. Stanton's office, and met the full Board of Trustees of the Home. The discussion lasted some time indeed it was near 8 when I left for home. The result is that the Building Committee are authorized to procure from me a fully matured set of Plans and Specifications on which to receive Proposals and go on with the work. Mr. Renshaw and others advise that my arrangement for 3rd. and 4th. stories be changed by substituting stud partitions for my brick transverse walls, and wooden for my Iron girders, to enable them to make smaller rooms and more of them. I am opposed to the change. Mine will make a stronger, safer & better building.

April 24   72° 76° 78°

Pleasant air from South East. Warm sunny sky.

The editorial corps that I invited to see our Bass [sic] reliefs have given a handsome and well written notice in their respective papers. Went after dinner to see Mr. Brown who has been severely injured by being thrown from his gig on the Carondelet Street pavement, fell on his head and remained insensible for five hours. Same horse that run away with us Feby. 28....

April 25   74° 77° 79°

Hot & sunny. Gathering clouds. South East wind.

Mr. Letchford called at the office with a sketch of the general arrangement of the "Seamen's Home" which he says they will all unite upon, and he authorizes me to go on and prepare the plans and specifications accordingly.[21]

Emily came at 3 O'clock and saw the Bas reliefs then rode up together to dinner.

After dinner Emily, Tommy & I rode up to see a piece of property near Mr. Robb's in Lafayette Tommy being a <u>very</u> important party to the investigation. Returning they got out at Robin Street, and I continued on to Mr. J. W. Stanton's office to tell him, at Mr. Letchford's request, the conversation that had passed between us in the morning, he being the President of the Association. He was much pleased with the arrangement, and altho' he prefers my Plan presented on the 23rd., yet as the rest of the Board will act together on the modifications of Mr. Day's plan suggested by Mr. Letchford, he will act with them, and I am to go on with a set of matured plans on that Basis, on completion of which $100 of my compensation as Superintendent will be considered due. Mr. Stanton will also notify the City Surveyor to furnish his certified Plan of Site immediately. Spent the evening in considering the new arrangement proposed.

May 6   80° 83° 80°

Very sultry. Clouds & hot sunshine. High wind from South East and light showers....

The meeting at Mr. Stanton's office this evening was a strictly business one. The resolutions passed important, and unanimous.

[21] William H. Letchford of W. H. Letchford & Co., dry goods, on Canal Street. NOCD 1857.

Leonidas Polk (1991.34.40 v), gift of Tom Lennox.

Amongst them were 1st. the entire approval and adoption of my last Plan. 2nd. authorizing the President and Building Committee to call for Estimates after the completion of the working drawings and specifications, and to accept Proposals, make the necessary contracts, and go on with the work. And 3rd. that the same gentlemen be authorized to provide the ways and means, by mortgage on the property, or otherwise say to the amount of $15.000 or $20.000. The survey of site has been received, so that the Plans go on without further delay....

May 8   72½° 75° 75°

Damp and cloudy. Cool air from North West.

Rode up to dinner in company with Bishop Polk and had a pleasant talk not having seen him for sometime.[22]

Mr. Brown, my landlord, called in the evening to see about some repairs required in the house. He offers to sell at $4000 Cash. I wish to accept it, and take a few days to make my arrangements. See if I can get all the money &c.

[22] Leonidas Polk, D.D., (1806-1864) became Episcopal Bishop of Louisiana in 1841 and was rector of Trinity Church from 1855 until 1860. He became a general in the Confederate Army and was killed in the battle of Pine Mountain, Georgia, on June 14, 1864. Trinity Church, erected in 1853 by George Purves, architect-builder, at the corner of Jackson Avenue and Coliseum Street, is still standing. *DAB;* Duncan, *Diocese of Louisiana,* 38.

May 16   78° 80° 82°

Very hot and varied with clouds and sunshine. North East wind.

At 11 crossed the river and walked up along the Levee to the Marine Hospital. Examined the repairs, and reported on them to T. C. Porter Esq. Collector, on my return at 2 O'clock.[23]

The River is very high and rising. The space between the outer and inner Levee filled up and the water percolating thro' the latter....

June 3   82° 85° 85°

Very hot and dry. South East wind. Showers at noon.

Yesterday was the Election day for Municipal officers. Scenes of violence and bloodshed at the Polls. Naturalized citizens were the objects of enmity and very often not permitted to vote at all. The result gives for Chas. Waterman (Mayor) Know Nothing 2020 majority.[24]...

June 12   81 1/2° 85° 87°

Clouds and sunshine, North wind.

Tickets of invitation to Miss Hull's distribution of prizes at the Lyceum Hall. We all went at 8, and returned home at 11. About 1000 persons present, and altogether a very graceful attractive affair. The graduating class appeared to great advantage. The music was uniformly good but Miss Mary Renshaw distinguished herself by an uncommonly fine execution of a passage from "Lucia di Lammermoor." A "melange" from "Le Domino Noir" on 4 Pianos 8 performers was delightful.

June 18   82° 85° 86°

Cloudy and threatening rain but turned out very hot & sunny. West wind....

We are sweltering under the blaze of a tropical sun but get relief by our trips to the Lake. Emily, Tommy & I went by the cars this afternoon at 5 and found the breeze delicious and the sunset on the pure sparkling water perfectly resplendent. Then we always find friends there and quite a lively group of visitors from town. A fine

Hotel, too, at the terminus with delicious lemonades for the ladies and children and radiant "smiles" for the rougher sex. Then the fishermen have a nice way of filling the wells of their boats with fine fish all alive, which they scoop up with a net, and string on Palmetto fibres in a twinkling as the numerous orders pour in upon them. We brought home a string of a dozen which were scarcely dead when we got to the house at 8, so that we had a delightful fish supper....

June 23   79° 82° 81°

Cloudy and very sultry. North East wind. Cleared off hot & sunny at noon but followed immediately by a sudden & very heavy rain. Cleared off again at 2 P.M.

Letter from the Honl. Secretary of the Treasury raising my Salary to $2000 per annum.

June 25   82° 85° 86°

Very hot and sunshiny. South West wind.

In the afternoon I took the 4 O'clock Train to Carrolton and got a carriage there to Mrs. Besançon's, had a very pleasant visit.[25] Stayed an hour and got back to Carrolton in good time for the 7 1/2 Train. Mrs. Besançon's place is a delightful spot. A fine spacious Southern residence with ample grounds, shadowy oak and choice shrubbery, retired from the river Bank about 300 yards with carriage drive terminating in a sweeping circle at the house, a charming Live Oak occupying the centre....

June 28   84° 86 1/2° 88°

Very hot and dry. North West wind.

Very pleasant letter from R. B. Morgan Treasury Dept. Answered by next mail. The Department has printed our monthly Report for May and sent it as a "Circular" to be adopted by all the Government Civil works in the Union. It is the general form I have used for the last 7 years with the recent addition of a Cash Statement. This is a decided compliment....

June 30   83 1/2° 84° 86°

Hot and very sultry. Floating clouds. South West wind.

A deep oppressive languor broods over the city, breeding head

[23] Thomas C. Porter was collector of customs in New Orleans (1854-1857), an appointee of President Franklin Pierce. He also served as agent of the Marine Hospital. Wilson, *The U.S. Customhouse in New Orleans*, 84.

[24] Charles M. Waterman (d. 1860) served as mayor from 1856 to 1858 when he was expelled from office following riots during which he deserted his post. Soulé, *The Know Nothing Party*, 77, 97-101.

[25] Mrs. Besançon's home was just below the site of the Huey P. Long Bridge. *Norman's Chart of the Lower Mississippi River from Natchez to New Orleans, 1858.*

View of New Orleans from the west bank of the Mississippi River, 1866? (1947.23.6).

aches and presaging a storm. After dinner commenced a "Specification" for the Carpenter work of a Frame Dwelling House about to be erected on Apollo Street by J. M. Reid.[26] Thus far the summer has been exceedingly healthy, and more agreeable than usual. The cold winter has no doubt contributed to the improvement in health over previous seasons. But the diminished emigration has had much to do with it. Emigration, as it has been conducted for many years past, has been the fruitful source of epidemic disease in the United States.

July 14   84° 87° 87°

Fine & pleasant, very hot. West wind. Heavy clouds gathered at 3.
Finished an Estimate of Funds to finish the building, called for by the Secretary of the Treasury. The following is an abstract.

For Materials &c. & workmanship	$1.945.314.59
Materials on hand and Balance of appropriations. June 30. 1856.	490.679.72
required to be appropriated to complete	1.454.634.87
Expended to June 30. 1856	1.773.404.15
Total Estimated Cost of the work	$3.228.039.02

July 22   83° 85° 83°

Gathering clouds. Calm & still. The prelude of storm. South East wind. Thunder at distance....
Major Beauregard subpoenaed to attend the Court of Claims, that is U.S. District Court before Commissioner Lusher to testify in the case of "Cronan v. U.S."[27] As the facts are all in my possession & I have already prepared a synopsis of them I went with him at 10 A.M. and on his stating the circumstance he was at once relieved and I remained to give the evidence under oath, which is done by written questions and answers signed by the attestor, the Counsel for Plaintiff dictating the enquiry, and the Commissioner making the written examination. It took nearly two hours and I gave them all the facts bearing upon the case from the commencement of the works at the New Custom House to the present time....

[26] James M. Reid was an architect at the Custom House and Wharton's partner in the private practice of architecture. Elijah Cox built Reid a two-story frame house on the west side of Apollo (now Carondelet) between Polymnia and Felicity streets. NONA, James Graham, July 12, 1856.

[27] Robert Mills Lusher (1823-1890), an architect and educator, served on the board of directors of the New Orleans Public Schools and was state superintendent of education (1856, 1876-1879). Lusher was the nephew of Robert Mills, noted architect of the Washington Monument. *DLB.*

August 1   82$\frac{1}{2}$° 77° 80°

Hot sunshine early in the morning. S. West wind. Floods of rain and heavy thunder from 10 to 11. Cloudy & damp afterwards with sudden reduction of temperature....
Mrs. Low had just heard the sad news that Miss Mary Renshaw was drowned in one of the Northern Lakes. The fine, accomplished young lady of some 17 [years], who graduated with so much credit at Miss Hull's in June. What a terrible blow to poor Mr. & Mrs. Renshaw after their recent loss of a young child but a few months ago.

August 2   79° 78° 79°

Damp and sultry. North East wind to South West and gloomy rains at noon....
Mr. Low called to say that Miss Renshaw's death is confirmed. She was in a pleasure party on Lake George. The Boat took fire and she was drowned.

August 4   79° 81° 86°

Bright sunshine. Cool North West wind....
Pleasant parting conversation with Mr. Low. He leaves today, and Mr. Payne also. I have taken the charge of Mr. Payne's Bible Class in his absence. At 4$\frac{1}{2}$ Mr. Boujellet, the contractor for putting up the Spire of the church, met me by appointment at home, and brought his sketches to determine the principal staircase in the Tower to the body of the Church. I showed him the drawing I had made for the same purpose, which seems to embrace all the points required with good architectural effect. He had no hesitation in adopting it....

August 6   83° 87° 88°

Hot and dry. North Wind.
All the officers of the Revenue moved over to the new building yesterday. The Collector tells me that they like their accommodations much. Mr. Soulé visited us this morning and I took him over the works & showed him the new offices &c.[28] Talking of political prospects he said, "property, you know, is always timid, but slave-property is a coward."

[28] Pierre Soulé (1801-1870) was a prominent attorney and pro-slavery Democrat. As U.S. minister to Spain, he was one of the authors of the Ostend Manifesto, which ended his diplomatic career. In 1854 he returned to New Orleans to practice law. *DLB.*

Pierre Soulé, February 18, 1854 (1974.25.27.408).

August 7 84° 88° 86°

Hot sunshine. West wind. Shower at 1 P.M.

Mr. Stewart sent by N. Richards to see if I would approve of certain modifications in the Sill Course of the "Home" with drawings.[29] Sent my views in writing, disapproving of the proposed

---

changes, and stating such admissions as I was willing to make, if acceptable to the Building Committee.

August 8 84° 87° 86°

Clouds and sunshine. Pleasant air from North East.

Mr. Newton Richards called again about that sill course, and I told him I could not admit his drawing.

August 10 80° 76° 78°

Sunday. High wind in the night and sudden dash of rain towards morning.

Got up pretty early & went to market.

Air somewhat chill, and clouds drifting heavily from the Eastward. Went to Sunday School and taught classes 2 hours before service....

The wind rose in the meanwhile and rain set in. At 1 P.M. it increased to a gale, blew down a large China tree in the next garden, tearing up the pavement & crushing the fence against which it fell, levelled the fence around the Public School on this Square, and covered the street around us with the fragments of Shade trees &c. &c.[30]

August 11 76° 78° 78°

The storm lasted all night, and at sunrise a strange glow filled the atmosphere making the wild clouds, the houses & trees appear as if seen thro' green glass. Soon after the torrents began to fall again and the wind from the South rose to a hurricane about 9. The Canal filled quickly and the street & square were soon under water. The force of the gale, however, soon spent itself, tho' the sky continued murky as ever with sudden dashes of wind & rain and a tendency to Westward. The last 30 hours must have been a fearful time on the exposed Gulf shore, tho' in town we are so protected that we scarcely feel it....

August 12 80° 80° 80°

The rain continues but the force of the wind is spent. It still blows from South East & South.

---

[29] Probably Samuel Stewart (1801-1868), builder of the Pontalba Buildings, who was awarded the contract for the Seamen's Home but withdrew before signing. Newton Richards, a native of New Hampshire, arrived in New Orleans in 1831. The most important granite dealer in the city, he erected the base for the Jackson statue in Jackson Square and designed the Chalmette monument. NOCD 1855; *ENOA*.

[30] Washington School for girls was at the corner of Magazine and Terpsichore streets. It became the Jackson School for boys and girls in the late 1860s; the site was extended to Camp when a new building was erected in the 1920s. Today the schoolyard extends along Camp to Euterpe, encompassing the lot where Wharton's cottage stood.

The storm gathering over Last Island [Ile Dernière], Destruction of the island, Frank Leslie's Illustrated Newspaper, *August 30, 1856 (1974.25.4.65–6).*

I saw the fine Steamer Capitol this morning minus her chimneys blown down.[31] The Papers already give the loss of some 14 lives by drowning during the gale....

August 14   78° 80° 78°

Gloomy and showers thro' the morning, South wind. At 2½ a violent rain set in. I tried to get home by the Annunciation Street omnibus but when I reached the head of the Street the flood was such that I had to return to the office. At 4 I took the Magazine omnibus, the rain having nearly ceased. Arrived at the corner of Magazine and Basin the water was still deep on Camp, but fortunately our Baker came along at the time and with the assistance of his cart and stalwart shoulders I succeeded in getting into the house dry. The water was at least a foot on the banquettes, but it all ran off by 6 P.M.

We have fearful accounts of the destruction of Last Island at the mouth of Berwick's Bay, and more than 100 persons who were spending the summer on the Island drowned. The details of the burning of the John Jay on Lake George, are now coming in and are more painful than I have read for many a year. Poor Miss Renshaw had still some warmth left when her body was recovered but all attempts to revive her failed.

August 15   80° 81° 84°

It has cleared off at last with a pleasant air from South West.

An Extra this morning gives the full particulars of the destruction of "Derniere Isle" [Last Island] on Sunday night 182 Victims have been already counted, belonging many of them to the best families in the State. Almost as many more were saved which seems little less than a miracle....

August 16   81° 84° 84°

Pleasant breeze from South West. Light clouds....

And to Messrs. Reynolds & Brown Builders in Natchez, to ascertain facts relative to the Galvan[ize]d. Iron roof of the Marine Hospital

preparatory to adopting it for our church.[32] Met Mr. Benson this morning and had conversation with him on the completion of the Church....

August 17   81° 84° 83°

Sunday. Very pleasant, warm sun. Cool North wind....

What a fearful calamity that was on the 10th. at "Last Island." All the buildings swept away and upwards of 100 human beings engulfed in the waters. At 10 O'clock that very morning I was illustrating to my Sunday class the striking parable of the "house without foundation built upon the Sand." How little did we think that at the very time the storm was then raging which in a few hours and within a few miles of us should furnish so terrible an exemplification of the force of the simile.

August 26   82° 87° 88°

Clear & very sunny. Pleasant air from North East.

I went with Major Beauregard and other friends to the City Hall to register our names and take our "voting certificate." Mine is numbered 6266. The lists will increase fast when the people return from the north....

August 28   82° 88° 88°

Very hot indeed, clear sky, pleasant air from North East.

Went with Capt. Duncan to see the repairs going on at the Branch Mint under his Superintendence.[33] Congress has appropriated $300.000 for the New Custom House for the current Fiscal Year, and we have a large Balance on hand.

August 30   81° 85° 86°

Cloudy & hot sunshine. Blustering wind from the North and intolerable dust.

[31] The badly damaged *Capitol* brought the first news to the city of the extent of the hurricane that completely destroyed Last Island on Sunday, August 10. *Daily Picayune*, Aug. 11, 1856. Last Island was a summer resort on the Louisiana coast with numerous vacation cottages and a hotel run by John Muggah. Almost 200 people, most of them natives of the New Orleans area, were killed in the hurricane. Charles L. Sullivan, *Hurricanes of the Mississippi Gulf Coast* (Gulfport, Miss., 1986), 21.

[32] Charles Reynolds and James Brown were prominent Natchez builders. Part of Reynolds's brickyard was acquired for the U.S. Marine Hospital site in 1850. Adams County Conveyance Records, 2:256.

[33] Johnson Kelly Duncan (1827-1862) of Pennsylvania served in the U.S. Army until January 1855. He moved to New Orleans where he worked as an engineer and architect and was later a brigadier general in the Confederate army. *DLB*. The United States Branch Mint on Esplanade Avenue was begun in 1835; William Strickland was the architect. In 1854, the building was fireproofed and strengthened by the addition of iron beams, masonry floor construction, an iron truss, and a corrugated iron roof.

U.S. Mint, John T. Hammond, lithographer, ca. 1858 (1954.9.4).

Mr. Renshaw sent for me this morning to consult me about a piece of Marble Statuary for "Mary's" Tomb. When I got to the office I sent for A. Defrasse & gave him a sketch embodying the general idea of the figure, and he is to bring me his complete design & proposals for the work on Monday. Mr. Renshaw handed me the letter from Mr. White which gives the particulars of the sad calamity. After the steamer took fire and neared the shore, Mr. White & Miss Renshaw both leaped, fell into the water and sunk together. He was recovered and resuscit[at]ed after being in the water 20 or 30 minutes, but when poor Mary was taken out life was extinct....

September 1   86° 87° 84°

Very hot & very dusty. South East wind. Cloudy and threatening at noon.

Renewed the lease of my house for another year. Mr. Defrasse brought his crayon sketch for the Statuary and proposed to do the work 3 ft. 6 in. high of 1st. Quality Italian Marble for $800 and for a design in plaster alone to cut from for $200, which I consider entirely too high and shall go and see Parelli (another able sculptor) tomorrow and also the Sicilian Consul Barelli, and see whether it may not be better to have it done in Italy.[34] I called in the evening at Mr. Renshaw's. They were all highly pleased with the design in crayon, and I gave Mr. R. the proposals I had received at the office in the morning, and told him how I intended to proceed in the matter.

[34] Achille Perelli (1822-1891) was an Italian-born sculptor whose works included busts of Robert E. Lee and Stonewall Jackson that were studies for the Monument to the Confederate Dead erected in Greenwood Cemetery, and a statue of Stonewall Jackson for the top of the tomb of the Louisiana Division of the Army of Northern Virginia in Metairie Cemetery. *ENOA.* Joseph C. Barelli, consul of Portugal and vice-consul of the Kingdom of the Two Sicilies, had a marble tomb erected in St. Louis Cemetery II in memory of his son, who was killed in a steamboat explosion. The tomb has a bas-relief sculpture depicting the explosion and is surmounted by five standing figures of angels, probably the statuary referred to on September 2. Barelli was also responsible for the erection of two major society tombs in St. Louis Cemetery I, the New Orleans Italian Mutual Benevolent Society tomb and the Portuguese Benevolent Association tomb. *New Orleans Architecture*, 3:9.

Street railroad car, Frank Henry Temple Bellew, delineator, September 1855 (1959.155.10), gift of Harold Schilke and Boyd Cruise.

September 2
84° 88° 86°

Very hot, dry & dusty, in the morning. South East wind, shower between 1 & 2, and fall of Thermo. to 85°.

Called at Mr. Barelli's office at 9. He kindly unboxed some fine statuary he has just received from Italy for his own Monument, and proposed that I should meet him at his office at 5½ this evening, and go together to see "Parelli" and also some fine specimens of Italian sculpture in the St. Louis Cemetery which he had imported on order, the prices of which are far below the figures given by Defrasse. After dinner I joined Mr. Barelli and went with him to the Cemeteries, saw the Marbles Mr. Parelli &c &c. and returned at 8 P.M. Called at Mr. Renshaw's & reported progress.

Drawing after tea until late.

September 3
84° 88° 85°

Clear & sunny. Very hot. Pleasant air from S. East.

Mr. Barelli & Parelli called at the office this morning, & spent an hour on the marble business both for the Statue and the Basso relievos of the Custom House, and Mr. Defrasse also....

September 4
84° 88° 87°

Sultry & very hot sun. South East wind. Gathering clouds.

Saw Mr. Parelli who will have two small clay models ready for me by Saturday, different in every respect from Mr. Defrasse' design, which I have returned to him. That is, the crayon sketch which he made from my dictation and the rough outline I furnished to him. After dinner we all went up in the cars, I to Carrolton, the rest to visit the "Hurlbuts" at Rickerville.[35] The Revd. C. Keener was in the cars and I went home with him at Carrolton had an hour's very pleasant conversation. Saw several very beautiful alabaster statuettes which he had purchased in Florence....

September 6
81° 84° 86°

Very hot sunshine. Passing clouds, South East wind.

Major Beauregard has had one of the marble capitals unboxed and set up complete on a base and a piece of shaft, in a good conspicuous situation. Each Capital consists of four pieces. The effect of the whole is exceedingly fine, and the bold innovations on the classic model quite successful.

September 9
82° 86° 87°

Hot, clear, dry and dusty. North East wind.

The sketch shows the principal dimensions of our beautiful white marble columns for the "Collector's Room." Corinthian from monument of Lysicrates, with certain changes, near the abacus, emblematic figures in place of the honeysuckle &c....

35 Rickerville, a small New Orleans suburb between Valmont and Joseph streets, was subdivided in 1849. It was a part of Jefferson City from 1850 to 1870, when it was annexed to New Orleans.

September 10 84° 86° 82°

Very hot, dry & dusty. South East wind. Showers in the afternoon.

Went to Mr. Parelli's to see his sketch in clay for the statuary and called at Mr. Monsseaux to see his fine groups executed in Italy.[36] He asked me the other day to come and examine them. Sent for Mr. Swan and wrote a specification of details for him to fill up as his proposal for covering the Spire of the Bapt. Church.[37]

September 11 82° 86° 87°

Clouds and sunshine. South East wind.

After [dinner?] Mr. Renshaw and I drove down, by appointment, to the Sculptor's to see his sketch in clay. Little Harry went with us and we called for Mr. Barelli on the way. The design is not satisfactory, and we ordered another in a different posture &c. We then drove on to Mr. Monsseaux's Marble Yard. Saw his specimens of Italian work, examined the monuments in two of the Cemeteries, & those that Mr. Barelli has in progress for his own family, and the Portuguese Society, the latter a fine Mausoleum. It was quite dark when we got back home.

September 16 82° 85° 85°

Very hot, dry and dusty. North East wind....

Spent 3 hours this morning with Mr. Roy at the Church examining the workmanship of the roof &c. &c. making measurements and calculations with a view to correct the many errors that appear in the construction as executed under the supervision and after the drawings of the original architect. After dinner commenced Plan & Elevation of a small building for Mr. Cox and worked at it until bedtime.

September 17 82° 86° 86°

Hot, dry, and very dusty indeed. East wind.

Drawing Plans after dinner and until quite late at night. The musquitoes troubled me a great deal, this is the worst month for them.

---

[36] Paul H. Monsseaux (ca.1808-1874), one of the most notable New Orleans tomb builders, executed many of the tomb designs of the architect J. N. B. de Pouilly. His marble yard was at the corner of St. Louis and Robertson streets. *ENOA*.

[37] J. L. Swan was a tinsmith on Circus St. (now Rampart). NOCD 1856.

September 19 81° 85° 83°

Hot, dry and dusty as ever....

Finished the Plans for Mr. Cox and made a sketch shewing the outward inclination of the walls of our Church taken by the plumb yesterday. It is sufficient to create the necessity for the Tension rods at the Foot of the roof-tresses which I shall strongly recommend as soon as Mr. Low returns, and also additional support to the floors, as I consider the present insufficient if extremely loaded....

September 21 82° 84° 82°

Sunday. Hot & dry in the morning. Cool Easterly breeze. Pleasant veil of clouds during the middle of the day. Today is the equinox, however, and true to its character did not pass without a change. At 2 P.M. a sudden dash of rain flooded the parched and dusty earth and filled the thirsty cisterns, and a strong wind drove the water into every dry chink that has been gaping for moisture for some weeks past....

The Cahawba from N. York on Friday evening brought Mr. White and the remains of Miss Mary Renshaw. I attended the funeral this afternoon. Almost every one I know was there and the line of carriages immense. The Revd. Mr. Rothenstein conducted the Funeral service and pronounced the address.[38] Meanwhile the rain fell freely and the shadows of evening began to fall, so when the procession moved from the house I returned home, which was only a few steps. Truly the real incidents of life are stranger than romance! What a termination to a gay and happy bridal party, that left here but 3 months ago for a northern summer of delight and enjoyment! I thought of the rooms but lately filled by the fine strains of Mary's rich and highly cultivated voice, now crowded with mourners and hushed to deepest silence broken only by occasional sobs and sighs of bitterest anguish.

October 6 74° 74° 73°

Gusty wind from the East. Dark clouds, prelusive drops in the morning, showers thro' the day.

Went after dinner with Mr. Renshaw to Parelli's to see his model in clay for Mary's statue. The conception is excellent and Mr. Renshaw has concluded to give him the order. It is to be of purest white Carrara marble, in the best style of art, and say 5.6 in height, at a cost of $1500.

---

[38] Charles F. Rottenstein became rector of the Episcopal Church of the Annunciation after the Rev. N. O. Preston resigned in July 1855. Duncan, *Diocese of Louisiana*, 13.

Bas relief on the Barelli tomb, St. Louis Cemetery II, Stuart M. Lynn, photographer, 1946 (1978.102.140), gift of Stuart M. Lynn; St. Louis I with the Portuguese Benevolent Association and Italian Society tombs in the foreground, Georges François Mugnier, photographer, ca. 1890 (1974.25.6.392).

November 5   58° 60° 61°

Lovely weather. Fine air from the North.

The Election returns show a large majority for Mr. Fillmore, say 3.383, of the 11.921 votes registered, only 8333 were polled. Much intimidation, it is said, was used in the latter part of the day and many outrages committed.[39]...

November 14   55° 58½° 58°

Lovely weather. Wind N. East to N. West.

Putting down floors in the Church Tower, levelling up, and "progressing" generally to satisfaction. Getting in hot air furnace &c. &c. Went to the Choir meeting in the evening.

November 15   56° 61° 60°

Beautiful day after a keen white frost in the night. North wind.

Examined the work on the new church Lafayette Square on my way home to dinner. The Spire is being constructed within the Tower & then to be raised into position.[40] Closed in the Tower of B. Church and had everything put in neat order in and around for Sunday. All fragments & rubbish cleared away from entrance & the whole levelled up and smoothed off.

November 24   70° 73° 74°

Damp & foggy. Very little air from South East, to South.

After the copious rains of yesterday I have the mortification to find that a defect in the bottom of our cistern lets the water out almost as fast as it flows in. I went round immediately for the carpenter. The cistern will have to be taken to pieces as the bottom is greatly decayed. It was all new but 2 yrs. 8 months ago. Like those broken "cisterns that can hold no water" to what purpose do the treasures of heaven flow in without the capacity to retain them, and to what purpose are we replenished with every advantage & every privilege if we lack the capacity to enjoy & improve them. The cistern when taken down showed the bottom in the last stage of decay & the sides perfectly sound. The former due to the fact that the foundation was built close without perforations for the circulation of the air within....

November 29   63° 64° 64°

Fine pleasant air from North West. Clouds & sunshine. This is a delightful change.

Fortunately my Cistern was just put up anew in time for the rain last night. The carpenters are getting along well at the Baptist Church and my main Entrance Staircase promises to meet with general favor.

December 10   60° 65° 58°

Rains in the night. Damp & close today. Showers & warm air from South East, increased to a gale from the South in the afternoon, with heavy clouds & twilight darkness, winding up with a storm of wind & rain at 4 P.M.

Wrote an article for publication urging the erection of a New Court House and recommending the present "Place d'Armes" for the site.[41] The subject was introduced in Council on Tuesday night by Alderman Reid in a Resolution &c.

December 12   49° 56° 57°

Keen white frost in the night. Beautiful weather today. South East wind.

My article on Court house appeared in the "True Delta" this morning with editorial remarks &c. recommending & enforcing it.

December 16   46° 50° 48°

Heavy white frost in the night. Bright & sunny. North wind.
Very pleasant visit from Revd. W. C. Duncan.
At 4½ P.M. young Mr. Harrod & Mr. Boyd called, and after

---

[39] The presidential election of 1856 pitted James Buchanan, Democrat, against former president Millard Fillmore of the American or Know Nothing party as well as John Charles Fremont of the newly organized Republican party. Fillmore's victory in Louisiana reflected the continuation of Know Nothing political power in New Orleans and a deep split in the state's Democratic party. Buchanan was elected president. Soulé, *The Know Nothing Party*, 82-83.

[40] The spire on the First Presbyterian Church on Lafayette Square was raised on Dec. 24, 1856. The spire, which weighed twenty-three tons, was the tallest in the city. *Daily Picayune*, Dec. 24, 1856.

[41] Wharton's article in the *Daily True Delta* (December 12, 1856) urged building a courthouse on Rampart Street on the axis of Orleans Street, in the space originally known as Congo Square, then called the Place d'Armes.

sitting awhile, looking over drawings &c. we went to see the New Church of St. Alphonse & Mr. Buckner's large new residence.[42]…

December 18   48° 56° 55°

Thanksgiving Day, and the works suspended at the N. Custom H. It is also the 5th. anniversary of our wedding day. Went to market before breakfast to provide accordingly &c. &c.

Lovely day with South East wind.

Short walk with Tommy after breakfast then spent the evening in making drawings for the proposed alteration in door of St. Paul's, until 3 P.M.[43] Then a short walk before dinner. Conversation with Mr. Pride on his plans for the Bank of New Orleans which he brought yesterday to the office for my examination &c.[44]…

December 22   40° 45° 48°

Hard frost at night. Ice ³/₈ inch thick. Bright & sunny. West wind to North.

Finished Report for Committee in Council on New Court House. The spire of the Presbyterian Church built & finished complete within the Tower is now all ready to be raised into place. The ropes are adjusted & every thing has been prepared under the management of E. McShaw, one of our foremen. Tomorrow the work will be attempted. The weight is 23 tons.…

December 23   38° 39¹/₂° 42°

Frost at night, and Ice. Cold North West to North East wind. Bright & sunny.

The "Spire" was successfully raised into place this morning. Walked home with Mr. Low and spent an hour with him before dinner at the Church examining the work &c., which is now nearly finished. The painters have commenced. After tea made working drawings for door of St. Paul's &c.

December 24   40° 48° 49°

Ice in the night. Cold air today, sunny sky. Wind South East to South West.

Went to market this morning to buy tomorrow's dinner in advance & met Mr. Keen loaded down with boughs of wild Orange, Myrtle Orange and Arbor Vita, the former covered with fruit.[45] All for our Christmas Tree tomorrow evening. The Report on Court House was adopted in the Council, and the proper Committee appointed to carry out its recommendations. Sat up until near midnight and wrote a full specification for the proposed change in the door of St. Paul's Church.

December 25   52° 57° 58°

Christmas Day. A lovely day with gentle air from the South East. Truly a happy and beautiful Christmas.

Drawing and coloring Plans all day until dark. Early dinner in approved manner, roast goose, plum pudding, mince pie &c., and the Christmas Tree in the evening loaded with presents and the golden fruit shewing between. Tommy was in ecstasies with it and sat up quite late amusing himself with his new acquisitions.

December 31   64° 68° 68°

Damp and gloomy. Thick mists. Drizzling rain. South wind. Bursts of sunshine & passing showers in the afternoon.

The year fades out amid gloom and shadows, the shroud of buried time, and the clouds shed drops of sympathy over its bier. Its events belong to history, its incidents to individual memory. Its pleasures, joys, hopes and sorrows have all floated off like bubbles on [the] bosom of the river of Lethe. Its deeds and its warning alone remain. The one a record of good or evil. The latter a treasury of wisdom & experience stored up for future use. Let thought and reflection, therefore, preside over the obsequies of the departing year, and gather maxims of value from a review of the past.

[42] Benjamin Morgan Harrod (1837-1912), son of Charles Harrod, became a prominent New Orleans architect. He designed the Southern Athletic Club at Washington Avenue and Prytania and directed the construction of Christ Church Cathedral (Episcopal) at St. Charles Avenue and Sixth Street. Henry Sullivan Buckner (1797-1883) of Kentucky was a cotton factor and financier. His residence, at the corner of Jackson Avenue and Coliseum Street, was designed and built by Lewis E. Reynolds. *Daily Picayune*, Dec. 20, 1883; NONA, H. B. Cenas, Apr. 23, 1856.

[43] Wharton's "Drawing of the proposed alteration in the Principal Entrance of St. Paul's Church, N. Orleans, T. K. Wharton, Architect" is in the Southeastern Architectural Archive at Tulane University.

[44] Charles Pride was a prominent architect-builder whose office was located at 301 Magazine; his residence was on Camp Street at the corner of Gaiennie. Among his important works are the Albert Brevard house at the corner of First and Chestnut, for which James Calrow was the architect, and the Richard Terrell house at 1441 Magazine. Both houses are still standing. NOCD 1859.

[45] Richard William Keen worked with Wharton at the Custom House and lived on Felicity, near Apollo. NOCD 1856.

Henry S. Buckner residence, Jay Dearborn Edwards, photographer, between 1857 and 1860 (1982.32.5).

Florance House Hotel, Mygatt & Co.'s Directory, 1857.

January 1 57° 54° 55°

Cold air from the South East. Clouds & bursts of splendid Sunshine....

Commenced my visits at the Florance House & St. Louis.[1]...

The streets filled with gentlemen passing rapidly from house to house, on foot or in carriages. I made during the day some 24 calls, closing at the St. Charles at about 10 P.M.[2]...

January 4 42° 46° 48°

Sunday. Charming weather. North wind.

Threw open my new staircase to the Principal Entrance in Tower of Baptist Church, roomy, solid and effective....

[1] The Florance House, built by A. T. Wood for Jacob Levy Florance in 1834, was a small hotel at the corner of South and Camp streets, overlooking Lafayette Square. NONA, William Christy, Jan. 27, 1834.

[2] The first St. Charles Hotel on St. Charles between Common and Gravier was designed by James Gallier, Sr., in 1835, destroyed by fire in 1851, and rebuilt almost immediately to the same design, with the omission of the dome which had been a city landmark. The rebuilding has been attributed to various architects, including George Purves. The second hotel burned in 1894 and was replaced by a third St. Charles Hotel designed by architect Thomas Sully, which was demolished in 1974. The site is now occupied by the Place St. Charles office building.

1857

St. Charles Hotel, Jay Dearborn Edwards, photographer, between 1857 and 1860 (1982.32.10).

January 14   40° 47° 52°

Ice and strong white frost in the night. The grass on Coliseum Place whitened over as if with a coat of snow. River full of ice 100 miles above Vicksburg. Change of wind to South & South West. Clear & sunny.

The Total Expenditures at the New Custom House up to January 1. 1857, amount to $1.940.526.20…

January 17   51° 56° 58°

Misty, gathering clouds, warm air from South East. Heavy rains set in about noon, and continued thro' the rest of the day.

At noon all came down to the office, Josy Cook with them and I took them to the Circus.[3] The performances were admirable, large attendance, chiefly from abroad, and every thing well managed. Tommy's excitement was intense. It was his first experience of a public entertainment. The church is the only public assembly he had ever seen and in talking about it afterwards he said he was afraid that the horses would be breaking loose among the "pews." But he dwelt more upon the music than anything else, even the very fine equitation.…

January 19   28° 33° 34°

Heavy ice formed in the night, in the most sheltered situation 3/5 of an inch, and on a vessel in an exposed site I measured it 1½ inch. The thickness is greater than I ever saw before of domestic origin and icicles and knobby masses lay about during the day in true northern fashion, tho' the sun shone cheerily, and the north west wind blew softly.

Invitations for the Ball at the St. Charles this evening.

January 27   58° 63° 64°

Warm sunny sky. South East wind.

Quite an exciting time in town this morning. A fire on the corner of Camp and Canal, and an adroit robbery of $50.000 committed on the Bank of New Orleans, by a very young man, a runner of the Bank, and an accomplice.

January 28   56° 62° 64°

Heavy fog from the river, cleared off very warm & sunny at noon. Clouded up with distant thunder at 3 P.M. Light East wind. Rain in the afternoon.…

The two youthful absconders were caught on the Steamer Cahawba outside the Balize & brought back to the city. Affidavits filed against them by Mr. Grayson of the Bank &c. &c.

Finished copies from cornices of Mr. Reid's house on Nayades Street, begun yesterday, A. T. Wood Archt., and reading Treatise on Stair Building.[4]

January 31   50° 53° 56°

Splendid sunshine, cool north wind.

Canal Street, Chartres &c. like a conservatory of tropical plants in full bloom.

Invitation to the Ball at the St. Charles on Monday. Engaged on working Drawings all the evening, to complete a set of Plans and details of Mr. Reid's house on Nayades Street, from the originals of A. T. Wood Archt. The house cost $6500 and looks exceedingly well in execution, besides being good durable work.

February 5   62° 67½° 68°

Charming weather. "The South wind blows softly."

There is welcome intelligence this morning of the upper rivers rising and ice breaking up. Also a dispatch from New York saying that the $50.000 stolen by young Stringer from the Bank of New Orleans was found in his State room on the "Cahawba" and placed in the care of the Chief of Police.

Drawing in the evening until late. After dinner went up the Spire of the Church to see the work on the Galvanized Iron covering &c. now nearly complete.

---

[3] Josie R. Cook was the daughter of Paul Cook (ca. 1808-1893), a family friend who lived on Magazine Street at the corner of Orange. Cook was a partner in the firm of Cook & O'Brien, wholesale dealers in provisions and western produce, at 40 Poydras Street. *Daily Picayune*, Feb. 7, 1893. The Three Circuses performed at Spalding and Rogers Amphitheatre and Museum on St. Charles near Commercial Place. *Daily Picayune*, Jan. 17, 1857.

[4] L. E. Reynolds, *A Treatise on Handrailing …* (New Orleans, 1849).

February 7   66° 70° 71°

Clouds. Bursts of sunshine spring showers and fresh breeze from East to South. Heavy showers at noon.

At 6¹/₂ Mr. Kearney drove round to take me to the Opera.[5] Emily had declined going. We took up Mrs. Underhill & Miss Phoebe Palfrey. The house filled rapidly to overflowing, and the audience presented a superb spectacle. Costumes of the utmost taste and beauty. A little faulty, however, in the distribution. Some segments of the voluminous skirts might have been spared to reduce the latitude & longitude of those upper regions which neither health nor elegance require to be so much exposed. Besides it is not pleasant to have the ladies turning a "cold" shoulder to you all the time. The music and representation of "Le Prophete" were beyond all praise. The duos & trio by "Moulin" and Mlles. Muller & Bourgeois, exquisite, and the choruses grand and impressive. The entertainment throughout faultless, and enjoyment banished criticism. Major Beauregard and relatives occupied the next box to Mr. Kearny's which by the way is one of the best placed in the deep circle, and many other friends were there &c. &c. It was very hot when we arrived, but a sudden change occurred which made it very pleasant within, but bitter cold without, and in passing from the House to the carriage at 11 O'clock the wind and rain swept by us with icy rigor. The change was complete from summer to winter during the few short hours that had been wafted away on the wings of harmony.

February 13   57° 64° 63°

Soft moist air from the South East. Clouds and sunshine, very warm and summerlike in the middle of the day.

Mr. Payne brought friends to go over the building and I spent an hour with them. One of them, Mrs. Prewitt, was at the laying of the corner stone on the 22nd. Feb. 1849, and has not seen the building since, and of course found everything exceedingly interesting. She was then Miss C. Shaw. I introduced her on that occasion to Mr. Clay which she recalls today with great pleasure.[6] By the

Henry Clay, T. Johnson, engraver, after Rockwood daguerreotype (1974.25.27.77).

commanding position he held among his countrymen and before the world, and his subsequent decease, every reminiscence of Mr. Clay is invested with peculiar sacredness, and deep interest.

February 19   66° 72° 70°

Warm and summer like. Hot sunshine. Showery in the middle of the day. South East wind.

Called upon H. Howard Archt. and saw the set of Plans and Specifications which he offered for the Bank of New Orleans &c. After dinner examined with the Builder the repairs going on at the Cupola and Portico &c. of St. Anna's Asylum. He is making very thorough work of it. Had I not seen it I could hardly have conceived the progress that decay had made in the joists flooring & general woodwork in less than 3 years, due both to inferior material and vicious construction.

---

[5] Alfred Kearney (1813-1877), a ship broker from New Rochelle, New York, was a member of the firm of A. Delagrave & Co., commercial merchants and dealers in paints, plaster, and other building materials. NOCD 1856; Civil District Court, Succession of Alfred Kearney, docket 5760, NOPL.

[6] Henry Clay (1777-1852) of Kentucky, as a senator, secretary of state, and presidential candidate, was one of the nation's most powerful political leaders. He had a strong connection with Louisiana because of his daughter's marriage into the Duralde/Claiborne family. *DAB*.

A Creole night at the French Opera-House, Alfred R. Waud, delineator, July 21, 1866 (1951.72).

New Marine Hospital, between 1862 and 1878 (1953.133.7).

February 20   69° 72° 72°

Damp, inclining to rain. Very sultry. Bursts of hot sunshine, and dark threatening clouds. High wind from the South East to South.

Drove out with Capt. Duncan to see the piling for his foundation of the new U.S. Marine Hospital.[7] They are about 10" or 12" square and drive 35 feet to a perfectly fine bearing. They have already driven 2100.

February 21   64° 66° 66°

Raw air from the North East. Cold rains in the morning, pleasant afternoon.

At 3 dined by invitation with Mr. Da Silva and spent the afternoon in examining his rich collection of coins & medals, ancient and modern, about 1600 in all and including fine specimens struck during the reigns of the 12 Caesars, and some as far back as

Alexander of Macedon.[8] A commemorative gold medal of the diet of Augsburg 1530, struck a century after say A.D. 1630 was particularly fine, with a head of Luther, and the motto, "Domini nomen fortissima terris." [The name of the Lord, most powerful on earth] The Roman coins were evidently genuine and in good preservation, the heads splendidly cut, and amid great variety preserving the general Roman character....

February 23   62° 67° 68°

Charming weather. East wind.

The Spire of the Baptist Church is finished and looks well, tho' I still think the Square finish would have been safe and equally effective. Sent Francis for Tommy at 12 and took him to the Museum &c. We found no one but ourselves in the room and after examining the collection Mr. Nellis (the man without arms) came in and kindly went thro' his extraordinary performances with his feet for our especial benefit, explaining his modes of executing the most

[7] The new Marine Hospital designed by Ammi B. Young, architect for the treasury department, was being constructed at the corner of Tulane and Broad, the site now occupied by the Criminal District Court building.

[8] Jean da Silva, a member of the Congregation Dispersed of Judah, was in the furniture business. He lived on St. Andrew near St. Charles. NOCD 1854, 1855.

delicate manipu- or "pedepulations" &c.[9] Thus an hour passed away without noticing it and Tommy was deeply interested, especially with his archery, pistol shooting & performance on the accordeon. He wrote our names on cards for us in clear bold hand and cut some admirable figures in white paper for Tommy to take home with him. He will be 40 next March but looks much younger and enjoys excellent health, and appears the very soul of good nature....

February 27   68° 71° 73°

Damp, inclining to rain in the morning. Sunny and warm in the afternoon, wind N. West to South East.

Went with Major Beauregard to see Herring's Picture of the "English Farm Yard" if "Landseer" can excel it he must be an "enchanter."[10] It is the most lovely gem in that walk of art I ever saw, rather crowded, however.

March 3   56° 60° 63°

Cool air from the South East. Dry parching dusty March weather. Warm sunshine.

Mr. J. W. Stanton called to say that they had at length made the necessary arrangements to go on with the "Seamen's Home" and had awarded the Contract to W. K. Day for $20.000.[11]...

March 16   52° 56° 56°

Warm and sunny, dry and very dusty, wind N. West.

Met Messrs. Stanton, Day & Coleman at the Seamen's Home at 9 by appointment to determine in regard to pulling down Mr. Coleman's party wall, recently built, which I had recommended. The agreement was soon made to the satisfaction of the parties, to pull down and rebuild according to my plans. Memorandum of which agreement I have since made for record. Our first correspondence

with the newly appointed Secretary of the Treasury Mr. Howell Cobb of Georgia, commenced today.[12]...

One of our sculptors made me a present of a fine medallion of Henry Clay which he has executed in a piece of our Carrara Marble. The likeness is admirable. The workmanship very fine, and set in glass, and gold & white frame. The whole forming an ellipse 6 in. by 8 in. of marble, exclusive of frame. Very busy drawing after tea, and on business of the "Home" with the builder.

March 23   65° 72° 73°

Very warm and clear. Mild air from the East.

At breakfast Mr. Bell brought me Tracings of the Plans of Seamen's Home completed, and I returned the originals to the contractor, and called at J. W. Stanton's on my way to the office to have the Tracings signed &c.[13] Mr. S. handed me a copy of the Contract &c....

March 28   68° 72° 76°

Very hot. Dry and dusty, scorching sunshine. Wind N. West....

Two notes from Mr. Stanton on business of the "Home." Wrote to Mr. W. K. Day acceding to his request of the morning to substitute shell for Thomaston Lime in foundations, owing to the great scarcity of the latter....

March 31   67° 68° 72°

Very dry and clouds of dust. South East wind. Scorching sun, clouds gathering in the afternoon.

Ticket to the consecration of the New Synagogue from Mr. Da Silva. Four tickets to the opera this evening from Mr. Kearney but had to decline as Emily had engaged to go to Mr. Young's & the Panorama. The Box of "Plans of Public Buildings" arrived today by express from the Treasury Department. After dinner drawing Plans, and saw Mr. Day on business of the "Home." After tea took the family & Mrs. Young to the Panorama of the Arctic regions.[14]...

[9] Mr. Nellis performed at the Spalding and Rogers Amphitheatre. *Daily Picayune*, Feb. 21, 1857.

[10] J. F. Herring, a landscape painter, exhibited at Mr. Norman's bookstore. *Daily Picayune*, Feb. 26, 1857.

[11] William K. Day (b. 1815) of Kentucky was a well-known builder who lived on Prytania near Urania Street. For several years he was in partnership with the architect James W. Calrow. Day was the contractor for the rebuilding of the Seamen's Home, which had been partially destroyed by fire in 1854. Plans and an elevation for this four-story brick building by J. Gallier & Co., architects, are in the Southeastern Architectural Archive at Tulane University. NOCD 1856.

[12] Howell Cobb (1815-1868) was elected to the United States Congress in 1842 and in 1849 became Speaker of the House. After serving a term as governor of Georgia, he returned to Congress in 1855. In 1857 President James Buchanan named Cobb secretary of the treasury. *DAB*.

[13] William H. Bell, an architect, lived on Apollo (now Carondelet) at the corner of St. Andrew. Many of his drawings are in the plan books at the Notarial Archives. NOCD 1859.

[14] Dr. Beale's *Grand Illuminated Historic Voyage of Dr. Kane's Exploration* was exhibited at Armory Hall. *Daily Picayune*, Mar. 28, 1857.

Quite a large audience and many points of interest, brilliant coloring and the usual display of gunpowder trickery.

April 1   67° 72° 67°

Hot & dry in the morning, South East wind, threatening clouds. Storm of wind at 2½ burying the city in "dust and ashes." Cold rains soon after from West and North.

Wrote to Mr. Ammi B. Young acknowledging the receipt of the Box of Plans from the Hone. Secretary of the Treasury. It is a noble work consisting of 31 Numbers, full folio, of fine line engravings of Plans, elevations, sections & details of all the Public Buildings in progress under the Treasury Department, or most of them, and 2 Volumes of Specifications. Mr. & Mrs. Penn returned this morning from Washington. Mr. Penn brings his Commission reinstating him as Commissioner as well as Disbursing Agent, with the additional $8 per diem, now $16. A pretty snug office with little to do, for which he is indebted to his indefatigable friend John Slidell....

After tea went to witness the imposing ceremony of "Consecration" at the new Jewish Synagogue. I was late and the great Iron gates were locked, but I communicated with my friend inside and gained admittance. The music was fine. The address by J. K. Gutheim quite eloquent.[15] The ceremonials simple and impressive, decidedly Mosaic. The arrangement of the interior similar to that of the great & ancient Synagogue at Amsterdam of which I have drawings. The Galleries were crowded with Hebrew beauty, the floor below with the gentlemen and the dignitaries of the house of God, all, including the minister, wearing their hats the whole time....

April 3   63° 66° 65°

Hot sunshine. Very dry & clouds of dust. N. East wind.

"Seamen's Home" on my way to the office. Mr. Day called about taking the water from the waterwork's Company for wetting brick, Making mortar &c. I directed him to connect with a 3 inch indestructible Pipe which can hereafter be extended into the court yard of the building for general use. Drawing after dinner and writing Specifications until near midnight. Very weary and eyes ache badly.

April 4   65° 67° 69°

Fine dry & very dusty. East wind, gathering clouds....

After dinner at the "Home" again for an hour or two. 12 Bricklayers laying in foundations fast to secure the benefit of the dry weather. Good stiff clay and firm bottom in the Trenches....

April 7   54° 60° 62°

Cool air from North East. Clear sunshine.

Mr. Low called with the Plans & Specifications, approved of. He leaves this afternoon to be absent a month. In the meantime he authorizes me to get in Estimates for his work, make arrangements for introducing the water works, surveying property &c. &c. Called upon Mr. T. Murray, builder, to meet me at the office tomorrow morning to get the Plans &c. for an Estimate.[16] After dinner at the "Home" with the Contractor &c. Rejected two Cast Iron Columns for bad materials & workmanship. Foundations going on well....

April 9   56° 57° 60°

Sudden change in the night. Storm of wind & rain from the North East this morning. Cleared off towards noon....

After dinner at the "Home" and on return the Contractor called on me and I went to his office and concluded to increase the footing under the Granite Pillar to 12 Bricks Square and under the Cast Iron Columns to 10 Bricks....

April 13   52° 57° 62°

Frost in the night and thermometer at 6 this morning 46°. Bright sunny sky. Cool air from N. West to West.

Met Mr. W. K. Day at the Seamen's Home at 9 O'clock. Foundations & sill course are laid and the first installment of $2000 less % due to contractor, which I gave him a certificate for this morning, and presented my Report of the Work to J. W. Stanton the President. The line of work thus far is decidedly better than is usual here on buildings of that class. I also notified the Contractor, Mr. Day, in writing that I would on no account accept the two Cast Iron Columns first delivered on the ground. After dinner went to the "Home" walls of the first story going up fast. Engaged to meet the Iron Contractors about the 2 Columns tomorrow morning....

---

[15] Rabbi James Koppel Gutheim (1817-1886) was a native of Menne, Westphalia, Germany. W. E. Myers, *The Israelites of Louisiana* (New Orleans, [1905?]), 30-32.

[16] Thomas Murray built a house at Jackson and St. Charles for Sewell T. Taylor and an icehouse for Stanton & Co. in 1853.

April 14 · · · · · 54° 60° 59°

Clear and sunny. Fine fresh breeze from the North East.

Met the Iron masters at the "Home" at ½ past 8.

Mr. Wheeler brought Mr. Grinnell of the firm of Leeds & Co. to act as his referee.[17] They seemed disposed to maintain with obstinacy the strength and excellence of the casting which I rejected on the ground of flaws & defective workmanship. But I explained to them fully & plainly my reasons for rejection, my calculations &c. and Mr. Wheeler agreed at once to withdraw the obnoxious casting. My objections to the other were only on the ground of finish not on defects that might impair its strength, so that it may be used in a position where the blemishes, which are not of great magnitude, will not shew. The effect of this little controversy will be to secure us superior Ironwork....

April 17 · · · · · 66° 69° 72°

High wind from the South East. Gathering clouds. Threatening rain.

This is one of my numerous Birth days, and I hoped to withdraw for the day from business and ruralize awhile, and pause while passing another of life's milestones. But there is no arresting the wheels of a vocation such as mine, so I must let them roll on. Went round by the "Home" on my way to the office. On application to Major Beauregard he kindly agreed to let Mr. Eastman have some 50.000 Bricks from our large pile, to be returned when the supplies from over the Lake begin to come in. We are out of Lake Brick at the "Home" and I discovered yesterday that the water in the Lake is ranging so low that schooners cannot come in with the usual supplies so I told Mr. Eastman yesterday that I would apply to the Major for a loan of sufficient to keep his numerous customers in material, & prevent the stoppage of several works in town, which he at once assented to....

April 18 · · · · · 72° 74° 74°

Hot dry and very dusty. Threatening clouds and gleams of sunshine.

Went to the "Home" before going to the office, and found every thing going on well. Very busy indeed at the office for awhile then Mr. Renshaw came by appointment and I went with him to Parelli's. He resisted my objections very obstinately but finally gave way. He will make the alterations and then call at the Custom House to let me know. Seamen's Home again in the afternoon. On the way Mr. Slark met me and showed me over his very handsome house and grounds which are arranged & furnished with great elegance.

April 23 · · · · · 57° 59° 60°

Cold harsh wind from North East, clouds of dust, clear sky.

Answered Mrs. Huling's letter. Instructions from the Treasury Department occasion many reductions in the pay of our subordinate employees, such as sub-overseers, stonecutters, laborers &c. and the discharge of our Foreman of Carpenters which I regret much. But changes are inevitable with an in-coming administration, when a shew of economy must be preserved to cover the widening of political leakages. Men must be paid for political services, no matter how incompetent for civil duties and the transaction of regular business. At the "Home" after dinner. Supply of brick and sand running short, pity this dry fine building weather.

April 25 · · · · · 60° 65° 64°

Mild & cloudy. South East wind. Rain in prospect.

At the "Home" on the way to the office. Found a load of yellow Salmon Brick which I notified the Contractor to have removed from the ground immediately. Again at the Building after dinner. Front Piers up and caps nearly set.

April 28 · · · · · 65° 70° 70°

Mild air from the West after warm fertilizing showers in the night, just enough to soak the thirsty earth and give a new impetus to the very backward vegetation.

Mr. Pierre Soulé came to the office, and I took him over the works, shewing him the Statuary in Italian Marble, machinery &c. &c. Took Emily and Tommy with me to the "Home" in the evening, and down to breathe the fresh air from the river &c. &c.

[17] J. F. Wheeler of the firm of Wheeler, Geddes & Co. operated the Shakspeare Iron Foundry at 208 Girod Street. Edward Grinnell lived on Foucher (now Constance) near Poeyfarre. NOCD 1856, 1857.

April 29 67° 70° 72°

Rains in the night & this morning. Pleasant air from South East, cleared off at noon.

At the "Home" after dinner, getting along well. At 9 P.M. went down to the St. Louis Cathedral to witness the marriage ceremony of Major Beauregard's sister. The richly frescoed Interior was highly illuminated and the Organ pealed thro' the vaulted cieling in rolling harmonies.[18] Numerous spectators and a short but very beautiful ceremonial. The bright moon hung low when I reached home again.

April 30 69° 69° 70°

Dark, frowning clouds, muttering thunder, dashes of rain and fresh breeze from the South East....

Proposals from C. C. Bier & Co. to do the Plumber work required at Mr. Low's house for $425.[19] Ticket to the "Orleans" from Major Beauregard. Mme. Bourgeois' Benefit, a brilliant affair and the house filled to suffocation. Delagrave's voice was superb.[20] At one time the boards presented a perfect hecatomb of roses, and voices innumerable fanned the dense and steamy air....

May 3 68° 69° 66°

Sunday. High wind from North and North West. Dashes of rain dark rolling clouds, muttering.

Got very wet in going to market before breakfast, and the morning was altogether so inclement that we resolved not to go to church for once. Mr. Calrow has lent me a dozen of J. Arnout's Lithotints of European Cathedrals, Litchfield, St. Paul's, Gloucester &c. & fine continental examples.[21] They are charming. I spread them out again & again. Our pigmy efforts at Gothic are in comparison as a child's wax figure to the Venus of Canova. Cold gloomy rains all the evening.

May 5 69° 71° 75°

Lovely weather. Mild air from South West.

After dinner young Mr. Harrod met me by appointment at the "Home" and spent an hour or so with me on the works then took him home to shew him those fine "Cathedrals." At night a children's party at Mr. Paul Cook's, with a very pleasant gathering of older people. Early supper for the young ones, who had a charming time. Good music, and dancing by both young & old. The latter sat down to an elegant table prepared by "Maurice" towards midnight, and laid in the wide upper gallery enclosed for the occasion.[22] Tommy's first large party was an era with him & he held himself up bravely resisting all our eloquence to induce him to go home before "the rest." Towards 1 O'clock tired nature could endure no longer, and he sunk into a profound sleep in my lap, and the company separating soon after....

May 14 77° 81° 81°

Clouds and sunshine. High wind from the South.

At the "Home" after dinner. Framing of the second story going on well. Iron Columns of dining room set, and putting on the girder 10 x 16, beautiful Lumber.

May 16 78° 80° 78°

Dark clouds, thunder storms, and hot steamy air from South East.

Walked down with Perry Nugent. He is just about building a store in connection with Mr. E. Peale.[23] The two together about $27.000. The Contract is given to Mr. W. K. Day, without an Architect. I made some very plain comments on that system, but told him that I thought him safer in the hands of Mr. Day, than those of any other builder in New Orleans. Mr. Slark is doing the same thing.

---

[18] Emilia Toutant (d. 1858) married Mortimer Belly of New Orleans. The frescoes were executed by Alexander Boulet when the cathedral was rebuilt in its present form. *ENOA*; *Daily Picayune*, May 3, 1857.

[19] The firm C. C. Bier & Co., plumbers, was located at 95 Camp St. NOCD 1857.

[20] A benefit for Mlle. Amelie Bourgeois was held at the Orleans Theatre. She sang the role of Odetta in *Charles VI* and Azusena in *Trovatore*. Delagrave was a tenor who sang at the Orleans Theatre. *Daily Picayune*, Apr. 30, 1857; *Bee*, Nov. 6, 1856.

[21] James Calrow, architect, designed the Albert Hamilton Brevard house at First and Chestnut streets and with W. K. Day built the Alexander Harris house at Prytania and Jackson. NONA, W. H. Peters, Jan. 3, 1857.

[22] A. Maurice, cakes, was located on Canal at the corner of Bourbon and on Royal at the corner of St. Louis. NOCD 1854.

[23] Perry Nugent of the firm of Robson & Allen, commercial merchants, lived at 63 Constance Street. Elijah Peale (1810-1874) of the firm Thomas, Henderson & Peale lived on Coliseum between Euterpe and Polymnia, across Coliseum Square from the Whartons. He was the ruling elder of the Prytania Street Presbyterian Church. NOCD 1856; Louis Voss, *Presbyterianism in New Orleans* (New Orleans, 1931), 201; U.S. Census, La., Orleans Parish, 1860.

St. Louis Cathedral interior with frescoes by Alexander Boulet, Vieux Carré Survey, Historic New Orleans Collection.

Henry Lonsdale residence, Louis E. Cormier, photographer, Illustrated Sunday Magazine, *ca. 1910 (1974.25.3.708 ii).*

The "Goodrichs" know better. They employ Mr. Howard, an excellent Archt. & Superintendent.[24]...

At Parelli's by appointment, at noon. Model greatly improved. He called yesterday at the office to say that the changes I had indicated had been completed, and I am glad to find with the happiest effect....

Sunday. Cool North West wind after the storms of the night, thick clouds and light rain.

Emily felt too tired to go to church. So I took a stroll into Lafayette as far as Mr. Lonsdale's new house, now near completion.[25]

[24] H. L. Goodrich of the firm of Goodrich & Co., wholesale grocers, contracted with Little & Middlemiss, builders, for their stores at Tchoupitoulas and Common streets. Howard and Diettel were the architects. NONA, G. Rareshide, Oct. 9, 1857.

[25] Henry T. Lonsdale (1809-1869) was a coffee broker. His house at the corner of Prytania and Third streets was built by J. K. Collins & Co., architects and builders, at a cost of $30,000. The house is still standing. NOCD 1855; *Daily Picayune,* Dec. 26, 1869; *Daily Crescent,* Oct. 21, 1856.

A huge, tasteless pile of Bricks, Marble, Iron and Stucco, but fine foliage around it and a sweet spot opposite with a garden as you seldom meet out of England. Walks, lawn, shrubbery and flower beds exquisitely arranged. The latter redolent with Sweet Peas, blue larkspurs, Nasturtiums and Centaureas, besides hundreds of species which belong exclusively to this latitude. Gardens, beautiful dwellings and the richest foliage every where in that charming Faubourg. I paused opposite Trinity (Bishop Polk's Church) while they were singing the "Laudate" with a fine Organ, and I felt more than ever impressed with the grandeur and beauty of our incomparable Liturgy. I fear I have yielded too far. There is a barrenness and inanity about every other ritual that I know of except the Romish and that is too idolatrous and absurd to be thought of for a moment.

June 2   75° 76° 78°

Clear & brilliant sky. Hot sun. Cool N. West wind....

Emily & Tommy came down at noon and I took them to the Daguerreotype Saloon. Had 2 Taken of Tommy, 3 of Emily & 1 of myself. All good and nicely finished in mat frames, &c....

June 11   81° 84° 86°

Very hot indeed, dry and dusty beyond measure. S. West wind....

The Contractor has taken care today to have good work done on Mr. Low's masonry and supplied good brick. A positive rejection, pulling down &c. well timed has a great moral effect....

June 19   76° 78° 81°

Very dry & clear. Cool wind from the North....

We went on to Parelli's to see the model of the Statue for Mary Renshaw's Tomb, which is now complete for the Marble. It is a graceful charming composition & eminently successful both as to likeness & design.

June 20   78° 81° 83°

Very hot sunshine, bright sky, cool north wind.

Took ten grains of blue mass last night and stayed at home today. Finished up a set of drawings of Barnstable New Custom House for young Harrod. Worked hard at them from 9 until near dinner at 3. But I am weak enough today....

June 22   81° 82° 82°

Hot & gathering clouds. East wind.

Letter from Mr. Bryant & roll of Plans of two works going on under his Superintendent. They are franked by the much talked of N. P. Banks.[26] Speaker of the house & M. C....

July 4   75° 78° 80°

Eighty first anniversary of American Independence. Our works are suspended. Throughout the city and suburbs pleasure and excitement will be the order of the day. And a charming North East wind is blowing which greatly reduced the heat of a glaring sun. No vestige of vapour stains the sky. I took Tommy to market with us, and sad to say our breakfast table was not cleared off until 10 O'clock. I then went to work on a set of Plans for the proposed Hotel on Lafayette Square, 150 x 150 and four stories high, and by 3 O'clock I had arranged the general features of the Plan and principal Front.

In this part of town the day passed as quietly as a Sabbath and in a walk with Tommy after dinner the streets were still, and free from excitement. The distant peal of cannon and the fireworks at night alone marked the Jubilee. The suburbs, however, and the populous 2nd. and 3rd. are the rallying points on Fete days.[27]

July 8   82° 86° 84°

Hot, & very dry. Dust again, annoying still air from North East.

At Mr. Low's before breakfast. Nine large & valuable produce stores were destroyed by fire between 12 & 3, just opposite the South East angle of the New Custom House. Our scaffolding was in some danger & we had the buckets, hose &c. all manned in case of emergency. It was a grand "spectacle" but extravagantly costly. Wall after wall fell outward with a loud crash, and hot as it was the firemen deserved great encomiums for subduing it as soon as they did.[28]...

[26] Nathaniel P. Banks (1816-1894), a member of Congress from Massachusetts, was Speaker of the House (1856-1857) and governor of Massachusetts (1858-1861). During the Civil War, he became a major general in the Union army and succeeded Gen. Benjamin Butler in command of Union troops occupying New Orleans in 1862. *DLB.*

[27] The second district was the old Creole area, today known as the French Quarter, extending from Canal Street to Esplanade Avenue. The third district extended downriver from Esplanade Avenue to the city limit.

[28] The fire began in a grocery store on Front St. (now South Peters), between Common and Gravier, and spread to adjacent buildings. *Daily True Delta*, July 8, 1857.

July 22 83° 86° 88°at 2 P.M. 84°

Very Hot sunshine, hot with a capital "H." Pleasant breeze from South East....

Finished my Annual Report of the works at New Custom House for the Fiscal Year, ending June 30. 1857. With Cash Statement for the same. And Estimate of appropriation of $350.000 to keep us moving thro' the F. Year 1858-59, to be transmitted to the Secretary of the Treasury. My books show an expenditure for the year just past of $342.932.84 and Total from the first $2.116.336.99....

July 23 83° 83° 83°

Shady clouds. Pleasant West wind. Showers at 10 to 2.

We are in the prime of our fruit season, figs, peaches, melons &c. For some time past Tommy has had his rich luscious figs every morning before breakfast fresh from the dewy gardens at Bouligny. Then in the evening he must have his ice cream with equal regularity. All cooling, however, & good for him, as his superfluous health attests....

July 24 78½° 81° 82°

Heavy rains in the night. Showery this morning. Gloomy clouds. South West wind....

Letter from Mr. T. Adams authorizing me to put Gas into the Seamen's Home and do certain Extra specified work which I had suggested. Replied immediately and gave Mr. Loeffler directions for laying the Pipes &c.[29] Went to see young Harrod. Has just finished an excellent drawing of the New Marine Hospital. He bids fair now to become one of the most accomplished architectural draughtsmen in the City. Called at the "Home" on my way to dinner. Flooring of 4th. Story & cementwork of blocking course going on, & grouting of store Floors. Every thing satisfactory from basement to Belvidere....

August 1 79° 83° 80°

Sultry, clouds & sunshine, showers at noon and in the afternoon with thunder and lightening....

---

[29] Thomas A. Adams was president of the Crescent Mutual Insurance Company and a trustee of the Seamen's Home. He lived on Prytania between Third and Fourth. Charles Loeffler of the firm Oehmichen & Loeffler, gas fitters, at 142 Chartres St. NOCD 1856, 1859.

Busy at the office closing up accounts for July public and private. I find I have received from the Government up to this time for my Services at the New Custom House $15.821.68, but my additional engagements in town have added materially to my income and kept me always in contact with the busy world around me....

August 14 80° 76° 79°

Mild & cloudy, with broad masses of sunshine. South wind. Rain set in at 10. Very heavy at noon & much lightening....

Just before I left the N. Custom House I had a severe fall by stepping hastily on a slippery plank. No great injury, however, but as rude a shock as is usual under the circumstances. It prevented me from going to the "Home" in the afternoon, but Mr. Calrow came to tell me that the lightening struck the Flagstaff and broke off six feet of it. It stunned the head-carpenter but fortunately did him no serious injury.

August 15 80° 83° 83°

Clouds & sunshine, distant thunder, South Wind.

Finished the last of my Annual Papers today at the Office. At the "Home" after dinner. Every thing going on rapidly. The lightening yesterday was evidently attracted by the Iron Bolt which secured the gilded Ball and Truck. It has left a very zigzag track plainly marked down the Staff on the Paintwork to the roof of the Belvidere where all traces of its course are lost, at the top of the South East corner post. Today has passed without rain.

August 23 80° 82° 83°

Sunday. Clouds & sunshine, pleasant air from the North East.

Emily, Tommy & I went in the morning to hear Dr. Palmer, who preached a wonderfully fine sermon from Zechariah 7.8 to 13.[30] Indeed I think the finest I ever heard. The church was quite full which proves his popularity. His style is forensic, clear, forcible, connected, more like my recollections of Lord Brougham as a counsellor than any one I ever heard....

---

[30] The Rev. Benjamin Morgan Palmer (1818-1902), a native of South Carolina, was installed as pastor of the First Presbyterian Church on Lafayette Square in December 1856. He was one of the city's most influential and distinguished clergymen. Thomas Cary Johnson, *Life and Letters of Benjamin Morgan Palmer* (Richmond, Va., [ca. 1906]).

Benjamin Morgan Palmer from The Life and Letters of Benjamin Morgan Palmer.

September 12   78° 82° 82°

Hot and dry, East wind. Nights very cold. Showery from 1 P.M. all the evening.

Visited the "Home" on my way to dinner, and found the top story finished both plastering & 2 coat[s] of Paint, looks remarkably well. Slate hearths set; Plumber work going on well &c. &c.

September 13   79° 76° 81°

Sunday. Clouds & sunshine, passing showers, South East wind.

Mr. Duncan preached two fine sermons on, "Draw nigh to God and he will draw nigh unto you." The Miss Cooks & Edwin went with us in the evening to witness the baptism of a lady which would have passed off unusually well but for a female friend of the lady who stood up with her on the platform, and who at the conclusion of the ceremony very absurdly took to screaming & fainting and hystericizing generally, to the great discomposure of the audience, and disturbing the impression produced by the preceding solemnities.

September 18   81° 84° 83°

Hot and steamy, South East wind.

Mrs. Abbott called at breakfast time to see if I could get her son, an excellent young man of 22, into the Custom House. She is feeble & helpless, with another child of 10 years, and the eldest supports the family. I called upon the Collector and urged the case strongly.[31] He received the application with much apparent interest, and will I think respond to it....

September 21   76° 80° 81°

Bright & pleasant. Cool North East wind. A most grateful change.

Visit from Mr. Da Silva to shew me a fine specimen of the ancient Hebrew silver shekel which he had just received. A silver coin of the size & about the value of a "half dollar." On one side the olive branch beautifully cast with the Hebrew inscription "Shekel of Israel" on the other, an urn with flame, and around it in Hebrew, "Jerusalem the Holy."...

September 22   75½° 78° 79°

Cool & breezy, light clouds, North East wind to North....

Emily & Tommy came to the office. Went to the Fancy stores in Chartres Street, made an investment for Tommy's birth day tomorrow, then home to dinner in the omnibus. The fine breeze today is very refreshing, tho' being due north at noon, rather trying to thin southern blood. Months have passed away without a breeze, save once or twice. Day by day and night by night, the same still, stagnant calm. No motion to carry off the gases of a populous, damp and almost tropical city. Still the general health has been good, and the West India plague, yellow fever, or whatever it may be named has been kept out — by Quarantine. This, rigidly enforced would save New Orleans a world of sorrow, yet there are hundreds so infatuated as still to deny its efficacy....

31 Possibly Lucinda Williford Abbott (1815-1866) who lived at the corner of Delord (now Howard Ave.) and Liberty streets. *Times*, Jan. 20, 1866. Francis H. Hatch (1815-1884) was collector of customs for the Port of New Orleans (1857-1862). *Daily Picayune*, July 20, 1884; Wilson, *The U.S. Customhouse in New Orleans*, 84.

September 28   77° 82° 82°

Dry and clear. East wind....

Saw A. B. Cammack just from England in splendid physical condition, and prepared to meet the great financial crisis now bursting over the land.[32] The dispatches from the North are bad, bad, bad.

At the "Home" the painting is in good progress.

October 2   72° 76° 76°

Pleasant air from the Eastward. Sunny sky.

Very busy indeed at the office, but am keeping well up with my work. Letters and Dispatches from the North calling for assistance in this great financial crisis. After dinner walked out with Tommy to see the finishing up of Mr. Harrison's handsome house on the other side of the Square.[33] It was built by Mr. Day 10 years ago, and he has just completed a thorough revision of it. The building is as sound as when quite new.

October 9   68° 71° 72°

Fine & clear. East wind.

Tho' warm in the sun I began today to walk up to dinner for the Season. So farewell to break bone omnibuses. Times are getting darker & darker & the financial clouds bred at the North are beginning to throw gloomy shadows over us here. One of our heaviest Contractors at the North, Messrs. Cooper, Hewitt & Co. write today that the "money market there is extinct" and express great anxiety about the proceeds of "Silas Grunman's" Beams &c. now at the Levee for us.[34] So I had the Iron inspected without delay & then signed & mailed Vouchers to them for the pretty sum of $12.852.83....

October 10   72° 74° 75°

Very warm & sunny. East wind.

Capt. Barrett of the "Sultana" has arrived with a large shipment of marble for us. He tells me that they sailed by many corpses of the ill fated "Central America," floating on the wide open ocean.[35] A sad sight indeed, but due ultimately to the money loving spirit of the age, that barters "strength" for "gain."...

October 12   73° 76° 76°

Warm & sunny. East wind....

Mortuary returns for the week 123 deaths altogether 12 of which of "Yellow Fever" evidently the ordinary "fever" of New Orleans, not the "plague" of the tropics.

October 14   72° 73° 75°

Cool North wind, cloudy inclining to rain.

At home carpenters &c. repairing & renovating. Emily putting down & fixing up, and the whole house in a state of unrest.

At the church the work going on well. The painters priming &c. At the "Seamen's Home," finishing up and preparing to turn over the work complete. Down town the "Mechanics' & Traders' Bank" & "Union" suspended, and others preparing to do likewise.[36] And any number of large Commission houses trembling on the verge of ruin.

October 15   68° 70° 74°

Bright & clear. North East wind.

Signed a certificate in favor of W. K. Day for $400 on his contract for fencing &c. around the church, which is going on well & the painting looks beautifully, I selected the color this morning. Heavy runs on the Banks today. The "Bank of New Orleans" has gone into liquidation, so that I must consider my stock for the present extinct, which is hard as I invested purely for safety, and to assist my family in case of need.[37] But it may be well yet....

[32] Addison B. Cammack was a prominent cotton broker associated with J. P. Whitney & Co. NOCD 1859. Fevered commercial speculation led to a business panic in August 1857. In the ensuing nationwide depression, businesses dafaulted on loans and banks failed, creating widespread financial distress.

[33] Jilson P. Harrison of the firm Payne & Harrison, commission merchants, lived on Coliseum Street at Race.

[34] Peter Cooper (1791-1883) and Abram S. Hewitt (1822-1903), his son-in-law, were iron manufacturers. Cooper's Cooper Union was chartered in New York in 1859 for the education of the working class.

[35] The steamer *Central America* sank after being struck by a hurricane in the Atlantic on September 11.

[36] The Mechanics and Traders Bank was at 101 Canal Street and the Union Bank was at 123 Canal Street.

[37] The Bank of New Orleans was on St. Charles at Union. NOCD 1857. All three banks recovered from this scare and continued in business.

October 16   59° 63° 65°

High wind from North East, cold blustering and dusty. Clear sky. The run on the Banks has ceased and confidence reviving....

October 17   62° 66° 66°

Delightful weather. Bright & health inspiring. Cool North wind but very dusty....

Sent off my report of the settlement of walls at New Custom House & Quarterly returns to the Secretary of the Treasury. The mean settlement during the past year is less that 1³/₄ inch and the maximum settlement from the first is a fraction over 19 inches, the ratio diminishing every year. At the Church, the fence and banquette are complete. Nothing to be done now but inside levelling & paving. Amongst business men the feeling is improving fast. After dinner at the "Home" nothing now remains to be done but graining Store Doors, marbling mantles, hanging Bells &c. &c.

October 21   59° 62° 64°

Cold North East wind. Dry and dusty. Clear sky....

Note to Messrs. Gallier Turpin & Co. introducing Mr. Hauvelman who comes recommended to me by my old friend Martin E. Thompson, Architect, of New York, and desires a situation in an Architect's Office. The feeling is so strong against Mr. Buckner Prest. pro tem. of the "Louisiana Bank" for his cold hearted policy during the present crisis that he stands in dread of personal violence....

October 29   58° 59° 58°

Cold air from the North East, threatening clouds....

Very busy today, and very unwell. After dinner went over Judge McCaleb's elegant new three story mansion on Apollo Street with the Builder Mr. Stewart.[38]

October 31   60° 63° 65°

Very fine weather indeed. West wind....

Lieut. Weitzel came up from the Fort, and brought for me a magnificent "Red Snapper" at least 2 feet long, and killed since 12

last night.[39] I sent it home immediately to be put on the ice for tomorrow. This fish is quite equal to "Salmon trout," and the flesh has a rich rose tinge, shotted with crimson outside. After dinner went over to Mr. W. K. Day's office &c. &c. The last day of October finds all my operations for the summer, outside my Government Office, fully completed according to contract, and I have reason to think in every way to the satisfaction of the interested parties. The Trustees of the "Sailor's Home" seem much pleased with their building, and the members of the church, as far as I have heard an expression of opinion are unanimous in their approbation of the way in which I have finished up their grounds &c. All this is very pleasing and I have every reason to be grateful for the success that has attended my summer work and the blessings of health & vigor that have attended me and my family thro' it. I have also been able to keep up the various business of the office, during Major Beauregard's absence, in its completeness, and every thing has met full & prompt decision.

November 14   60° 63° 64°

Very fine & clear. North East wind.

Went over Mr. James' mansion on Tivoli Circle with the architect L. E. Reynolds.[40] The inside very elaborate indeed. The Corinthian Caps made 10 minutes higher than the order, and, for interior work, look much better. We have treated the example of "Andronicus Cyrhestes" at the Custom House, with similar freedom, and with evident advantage. The house is undergoing entire renovation with 4 coats of Zinc paint on all woodwork admirably laid.

November 22   53° 58° 59°

Sunday. Lovely weather. West wind.

A loud alarm of fire last night turned out to be a long two story wooden Block on Magazine Street 3 Squares above us. Returning from market this morning I found Ed. Tisdale one of the sufferers and invited him to take breakfast with us, so we hastened home together.[41] It was lucky that I happened to go round that way, for his prospects for

[38] Theodore Howard McCaleb (1810-1864) was judge of the U.S. District Court and a law professor at the University of Louisiana (now Tulane). *DLB*.

[39] Godfrey Weitzel (d. 1884) was from Ohio. Heitman, *Historical Register*.

[40] Andrew Broadus James (d. 1869), a dry goods merchant, lived on St. Charles, corner Tivoli (now Lee) Circle. *Daily Picayune*, Dec. 28, 1869; NONA, T. O. Stark, May 23, 1854; NOCD 1857.

[41] A fire that started in a house at the corner of Magazine and Richard streets destroyed the building and its contents and damaged the upper portions of some adjoining apartment buildings. Ed. Tisdale lived in one of the apartments. *Daily Picayune*, Nov. 23, 1857.

coffee and comforts were but slender amid the smoking ruins that he had been groping amongst since 2 in the morning, helping his fellow sufferers to save their property & movables &c. &c....

November 24   48° 51° 52°

Pleasant weather. Quite cool. Wind North East....

Pleasant walk up with Mr. Low. At the "Seamen's Home" after dinner to examine kitchen range & flue &c. at the request of Mr. Stanton. Then went to see the Contractor &c. Drawing after tea until abt. 9.

November 25   50° 54° 56°

Beautiful weather. Cool wind from North East....

After tea went over for Mrs. G. M. Pinckard and then with her and Emily to the Prayer meeting, which was unusually interesting.[42] It cannot be concealed the Baptist church principles are taking a strong hold upon this community, the simplicity of their observances, their purity of doctrine, and especially the giving prominence and a sphere of active labor to each individual member, all are elements of strength, and greatly affect the "average mind" without the concomitant aid of excitement, revivals &c. especially where the[re] is no anterior attachment to other systems, such, for instance, as that which involves an established liturgy, diocesan ordination &c. &c.

December 10   52° 52½° 54°

It has cleared off very cold and bright with a clear joyous atmosphere & North East wind.

Called upon the Hone. J. C. Breckenridge the Vice President at the St. Charles, with a relative of his and had a very pleasant visit, but I made it short as he leaves again for Washington in the Mail Boat this evening.[43]

December 11   51° 54° 54°

Heavy white frost during the night. Cold & clear today. Wind North to North East.

A dispatch announcing the suspension of payment at the "Treasury Department" in the morning Papers excites much enquiry. I think it applies only to certain works of acknowledged inutility. After dinner went to see the new works in the Fourth Dist. handsome dwelling houses &c.[44]

December 14   50° 54° 57°

Fine and clear with chilly air from the North East....

President's message is out today with admirable suggestions on the Banking operations of the country, and recommends to Congress a loan to provide for any temporary deficiency that may occur in the "Treasury Department." By the by, the dispatch the other day stating that the "Treasury" had suspended turned out, as I supposed, to be erroneous.

December 16   55° 60° 60°

Thanksgiving Day and works at the N. Custom House suspended. Lovely weather. North East wind.

Got Ellen & Tommy up early & took them with me to market to buy the "Thanksgiving Turkey" &c. &c. Found every thing abundant, good, and thanks to the returning good sense of the community, quite cheap. Indeed while our recent troubles are to be deplored they will certainly have one good effect, to arrest the wild career of extravagance and profuse expenditure that have so long been the bane of the country. People of moderate means will now be able to live in superior comfort and free from corroding anxiety....

December 18   55° 56° 58°

Cool air from North West, light clouds.

The failure yesterday tells heavily on factors' business today, and money is hard to reach on the highest grades of paper. Commenced a

[42] Sarah A. Pinckard (b. 1809) was the wife of wealthy planter George M. Pinckard (ca. 1799-1864), who also was president of the Bank of New Orleans. The Pinckards were neighbors of the Whartons at the corner of Coliseum and Polymnia streets. *Daily Picayune*, Jan. 19, 1864; U.S. Census, La., Orleans Parish, 1860.

[43] John C. Breckinridge (1821-1875) served as James Buchanan's vice president (1857-1861). He was an unsuccessful presidential candidate in 1860 and later served in the Confederate army.

[44] Among houses built in the Fourth District in 1857 were those of Thomas R. Chew at Magazine and First; Joseph W. Boyle and Nathaniel Williamson, both by George Purves, on Jackson between Magazine and Constance; Lawrence G. Bien on Camp, between Philip and First, by Joseph Moorehouse; and Nels Anderson on Fourth, between Magazine and Camp, by John Cude.

Turkey peddler in New Orleans, Hyde, engraver, Frank Leslie's Illustrated Newspaper, *December 12, 1885 (1983.187).*

report for the "Committee on Education" to urge the immediate construction of a new School-house in the 7th. Precinct at a cost of $12.000.

December 22   51° 51° 52°

Cool air from the North West, light clouds.

We are not receiving our usual monthly remittance from the Department at the proper time, which creates the impression that the U.S. Commissioner of Customs is awaiting the fate of the Treasury Note Bill now before Congress.

December 25   44° 46° 48°

Christmas Day. Cold north west wind & grey clouds but dry and not unpleasant.

Went myself to market to lay in the Christmas dinner which entailed a free and easy breakfast until 10, when I sat down to my Plans &c., and the sun in the meantime beginning to shine cheerily in at the dining room window. Drew until dinner. Then a walk with Tommy in the evening....

December 29   60° 62° 61°

Gloomy rains. South East wind, to South West.

Finished the report of the Committee on Education increasing the recommendation to an appropriation of $33.000 for building a school house in each of the 4 districts, in consequence of the action taken at a called meeting last evening. I have just read with as much interest as a school boy when he first gets hold of Robinson Crusoe, Dr. Kane's narrative of his Arctic explorations in '53, '54 & '55.[45]...

December 30   55° 55° 54°

Dark & gloomy. Cold rains from the North East. Dripping, dripping, until about 2, when the rain stopped but dull leaden clouds still obscured the sky.

The Treasury Note Bill has passed, and we received notice today that our requisition for $15.000 for December was referred to the accounting officer for transmission. This with our balance on hand will see us safely thro' our disbursements.

December 31   51° 54° 56°

White frost in the night followed by a lovely day & pleasant elastic air from the North.

Very busy at the office closing up the accounts of the year &c. &c. Great activity at home and among the "rest of man and woman kind" in preparing for the festivities of tomorrow....

---

[45] Elisha K. Kane (1820-1857) was a naval officer and world explorer. He survived two winters in an ice-locked ship close to the North Pole before walking 1,300 miles to the nearest settlement. His account of his adventure, *Arctic Explorations in the Years 1853, '54, '55* (Philadelphia, 1856), sold 65,000 copies the first year.

January 1   56° 60° 62°

The new Year opens with a light springlike air from the East, and a dappled sky with gleams of sunshine streaming thro' the crevices.

We commenced the year rather leisurely with a 9 O'clock breakfast but our late vigils last night fully justified it. In no city that I know of is so much genuine pleasure drawn [from] the custom of "New Year's visits" as in this....

Joyousness & good humor were in the ascendant every where, and the streets were gay without boisterousness, or any approach whatever that I saw to indecorum or visible intemperance, & the same remark was made by one of our ex-aldermen friends who habitually notices such things. Altogether I never spent a "happier New Year."

January 5   53° 54° 58°

Pleasant & cold. North wind.

Approved Mayer & McIntyre's Bill for Plumber Work at the "Home" as per Contract $290.[1]

Major Beauregard left yesterday for Pensacola, so that I am comparatively alone today at the office. Yesterday's payments in Bank amounted to over three millions. 3 prominent houses failed.

January 15   69° 72° 62°

Warm South wind. Threatening clouds. Heavy storm of wind and rain between 1 and 2 P.M. drove several vessels of large size from their moorings at the Levee, and continued to rain after the wind subsided....

January 16   55° 56° 58°

North wind. Cold with cloudy sky in the morning. Cleared off at noon very pleasant.

The tornado yesterday did a great deal of damage in a very short time. 8 lives are known to be lost. 40 ships & 3 steamers parted from their moorings and went across or down the river. Two steamers had their chimneys blown down. A Methodist church in Jefferson blown down, and more or less damage done in every quarter of the city.[2]...

---

[1] The firm of McIntyre & Mayer, plumbers, was located at 125 Camp Street. NOCD 1857.

[2] Jefferson City, incorporated by the state legislature in 1850, extended from Toledano Street to Joseph Street and centered approximately on Napoleon Avenue. It was annexed to New Orleans in 1870. *New Orleans Architecture*, 7:27.

1858

January 23   56° 60° 62°

Beautiful weather with North East wind, which rose high in the afternoon with clouds of dust.

Called at Mr. Renshaw's office about the Marble Block for his Statuary....

Emily, Tommy & Ellen came to the office at 2, and I took them to see Rosa Bonheur's famous picture "The Horse Fair" by far the finest production in its line that I ever saw.[3] It is simply "wonderful". It is warm breathing palpitating life, and bathed in floods of lucid sunshine.

January 25   65° 69° 68°

Rains in the night. Dull gloomy clouds, showers, and East wind this morning. Cleared off at noon with high wind from South East....

Took Major Beauregard to see Rosa Bonheur's picture. She has cast all scholastic conventionalism to the winds, and produced a magnificent expression of genuine "nature".

January 31   52° 54° 55°

Sunday. Gloomy and damp North East wind.

Our market was destroyed by fire last night, so we went this morning to St. Mary's and found everything I wanted of the best quality & cheap.[4]...

February 2   46° 50° 50°

Brilliant atmosphere. North West wind.

The Treasury Department is again responding to our requisitions for funds. We received the other day $15.000 in new Treasury Notes of the denominations of $1000 and $100, and Major Beauregard & Stevens have received $18.000 for the Forts, and the balance on hand was sufficient for the rolls of last month. So that our disbursements at the New Custom House have been undisturbed by the monetary troubles....

Charles Gayarré, Jules Lion, lithographer, between 1837 and 1847 (1970.11.119).

February 6   44° 50° 52°

White frost in the night. Beautiful weather today. North East wind.

Rosa Bonheur's Picture was largely attended today & I met several friends there, among the rest Mr. Charles Gayarré the historian of Louisiana, whose European travel & fine taste enable him to set a due Estimate upon such a work as this.[5] After dinner went to the "Home" at Mr. Stanton's request to see about placing the new cistern, as the Trustees have made a contract for completing the Pavement of the Court yard with German flagging. Tommy went with me and had a good time generally in seeing the departure of the evening boats, of which we had a fine view from the roof & Belvidere.

February 10   57° 56° 55°

Gloomy morning, wind due North. Cleared up in the middle of the day. Quite cold.

Spent an hour very pleasantly at the examination of the

---

[3] *The Horse Fair* by Rosa Bonheur was exhibited in the lecture room of Odd Fellows Hall under the patronage of the queen of England. *Daily Delta*, Jan. 23, 1858.

[4] The fire broke out at about 1:00 A.M. in a dry goods store at Magazine and St. Mary streets, destroying a number of other stores as well as the Magazine Market. *Daily Delta*, Feb. 1, 1858.

[5] Charles Gayarré (1805-1895), noted Louisiana historian and politician, served in the state legislature and was attorney general of Louisiana (1846-1853). His *History of Louisiana* in four volumes was first published in 1854-1866. *DLB*.

Washington School, James Earl Taylor, delineator, Frank Leslie's Illustrated Newspaper, *October 12, 1867 (1979.298 i,ii).*

Washington School.[6] After dinner went to see the house Messrs. Day & Calrow are building for Mr. Harris. The Columns on front and flank are up, and it promises to be the handsomest piece of work in the District. At Prayer meeting in the evening.

February 12   62° 65° 67°

Wind changed to South East, and comes up from the Gulf like a gush of tepid steam, with dull rain clouds. Heavy showers at noon.

[6] Washington School for girls was located on Magazine Street at the corner of Terpsichore, around the corner from Wharton's house. NOCD 1859.

Sent Francis for Tommy at 1 by the omnibus, and then took him to see the "Picture" for the last time. It will be taken for exhibition at St. Louis tomorrow. He wanted very much to see those wonderful horses again. I have studied this picture very carefully and while I discover new excellencies all the time I have yet to find the first serious blemish. There is an engraving of it by T. Landseer for distribution to subscribers at $50 & $40 for proofs. But an engraving, even the best, would be a poor substitute in the absence of the picture itself, about the same as the portrait of a friend after the removal by death of the original, but a melancholy satisfaction.

Second annual Mardi Gras parade of the Krewe of Comus, Henry M. Snyder, delineator, London Illustrated News, *May 8, 1858 (1959.172.12), gift of Harold Schilke and Boyd Cruise.*

February 16   55° 60° 61°

Still very fine indeed. North East wind.

The brightness of the weather brought out the "Mardi Gras" masks in swarms, and the streets were more thronged than they have been for years on this anniversary. Tommy had a lively time of it....

February 19   62° 64° 64°

Beautiful weather. South East wind, to North West.

At 1 I sent Francis home for Tommy, and took him to see the machinery at the chocolate maker's, the aviaries, the monument at Jackson Square, interior of St. Louis Cathedral, the picture stores & every thing worth seeing in the French quarter, not forgetting to visit "Bellanger's."[7] Then home to dinner.

---

7 Bellanger & Co., confectionary, Orleans corner Royal. NOCD 1857.

March 20   70° 73° 72°

Mild & cloudy. South East wind.

Call at the office from Mr. R. H. Browne to introduce Mr. Whitehead of Virginia, the gentleman for whom I am to superintend the erection of 4 new Warehouses.[8] Had a long conversation on the proposed details of the work &c. and recommended an immediate survey of the property, as an essential preliminary. The ground is about 122' by 100', going thro' block from Fulton to Front Street and about 25 feet from the corner of Julia Street....

---

8 Richard H. Browne (b. ca. 1830), an attorney with offices at 54 Camp Street, and his wife Sarah (b. ca. 1835) lived in the same house as James H. and Maria Low. U.S. Census, La., Orleans Parish, 1860; NOCD 1857. Colonel W. B. Whitehead's plantation was on the right bank of the river, about 33 miles above New Orleans. *Norman's Chart.*

Stereoscope with stereographic views, Jan White Brantley, photographer, 1999.

March 21   70° 74° 72°

Sunday. Mild & cloudy, with gleams of hot sunshine. A "soft summer air" from South East.

On my way from St. Mary's market before breakfast I called at the Sailor's Home. The Court yard, new cistern & leaders are all finished & every looked so clean & airy & substantial, and large groups of seamen about so orderly and well dressed that I felt well repaid for all the pains I have taken with the work....

March 24   63° 66° 67°

Beautiful weather. Cool air from North West.

Emily & Tommy came to the office at 1 and I took them to see some beautiful stereoscopes at Duhamel's.[9] They reproduce nature more exquisitely than by any other contrivance of art. I made a selection which I will complete at leisure....

March 27   65° 69° 70°

Lovely weather. East wind.

Emily's 23rd. Birthday. Did not go to the office as usual....

I got one of those stereoscopes for Emily, and the views I selected are perfectly exquisite. You are brought face to face with the reality,

[9] A stereoscope is an optical instrument with two lenses for creating a single, three-dimensional image from two photographs of the same site. The photographs, taken from slightly different angles, are mounted on a card which is inserted into the stereoscope for viewing. Clement Duhamel was an optician at 50 Chartres Street. NOCD 1859.

no painted shew but genuine air-encircled masses, the splendid alcoves of Elgin, the ivys of Kenilworth, the glorious trees over the old bridge at Warwick Castle, and the simple farm yard scene at Tintern Abbey are all apparently real, real. The last is beyond all description charming. No need hardly to travel, with such an instrument as this at home, and such scenes imprinted as you would desire to visit....

March 30   61° 63° 64°

Change of weather in the night. Storm of rain wind & lightening from the Eastward, dark and gloomy. A tempest of rain and wind from 8 to 9 & change to North. In less than an hour the whole square opposite presented an unbroken sea of turbid water. The street lines marked only by the fences & trees the water stood 9 inches just inside my front fence and effectually imprisoned me in the house....

Availed myself of my confinement to the house until noon to make good progress with my Plans. Afternoon and evening until 9 chiefly engaged in making up documents for the Treasury Department. Mr. J. W. Stanton's report of the Sailor's Home appeared in Saturday's "Bulletin" he alludes very pleasantly to my service as Architect.[10]

March 31   62° 64° 64°

Cold and cloudy. South East wind. Cleared off in the afternoon.

Col. Whitehead called at the office, and I read over with him the contract & specifications for his Warehouses, amounting to $14.000 & upwards. The contract is made with Mr. Huyghe, the Builder, and duly signed, and provides that it shall be executed under my Superintendence, as Architect.[11]...

In talking over the details of the Whitehead Warehouses, I strenuously insisted that the Foundations should be 8 Bricks wide, but Col. Whitehead has determined that they shall be but seven bricks in width. This I deem insufficient in view of the maximum load to which the floors will be subjected. But he seems to be perfectly satisfied with his view of the subject.

[10] *Commercial Bulletin*, Mar. 27, 1858.
[11] Robert Huyghe (1813-1877), a prominent architect-builder, also built the villa designed by Howard and Diettel, architects, for Col. Robert Short at Fourth and Prytania (1859) and designed and built the Lafayette Presbyterian Church on Magazine between Jackson and Philip (1866-1867).

April 3   64° 68° 70°

Very lovely weather. North West wind.

Unusual press of work at the office until dinner at 4. After tea drawing foundations of the "Whitehead Warehouse" until half past 10. The contract requires inverted arches from Plinth to Plinth in the cross foundations. The Plinths of Granite 17" x 17" and 10" in height.

April 10   75° 76° 78°

Mild & cloudy. East wind. Blowing hard in the middle of the day....

At the foundations of the new building after dinner. They are dry at the required depth and composed generally of good Batture sand and clay. A piece of oak Plank and a heavy Pine post that have evidently been buried a long time (being portions of the old wharf) were quite sound.

Drawing sections of foundations until 10 at night.

April 11   65° 68° 68°

Sunday. Heavy gale of wind from the South East all night, bringing vast accumulations of cloud, and driving the water of the river over the Levee....

The river is now quite full and in some places running over, so that the Levees above the city must have suffered during the gale of last night. Fine & clear in the afternoon. Walked down to the Levee and found the River stealing over the Levee at the foot of Robin Street and at other depressed points....

April 12   60° 64° 64°

Brilliant weather. Pure blue sky & high wind from North West, cold and bracing. All nature cleansed and shining in the brightest green after the floods of yesterday.

On my way to the office stopped at the foundations of the new building. Found the workmen pumping out the trenches which are full of water. Conversation with Mr. Huyghe on the arches &c. Visit from Mr. Stauffer one of the Directors of the Canal Bank.[12] Explained to him our system of Iron floors &c. which they propose to introduce into the New Bank....

[12] Isaac Hull Stauffer (1813-1903) was with the wholesale hardware firm of Slark, Stauffer & Co. *Daily Picayune*, Nov. 15, 1903; NOCD 1858.

Bell crevasse (or break) in weakened Mississippi River levee opened by high water, 1858 (1974.25.11.2).

April 15   65° 70° 71°

Mild & light clouds. West wind. Cleared off hot & breezy.

Met Messrs. Browne & Huyghe by appointment at 10 at the building to survey the north wall. The city surveyor, however, was called suddenly to Carrolton and could not meet the appointment. After dinner we met again, with Mr. Pilié the City Surveyor, who was of opinion that the half of the north wall should be condemned and will give a certificate accordingly.[13] The whole wall, however, will have to come down as it is insufficient for our building....

April 17   71° 76° 76°

Dry and clear and dusty. Fresh air from the S. West....

Emily Tommy & Ellen came to the office at 2½ after having been to the "Panorama of Italy" again, and we all rode home to dinner at 4, which was distinguished with more than usual care, presents, champaigne &c. in honor of my 44th. Birthday.[14] After dinner we all took a pleasant ride in the omnibus to the upper Line of Jefferson City, and got amongst the bright green fields, redolent with the scent of innumerable clover blossoms, and the pure air was laden with the sweets floating over the country from the gardens and orange groves....

April 19   74° 77° 76°

Clouds threatening rain. Strong breeze from the South.

I was awakened by the fire alarm at 5 O'clock, and as it was near, dressed & went to the spot. It was Annunciation Square church which we formerly attended. It was entirely destroyed by 6 O'clock.[15]

At the building on my way to the office, and again at 12.

Note to Mr. Brown about the North Wall, and visit from him at the office. The sill course is being set. Ordered cement to be used instead of common mortar....

April 20   76° 79° 80°

Cloudy threatening rain. Fresh breeze from the South West. Hot sun after 12 M....

The River is still rising. The crevasse on the opposite bank widening, and the water fast encroaching upon the town of Algiers.

[13] Louis H. Pilié (1821-1884) had followed his father Joseph Pilié as city surveyor. As architect for the city, Pilié designed the fence around Jackson Square and the wrought-iron entrance gates of the Cabildo.

[14] The panorama entitled *Waugh's Italia and the Italian Fantoccini, A Panoramic Voyage from Boston to Rome and Home Again, from Naples to New York* was exhibited at Armory Hall. *Daily Delta*, Mar. 13, 1858.

[15] The fire at the Episcopal Church of the Annunciation was believed to have been of incendiary origin. A new site for the church at the corner of Camp and Race streets was purchased in 1860, but the new church was not erected until 1873. *Times-Picayune*, Oct. 10, 1915.

Bell crevasse, April 11, 1858, with steamboats passing on the Mississippi River (1989.133).

Thomas C. Gilmour residence, Tina Freeman, photographer, 1982 (Mss 98-9-L).

It can be seen distinctly from the top of the New Custom House gradually & surely extending the area of Submersion.[16]…

April 23   70° 73° 74°

Hot dry & very dusty. South West wind.…

At the prayer meeting in the evening. Excellent remarks from Mr. Duncan on the difference between genuine, wide-spread, deep seated interest in religion and those popular periodical excitements

16 A crevasse is a breach in the river levee. On April 11, 1858, a serious crevasse opened on the west bank of the river, opposite Louisiana Avenue, at the plantation of John M. Bell. *Daily Delta*, Apr. 17, 1858. On May 13, 1858, the *Daily Crescent* published a letter from John Roy, Wharton's associate at the Custom House, on the crevasse and his proposal for closing it.

which are as easily mistaken for it, and as easily produced by the usual agencies of exciting preaching, exciting conversation, exciting singing, and excited gatherings of excited people &c. &c.

April 25   64° 65° 65°

Sunday. Cold East wind. Clear sky. Hot sunshine.

Mr. Duncan preached morning & evening. 5 new members were baptised after the night service. After dinner walked to the beautiful places of Mr. Lonsdale & Mr. Gilmour.[17] Their gardens are in the

17 The house of English cotton broker Thomas C. Gilmour on the corner of Prytania and Third was built by Isaac Thayer in 1853. It was restored in 1985-1987 by Koch and Wilson, architects, for Mr. and Mrs. William K. Christovich. NOCD 1855; NONA, John Claiborne, Jan. 11, 1853.

finest condition, with the sweetest of sweet peas, verbenas, gladiolus, amyrillida, nasturtiums &c. &c. in full flower, and the usual large intermixture of fine roses which are here always in bloom, and the purest blue overhead.

April 26   70° 73° 68°

Light clouds preparing for rain. South East wind. Clouded up at noon and looked dark & threatening. The river has risen considerably since Saturday & the news this morning shows it still rising at all points above. The country on the opposite shore as far as the eye can reach from the top of the Custom House appears under water....

Took Tommy and Emily up to the River Bank, at Louisiana Avenue and had a good distant view of the crevasse on the opposite side, and the submerged country, from the upper deck of a large steamer lying at the Landing....

April 28   62° 67° 68°

Dry, clear, & very dusty. North East wind. Light frost at Memphis yesterday morning.

At the building at 9. Workmen pulling down the North Wall. In the afternoon laying down the Granite Plinth, and beginning to raise the 12"/12" Posts. Went from the Building to the "Sailors' Home" and measured the work included in Mr. Klein's Bill for flagging &c.[18]

April 29   68° 72° 68°

Warm, dry & dusty. South East wind. Very clear. Wind rising....

After dinner took Emily Tommy & Ellen up to the upper line of Jefferson city and a short & pleasant walk down a grassy lane brought us to the river bank. The current sweeping onward with wondrous force and quite full up to the brim of the Levee which seems but a feeble barrier to restrain such a mass of waters. Indeed they are working their way insidiously thro' it in many places and I should not be surprised at any moment to hear of a rupture on this side similar to the great "Bell Crevasse" on the other. On which by the way the operations are becoming daily more hopeless. I felt satisfied from the first that nothing but a fall of the river itself would stop it....

April 30   70° 74° 76°

Hot, dry & very dusty, but signs of approaching rain.

Went to St. Mary's Market before breakfast, thence to the building. First Tier of Joists laid on one fourth of the space. Skewback arches on Fulton Street very neatly put in, and the foundations of half the old north wall all taken out, &c. &c. Objected to some of the joist pieces as having considerable sap &c. Door frames on Front Street up. Called at the "Sailor's Home" on my way back and completed some measurements &c....

May 1   72° 74° 76°

Hot, dry & very dusty. South East wind. A little rain at noon. Cleared up immediately very hot & sunny.

Received from Mr. Bryant printed report on the Alms House at Deer Island & State Prison at Charleston &c. &c. which will be valuable to me in making Designs for the "Touro Alms House."[19]...

May 2   73° 75° 75°

Sunday. Gathering clouds. South East wind. Rain set in on my return from market in quiet fertilizing showers. Cleared off again at 10.

Stayed at home this morning & read "Curtis' on the progress of Baptist principles."[20] Finished the book after tea. His arguments shewing the unscriptural nature of Pedobaptism [infant baptism] and its dangerous tendencies, leading to an unconverted church membership &c. appear to me irresistable. Also against mixed communion, and the chapters shewing that Baptist principles spring directly from the New Testament in its simplicity, and underlie the entire structure of religious & even civil liberty, and have been the originating sources of the great religious enterprises of the last century, the diffusion of the Bible and Christianity among the heathen; are exceedingly fine and abound in the most convincing & eloquent passages I ever met with. He has opened up the whole subject with a fairness, candor & power which cannot be excelled.

[18] H. M. Klein, contractor for flagging, 111 Julia and Dryades opposite market. NOCD 1859.

[19] The Touro Alms House, a large Gothic structure designed and built by William A. Freret, was named for Judah Touro (1775-1854), who left funds for its construction. It was located on Levee Street, between Piety and Desire. In 1865 the still unfinished building was destroyed by fire while occupied by Federal troops. *Daily Crescent*, Sept. 12, 1859.

[20] Thomas F. Curtis, *The Progress of Baptist Principles in the Last Hundred Years* (Boston, 1855).

May 3   72° 68° 71°

Cleansing rains in the night. Full cisterns and all traces of the drought washed away. Cloudy & sprinkling this morning with South East wind. At 10 heavy showers set in with dark scowling clouds & distant thunder. Ceased about 1 P.M.

At the Building at 9. A second row of 12/12 Posts set. The view from the top of the Custom House becomes daily more aqueous. The sharp line of the Levee formed by the wharves is obliterated and broken into bays & inlets flowing over on the shore. In the evening the river poured down Robin & Basin Streets on either side of us quite freely. But a large force succeeded in leveeing it out before night.

May 4   68° 72° 72°

Bright & clear. Pleasant air from the East, to North. Every thing clean & cheerful after the rain.

The morning paper announces a bad crevasse at the LaBranche Plantation on the other side of the River 25 miles above.[21] Wrote to Mr. J. W. Stanton & enclosed Klein's Bill for Paving examined, and my own a/s for Superintendence. At the Building on my way to the office. All hands at work to make up for time lost by the rain. After dinner went down again and took Tommy with me. After looking over the work with the Contractor, we went on board the "Ingomar". He wanted to see the 5 O'clock boats leave which they did in grand style, the "Princess" the "Falls City" & the "J. D. Newcomb." When the last boat got out into the stream a skiff pushed out for her with a passenger who "was too late." She stopped her way & the skiff was at her bow in a few seconds. Trunk handed up, and the owner siezed the large moulding of the [rim?] just above the stern post. The current swept the skiff away from under him and in an instant he was overboard striking out boldly for the shore. Some minutes passed before the skiff was headed up towards him but he sustained himself until she came up, and he was dragged on board safely and apparently but little exhausted. But it was a time of deep suspense to the multitudes who saw him struggling with the fierce eddies from the long row of steamers lining the wharves. He prudently declined trying it again, and hailed the steamer, which still awaited him, to go on her way, while the oarsman hastened back with him to the shore....

---

[21] The plantations of Mme. J. M. Labranche and Ambrose Lanfear, in St. Charles Parish opposite Destrehan, were in danger of being flooded. *Daily Delta*, May 4, 1858.

May 7   70° 73° 74°

Beautiful weather, cloudless sky. North wind.

At the Building from 9 to 10. South party wall second story commenced with Batture brick. Taking out foundations under the weak part of old north wall. They rest on a soft wet filling of shavings, street sweepings & rubbish of all kinds. After dinner I went down again and before I left at 6 the workmen had found the bottom of the gully after throwing out a huge pile of shavings, and soft offensive matter in a state of partial decomposition. The woody fibre, however, seemed to be in good preservation owing to the wetness of the situation. The bottom was as firm as is usual. A mixture of sand & blue clay and varied in depth from 20 to 28 inches below the plank footing of the old foundation, and as it evidently slopes off gradually to the deepest place (which probably occurs near the north line of the Square). I anticipate no further trouble in obtaining a sound foundation for the new wall....

May 8   72° 74° 76°

Warm & sunny. Dry North wind, to North East.

At the building at 9. Bottom of the Trench dug yesterday, all levelled and Plank laid for the new foundation on firm ground. A serious break occurred in the Levee at Algiers this morning. The river appears higher on this side at foot of Custom House Street than ever before. I am in hourly expectation of a break in the bend at Carrolton which would be disastrous to the city.[22] After dinner went down to the Building. The South wall is up to the Cieling Joists, and the last Section of the Foundations of the North Wall are in, except a few feet in the North East angle....

May 10   70° 72° 73°

Rain set in at 2 A.M. with thunder lightening and strong gusts of wind, and continued till daybreak. Still cloudy this morning with light air from S. West. Cleared off very pleasant at noon....

At the Warehouse at 9. Stated to Mr. Huyghe my objections to allowing any part of the angle Pier of old wall at East end to remain, but he assured me that with the precautions he has taken by wedging

---

[22] The bend in the river at Carrollton was the site of a disastrous crevasse at McCarty's plantation in 1816, when a large area to the rear of the city was flooded.

Bell crevasse, with sightseers on the levee, Picayune Supplement, *May 16, 1858 (1953.130).*

up the small piece of angular foundation, and by making our own wall receive all the weight that will come over the corner, he is willing to take the entire responsibility of the shred of old brickwork that remains, and also of a few feet of filling with batture sand & clay under the north end of the front foundation. I fear the effect of compression at that point after the whole weight of the wall comes upon it, altho' that weight is inconsiderable....

May 14 72° 76° 76°

Dry clear & dusty, pleasant air from South West....

At the building after dinner, framing of second story commenced. Pointed out several joists (4 at least) which I wish to have taken out and replaced by better timber. And objected especially to one of the Girder-joints which comes on one side instead of directly over its post. And also the omission of the framer to bevel the ends of several joist pieces where they enter the wall....

May 18 76° 80° 80°

Pleasant from the South West, after a terribly hot night, and unimaginable myriads of musquitoes. Floating clouds.

Strong efforts are being made by the best men in the city to draw out Major Beauregard as an independent candidate for the "Mayoralty" but he cannot serve without resigning his honorable position in the army, which he is unwilling to do. The dispatches from headquarters to that effect are positive. And the Major's "ultimatum" today equally peremptory, acknowledging the compliment but declining the overtures, for him to abandon a distinguished military for precarious civil & political career would be to verify the line in Dante. "Vai ch'entrate agni speranza lusciate."[23]...

23 Trans.: Abandon hope all who enter here.

162

May 20   77° 81° 82°

Hot dry & dusty. Pleasant air from North West....

The Department Telegraphs Major Beauregard that he can retain his superintendency at the New Custom House if elected Mayor. He will no doubt yield to pressure and consent to run. At least so he tells me this morning, if the guarantees that he requires are made satisfactory. This morning he handed me his notes of an address to the "Committee of nomination" defining his views in very firm and decided language, and I put them into complete shape ready for presentation before I left the office at 3.

After dinner Emily Tommy & I & the rest took the omnibus to the Gretna Ferry, crossed the river, and a pleasant walk of ½ a mile on the Levee brought us to the great "Bell crevasse" which has been pouring its relentless flood, for more than a month, into the opposite country, which now lies buried under a brown, soaking deluge as far as the eye can penetrate thro' the woods and many a weary mile beyond. The "crevasse" itself is several hundred feet wide, and the river rushes thro' the opening with terrific force, assuming the general appearance of "rapids" on northern rivers in all respects except the want of clearness & lucidity in the current. Quite a number of familiar faces from the city had been, like ourselves, attracted to the spot. And fishermen were there with their landing nets scooping up myriads of shrimps and the large coarse varieties of fish which abound in the river. About an hour before we got there two men had been drawn into the furious torrent and have not been seen since. On Monday last, it is said, two others shared the same fate, and another was drowned a few days after the break first occurred by missing his footing on the edge of the vortex. So that life, as well as millions of money-value has been sacrificed to this fatal flood. We reached home about dark, tired indeed, but amply repaid by our visit to the "Bell Crevasse."

The idea of closing it is now wholly abandoned. The fall of the River alone can do it. Efforts, however, are still being made at the "Labranche crevasse," 12 miles above, under the direction of our Mr. J. Roy.

May 21   76° 80° 81°

Hot, dry, & dusty. Pleasant breeze from the North East....

Major Beauregard deep in with Committee men &c. &c. preparatory to running for the Mayoralty. A dispatch from the Department says that he can retain his Superintendency at the Custom House if elected but will have to resign his military Commission. After dinner I found that two of the foundations of Posts for inclined Plane had been put in with only 5 Brick base instead of 6 so I had them taken out again. Outside walls levelled up to cieling joists.

May 22   78° 82° 82°

Hot, dry and dusty. East wind.

At the Building, framer is cutting the rafters, and the foundations of Posts to inclined Plane finished ready for the Granite Blocks. Grading well advanced to receive the Pavement of ground Floor. Spent 4 hours in close writing preparing the Major's "address" accepting his nomination to the Mayoralty....

May 24   78° 78° 80°

Rain fell thro' the night but the sun shines out brightly this morning and all nature looks refreshed and joyous. But the South East wind bodes more rain still. Showers at intervals thro' the day.

After dinner spent an hour at the Building with Mr. Robt. H. Browne, the Agent, the rafters are on two of the roofs and the paving of ground floor commenced. They had committed an error on Front street in raising the floor above the sill only 4½ inches instead of 7", in the 4 foot slope next the street. Fortunately it was only just laid out so the correction involves no loss of time.

May 25   79° 82° 82°

Fine & breezy. Bright sunshine. South East wind. Every thing sparkling & flushed with color after the rain.

Found Mr. Huyghe at the building at 9. He misunderstood the decision fixing the front sill course at 2" & the rear at 4" above the Banquette, instead of 1" and 3" as he at first proposed. Says he thought the additional inch was to be taken out of the height of floor above the sill course, which the contract fixes at 7 inches on both fronts. I told him that I would accept 6" on both fronts for the height of floor at the top of the 4 Foot slope, and orders were immediately given accordingly. This figure (6") is the height called for by Mr. Whitehead in an appendix to the Contract, at my suggestion. Committee waited on the Major this morning on the subject of the Mayoralty and a large meeting will convene at the St. Charles this evening....

Alexander Harris residence, Rudolf Hertzberg Photographs, Southeastern Architectural Archive, Tulane University Library.

May 26   80° 78° 82°

Pleasant air from the South East. Rains 11 to 1.

The meeting at the St. Charles last evening was an enthusiastic one and Major Beauregard's nomination for Mayor is now formally made and accepted. The press comes out warmly in his favor this morning, that is, the "Delta." The other papers have not spoken out yet....

May 27   80° 82° 82°

Hot sunshine, floating clouds, pleasant air from South East.

Went to St. Mary's Market before breakfast, and thence to the Warehouses where every thing goes on briskly. All the rafters on, and one Section of roof sheathed, and the pavement corresponding to that Section laid. Breakfasted late and did not reach the Office until 10. Custom House business pretty engrossing today. After dinner went with Mr. Calrow to see Mr. Harris' new house which is nearly finished, and is a highly creditable performance to the Contractors.

Messrs. T. Thornhill & McIlhenny came in while there, and after a general survey of house & grounds I accompanied those two gentlemen in a walk thro' the best improved parts of the 4th. Dist. which is richer in flowers and tastefully adorned residences than any other suburb I know of except Brookline near Boston, and all flush with the glowing colors of May.[24]

May 31   81° 84° 84°

Hot, very hot, dry and very dusty, South East wind....

At the Warehouse after dinner. Slating commenced & copper gutters nearly finished. Invitations from the Renshaw's to attend the distribution of prizes &c. at the Lyceum Hall to the classes of Miss Hull's School. We all went & called for Mrs. G. B. Young on the

[24] Thomas Thornhill (d. 1870), a Natchez plantation owner, lived in New Orleans for some years. *Daily Picayune*, Aug. 28, 1870. Alfred McIlhenny lived at the corner of Camp and Terpsichore streets. NOCD 1858.

way. The musical performances and general appearance of the young ladies were charming and Miss Medora Renshaw graduated with distinguished honor....

June 1   81° 84° 84°

Hot, dry, and dusty. South East wind.

At the building at 9. Handed Mr. Huyghe a notification to replace with good material the Second Post of inclined Plane, and called his attention to a mistake in the height of Chimneys on the South side. Wrote to Mr. Browne defining my construction of Specific Clause No. 18 and general clause No. 24 of the Contract, taking the ground that a general clause in a contract, gives new force to, and provides in a measure for omissions in, a specific clause, but cannot add a new and important feature to that clause. Pleasant trip with Tommy to the Lake after dinner.

June 2   82° 84° 84°

Hot, dry & dusty. South East wind.

At the building at 9. Copper gutters nearly finished. Slating & cornice going on rapidly and the Flooring of second story commenced. At the office the approaching election is an absorbing theme. Those who never talked politics before are eloquent now. The independent movement is spreading with giant strides, and Major Beauregard's success is considered certain....

June 3   82° 86° 86°

Last night was one of hottest within the recollection of "This City." Today still more so and very dusty. Musquitoes swarm, and the sun shines with a glare of absolute ferocity. Wind still South East, but no symptoms of rain yet.

At the Building at 9 with the Contractor. Every thing going on well. The Vigilance Committee are fully organized and have commenced the most vigorous measures for the restoration of order & security, and to free the city from ruffianism, to which it has long been a prey.[25] After dinner went down to the Warehouses. The day has passed without any overt act of hostility to the "Vigilants" who are in the meantime strengthening their position every hour.

June 4   82° 84° 83°

Hot, dry and dusty. South East wind. Shower at 9 and again at 3½....

At the Building every thing goes on well. Exciting times down town. At 1 O'clock an armed force went down to attack the entrenchments of the Vigilance Committee but wisely retreated without striking a blow. An attack also was threatened at the Custom House, but our small force was immediately put under arms, and with Major Beauregard at the head, not a man could have entered the building alive. But one shot was fired at the building and that apparently in bravado. In the meantime the Mayor entered into an arrangement with the "Vigilance Committee," which it is probable will immediately restore order and confidence. Went down to the warehouse after dinner. Every thing going on well at the Building. Then went to Lafayette Square, the gathering ground of the "Thugs" &c. and found all quiet. Got an extra "Delta" down Camp Street, giving in general terms the arrangements made for the restoration of complete order & security throughout the city and then returned home to supper. Heavy rain at noon.

June 5   80° 79° 82°

Showers in the night. Pleasant this morning, but hot, with South East wind.

The "Vigilance Committee" under the command of Capt. Jos. K. Duncan have achieved a signal tho' thus far bloodless triumph. They number now fully a thousand men, occupying an entrenchment absolutely impregnable to any of our "civic military" bodies, no matter how numerous, and still more so to undisciplined lawless ruffians. Every thing is arranged with the most scientific skill, & the

[25] The city of New Orleans, divided into three separate municipalities in 1836, was reunited in 1852 with the addition of the suburb of Lafayette. Fiercely partisan politics dominated elections, particularly after the rise of the Know Nothings, an anti-immigrant, anti-Catholic party led by American businessmen who opposed the Democrats, dominated by Creoles and Irish and German immigrants. Electoral violence, stolen ballots, and street fighting were common throughout the 1850s. In March 1858 a Vigilance Committee, largely made up of Democrats, was formed to ensure that they were not disfranchised in that year's election; they supported the candidacy of P. G. T. Beauregard. At three o'clock in the morning of June 3, the "Vigilants" under the command of Johnson Kelly Duncan seized the Arsenal, armed themselves, and set up camp in Jackson Square. The mayor was unable to dislodge them, and their opponents formed another armed camp in Lafayette Square, but the election of June 7 proceeded fairly peaceably. After another Know Nothing victory, the Vigilants disbanded with virtually no attempt made by the city to punish them. Soulé, *The Know Nothing Party*, 92-104.

Louisiana State Arsenal by James Dakin, 1839; poster reproduction, 1980 (1980.83), gift of Stanton M. Frazar.

whole organization moves like clockwork. The Mayor and Major Genl. Lewis (Superintendent of Elections) waited upon the "Committee" yesterday at the Arsenal, and signed a Treaty with them accepting their services as a special Police for a least 5 days to come, and legalizing their acts for the entire extirpation of "ruffianism" and "thuggery" from the city. They to retain their organization complete, and full possession of their stronghold as now, until a post equally advantageous shall be selected. Thus the triumph of law and order, and the <u>will</u> of the best part of this long suffering community, is at length guaranteed, and bright prospects open out before. The terrorism of the last 3 years is virtually at an end. The assailants dared not, with all their hardihood, rush upon certain destruction as they would have done had they attacked yesterday. Called at the Warehouse at 9. Found the error that I complained of in the chimneys corrected. The header in front of chimney breast on the north side has been put in as directed, but the objectionable post in the framing of the inclined Plane remains untouched. I told Mr. Huyghe that I should insist upon compliance with my notification. At the office and down town things are altogether too stirring to write about with pleasure. Did not get home to dinner till between 4 and 5....

June 6 — 81° 83° 85°

Sunday. Hot and sunny. West wind.

The Plot thickens. The city council late last night impeached and deposed the Mayor, and appointed H. M. Summers (Ex-Recorder) to act pro Tem. In the meantime the Vigilance Organization is complete, numbering 1200 men within the lines, thoroughly trained, and ready for action. Besides strong bodies diffused thro' the city, important arrests of notorious ruffians are also being made. All of which tend to rivet the hopes of perfect quiet & security in the voting tomorrow. Major Beauregard's address appears in all the papers this morning, shewing his entire freedom from all political bias whatever in accepting his nomination. Mr. Duncan preached an admirable sermon on the text "and when he beheld the city he wept over it." Painting eloquently the <u>then</u> prosperous condition of Jerusalem and her <u>then</u> approaching doom, and shewing the sorrow which should fill every Christian bosom when he sees a large city around him full of wickedness, and the exertions he ought to make to save those around him from their certain spiritual doom if unrepentent. At 5 went down in the omnibus to the Custom House to get my "registry." Found the building occupied by a detachment of United States troops, and in the office Major Beauregard & Mr.

Members of the New Orleans Vigilance Committee guarding the barricades surrounding Jackson Square, July 10, 1858 (1959.159.28), gift of Harold Schilke and Boyd Cruise.

Penn, entertaining the commanding officers & several friends. Remained a short time and then returned by Lafayette Square, the head quarters of the opposition, which I found strictly guarded by artillery, and the usual crowd around the Hall. I understand a reckless attack was made upon the "Vigilants" last night which was attended with the loss of 3 or 4 lives, tho' the accounts varied....

June 7   81° 85° 80°

Hot and clear. Wind due South. Clouds gathered at 9 and refreshing showers fell at intervals thro' the day.

This is the day of the great struggle. I was at the Polls at 8 and voted. Met a good many friends and talked over prospects &c. for half an hour. Mr. Reid was there just from the Custom House, and reported that no work would be done owing to its occupancy by United States troops, and, of course, no office business. So I returned home and went to work on a drawing for the Warehouses. Finished that by 11 then put the flower borders in good condition, and just finished when a smart shower put an end to all out door work. The Vigilance Committee have failed to yield the protection promised, but as far as I have seen up to this hour (12 O'clock) it has not been needed. And the rain now falling will throw some little cold water on the heated passions of the more belligerent contestants. But the palpable imperfection of the general arrangements throws a dark shadow on the prospects of Major Beauregard. The "American" party seemed in possession of the polls where I voted this morning and there were no tickets to be had for the "Independent" party. Those of us who voted that ticket either went provided, or obtained them from others who had a number in their possession. On inquiry I found that Mr. Marks who was entrusted by the Executive Committee with the tickets for our Precinct had not been able to find a man bold enough to take charge of a stand for their distribution. After a heavy shower at 3 the sun came out bright and I went round to the Polls at our precinct. Every thing in excellent order, and the hour of closing (4 O'clock) then near. The voting close. I then took the omnibus to the Custom House. Remained there awhile and on my return the Polls had closed, with a result at our precinct of 100 for the Major, against 91 for Stith.[26] From all that I could learn below things have been conducted with uniform quiet thro' the day. Upon the whole [th]is has been the <u>calmest</u> Election day ever known in this city.

<hr/>

[26] Gerard Stith (1821-1880) was mayor of New Orleans from 1858 to 1860. He also served on the city council (1854-1856, 1860-1862) and as city recorder (1856-1858). NOCD 1859; *DLB*.

June 8   80° 83° 83°

Hot and clear. Wind due South. Thunder shower at P.M.

The result of the Election is now known. Mr. Stith's majority over Major Beauregard is estimated at 290. Chiefly attributable, it is said, to the defective arrangements of the "Independent Executive Committee."

Read all the papers before breakfast, with their varied expressions of chagrin or triumph. Men, however, will now return to their customary employments, and the wheels of the city government will again move on. The only exception seems to be the "Vigilance Committee" which still retains its organization at the Arsenal according to the Papers. Called at the Building at 9 and found every thing going on well. At the Custom [House] the military are still on duty but the works went on as usual, and Major Beauregard smiles over his defeat. The "Vigilants" it appears disbanded early this morning and the Police are hunting them down every where, about 50 arrests are said to have been made. Both the "Independent" and "Vigilance" measures have resulted in the most disastrous defeat. But it is to be hoped that a general salutary impression has been produced. The formidable and intense display of public feeling which has prevailed for the last 10 days will show the officers elect that the broad, wide-open, glaring eye of the Public is upon them and will inspire them with the most scrupulous caution in all their movements....

June 9   81° 83° 82°

Very pleasant weather with fresh air from the South.

Things have settled down again to their normal condition. The arrests made of Vigilants yesterday were unsupported by suitable affidavits & the parties soon dismissed. The general effect will be salutary, an awful & mysterious warning to the fiends who have heretofore been employed for party purposes and suffered to go unpunished. Many, I am told, have left the city for other fields of "labor"!...

I ver[il]y believe that in any other city of the Union the bloodshed would have been frightful. But the tone of feeling in New Orleans is of a higher character than is found elsewhere, and I have the utmost confidence in it. And as a proof of it I have gone about during these exciting two weeks just the same as ever without carrying any means of defense of any description, not even a pocket knife....

At 10 O'clock the Drum called the troops into rank, and they withdrew from the Building in admirable order, and proceeded to the Steamer for head quarters at Baton Rouge....

June 10   81° 83° 81°

Beautiful weather. Wind due South. Light showers....

The official returns are in and the majority against Beauregard after all is only 131. A very little additional energy on the part of his blundering executive committee would have secured his election....

The Major left town today for a little rest after the pressing excitements of the last two weeks....

June 12   78° 80° 80°

Dark clouds gathered at 7½ A.M. with South West wind. Heavy rains at 8 and 11 A.M. and 3 P.M.

At the Building at 9. The rain storms have no effect whatever on my roofs which are perfectly watertight....

Mr. John Roy has failed in his attempt to stop the LaBranche crevasse, and has abandoned the work. The [river?] still quite full....

June 15   74° 78° 80°

Very fine indeed. Cold air from North West. Windows all shut, and blankets in demand at night.

At the building at 9. Flooring, banquette, & painting, all going on well. Major has returned & is beset on all sides to contest the Election but stoutly refuses to have anything more to do with it. His friends claim a majority for him in behalf of a large number of "general tickets" thrown out in consequence of inaccuracy in the names on the respective Ward Lists....

June 17   78° 81° 82°

Beautiful weather. North East wind.

At the Building at 9. Painting, glazing, Inclined Plane, Plumber work &c. &c. all going on rapidly. The objectionable Post which I declined to receive has been taken out, and replaced with sound Cypress....

June 22   80° 79° 82°

Clouds & hot sunshine. East wind. Dark clouds, thunder and some rain at 12. Soon cleared off....

Letter from Messrs. Cooper & Hewitt to Major Beauregard states that the "Conference Committee" on appropriations agreed to give us $250.000. I also find it announced officially in the

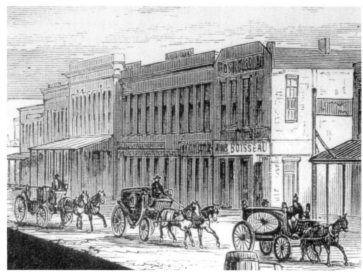

Funeral procession, late nineteenth-century New Orleans (1974.25.6.549).

Washington Union of the 16th. so this may be considered a "fait accompli" and will be equal to about $400.000 available to us for the approaching Fiscal Year, inclusive of Balance on hand....

June 23   79° 80° 78°

Clouds and bright sunshine. Pleasant air from the South East. Rain at intervals thro' the day....

Saw a sad sight this morning, a father and his two poor little boys laid out in their coffins at the Rainbow Hotel corner of Levee and Notre Dame. They were victims of the explosion of the "Pennsylvania." The father was the proprietor of the Hotel, Mr. John P. Betz.[27] In going from the Warehouses to the office I noticed quite a gathering round the Hotel and found this to be the cause of it. When will our legislation be sufficiently stringent, and surely carried out to prevent such unnecessary and wholesale Slaughter? Walking down to the Warehouses after dinner I met the funeral procession of Mr. Betz which was one of the largest I ever saw, extending many squares along Magazine....

[27] Mrs. John P. Betz was the proprietor of the Rainbow Hotel. Betz was a baker with the firm of Jenni & Betz on Notre Dame Street near Fulton. NOCD 1859.

Depiction of an earlier steamboat explosion, the Louisiana, *G. Tolti, delineator, 1849 (1991.128), shows the tremendous force of the bursting boilers.*

June 25   79° 80° 78°

Very pleasant morning. East wind. Thunder showers in the middle of the day. Violent rain with heavy thunder at 12 to 1....

Rainy afternoon, yet I went thro' it after dinner to the Warehouse, and found the 10 spouts & heads all on the ground and 5 of them on Fulton Street already up and looking extremely well. Unfortunately, however, they were 4 instead of 5 inches in diameter (as required by contract) making a difference in Sectional area between 12.566 and 19.635. Of course I could only reject them, which I [did] with much regret, especially as it will delay the building several days, and I fully hoped to turn it over finished and complete tomorrow night.

June 29   81° 84° 84°

Fine and clear. Very pleasant air from South.

At the Building at 9 and gave directions to the painter about putting on the name on both Fronts "Whitehead Warehouse." Also about some little finishing up in paintwork &c. The whole of the spouts will be replaced today with 5 Inch. The 4 Inch which I rejected having been taken down. Mr. Huyghie called at the office, and I gave him a certificate for his final payment as the work covered by the Contract is now complete. I also checked & examined his Bill of extra measurement owing to the difference between the dimensions of the contract and those of the actual survey, amounting to $348.85, which with his claim for extra foundations in the gully on the north line makes altogether $405.55. The Buildings now finished have cost (exclusive of the ground) about $15.000 and the work is decidedly superior to that of the Montgomery Warehouse which is referred to in the Contract as our Standard.[28]...

July 3   80° 82° 83°

Showers and sunshine. South East wind....

The Levee business has sunk down to the summer standard, very little shipping either above or below, and only 20 Steamboats, all small except 2 first class, and 3 Steamships. The river is about 10 or 12 inches lower than it was at the top of the flood but the country opposite is still submerged as deep as ever....

[28] The Montgomery warehouses were located on Fulton Street, between Julia and St. Joseph.

July 6   84° 85° 88°

Hot & clear, South West wind. Light clouds floating across the sky.

The returns of the interments for the week ending July 4th. shew as follows. viz.

Various diseases.	134
Yellow fever.	8
Total	142

July 7   82° 78° 77°

Rains in the night. Pleasant this morning with Wind from the West.

The Board of Aldermen & Assistant Aldermen went into joint session last evening for the election of City Officers. Whatever may be their opinion of the Politics of the New Custom House, they have certainly exhibited a very favorable opinion in other respects, in the election of Mr. J. M. Reid and myself as directors of Public Schools for the First District. As far as I am concerned the action of the Council is entirely spontaneous, as I have in no respect whatever sought the office. I may, however, be able, now & then, to offer a suggestion, or propose a measure that will not be without advantage. Dark and gloomy rains set in at 9$\frac{1}{2}$ and continued thro' the morning and middle of the day, with occasional lightening, and change of wind to the North East. The thermometer fell 4 degrees and so dark was it, that candles were lighted in the offices....

July 12   80° 79° 79°

Beautiful weather, cool breeze from the S. West. Cloudy and showery after 9 A.M. with very cool air....

Letter from the Department advises Major Beauregard that by the recent law of Congress Mr. Penn's Commissionership & Disbursing Agency expired (alas for him) on the 30th. Ulto. and that Mr. F. H. Hatch, the Collector of the Port, will hereafter perform our disbursements "ex officio."...

The law of Congress above stated abolishes a sinecure of $16 per day which has been a drain upon our resources since 1853, for mere political service. It also demolishes all similar "disbursing agencies" throughout the United States, all of which are utterly useless and have been attended with immense expense to the Government....

July 14   82° 84° 86°

Warm and sunny. Pleasant West wind, to North East....

Then called at the Warehouse, now occupied, and looking extremely well. Found Mr. Bennett loading up the second floor with oats 14 Tier high, which is too great a strain for new work and produces a perceptible curvature of the timbers, and a small depression of the foundations. I told Mr. Bennett that for some time to come he ought to distribute the load more uniformly on that floor and not pile so high by several tiers, until the wood seasons and comes to a bearing.

July 15   82° 84° 86°

Fine, hot and sunny. North East wind.

At the Warehouse at 9 and pointed out to the Lessee the danger of overloading the second floor before the work is properly set. My annual & Quarterly papers are now complete. They shew total disbursements on the building from the first $2.534.339.30
    Expenditures for the Fiscal Year
    ending June 30. 1858 $407.368.20
    Balance in Treasury $146.952.97
    Appropriation for this year   250.000.00 $396.952.97
    Total available for Year ending June 30. 1859 $396.952.97

July 16   83° 86° 87°

Very warm and sunny. Light air from the East.

Call from Messrs. Hall & Kemp to meet them at their office at 9 to 10. Went over. They had determined to accede to my terms, and put the erection of their stores into my hands.[29] Talked over the general details &c. The building is to cost about $9000. Notice from the Secretary of the School Board of the first meeting on Monday night next, and went at 12, with Mr. Reid to the Mayor's office to be qualified....

July 19   85° 79° 82°

The heat and the musquitoes last night were something more than even we are accustomed to. And today the air is dry & hot with

[29] Hall, Kemp & Co., grocers, was located at the corner of Tchoupitoulas and Canal streets. NOCD 1858.

South East wind. Violent storm of wind, rain, and thunder at noon with fall of thermometer several degrees....

The School Board of the 1st. Dist. met this evening at 7, for organization in the council room of the Board of Assistant Aldermen at the City Hall. The chairmen of the different standing committees for the year were elected. The Chairmanship of the Committee on the "Lyceum & Library" fell to me. Some discussion arose relative to the Plans before the Board for the new Fisk School.[30]...

July 22   84° 85° 84°

Pleasant air from the West. Dry and sunny. Light shower at noon and thunder shower at 3½.

Settled details of Plan for New Store. I am only waiting now for a certified copy of survey from the City Officer defining the lines and angles &c. After dinner went to Nicholson's yard to see his granite sills &c.[31] Then to Mr. Thiel about the plans.[32] I have employed him as draughtsman to assist me with them.

July 23   84° 86° 90°

Brisk breeze from south west. Clouds sweeping across the sky. Very hot in the sun thro the middle of the day.

No survey yet from the City Surveyor. Slow work. Met Messrs. Reid & Rogers at the City Hall in the evening & examined drawings &c. for the new School House &c. and visited the Library &c. &c.[33]

July 24   84° 88° 91°

Fine breeze from the West. Clouds & sunshine. Thermo[mete]r. rose to 90 at 3, within the thick walls and shadows of the New Custom House.

Call from Judge Huling at the Office. They have bought a pleasant place at Amite City and want us to go up and see it, and

[30] The Fisk School was at the corner of Perdido and Franklin streets. NOCD 1859.
[31] Nicholson & Co.'s Granite, Marble, Stone and Slate Yards, corner of Magazine and Robin streets, were directly in back of Wharton's Camp Street house. NOCD 1859.
[32] William Thiel (1821-1870), an assistant architect for the new Custom House, lived on Prytania near Euterpe. After the Civil War, he was architect for a number of buildings, including a hall for the Turner Society which still stands on Lafayette Street at the corner of O'Keefe. NOCD 1859; NONA, J. Cohn, Aug. 18, 1868.
[33] William O. Rogers was superintendent of the first district schools from 1856 to 1862. In 1865 he became superintendent of city schools.

Advertisement for the New Orleans, Jackson & Great Northern Railroad, 1871 (1974.25.37.54); Girls High School, Plan book 86, Folio 37, April 20, 1852, New Orleans Notarial Archives.

visit them from time to time thro' the summer.[34] It is a trip of about 3 hours by the Jackson Rail road....

July 27   84° 87° 84°

Hot and dry. North East wind. Showers at noon.

Notice to meet the "Joint Committee on Finance & Building" of 1st. Dist Pubc. Schools at 5 P.M. Met the gentlemen at the City Hall. After looking over the various drawings before us, and hearing the remarks of others, I represented to them that the designs submitted being only sketches, tho' containing admirable features were insufficient to base a decision upon, and wholly so to build from. I recommended, therefore, that without further loss of time, Architects should be invited, thro' the papers, to present complete plans & specifications, in competition, and send them in by the 15th. of August. And, for this purpose, that 5% of the appropriation, say

$500, should be set apart, $150 as a premium for the Plan adopted $50 for the next best. And the remaining 3% to pay a superintendent. This was unanimously concurred in. The advertisement at once written, and tomorrow morning it will appear in four of the leading Journals.

August 5   84° 88° 84°

Clouds are gathering for a change of weather. North wind. High wind, thunder, clouds of dust and prelusive drops of rain at 3 P.M.

The School Board met this evening from 7 to 9. A Quorum present. I am on three standing Committees for the year. The Lyceum & Library, Commee. on Teachers, and Comme. on Girls' High School, and am continued on Joint Committee for receiving and adopting a Plan for the New School House.[35] Calling for bids from Builders &c.

---

[34] Amite City (now Amite) was a small resort town in the pine woods north of Lake Pontchartrain.

[35] The Girls High School was on Clio Street, between St. Charles and Prytania. NOCD 1859.

Attempts to halt the spread of yellow fever by destroying items presumed to be infected by victims, 1870s (1974.25.11.123).

August 6   83° 87° 87°

Dry and clear. North East wind.

The subject of Yellow Fever is beginning to excite attention; the rapid increase of deaths in the Hospital during the last few days shews its epidemic character, and there is no doubt, that it bears the genuine West-India type.

August 7   84° 89° 88°

Hot and dry. North East wind.

Wrote to Messrs. Hall, Kemp & Co. giving Points to embrace in their Building Contract. After dinner Emily Tommy Ellen & I took the cars to the Lake, where the wreck of the Steamer Virginia, which blew up this morning at the wharf, was attracting hundreds of our citizens. The cars were very full both in going and returning, and several friends were there. The boat is sunk to the guards, and the saloons and whole middle sections exhibit the most frightful heap of ruins I have ever seen except in the case of the "Louisiana" some years ago. The demolition is complete and several lives were lost, 5 or 6 at least, and many others severely scalded. Fortunately the passengers had not assembled for the morning's trip when the accident occurred.[36]

---

[36] The steamboat *Virginia* was scheduled to depart from the lake end of the Pontchartrain Railroad for Ocean Springs, Mississippi, at noon on August 7, on the arrival of the railroad cars. *Daily Delta*, Aug. 8, 1858.

August 10   83° 86° 87°

Hot and dry. East wind.

Yellow fever is on the increase. We have hitherto lost but two hands from the works. The Telegraph announces the Atlantic Cable laid perfect and complete in connection from both ends.[37]

August 11   82$\frac{1}{2}$° 85° 86°

Hot and dry. North East wind.

Mr. Pattison called to request that I would consent to modify the specifications & plans for the New Store.[38] I agreed to dispense with 3 of the Cast Iron Columns & corresponding Posts &c. and to substitute Brick for Iron Pilasters, with Cement Caps except at the Door Jambs. The Firm then closed a Contract with Messrs. Crozier & Wing for $12.700 and left the Plans with me to be copied etc. etc.[39] After dinner and at night copying Specifications.

At 7 P.M. met the Committee on Teachers at the City Hall.

August 13   84° 88° 84°

Hot and dry. West wind....

Yellow Fever is increasing rapidly and Quarantine established at Natchez....

August 16   82° 82$\frac{1}{2}$° 80°

Hot & dry. East wind. Rain and heavy clouds with thunder at noon....

Commenced opening the Trenches for the New Store.

Interments for the week are

Yellow Fever	286
other diseases	<u>171</u>
Total	457

Met the Committee at 6 to adopt a Plan for the New School House. 9 were offered, some of them very fine indeed. After about

---

[37] In 1858 a telegraph cable was laid on the ocean floor from Newfoundland to Ireland, briefly revolutionizing communication between Europe and America. Because international news had formerly required several weeks to arrive, there were worldwide celebrations of this technological feat. Unfortunately the cable functioned for only a month; permanent telegraphic communication was not achieved until 1866.

[38] William J. Pattison was with Hall, Kemp and Co. NOCD 1858.

[39] Robert Crozier (1806-1867) and Frederick Wing (1814-1895), builders. *New Orleans Architecture*, vol. 2, Mary Louise Christovich, Roulhac Toledano, Betsy Swanson, and Pat Holden, *The American Sector* (Gretna, La., 1978), 223.

3 hours examination, discussion, reading specifications &c. the vote was taken and resulted in favor of Mr. Lusher's. I preferred Mr. Thiel's & voted accordingly. For second best the vote was a tie between Mr. Thiel's & Mr. Roy's. We adjourned until tomorrow at 6 P.M. In the meantime Messrs. Reid & I are to revise the Specifications. Delicious iced Champaigne at Mr. Solomon's house on my way home.

August 17 81° 78° 76° 78°

Cool and cloudy. East wind. Violent rain and very dark indeed at 12 M. with fall of thermo to 76° by 1 P.M. Heavy rains after nightfall.

At the Building at 9. Digging going on, and excellent brick delivered for the Foundations. Took the Plans, & copies of same, over to Messrs. Hall, Kemp & Co. for signature at 10. Met at the City Hall at 6 to complete the business of the Plans. Our amendments of specifications were adopted. W. A. Freret appointed Superintendent at a compn. of 3%, and proposals for the work called for from 7 selected Builders, to be in by the 30th. Inst. Mr. Thiel's Plan was adopted second best, and on suggestion of Mr. Lusher, who conceded $50 of his compensation for the Plan adopted. Mr. Roy's plan was accepted as third-best at a premium of $50, owing to the many valuable & original features it contained, which rendered it important that it should become the property of the Board. Walked home thro' a dreary rain at 9. As the moon ought to have shined. No gas.

August 18 77° 79° 82°

Heavy rains in the night, and continue this morning. West wind. Struggle between rain & sunshine thro' the day, with change of wind to North....

At the Building at 11. Trenches full of water. Operations suspended. A grand salute was fired today in honor of the great event, the completion of the submarine Telegraphic Cable.

August 21 82° 87° 86°

Hot and dry. East wind.

Major Beauregard has lost his sister by Yellow Fever this morning.... At 6 P.M. attended the funeral of the Major's Sister. It is a sad event. Only 16 months ago I attended her wedding at the St. Louis Cathedral to Mr. Mortimer Belly. The cortege was a very large one. The traces of the epidemic are stamped much more legibly in the heart of town than in our more salubrious locality. Several funerals

Shepherd Brown residence, 1895 (1979.313.11.10i), gift of Mr. and Mrs. Robert Develle.

preceded that I was attending, and the air was stifling and palpably laden with the germs of disease....

August 24 83° 87° 87°

Hot and dry. East wind. Cloudy afternoon. Sultry and very oppressive.

Twice at the new building. Foundations of north wall well put in. Trenches firm & solid, batture sand, with small admixture of clay, no weak wet place. Old wooden spiles & pieces of wharf, when uncovered, were found with but very little decay & in good condition. In the afternoon spent an hour with Mr. W. K. D. looking over the foundations, and examining the Plans of a fine $30.000 mansion he is building for Mr. Shephard Brown, on the South West end of our Square.[40]

[40] Shepherd Brown (ca. 1801-1883), a member of the firm of Rotchford, Brown & Co., cotton factors, was later engaged in the banking business. Henry Howard was the architect and William K. Day the builder of his house on Coliseum Street, between Urania and Felicity. *Daily Picayune*, Feb. 9, 1883.

August 28   83° 82° 81°

Warm & sunny morning. East wind. Showers at noon.

At the new building at 10. Every thing ready for the Granite Sill Course. Major Beauregard left this morning for a week's absence at the Forts below. At 7 we had a special meeting of the School Board, to consider the propriety of extending the present vacation a month longer (to Oct. 4) owing to the serious epidemic prevailing in the city. A quorum being present a resolution to that effect was discussed and adopted.

August 30   72° 75° 74°

Cold North wind in the night. Clear & bracing this morning. Severe weather for the sick, but very pleasant indeed to the healthy.

At the new building at 9. No work waiting for the Granite Sill Course.

Mortuary returns for the week are very large. viz

of Yellow fever	402
other diseases	184
Total.	586

Met the special committee at the City Hall at 5 P.M. to open the bids for the new School House. As the proposals had not all been sent in we adjourned the business to the regular meeting of the full Board on Thursday. The odd & the sad are sadly mingled during an epidemic. In walking down Camp Street I observed the following written notice on a closed store. "This schop is closet on the count of sicknes." In the next house (Dr. Peniston's) two children had just died of the fever, and a few steps further lived a family in affluent circumstances, in which six members are lying sick of the same disease.[41] It is everywhere! In the houses of the rich and the houses of the poor.

August 31   74° 77° 80°

Clear Sunshine. Cool North wind.

The Granite for the sill course is on the ground, and of excellent quality. Notified Contractors of a departure from Specifications in regard to the "wash." Mr. Wing called immediately and I arranged it with him, accepting an equivalent. The "Yellow Fever" has become deeply rooted among us. The deaths yesterday were nearly 100. Yet Providence has dealt kindly with us as a family, for we all retain our usual good health....

N.B. The Thermometer is taken daily at 9 A.M. 12 M. & 4 P.M. My instrument is placed strictly in the shade, within a corridor of the New Custom House, open to the external air.

September 1   77° 81° 83°

The month opens with a sultry summer air, and cool north wind. The worst possible combination during an epidemic. Even those otherwise well feel its enfeebling influence.

Walking down to the office I saw the hearse opposite the door of the frame maker's on Camp Street whose shop I have noticed "closed" for two or three days past. He & his wife both dead....

September 2   80° 83° 84°

Warm & clear. Light air from the South East.

Had to spend some time in the burning sun this morning at 10, measuring the Granite course with the 10 foot rod, and found it correct. Notwithstanding the great heat I never felt better in my life than today. The air is so bland & cheerful.

The "Yellow Fever" is making sad inroads. This morning on the way to the office I noticed white crape on the door of a handsome house just opposite where the deaths occurred at Dr. Peniston's, and the Frame maker's. It was for a young stranger aged 18. The son of W. K. Day has it, and a young child of Capt. J. W. Smith, of the New Custom House. His house is on Euterpe Street, opposite to ours over the Square. Among the deaths today is that of Edward Deslondes, who belongs to one of our most prominent Creole families, related to the Hone. J. Slidell and R. W. Adams, his brothers André and Adrian were at Dr. Muhlenberg's on Long Island when I was there.[42]

At 7 went to the City Hall, but there being no quorum, the regular meeting of the Board was adjourned to Monday night. Our "joint Committee" on School Houses, however, drew round a Table in one part of the room, and we opened the bids for the new building, adopting unanimously, (at second ballot, the first being a tie) the lowest bid of Mr. Murdy $11.675.[43] The highest offer was

---

41 Dr. Anthony Peniston (ca. 1825-1863) was an adjunct professor of anatomy at the New Orleans School of Medicine. His residence was on Race Street at the corner of Magazine. Duffy, *Matas History of Medicine*, 2:261; Leonard V. Huber and Guy F. Bernard, *To Glorius Immortality: The Rise and Fall of the Girod Street Cemetery* (New Orleans, 1961), 27; NOCD 1859.

42 Edward Deslonde (ca. 1834-1858), P. G. T. Beauregard's brother-in-law, lived at the corner of Dumaine and Bourbon streets. *Commercial Bulletin*, Sept. 3, 1858.

43 John H. Murdy lived on Constance near Josephine. NOCD 1858.

$14.000. On leaving the Hall I met Mr. W. P. Campbell, one of the directors, he told me that his absence this evening was owing to his little child having been taken with "Yellow Fever" and he was then going for a physician.[44]

September 3   82° 85° 84°

Hot and dry. South East wind.

At the request of Mr. Browne I called at the "Whitehead Warehouse" on my way to the office. It was loaded with heavy storage, corn &c. both 1st. and 2nd. story, to its utmost capacity, and I was surprised to find so few evidences of settlement, under the severe strains to which such <u>new</u> <u>work</u> has been exposed. Sent a note to Mr. Browne when I got to the office....

September 4   79° 81° 81°

Rain storm in the night. Thunder and lightening unusually severe. Fresh and pleasant this morning after the rain. Wind due South. Clouds & light showers.

In measuring the Granite Course at the Store this morning I discovered an error in length, made by the sub contractor, of $2^{1}/_{2}$ inches. I altered it at once, and sent for the Contractor, Mr. Wing, and had it arranged officially.

The "Yellow Fever" returns this evening show a serious mortality for the last 24 hours, 77 interments & 12 waiting for burial. The city looks subdued and still, more like a village in summer tide, as far as human action is concerned, which contrasts strangely with the long rows of tall buildings and piles of brick & mortar. Writing Specifications after dinner, and at night.

September 5   83° 84° 83°

Sunday. Hot sunshine, floating clouds. N East wind....

Towards evening I walked down to Lafayette Square & back. The streets and square looked very cheerful, and well lined with people & children, and a fresh, balmy air stirring among the trees. No indications of the "Destroyer" save a solitary hearse on Girod Street, and a little coffin (carried by two boys) covered with white satin, and decked with ribbons, for some young child just perished.

44 W. P. Campbell was a member of the First District School Board and chairman of the standing committee for the Girls High School. NOCD 1859.

Mass burials by torchlight during a yellow fever epidemic in New Orleans, from History of the Yellow Fever *(Philadelphia, 1854).*

September 6   82° 80° 80°

Hot & dry. North East wind. Rain & thunder set in at 10 A.M. Cleared off at noon. Then poured down again at 2 in time to accompany me home to an early dinner.

At the new building putting in foundations of interior Columns, and backing up Granite Water Table. Mortuary returns for the week shew as follows viz.

Yellow fever	449
other diseases	<u>197</u>
Total	646

A very serious report. The case of Miss James, a young girl of 14, living 2 or 3 Squares from us, is a singular one. She has had black vomit for 3 days & nights until yesterday morning, when it ceased and she is now likely to get well. In going to the office this morning I saw a tall German taken with the fever on the Street just opposite Mr. James' house. He fell down from pure weakness and his skin was very yellow & livid....

September 8   80° 83° 81°

Warm sunshine. East wind. Wet and muddy, unfashionable weather for September which is usually our dry month.

The castings for the Store are arriving but in the meantime the work is at a stand. In walking to the office saw 2 white Plumed hearses at the same dwelling on Camp Street. The evening report shews no diminution of the "Fever."...

September 9   80° 83° 83°

Cloudy & threatening, South East wind. Hot sunshine.

At the Building, the Cast Iron Pillars & Lintels on Canal Street are set, and look well. The Water work's Co. are at last laying their pipes in front of our Square to give us the river water. Dr. Barton's theory is that it increases danger to disturb the earth during the summer months, and especially during the prevalence of an epidemic, but I do not think the facts sustain him. The truth is, the same agency which will produce agues and intermittents so freely on the lofty banks of the Hudson River, will produce "yellow fever" on the depressed shores of the Mississippi. After dinner writing and then a walk to the Library &c.

September 11   79° 80° 83°

Cloudy and unsettled. High wind from the North.

At the Building with Mr. Wing at 9. Brickwork going on well. Yellow fever continues very fatal. Deaths varying from 60 to 80 per diem, for the 24 hours ending yesterday at noon 85. After dinner the cool north wind blew freshly, and the afternoon was so inviting that "outdoors" was decidedly preferable to the house. I took Tommy and Ellen down to the Library at the City Hall & spent some time very pleasantly and an equally pleasant walk home under a glorious sunset, taking in a supply of good things on the way, and among the rest a perfectly ripe Pine apple, fresh from Havanna.[45] High wind from the North all night. It will be fatal to many a "fever" patient.

September 14   77° 79° 80°

Change of weather in the night. Rain storm from the North East, and quite cool. Steady hard rain this morning until 9 A.M. The Canal, as usual, over its banks and our Banquette several inches under water. So that I stayed at home writing until it subsided sufficiently to let me go down to the office between 10 and 11. Clouds & showers for the rest of the day.

At the new building I found them hauling bricks and castings, but, of course, no work while the rain lasts....

[45] The Lyceum Library, a public library located in City Hall, was under the jurisdiction of the First District Public School Board, but was used by public school pupils in all districts of the city, as well as adult subscribers. The library contained more than 11,000 volumes. NOCD 1860.

September 16   74° 76° 78°

Cold and clear. North wind. The sky is perfectly lovely today, and the breeze very cheering to well people. But severe on the poor victims to "fever" 74 of whom died yesterday.

Mr. Wing called at the Office and I gave him a working drawing for the Cornice of First Story Entablature. The work at the building goes on well. About a dozen hands employed in raising the Iron Front on Fulton Street and running up the Brickwork....

September 18   73° 75° 76°

Pleasant air from the Eastward, clouds threatening rain.

At the Building at 9 with Mr. Thiel, who liked the work much. Mr. Church the sub-contractor for Brickwork came to the office & I directed him about the Flues which I propose to change somewhat from the Plans....

The "yellow fever" report of yesterday shews a still further decline. The three days have been, 74. 63. 57. deaths. Mrs. James, a lady of 56, near us, took it last night. Opposite to us yesterday, on Euterpe Street, a child was buried. All the other children of the family have had it but recovered. They have been born here. Mr. Thiel, buried a servant yesterday of fever, she was a new comer from Germany and he says her death struggles were perfectly frightful.

September 21   72° 76° 78°

Cool East wind. Clear & very dry. Hot sun.

At the Building the Lumber is being delivered of excellent quality. And brickwork of Entablature, relieving arches &c. going on well....

The Yellow fever seems more violent than ever. 107 deaths are reported for the 30 hours ending yesterday at noon. Poor Mrs. James died yesterday, and the funerals today seem unusually frequent....

September 22   76° 80° 82°

Hot sun, dry parching North wind.

The very worst class of fever weather, as shewn by the continued great mortality of yesterday. 80 deaths. 4 clerks in the Bank of Louisiana are attacked today, severely. Creoles are no longer considered safe. At the store the Brickwork of 1st. story Entablature is nearly complete, and the framing going on. The Lumber is Clear

Lake yellow Pine, which is the best Timber that I know of for framing. In the evening spent 2 hours at the City Hall examing an applicant for teachership, with Messrs. Lusher & Rogers.

September 23   76° 79° 80°

Hot sun. Dry parching air from the North blowing quite fresh....

Mr. W. P. Campbell called, and brought the "Circular" for Pubc. Library, which I had sent to him for perusal & signature. He concurs in it fully, and also in my general plan of instituting a course of 5 Lectures during the ensuing season for the benefit of "Library."

September 24   76° 80° 78°

Damp river fog. North East wind. Changed to south East in the afternoon with strong gusts.

At the Building first entablature finished & laying joists of second story.

At 5½ P.M. I met Messrs. Lusher & Rogers to examine a candidate for the Principalship of the Girl's High School. She went thro' a very searching examination until 9. On Reading & definitions, Grammar, Rhetoric, Intellectual Philosophy, Natural Philosy. Universal History, Chemistry & Astronomy, but when we came to the Mathematical course she requested to waive it, as she acknowledged deficiency there, tho' she had, on the other branches, acquitted herself very creditably. This will deprive her of any chance whatever, unless a modification of this feature in the course of study should be determined by the Board. During the evening I looked out of the window and had a fine view of "Donati's" Comet in the West North West, with its beautiful curved train well defined, thus. It was the loveliest of moonlights when we walked home and it was hard to persuade ourselves that such a radiant atmosphere should be instinct with the seeds of death. Yet so it is. The mortality by fever is still about 70 per day. Many, however, are strangers who persist in rushing to the city in quest of situations, which is simple suicide.

September 25   76° 80° 81°

Warm & sunny. South East wind. Very dry and dusty.

At the Store the framing of second Floor &c. going on well, and window frames being delivered. The subcontractor for the brick work, Mr. Church, lost his little boy by yellow fever yesterday. Mr. Norman's little boy was taken last night, and Mr. Hurlbutt's little boy is still in an unsafe condition. All born here, adding evidence to that fact that "Creolism" is a feeble reliance. Mr. Poinier, a member of the Baptist church, was buried this morning, and there are many cases in our immediate neighbourhood.[46] The epidemic is still in the ascendant, and the "mourners go about the streets." (Yet with the acclimated every thing moves on as easily and uniformly as ever, and the general appearance of the city, apart from the funerals, is cheerful and pleasant, with strong indications of autumnal renaissance.)...

September 27   77° 81° 82°

Hot sunshine, dry and very dusty, North West wind.

From 5 until 9 P.M. at the "Hall" examining Miss E. Perry for the Principalship of Girls' High School.[47] She showed a thoroughly well trained and cultured mind, an extensive acquaintance with general literature, Universal history, & Intellectual Philosophy, prompt and accurate in the exact sciences, and passed by far the most satisfactory examination of all that have yet applied.

September 30   75° 78° 79°

Hot, dry & dusty. East wind....

Note to Mr. Lusher, advising him to call a meeting of the School Board immediately to defer the opening of the schools to the 18th. Proximo, in consequence of the slow decline of the epidemic. At the Custom House we have suffered very little by the fever, only three cases and one fatal. The turning point has evidently been reached, and, we hope, passed; but the decrease is very gradual, and the character of the disease is very malignant. The prevalence, too, of other dangerous forms of disease, typhoid, congestive & intermittent, has been uncommonly great. The deaths in the Charity

[46] G. W. Church, mason, lived on Josephine Street, near Rousseau. NOCD 1859. Levi Hurlbutt lived on Magazine at the corner of Race. NOCD 1859. J. R. Poinier. *Daily Crescent*, Sept. 25, 1858.

[47] Miss E. A. Perry received a salary of $1,200 as principal of the Girls High School. NOCD 1859.

Paulding School, Louis E. Cormier, photographer, Illustrated Sunday Magazine, *ca. 1910 (1974.25.3.699i).*

Hospital alone during the past month have been 521 in all, of which 442 were of yellow fever.

October 1   75° 77° 79°

Hot, dry & dusty, East wind. The air is very pleasant but the sun scorching.

At the Building there are 25 hands actively engaged on the 2nd. Story. At 7 the School Board met, and having a quorum, proceeded at once to examine the propriety of continuing the vacation to the 3rd. Monday in this month owing to very slow decline of the epidemic. The preamble and resolution to that effect were finally adopted with but one dissentient voice. Mr. Lusher offerred a series of resolutions affecting the New School House, one of which provided for the continued supervision of Mr. Reid and myself. I strongly objected and stated my reasons briefly but was overruled, so I suppose we shall have to act, until the completion of the work, on that Committee also.

October 5   78° 80° 79°

Damp & cloudy, with warm bursts of sunshine. South East wind. Dark clouds, & showers at 3 P.M.

At the Store we have commenced framing the 3rd. Story Floor. At the Custom House I have closed my books for the Quarter ending Sept. 30th. and find the total disbursements of the Work from the first to be <u>$2.577.402.51</u>....

At the Custom House Mr. Roy's child, and servant have died. Mr. Thiel's servant and a Prussian friend. Mr. Keen's wife is attacked with the disease, and Capt. Smith's wife is getting worse. Many other cases are around us and deaths every where!! Up to Sunday the deaths by yellow fever in this city alone are reported at 3.491, with an unusually small unacclimated population....

October 7   78° 80° 82°

Heavy rains in the night. This morning very unsettled weather, clouds and sunshine, and warm South West wind.

At the Building the walls of the third story are commenced. The yellow fever continues very bad, 56 deaths yesterday. No less than 5 funeral notices were posted on the Doors of the Post Office. A little creole child died on the next square, and Mrs. Smith on Euterpe Street opposite to us is given up by Dr. Graham. At 7 the monthly meeting of the School Board convened at the City Hall. I opened the proceedings by reading my Report on Library & Lyceum, and the Circular which I had prepared for distribution thro' the city, with a view to excite new interest in our Library, all of which was unanimously approved. A good deal of miscellaneous business was disposed of. Mr. Lusher was elected Chairman of Committee of boy's High School.[48]

Miss E. A. Perry, was presented by the committee on Teachers for the Principalship of the Girl's High School, and elected after much discussion growing out of the opposition of two members. Mr. [U. H.] Pearce was elected 1st. Asst. of Paulding School.[49] I then made a few remarks introductory to the following Preamble and Resolution, which I offered with a view to remedy certain disadvantages under which our Public School System now suffers. Preamble. Whereas the experience of the last half century has shewn the month of July to be comparatively a safe and salubrious month in this city; and the month of September, even in the healthiest seasons, to be marked by a degree of mortality greatly exceeding the normal standard; therefore, Resolved, that the commencement of the Summer vacation be transferred from the Friday next preceding the 4th. of July, to the 1st. Friday in July, and that the reopening of the Schools shall be changed from the 1st. Monday in September, to the 1st. Monday in the month of October. This met with the cordial support of the entire board, and it was moved to dispense with the Rules and adopt it at once. But as it involves the change of an existing rule, it is obligatory to postpone final action for one month, when there will be no doubt of its being passed unanimously. Board then adjourned.

[48] The Boys High School was at the corner of Camp and Melpomene. NOCD 1859.
[49] Paulding School was located on Gaiennie, corner Constance. NOCD 1859.

PLATE 12. *Port and City of New Orleans from Mandeville Street by Marie Adrien Persac, between 1858 and 1859 (1988.9), Clarisse Claiborne Grima Acquisition Fund purchase. Details shown on the levee in the foreground include the Third District Market, wharves, a ferry at dock, and bales of cotton (some covered with a tarpaulin) ready for loading.*

PLATE 13. *French Market and Red Store by Louis Dominique Grandjean Develle, between 1840 and 1850 (1948.1), showing vendors and peddlers on the levee.*

PLATE 14. *New Orleans from the Lower Cotton Press, Bernhard J. Dondorf, delineator, engraver, 1852 (1949.17). The typical mixture of business and pleasure on the city's levees is depicted in the left foreground: stevedores loading bales of cotton and hogsheads (perhaps of sugar) onto a ship, drays, pedestrians out for a stroll, gentlemen on horseback, and a sporty carriage.*

PLATE 15. *Fire Protection on Parade – 35th Annual Parade of the Firemen of New Orleans by Paul Poincy, 1872, reproduction (1974.25.2.211). The Firemen's Charitable Association wielded considerable political and economic power, controlling pension funds and cemeteries; the firemen are assembled at the Henry Clay statue on Canal Street for their annual parade through the city.*

PLATE 16. *Bird's-eye view of New Orleans from the Lower Cotton Press, John William Hill and Benjamin Franklin Smith, Jr., delineators, David William Moody, lithographer, 1852 (1947.20). With the city viewed from a height, much of Algiers, including the Belleville Iron Works, Holy Name of Mary Church, and the old Marine Hospital, as well as the sweeping crescent of the Mississippi can be seen.*

PLATE 17. *Bird Store, 626 Royal Street by Boyd Cruise, 1945 (1946.3). Royal and Chartres Streets were the elegant shopping thoroughfares of the 1850s; the Whartons browsed and purchased Christmas and birthday presents there.*

PLATE 18. *French Opera House by Marie Adrien Persac, between 1859 and 1873 (1939.5), one of the major cultural institutions of the Creole city.*

PLATE 19. *Seventy-two rue de l'Hôpital, New Orleans, Louisiana, by Boyd Cruise, 1948 (1950.6), representation of a nineteenth-century French Quarter residence.*

PLATE 20. *French Opera House, postcard, ca.1900 (1982.135.32).*

PLATE 21. *Farragut's Fleet Passing the Forts below New Orleans by Mauritz F. H. De Haas, between 1863 and 1867 (1974.80). De Haas, who never visited New Orleans, painted this accurate depiction from descriptions provided by his friend David G. Farragut. It shows the nighttime battle with its artillery duel between Forts*

Jackson and St. Philip and the Union mortar boats, blazing fire boats, the Confederate ironclad ram Manassas *(the armor of which was fabricated in the Custom House), and the Union fleet passing through the defensive ship hulks and broken chain barrier that had blocked upriver access.*

PLATE 22. U.S.S. Pensacola *at Anchor in the Mississippi River at New Orleans by Edward Everard Arnold, 1864 (1983.1). The* Pensacola *was one of the Union ships that arrived at the city April 25, 1862, after running the gauntlet of Forts Jackson and St. Philip; it is depicted from the lower part of New Orleans with the west bank in the background. Captain Henry W. Morris with two squads of marines, probably shown in the boat going ashore, raised the American flag over the U.S. Mint on April 26.*

St. Patrick's Church (1974.25.7.81).

o[r]phans from the Catholic Asylums were present. The ceremonies ended we took one of the long file of carriages, and proceeded to the Graveyard (St. Patricks) about 4 miles from town, on the Metairie Ridge.[52] The Cemetery looked so peaceful and inviting under the sweet mellow light of the summer sunset. And beautiful trees waved every where over the thick sown tombs. At the grave the ceremonies were short, and we drove back to the city before 7. Mrs. Fox was upwards of 70. She died at the Bay of St. Louis, where she owned a summer residence; her remains were brought over last night by her son in law, E. Tracey. She leaves a handsome property.

October 16   72° 76° 75°

Warm and sunny. East wind. Wind rising and clouding up for rain during the day.

At the Building putting on cieling joists. After dinner took Tommy up to Fleming's to get him some little books.[53] The fresh breeze blew cheerily, and the rich green trees around us begin to shew an occasional tinge of autumn. The beautiful comet that has been with us so long is gradually fading out of the South Western sky. Not many evenings ago the young moon, Venus, & the Comet, all in the same quarter of the heavens, formed a Stellar combination

October 14   72° 75° 76°

Cool morning, with early mist. North East wind. Very hot sunshine. Building going on rapidly….

We received notice today of the death of Mrs. Fox (Mrs. Elisha Tracey's mother).[50] After dinner Emily, Mrs. Ladd & I went to Genl. Tracey's. The funeral address was deliv[er]ed by Father Mullen in full canonicals; and the obsequies performed by him, Father Lacroix, and another priest.[51] A large number of male & female

[50] Mrs. Patrick E. Fox died in 1858 in Pass Christian, Miss. *Daily Picayune*, Oct. 12, 1858.

[51] The Rev. James I. Mullon (1793-1866) was pastor of St. Patrick's Church on Camp Street. The Rev. Cyril Delacroix was his assistant. Samuel Wilson, Jr., *St. Patrick's Church, 1833-1992* (New Orleans, 1992), 54-55.

[52] St. Patrick Cemetery was founded in 1841 by St. Patrick's Church to accommodate its many Irish immigrant parishioners. It is located at the end of Canal Street near Metairie Ridge. *New Orleans Architecture*, 3:32-33.

[53] William Flemming, bookseller, was located on Magazine Street at the corner of St. Andrew. NOCD 1858.

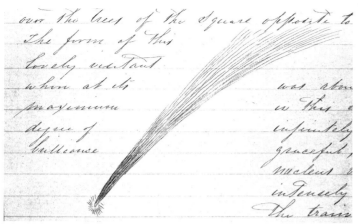

of rare beauty. Somewhat thus, as seen over the trees of the Square opposite to us. The form of this lovely visitant when at its maximum degree of brilliance was about as shewn in this sketch but infinitely more graceful; the starry nucleus became intensely bright, and the train gradually widening in a curved line, and diminishing in clearness. As it retired far far away from the luminous vortex, became at last so rare and filmy that other luminaries could be clearly discovered thro' it. Seldom has it been our lot to witness so superb a phenomenon. "The heavens declare the glory of God."

October 23   72° 75° 76°

Warm & cloudy. Wind due north. Bright sunshine in middle of day.

At the Building copper gutters going in and brickwork nearly finished. Drove out with Major Beauregard to the New Marine Hospital, examined the work, and extended our drive to the new square on the Metairie ridge, & back by Bienville Street Shell road.[54] A very pleasant variety to the daily routine. Got home to dinner at 3, and much distressed to find Tommy with high fever.

October 24   74° 70° 73°

Sunday. Mild air from the South East. Clouds and sunshine. Rains in the afternoon.

Yesterday when I got home and found Tommy with such a raging fever, I at once took the omnibus & went for Dr. Wood, who was

soon in attendance, and put him immediately under a course of treatment for yellow fever.[55] He had already taken the usual mustard foot bath. He took his medicines very well, and Emily and Mrs. Ladd watched him closely all night, so that this morning he is quiet, with very little fever, and apparently doing as well as possible. Dr. Wood called morning & evening, and represented his condition as very good indeed.

October 25   72° 75° 75°

Warm & sunny. South wind after dashes of rain in the night. Very hot at noon.

Tommy passed a very easy quiet night, but from time to time complained of thirst. Dr. Wood came at 8 and was perfectly satisfied with his condition. No fever. No symptom of inward irritation, but an uncontrollable appetite, and desire to get up. The former we must appease for the present with soda-biscuit and corn-starch. The latter by supplying means of amusement in bed. At the Building twice this morning. Cornice & roof work going on well. Rejected a number of yellow brick.

Mortuary returns for the week are.

Yellow fever	265
other diseases	145
Total.	410

When I returned to dinner found Tommy entirely free from fever. No debility or internal irritation and much delighted with the things I brought him, and when Dr. Wood came in the evening he seemed much pleased to see him in the same hopeful condition without any fever whatever.

October 29   65° 68° 67°

After a very cool night the morning opens very pleasantly with South West wind. Changed to West at noon.

Tommy has had an excellent night and is very much better this morning, his recovery is advancing most satisfactorily.

Work goes on well at the building. Iron Scrolls well executed. Hall & Kemp have leased it today for one year to C[harles]. H. Bradshaw, wholesale and retail grocer. At $2.200 per ann. which makes the investment a good one.

[54] This square may have been City Park. The city had contracted with James Lindsey to build a common bar, fence, and keeper's lodge under the direction of Louis H. Pilié, city surveyor. NONA, Eusebe Bouny, Apr. 14, 1858.

[55] Dr. William B. Wood lived in Wharton's neighborhood, on Magazine St. at the corner of Josephine. He was one of five doctors appointed to a special board of health by the city council in 1853. Duffy, *Matas History of Medicine*, 2:180.

Say. for ground.	$ 8.000
" Building	<u>12.700</u>
	$20.700

Visited the Girls' High School, and spent an hour during the opening exercises. The whole most admirably conducted by the talented principal, Miss Perry. 80 Pupils were in attendance, divided between the Principal and 3 Assistants, and a better conducted, and more carefully arranged school I never saw....

October 30   65° 68° 67°

Beautiful weather, with pleasant cool air from the north.

Tommy has had an excellent night, and is fresh and lively this morning. The Doctor allows him to sit up out of bed today. It is just one week since he was taken and I feel very thankful indeed to think that he has got so easily over it, especially as the first attack was so severe.

At my building one pediment is finished and the Iron Scrolls in place, and the effect is decidedly good. Mr. Reid and I paid an inspecting visit to the new school house, corner of Palmyra and Prieur Streets. The brick piers are up and first tier of joists on, and the work generally creditable to the contractor....

October 31   64° 67° 68°

Sunday. Dark gloomy clouds, dripping rains, North East wind. Gleams of sunshine.

Carpets down yesterday, and a comfortable fire in the dining room today....

Dr. Wood has not called today which I consider a plain indication that he thinks Tommy perfectly safe. Indeed he has been all day as lively and apparently strong as usual, for which I feel deeply thankful.

The mortuary returns for the week are

Yellow Fever	174
other diseases	<u>164</u>
Total	338

Shewing a very marked decline. The total mortality by "fever" alone to this time is 4.628. And it lingers among us so long. Day after day, new and unexpected cases have sprung up in our neighbourhood for weeks past, so that we shall hail the return of full general health as the desert pilgrim the "diamond Fountain." At the New Custom House during the past very dangerous month we have been highly favored, only three cases and one of them fatal.

November 6   51° 51° 54°

After a long delay, the frost came unmistakably last night, and the grass was well crisped early this morning. The sun rose clear and the North wind breathed keenly over the streets. The scourge of the summer is vanishing rapidly....

At the building a good deal today. 3 times on the roof. Met the contractor and Mr. Hall, one of the proprietors. Every thing going on actively and to my full satisfaction. Slating the roof commenced this morning. Found them neglecting the <u>mortar clause</u>, and took the contractor up immediately and had it rectified. I consider it very important on such a warped roof to bed & point the upper line of the slate carefully with good cement or white mortar.

November 10   46° 47° 49°

Very cold North wind. Light clouds.

Tommy is almost quite well now, but we still keep him in the room by a good warm fire. At the Building the roof is finished and looks extremely well. Gave certificate for the 4th. Payment. Visited the Girls' High School, and much pleased with the recitation of Mrs. Abbot's class on the history of Europe during the early part of the 12th. century. Last Wednesday I heard one of the Papers, edited by the young ladies of the 2nd. Course, read admirably, and full of good articles. Name "The Wave." Today the paper of the 3rd. Course was read, "The Arrow," and was very creditable but uniformly exhibiting less ability than the rival sheet. Mr. Lusher and Mr. Campbell were also present (joint members with me on the Committee) and the visit throughout was most satisfactory.

November 15   60° 60° 56°

Heavy rain this morning. North West wind. Wet and gloomy all day.

Work at the Building confined to the inside. Our contract requires delivery today, but the disabilities from the epidemic compel us to call for indulgence.

Saw Mr. Lusher on business of the schools. Proposed to reduce the extent of daily lessons at present imposed on pupils, by extending the time assigned to the aggregate course. The amount of labor now required from them is too great, both mentally and physically considered, Mr. Lusher fully agrees with me.

Mortuary returns for the week shew.

Yellow Fever	66
other diseases	<u>164</u>
Total	230

November 17   46° 52° 52°

Beautiful weather. Cold North wind.

Store finishing up rapidly. Met Mr. [Alfred] Morel at the Office of Amadée Ducatel at 12 and went to appraise the succession of Major Beauregard's sister, M[adam]e. Emilia Toutant Belly. We shall have to meet again, as part of the Property was not presented.[56] Spent half an hour at the High School with Mr. W. O. Rogers, the Superintendent. On my way home to dinner, walked up part of the way with Dr. Palmer who is recovering slowly from "yellow fever" and still feeble. Mr. Rogers is weak but nearly well.

Dr. Palmer says he will be prepared to deliver a lecture for us at the Lyceum on any day from the 10th. to the 15th. December. His subject "the importance of a more thorough acquaintance with the English Language in the community." Mr. Cohen told me this morning that he was ready to follow the Dr. on any day that I should appoint in December.[57] Answered sister Marianne's letter. After dinner walked up to Bishop Polk's to return him "Hodge's book on Infant Baptism."[58] I had a full and very interesting conversation with him on the Book and the subject generally. This work is a "finality" it settles the question in favor of my ancestral belief beyond the possibility of its being again undermined.

November 22   47° 49° 50°

Cold wind from the North West, driving the clouds across the sky, and sweeping the withered yellow leaves from the China Trees....

At the new Building painting and Banquette going on briskly. The Banquette 25 feet wide with slope of ¹/₂ inch to the foot, of North River "dimension" flag will be an admirable piece of work....

[56] Amadée Ducatel was a prominent notary whose records run from 1836 to 1890. His office was at 60 Toulouse Street. NOCD 1858; NONA, Amadée Ducatel, Nov. 17, 1858.

[57] M. M. Cohen was an attorney at 22 Exchange Place. NOCD 1858.

[58] William Hodges, *Infant Baptism Tested by Scripture and History* (Philadelphia, 1844).

Judah P. Benjamin by Adolph Rinck, 1853 (1959.82).

November 23   45° 46° 49°

Strong white frost in the night. Bright sunshine. West wind.

The extreme beauty of the day drew out several lady visitors to the New Custom House to see the superb Corinthian Capitals now fully set, and lustrous with sunshine, and the fine views from the top of the works &c. &c....

November 24   44° 46° 48°

Heavy white frost in the night. Charming weather. North West wind.

At the Building stairways nearly finished and awnings &c. &c. going on briskly. At 12 to 1 went to St. Louis Street and appraised the succession of Major Beauregard's sister at $13.417, for partition among the heirs, on a cash basis, and of course, much within actual value....

November 25   44° 49° 52°

Heavy white frost in the night. Cold air from North West. Bright sunny sky.

Work at store advancing fast. Letter to Senator J. P. Benjamin, with list of Books, published by the Government, which are wanting in our Library & which he has kindly promised to send me.[59] Took Senator Slidell over the work; he was much gratified, especially with the splendid marble capitals, all glistening in the lustrous sunshine.…

After dinner Mr. Wheeler called for me to go to Shephard Brown's handsome new house, going up at the end of our Square, to consult about the arrangement of a hot air furnace, flues &c. "Chilson's new conical Patent." Met Mr. Brown there, and Mr. W. K. Day, the builder. Decided position of furnace, branches, registers &c.

November 27   54° 60° 58°

Beautiful weather. Cool air from the East clouding up in the afternoon.

The Banquette round the new store is finished and looks very well indeed. Stairs, also &c. &c., and the Tenant is more than ever pleased with his stand. Met Mr. A. H. May, one of our Directors.[60] Told me he had just lost a child, and was deeply affected. It made me more grateful than I was before, if possible, that Tommy had so completely recovered from his yellow fever attack. In the evening at Nicholson & Co.'s office about the stone of Banquette &c. After tea arranged a Portfolio full of drawings.

November 29   62° 64° 64°

Damp and foggy. South East wind.…

The dreadful epidemic of 1858 is evidently now at an end. The total mortality to this time has been 4.852 by yellow fever alone.

November 30   50° 52° 54°

Heavy rains in the night, and change of wind from South East to North West. Cold and gloomy this morning with raw air from the North West. Cleared off pleasant in the middle of the day.

On my way to the Office spent an hour at the High School, and went over two or three Propositions in 6th. & 7th. Book of LeGendre's Geometry, with the Principal's first class.[61] The demonstrations were decidedly good.…

The month of November happily closes the epidemic season, which may now be considered extinct. The air has resumed its wonted buoyancy, and sorrow and sighing have fled away. The Disease has been marked by the highest point of mortality, in proportion to the extent of the unacclimated population, ever reached in this city.…

December 1   50° 54° 54°

Cold bracing air from the North East. Very pleasant. Passing clouds & bright sunshine. Cloudy in the middle of the day.…

Note from Mr. Charles Gayarré in reply to mine. He will be unable to deliver a Lecture in our Lyceum, as his whole time this winter will be devoted to the completion of his History of Louisiana.…

December 2   56° 60° 60°

Dull cloudy weather. Raw air from North East. Sprinkling rain in the middle of the day with bursts of sunshine.…

At the Office monthly Reports &c. for November. The amount of work performed is unusually great, and the beautiful Corinthian Capitals of Collector's room are now all set. And preparations making for the heavy, double faced Entablature to come over them. During the long and malignant epidemic we have been greatly favored. Out of 200 persons, or thereabouts, always on the work, we have had but 8 cases of yellow fever, 4 of which proved fatal. In the Offices Major Beauregard, myself, Mr. Andrews, Mr. Guesnon and Mr. Deacon have never had the "Fever" and yet we have enjoyed our usual good health all thro' this fatal season.[62] Monthly meeting of the Board this evening. My Programme of Lectures approved, and after the meeting I made all necessary arrangements with the Superintendent & Librarian to carry them forward. I offerred a Resolution to allow Teacher's Salaries when absent from sickness and from death of relatives, under proper restrictions. Referred to Committee on Teachers.

[59] Judah Philip Benjamin (1811-1884), an attorney, was a United States senator before the Civil War and served in the Confederate cabinet as attorney general, secretary of war, and secretary of state. *DLB.*

[60] A. H. May, a commission merchant and cotton factor, lived on Prytania near Urania. He was a member of the First District School Board. NOCD 1859.

[61] *Elements of Geometry and Trigonometry* by A. M. Legendre, first published in 1819 and frequently republished.

[62] Joseph Andrews was a member of the First District School Board. NOCD 1859. Antoine Danvillier Guesnon (ca. 1803-1879), a customs warehouse clerk, lived on St. Claude near Barracks. NOCD 1856; *Bee,* Jan. 18, 1879. William Deacon (ca. 1808-1861), a clerk at the Custom House, lived on Camp St. *Daily Picayune,* Mar. 7, 1861; NOCD 1854.

Seamen's Home by J. Gallier & Co., Labrot Collection, Southeastern Architectural Archive, Tulane University Library.

December 6   72° 72° 73°

Mild & cloudy. South East wind....

After dinner went to the "Sailors' Home" at the request of Mr. M. Rice to examine an appearance of settlement in one of the floors.[63] I found some trifling evidence of curvature where the parlor floor crosses a dwarf wall, and some cracks in the plastering of 4th. story, due to the shrinkage of so extended a system of wooden framing enclosed within heavy brick walls which have not subsided at all. After the business season is over it will be well to bring the floor to proper line again, point up &c. &c. I think by that time every thing will have reached its true bearing....

December 7   72° 73° 74°

Mild & pleasant. South East wind. Very warm, sunny and debilitating in the middle of the day....

On my way home called at Dr. Palmer's and had an interview with him preparatory to the "opening Lecture" of our course on Friday for which I have made ample arrangements, &c. &c. and in addition to the regular paying tickets, have issued a large number of Complimentary Tickets for the Course to the Clergy, the Press, and friends interested in the cause of Public Education, and the establishment of a literary "Centre" in our City. At 3½ got home to dinner very weary with warmth and walking....

December 10   44° 49° 50°

Lovely weather, with cold bracing North wind....

At half past 6 took a carriage, and called for Dr. Palmer, whom I found ready and in excellent voice. Drove to the City Hall, and found our handsome Lecture room filling up fast. By 7 the seats were nearly all occupied. Dr. Palmer and the committee ascended the Platform, and as Chairman I rose and introduced the Lecturer to the audience, which was very large and select, and the greater part composed of "familiar faces." My only regret was that I had failed to induce any one of my own family to accompany me. The Lecture "on the claims of the English Language" was one of extreme beauty, rising at times to summits of lofty eloquence, and was listened to throughout with profound attention, and well applauded at the close. Altogether a most gratifying exordium to our "Course."...

[63] M. T. Rice of the firm Rice & Hathaway & Co., commission merchants, at 37 Natchez. NOCD 1858.

December 11   52° 54° 57°

Dull and cloudy. Raw North wind.

At the New Store. The last painting on cornice, antae caps & first story walls is going on. Was there at 11, and hands all busy. Rains set in at 9½ and continued thro' the morning. Very dreary, muddy & hateful. The Press today abounds in beautiful and flattering notices of our first Lecture at the Lyceum, last evening. It was very successful. This morning had an application for our room on Monday evening, to be used by G. D. Prentice (the famous orator & poet) to deliver a Lecture on the "present aspect of the politics of this country." The "ordinance" requires that no Lecturer shall use the room without the Sanction of the Board, so I immediately enclosed to Mr. W. O. Rogers, a circular addressed to the Board for approval and signature, requiring that at least 11 names should be attached to it. I also, at 12 M. when Mr. Rogers called upon me, addressed, and handed to him, a note to Mr. Robt. J. Ward (acting for Mr. Prentice) in which I quoted the stringent language of the ordinance under which we act, limiting our Lectures strictly to "Science & belles lettres" and prohibiting "religious and political discussions," and expressing an earnest request that Mr. Prentice would accordingly give a general, comprehensive, and poetic treatment of the subject chosen, (which he so well knows how to do) so as not to contravene the intention of the ordinance.[64]

December 16   56° 59° 60°

Thanksgiving Day. Works at the Custom House suspended as usual. Lovely weather with cool bracing air from the North West.

Tommy and I got up earlier than usual, and went with the servant to market. Found the Red Fish exceedingly fine and fresh from the water, with blood red gills, vegetables, too, of superior quality. Filled up the basket handsomely to help out the Thanksgiving Turkey. It was with the "deepest thankfulness" that I saw Tommy trotting along so hearty and well by my side after the fearful ordeal of last summer. Spent the morning in finishing up a set of working drawings for the New Store to keep on record. Then at noon went over to W. K. Day's to see the drawings of cornice for Shephard Brown's house, which he invited me to examine, the other day. After dinner went over the work itself, the cornice being actually in hand, cieling joists laid &c. &c. It will be a fine structure, and the locality is one of the

[64] Robert J. Ward of Ward, Hunt & Co., commission merchants, 100 Gravier Street. NOCD 1859.

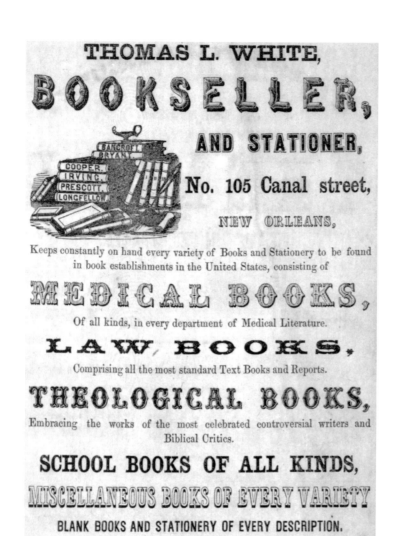

Keeps constantly on hand every variety of Books and Stationery to be found in book establishments in the United States, consisting of

MEDICAL BOOKS,

Of all kinds, in every department of Medical Literature.

LAW BOOKS,

Comprising all the most standard Text Books and Reports.

THEOLOGICAL BOOKS,

Embracing the works of the most celebrated controversial writers and Biblical Critics.

SCHOOL BOOKS OF ALL KINDS,

MISCELLANEOUS BOOKS OF EVERY VARIETY

BLANK BOOKS AND STATIONERY OF EVERY DESCRIPTION.

Dealers Merchants and Teachers

Would do well to call and examine the stock offered.

☞ A liberal discount made to those buying to sell to Universities, Teachers and Students.

Advertisement, Gardner & Wharton's New Orleans Directory, 1858.

choicest in the city. The view from its lofty blocking course is without exception the most picturesque and varied that I have yet seen in this district; and the house itself will add greatly to the beauty of our Square.

December 29   53° 56° 61°

Damp and cloudy. East wind. Cleared off at noon.

Called at High School, where the graduating class is attending daily from 9 until 3, reviewing their principal studies, altho' this is Vacation week. The Principal finds them all punctual and well prepared. Called at the new store, finished for Hall & Kemp, and found every thing in good order as to the Building, and the Banquette around perfectly solid, after the severe strains that it has been exposed to, by rolling sugar Hogsheads over it, since the Lessee took possession. Settled up in full with Hall & Kemp. Very busy at the Office in closing up the month &c. Meeting of the Committee on Teachers at 6 P.M.…

December 31

Heavy rains in the night, with change of wind to North. Cold, raw, cloudy, & rainy this morning, with mud of the utmost tenacity &c. &c. Cold rains from the North thro' the morning: rather better in the afternoon, with an attempt to clear up.

Very busy at the Office with my accounts &c. for the end of the Year, and the close also of the Financial Quarter. Yesterday I bought a very nice box of good Tools for Tommy, and I never saw so large an amount of real happiness drawn out of an equal investment before. This morning he was up before any of us, and hard at work with them, and went at it again immediately after breakfast. Again when I returned to dinner at 3½. The tools were still before him. In the morning Major B. & I went off for half an hour to "Steele's" & "White's" and out [of] the stores of elegant volumes for the New Year selected each a "gem."[65] Walk after dinner, and retired very early after tea. Wearied out with the fatigue and gloomy weather of the past week, and determined to get a good solid rest, and open upon the New Year thoroughly refreshed. "Tired nature's sweet restorer" &c. &c.

65 J. B. Steel was a bookseller and stationer at 60 Camp St.; Thomas L. White was a bookseller and stationer at 105 Canal St. NOCD 1857.

Wagon sunk in the mire of an unpaved New Orleans street, Edward L. Wilson, photographer, ca. 1884 (1987.172).

January 1   47° 50° 51°

The North wind has done its duty: the first opening of the shutters threw in a flood of sunshine: the square opposite powdered over with white frost. The sky unsullied, and the air elastic and springy. All in brilliant contrast with the dull grey curtains, and dripping mists of the dying old year....

At 12 commenced the regular <u>business</u> of the day. Business & pleasure combined in careful proportions. Business, walking, pleasure, calling. The day was so pleasant that every body was on the alert, and the stream poured on until night closed the scene. The visitors at home outnumbered my visits abroad, but I made 21 calls and I thought that was doing pretty well when those calls were extended over a lineal space of three miles. All on foot. As to those who rode, I pitied them. The mire was worse than a storm on the Atlantic....

1859

January 8   38° 42° 42°

Anniversary of the Battle of Orleans.

Works at the Custom House suspended.

Heavy frost in the night. Ice formed on the pools of the Square opposite quite thick for this latitude, ⅛". Brilliant sky overhead and sharp North wind.

The day was ushered in by the booming of cannon as usual. Today the festivities receive an additional interest from the presence of the veteran General [Winfield] Scott....

At 11, took Tommy, Ellen & Miss Tallulah Low to the City Hall to see the assembling of the great people of the day at the Mayor's Room.[1] Then as the cortège marched to the platform on the Square opposite, we passed out by the side door, and clearing the crowd, took our position with about 100 ladies and gentlemen on the Verandahs of the Florance House, which commanded a fine view of the evolutions on Lafayette Square, and then of the entire procession which passed under the galleries at between 12 & 1. General Scott & the Mayor with Genl. Twiggs & aid occupied an open-carriage drawn by 4 white horses, in about the centre of the long file.[2] He appeared strong and hearty, tho' so advanced in life, and returned the greeting from our gallery with a graceful bow....

January 10   44° 48° 50°

Beautiful weather. Cold West wind....

Call at the office from Lieut. Col. Lay to obtain the use of the Lyceum Hall for "Readings" by a Mrs. Blunt, strongly recommended by Genl. Scott, Bishop Polk, and others.[3] I stated to him the limitations imposed upon us by the ordinance of council &c. and the proper mode of making the application by the authorized Agent of the Lady, in order to obtain the required Sanction of the Board &c.

[1] The Mayor's Room, now generally known as the Mayor's Parlor, is located in the corner of Gallier Hall (the former City Hall), overlooking St. Charles Avenue and Lafayette Street. It is still used for civic receptions.
[2] Winfield Scott (1786-1866), hero of the Mexican War and Whig candidate for the presidency in 1852, had been commanding general of the U.S. Army since 1841. *DAB*. David Emanuel Twiggs (1790-1862) lived on Prytania Street, opposite Margaret Place. Later a major general in the Confederate army, Twiggs was in command of the military district headquartered in New Orleans. *DAB*; NOCD 1856.
[3] George William Lay (d. 1867) of Virginia was aide-de-camp to Winfield Scott (1855-1861). Heitman, *Historical Register*. Ellen Key Blunt (b. 1821) was the daughter of Francis Scott Key and Mary Tayloe Lloyd Key. George A. Hanson, *Old Kent: The Eastern Shore of Maryland* (Baltimore, 1876), 38-39.

&c. This application signed by Bishop Polk, Major Beauregard and several eminent citizens was brought up to me by Grey just after dinner, when Mr. D. Cronan also called on business. I went down to the City Hall and wrote a letter to the members of the Board laying the subject of the above interviews & application before them &c. &c....

January 11   46° 48° 49°

Raw, cold & cloudy: dripping rains. North East wind. Dreary, dreary all day....

Bishop Polk called at the office to learn the progress of negotiations in reference to the application of yesterday. I told him that as soon as my messenger returned with the proper number of signatures from the Board, I would address him at the "St. Charles" which I did at 1 P.M. offering the use of Lyceum Hall for tomorrow evening to Mrs. Key Blunt for her "Readings" "free of charge."...

January 12   52° 52° 53°

Rains all night, and again this morning damp and cheerless, with East wind....

After tea went to a meeting of the Committee on Teachers at the City Hall. Met Messrs. Lusher, Clark, Poindexter and Rogers.[4] At 8 adjourned to the Lyceum Hall to he[a]r Mrs. Blunt's readings which we found quite well attended for such a wretched evening. Her "Evangeline" was good, but her best were "Poe's Raven" and her father's "Star Spangled Banner."...

January 14   58° 58° 60°

Mild and pleasant air from the South West. Sun shines out again at last.

Visited the 6 rooms of the Washington School. Found everything in good order as to classes, and studies, made note of necessary improvements in rooms &c. &c. Corrected "article" for "DeBow's Review" on N. Orleans New Custom House &c. &c.[5] Visit from Mr. Low at the Office about proposed embellishment of his property and engaged to meet him at the Sailor's Home at 5 this evening to consider with the Trustees certain additions proposed.

[4] James S. Clark of the firm Clark, Mosby & Co., commission merchants, was a member of the First District School Board. In 1859 he lived at 25 Terpsichore. J. G. Poindexter was also a member of the board. NOCD 1859.
[5] "Commerce of New-Orleans" in "Notes on Southern Cities, Etc.," *DeBow's Review* 26 OS (May 1859): 596.

Chalmette battlefield, Jacob A. Dallas, delineator, Frank Leslie's Illustrated Newspaper, *January 23, 1858 (1974.25.5.26).*

Answered cousin Fanny's letter of Decr. 21. 1858. At 5 Mr. Low called for me and we had a most gratifying visit to the Sailor's Home, which is under excellent management, and in full tide of prosperous operation. I indicated a piece of ground on the property about 35' x 18', and proposed that $2000 should be appropriated by the Trustees for the erection of a Two Story Brick Reading & Sitting Room, which the Sailors much need. It meets with warm support from Mr. Low, and the Superintendent.

January 15   48° 50° 52°

Pleasant change in the weather. Cold North West wind. Clear lucid sky. Bright and joyous.

Met Mr. & Mrs. Low, who were much pleased with drawings of a front I designed last year, and which they sent for yesterday to examine with reference to their proposed improvements. They say it will be just the thing, but I advise to defer the contemplated changes until another season. Their recent outlays have been great, and it is best to breathe awhile before encountering fresh expense. In the meantime the whole plan can be matured so as to meet every point in the best manner. Mr. Low fully agrees with me.

After dinner went over the two buildings, still unfinished, of Mr. Robinson and Mr. Brown.[6] From the roof of the latter's house the view is exceedingly fine, but unfortunately he has omitted to frame a Belvidere, so that the top of the house will be inaccessible except by a mere scuttle.

January 18   43° 46° 48°

Cold wind from the north. Clear sky....

I have closed my Books for the fourth Quarter of 1858 and find the total disbursements at the New Custom House to Decr. 31. 1858
        $2.603.336.79
and the amount still available to the 30th. June 1859, from Jany 1st. is $327.955.48....

January 22   46° 48° 50°

Cold north wind. Still cloudy, with gleams of sunshine. Severe change of 16 degrees in 24 hours.

Called at "Normal School" fine classes under the admirable direction of Mrs. Pagaud and Mrs. Waugh. Note to Mr. Hoffman

---

[6] The residence of Emmett Toole Robinson, later Miss Sophie B. Wright's Home Institute, still stands at 1465 Camp Street.

declining his application to admit his child as a pupil of the Washington School, as he resides <u>out</u> of the District. Note to Mr. Lusher, recommending a negotiation with Mrs. Blunt to admit the pupils & teachers of our "Normal" and "High Schools" to her "Readings" on moderate terms, and the promotion of Miss Allston of the Washington School, when an opportunity occurs.[7]...

January 26   49° 52° 53°

Still dull and gloomy but without rain: North East wind. Rain, however, at noon....

Received an order from Mr. Low to commence Plans for a new Baptist Church (about $25.000).

Made a trial ground Plan for the Building after tea, providing 108 fine large pews, 3' by 9' accommodating with roomy sittings 550 persons.[8]

January 27   58° 64° 66°

Rainy and warm. Dark and gloomy. East wind. Struggled hard thro' the morning to clear up, but the rain came down heavily in the afternoon, and the mud is perfectly intolerable....

Met Mr. M. Rice, who stated that the Committee on "Orphan Asylum" has purchased a Square, on which to build a new Asylum and wished to know if I would offer a set of plans in "competition;" to which I unhesitatingly replied, no, as late examples have shewn that "competition" simply means getting the elaborated efforts of the best architects, and then giving the substantial profits to some favorite already determined on....

January 31   50° 53° 54°

Beautiful weather. Wind N. N. East....

Spent the evening on a pencil drawing of the present appearance of Mr. Low's house with its surroundings, trees &c. He proposes to replace the present front &c. with more tasteful and decorative work,

---

[7] The Normal School, of which Mrs. L. A. Pagaud was principal, was located in the Girls High School on Clio Street. Mrs. A. Y. Waugh was associate principal. Miss E. Allston was second assistant at Washington School. NOCD 1859.

[8] The plans were probably for a building for the First Baptist Church, which was holding services at the Coliseum Place Baptist Church. In July 1861, the First Baptist Church purchased the old Lafayette High School building at the corner of Magazine and Second streets, which served the congregation until April 3, 1892, when it burned.

and I have made the present drawing as a study to lead to the best mode of introducing the intended changes.

February 2   61° 63° 63°

Clouds and sunshine. South West wind. Turned out very pleasant in the afternoon....

At the office just driven to death with business. Indeed I never had so much of detailed and miscellaneous calls upon me as at present, and think seriously of resigning from every thing, and devoting myself exclusively to rest and the "fine arts."...

February 5   51° 56° 54°

Fine and sunny with light clouds gathering. East wind.

Visited the normal school on my way to the office.

At 11 Ellen and Tommy came to the office, and I took them to the Circus, in respondence to innumerable petitions during the last two or three weeks. The performances were fine, the "spectatorial corps" immense, and the general hilarity and enjoyment unbounded. All possible equestrianism, and callisthenics of the most difficult description, good music &c. &c. all well executed, and covering about 2½ hours.[9] Returned to the office, and then home to dinner at 4. Tommy stood during the whole performance at the Circus, with his eyes rivetted on the arena, and as completely fascinated, as a bird by a serpent.

February 9   51° 50½° 50°

Cloudy. With fresh breeze from the West. Quite cold. Cleared off at noon. Turning colder.

Answered "subpoena" to 5th. Dist. Court at 10, in case of Costa v. Whitehead.[10] My report of yesterday was so completely in opposition to the defendant, that his counsel, by whom I was "subpoenaed" thought he could get along better without me, so that I was fortunate in having but a short detention. The terrific lightening flash that

[9] The circus was held at Spalding and Rogers Amphitheater. *Daily Delta*, Feb. 5, 1859.

[10] The Fifth District Court of Judge H. B. Eggleston was held in the Presbytere on Jackson Square. Marie M. Costa filed suit against William B. Whitehead and J. W. Carroll charging the unauthorized use of her building as a party wall and asking for reimbursement. Judgment was rendered in favor of the plaintiff. Fifth District Court, Marie M. Costa vs. William B. Whitehead and J. W. Carroll, docket 12826, NOPL.

Advertisement, Spalding & Rogers New Orleans Circus (1974.25.30.679).

stunned us last evening, was fatal to a negro servant not many squares from us. It killed him instantly. Walked down after dinner to the library in company of Mr. R. Browne. He says the "Costa" case was opened this morning, and then laid over so that I shall be called upon probably by his opponent.

February 17   68° 74° 74°

Warm and foggy. East wind. Cleared off hot and sunny, and very dusty.

Last day of the examination at Girl's High School.

Large concourse of visitors. Took Major Beauregard and Mr. Low. The examination in Geometry was superb, and the Major was reminded of West Point days. Astronomy, too, excellent. The universal feeling was that sound scholarship, and the most complete discipline were the ruling features of the Institution. Beautiful compositions, and pleasant music closed a series of examinations that are equally a credit to the Principal, her assistants and the pupils. We are proud of this school, and I ought to take special interest in it as my wife is one of its graduates. After tea went to the City Hall to a special meeting of the School Board, on points connected with the opening of the new school house &c. &c.

February 19   68° 72° 74°

Damp and misty early in the morning with warm air from the South East. Hot sunshine high wind and dust in the middle of the day.

The schools assembled today at the Lyceum Hall to go over the programme for the 22nd. Feb. They met at 10. The superintendent, and some directors present. We first went over the music, then dismissed the Dist. Schools, retaining the graduating Classes of Boy's & Girls' High Schools. Mr. Rogers & I went over the compositions & orations of the entire Programme making notes as each speaker successively took the platform, and suggesting afterwards such improvements as we deemed desirable. The general tone of the writings and the delivery was highly pleasing. Nothing turgid. No declamatory violence, but earnest strength, and clear, lucid language....

The whole thing promises a handsome display on the 22nd.

February 21   52° 57° 58°

Cold North wind. Sunny sky. High wind and clouds of dust.

Went down to the Courts at 10 and got almost blinded by the fine detritus of the Granite pavements round the Cathedral of St. Louis....

February 22   57° 63° 63°

Washington's Birth Day. Works at the New Custom House suspended as usual.

Pleasant weather. Cool East wind.

The Exhibition of the Schools was held this morning at the Lyceum Hall. The room was crowded to its utmost capacity, floors, Galleries & Corridors, nearly 2000 present, and throughout the three hours perfect order prevailed. Every thing passed off uniformly well. The music subdued and harmonious. The speeches and compositions well delivered, and very well written. The address by the President of the Board, Dr. Lindsay, feeling and appropriate.[11] The whole proceedings characterized by deep, solid earnestness, shewing the intense interest felt by the public in our noble system of Public education....

February 28   68° 70° 68°

Damp and foggy. Warm air from the East. Heavy rains thro' the day. Got very wet in a violent storm of wind and rain between the omnibus & home at dinner time.

Dreadful calamity telegraphed this morning. The total destruction by fire of the fine Steamer "Princess" with much loss of life. Met the Standing Committee of Girls' High School, by appointment, at 8½, at the school, and determined the promotions &c. from course to course, on the reports of the Teachers and representations of the Superintendent. Call at the Office from Mr. P. Soulé, who regrets much his inability to prepare a Lecture for me at the Lyceum owing to pressing engagements, but will take his leisure moments during the summer to have one in readiness for next season. The storm subsided soon after dinner and the sun set amid the richest tints. The deepest purple to the palest violet. The deepest blue toned down to the lightest sapphire, and grand draperies of crimson and gold flung across the western sky. No climate can surpass ours in the beauty of its sky painting. If we only had scenery to match!

[11] Dr. William B. Lindsay lived at 40 St. Thomas Street. NOCD 1858.

The Princess *docked in New Orleans, Jay Dearborn Edwards, photographer, between 1857 and 1859 (1982.32.1); explosion of the* Princess *at Conrad's Point on the* Mississippi, Harper's Weekly, *March 12, 1859 (1974.25.30.471).*

March 1   65° 66° 66°

Damp and misty. North wind.

When I picked up my paper this morning early I found the details of the "great calamity" even more appalling than stated yesterday. Over 100 killed or missing besides the many sadly wounded. The number of missing, however, may yet be greatly reduced. The "Princess" was considered one of the best managed boats on the River....

March 7   56° 59° 62°

Bright and sunny. The clouds have vanished, and the air blows fresh from the north....

After dinner went over to Mr. Robinson's new house and found that his fine new brick cistern of 6000 gallons, cement & brick & half thick, had burst during the storm the other night, and spread ruin & destruction over 15 or 20 feet around. Fortunately no one was near at the time. The cement mortar that I examined was soft and but imperfectly set, and the brick a soft quality of our batture bricks known as "Delassize Bricks."[12]

March 8   56° 58° 61°

Lovely weather. Cool South West wind.

Visited Washington School on way to the office.

At 11 Major Beauregard & I went up to see the collection of pictures &c. &c. now for sale at Mr. Robb's great mansion in the 4th. Dist. (Sic transit gloria mundi!) The best pictures are those which graced Mr. Robb's gallery in the old house in St. Charles Street, chiefly purchased at the sale of Joseph Bonaparte at Bordentown. Joseph Vernet's great picture of mist, sunrise, ships, and sea shore figures. St. Denis' "falls of Terni," and "Bay of Naples." Two other pictures by Vernet, "falls of Tivoli" and "falls of Terni," and a fine picture by Natoire "the toilet of Physche." To these add 2 very fine pictures by David Huntingdon, "the Communion of the Sick" and "Imprisonment of early Christians at Rome." The "Cathedral at Burgos" by David Roberts of London is a charming picture, and the "Monastery in Madrid" (water color) by Louis Haghe of London, also very fine. The bronzes, vases, furniture, porcelain, &c. &c. Dresden, Sevres & Bohemian ware exceedingly elegant and tasteful.

[12] The L. T. Delassize brickyard was located on the Old Basin Canal at Claiborne Avenue. It dealt in brick, lime, and sand. NOCD 1859.

The Frescoes on walls, cielings &c. wretched! Badly drawn, worse in color. Worst of all in contrast with the artistic gems which half conceal them. The house itself is an unwieldy mass of bad taste, and common, inelegant finish. The grounds, however, covering the entire square are fine, and the serpentine gravel walk quite English. There is but little statuary. The "angler" by Steinhamer, is the best, and the 2 porphyry vases, in [the] basement are very beautiful. These, too, were purchased at the Bonaparte "Sale" and are said to have been the gift of Bernadotte to the Ex-king and executed in Sweden. These and the "St. Denis'" "Vernet's" and "Huntingdons" I saw 10 years ago, when Mr. Robb was living in his old establishment in St. Charles Street, now the "Orleans Club House." His day dream of wealth and gilded splendour is now fading out, and this is the last closing scene of the gaudy drama.[13] The visitors today were numerous, among whom I found many friends. After seeing all the Major, Mr. Dunn & I took a turn among the many tasteful & costly residences of the 4th. Dist. gardens &c. all lustrous with glowing sunshine, and decked with "azaleas" and other charming spring flowers & then took the omnibus for the office at 2 O'clock. When I returned home to dinner at 3½, Tommy was full of his exploits during the morning. Today is "Mardi Gras" and he takes his share, of course.

March 10   60° 64° 66°

Damp and cloudy. East wind....

After tea attended a called meeting of the Board of Directors, at City Hall, in private session, to act upon the Report of the Committee on Teachers, for the ensuing scholastic year, that is, the distribution of Teachers, transfers &c. &c. Full attendance, and an exciting debate, on a recommendation to establish the principle that female teachers in the District Schools on contracting marriage, should be considered as tacitly resigning their position, and that in all vacancies to be filled, the alumni of our Normal Schools should be entitled to the preference. The principle in both cases was

[13] During most of James Robb's career, he lived at 17 St. Charles in the first block off Canal Street. There he became the city's leading art collector; his purchases at an 1845 sale of artworks from the collection of Joseph Bonaparte, Napoleon's brother, included a Rubens. Because of crippling financial losses following the panic of 1857, much of his collection was sold at auction in March 1859 by art dealer Charles Galvani. *The Toilet of Psyche* by Charles Joseph Natoire is now in the New Orleans Museum of Art. Robb also sold his grand mansion on Washington Avenue, containing frescoes attributed to Dominique Canova (1800-1868), and moved to the North where he eventually recouped his fortune. When Robb's house was demolished in 1954, the frescoes were removed in pieces by architect Henry Krotzer to the Louisiana State Museum. Schmit, *Robb Papers*, 3-4, 13.

One of the prizes of James Robb's art collection, The Toilet of Psyche *by Charles Joseph Natoire, 1745, New Orleans Museum of Art: Museum purchase through the Bequest of Judge Charles F. Claiborne.*

Frescoes from James Robb residence, attributed to Dominique Canova, Stuart M. Lynn, photographer, 1954, Louisiana State Museum.

adopted, but in the former I strenuously opposed any attempt to make it retroactive or in any way whatever to in[ter]fere with the present position of 5 married teachers of excellent abilities now in the schools. It was, therefore, made purely a <u>prospective</u> measure, and the cases of the married teachers now in the schools carefully guarded by a distinct "resolution" appended to the report, after striking out the clause from which I dissented.

March 12   59° 59° 57°

Cloudy & cool. North East wind. Gloomy rains set in at 11 and continued thro' the afternoon....

A sad, sad accident occurred at the N. Custom House last evening at 4 O'clock James Cannon (a laborer) fell from the hoisting frame work of the Collector's room to the Floor (a height of near 60 feet) and was instantly killed. He was an Englishman by birth, about 40 years of age, and leaves a wife and two children (now in Philadelphia) to mourn his untimely end. This is the first serious accident that has to be recorded on the work and I fervently pray that it may be the last. It has thrown a deep gloom over all.

March 15   56° 58° 60°

Beautiful weather: cool wind from the North.

Visited the Franklin School on my way to the Office.[14]

Called at A. Duncan's and arranged with him about Plans & specifications for an improvement of property he proposes making. On Canal Street I saw a poor fellow, a driver of one of the "St. Charles'" Coaches, lying on the banquette with his leg broken, having been thrown down and the wheels passing over him. The people in the adjoining store were rendering such aid as the case required. At the Custom House we have had another day of overwhelming calamity. Near noon I was standing with Mr. Reid in the Collector's Room nearly under an architrave Piece of white marble of 10 Tons which was swung to the heavy Central Derrick and was being raised slowly into position. Mr. Reid was explaining to me more minutely than before how the accident of Friday occurred. The heavy block meanwhile gradually rising. He wanted me to stay longer, but I told him I had an important letter to write to a northern Contractor & returned to the Office. About 12 I heard an alarm of fire, and went immediately up to the top of the Building to see where it was. I mounted to the top of the wall of [the] "Collector's Room"

14 The Franklin School for Girls was on St. Charles near Julia. NOCD 1859.

and there I saw the great Block of Marble nearly up to its place (about 40 to 45 feet above the floor) and two laborers, Saml. Newton and James Kelly, standing upon it. In an instant the great hook parted, and the whole mass fell to the floor, with a terrific crash, and white clouds of marble dust rose from the fragments and enveloped the spot completely so that it was impossible to see the effect of the catastrophe. I hurried down stairs, and found every body rushing to the scene of the accident. When I got to the entrance of the great room I met 6 men carrying off the dead body of poor Newton, sadly mutilated. Then a few steps further, others carrying J. Kelly so much injured that it is impossible for him to survive many hours. It appears the Major had given this morning the most positive orders that the men should not stand on the blocks when in the act of being raised, and these very men had been ordered off the block but a few minutes before by Mr. Roy. Had they obeyed the order no injury would have accrued to any one. The accident was due to a flaw in the great hook which sustained one fourth of the whole weight say $2^{1}/_{2}$ Tons. It was in the core of the neck, and could not be detected. The same hook had been used already with a strain of 5 Tons, and was calculated, if perfect, to resist, with entire safety, 11 Tons. When removed from the ruins the poor fellow that was killed presented a hideous spectacle; and the other hardly less so, though his wounds did not shew so much on the surface. I trust I shall never witness such a scene of human suffering again....

March 16   57° 58° 58°

Dark and rainy. North wind.

Works suspended in the afternoon, to allow the men to attend the funerals of poor Newton and Kelly. The latter died at $4^{1}/_{2}$ yesterday afternoon in great agony. Every thing about the building seems wrapped in gloom....

March 18   52° 54° 56°

A strong West wind all night has driven away every vestige of cloud and today the sky is glorious....

At $6^{3}/_{4}$ P.M. I drove up for Mr. Bolles, and we reached the City Hall just as the audience had assembled.[15] It was not large. Say about 150, but select, and deeply attentive. The Lecture was admirable. "Piccolomini" at the opera and evening services at some churches, reduced our numbers.

15 The Rev. E. G. Bolles was minister of the First Congregational Unitarian Church. NOCD 1859.

March 19   53° 57° 59°

White frost in the night. Bright and sunny today, with North West wind.

Walked down with Mr. Low and deplored together the lack of interest shewn in enterprizes of an intellectual character here, exemplified by the fact that last night but <u>two</u> of our Directors besides myself were present, which troubled me more than the thinness of the house. For how can we succeed in establishing anything like a literary centre among us unless those engaged in the effort stand by each other. It is <u>very</u> discouraging! The Revd. Mr. Howard, who came with Mr. Low last night, remarked that in Chicago the thing would be considered a failure, from the thinness of the house, and yet the Lecture was as good probably or even better, than those which draw crowded houses <u>in Chicago</u>.…

March 21   64° 65° 67°

Cloudy and damp. East wind. Threatening. Rains set in at noon.…

Letter from the Department announcing that the appropriation failed, and that Congress requires the Balance on hand, say $220.273.51 to be expended on the Building to prepare it for use. (a manifest absurdity) It goes on to require in accordance with this Act of Congress, an immediate reduction in force, and general operations, and a scale of expenditure brought down to the most economical limits. The Balance on hand as represented by the Department differs from mine by a small sum due to certain disbursments made at the Dept. since June 30. 1858 and which have not been yet referred to our Office.

March 22   68° 70° 73°

Rainy night, and damp close air this morning. Wind South East. Sun very warm at noon and in the afternoon.

Major Beauregard has settled this morning the details of the reductions called for by the Department, which will make an aggregate reduction, on Pay rolls alone, of $22.000 per annum. He dispenses with the Disbursing Clerk (Mr. Guesnon) at $180 per month, whose duties will devolve upon me, and the overseer of Laborers at $150 per month, whose duties will fall to Mr. Reid. 35 Mechanics and Laborers will also be discharged.…

March 23   68° 71° 72°

Damp and foggy. South East wind. Warm and sunny at noon.…

Driven almost to death, at the Office, by an accumulation of miscellaneous business increased by the late absurd action of Congress in cutting off our appropriations, and changing the natural current of our daily transactions. The removals from office, too, springing out of it, are painful both to the parties, and to all cognizant of the facts. The work was advancing admirably under a well digested system of operations, but now the reduction of force, and delay in orders for material will apply most injuriously; and greatly retard the completion of the whole.…

April 2   72° 75° 76°

Damp and cloudy threatening more rain. South East wind, warm & steamy. Bursts of hot sunshine.

At the Office I assumed today the duties of Mr. Guesnon, who has been discharged; and disbursed nearly $3000 on the mechanics' roll between 12 and 1$^{1}/_{2}$. These duties will be in addition to my own, and at present at least without additional compensation so that the saving to the Government will be $180 per month.

After dinner took Tommy to see the ruins of the "Planter's Press" which was partially destroyed by fire night before last.[16] Loss in Cotton, Steam Press and Building about $200.000.

April 7   58° 60° 62°

Cloudy & threatening. East wind.

Pleasant visit to the Franklin School on my way to the Office. There was a heavy fire yesterday at the Lower Cotton Press, and at noon today at the "Hale Warehouse".[17] The losses to the Insurance Companies by these, and the fires of the week previous, will reach the sum of $700.000. The total loss, however, will be greater, as much of the property was uninsured.…

[16] The Planters Cotton Press was on Annunciation Street between Richard and Market. *Daily Delta*, Apr. 2, 1859.

[17] The fire at the Lower Cotton Press, on the river between Montegut and St. Ferdinand, was said to have been started by cotton bales removed from the fire at the Planters Cotton Press. Hale's warehouses, bounded by Levee, Fulton, St. Joseph, and Julia, were built in 1852 by John Sewell from plans by Henry Howard, architect. After the fire, Samuel Stewart contracted with Charles Pride, builder, to rebuild the warehouses at a cost of $13,200. *Daily Delta*, Apr. 7, 1859; NONA, Theodore Guyol, Apr. 16, 1852, Selim Magner, Apr. 26, 1859.

Burning of the Alabama Cotton Presses at New Orleans, Illustrated News, *March 19, 1853 (1976.135.2), gift of Ralph M. Pons, shows the near impossibility of bringing a cotton press fire under control.*

Carrollton Gardens, ca. 1875 (1974.25.29.64).

April 24   59° 64° 66°

Sunday. Very beautiful weather, dry and sunny. Pleasant West wind.

As sister Emily is a member of the Episcopal Church, we attended "Trinity" this morning, and being Easter Sunday, and the communion administered, the services were three hours long, but Tommy shewed no signs of weariness, and indeed preferred it to the simpler modes of the Baptist Church. The sermon, however, I am sorry to say, was the most complete example of diluted, infantine, nay pitiable imbecility, perhaps ever spread before an audience....

April 30   70° 72° 76°

Lovely weather after the rain, pure air from the West.

Very busy at the Office. Paid Officer's Pay rolls for the month. &c. &c....

After an early dinner we took the 4 O'clock Train to Carrollton. Emily, sister Emily, Ellen, Tommy & myself. And after walking thro' the gardens, and on the river bank, took the Lake Train to the end of the road, enjoyed the fine breeze from the water. Saw many friends &c. and returned to supper at 8 P.M. The river at Carrollton looks more formidable than I have ever seen, even at the worst of last year's flood. The outer Levee is quite covered, and at the inner line it is brim full. Last year when at the highest there was always a dry walk on the outside Levee. A break at or near Carrolton would be disastrous in the extreme and deluge not Carrolton only but the rear of New Orleans. It may happen at any moment, as the pressure on the Levee at that point is enormous....

May 2   69° 70° 71°

Dark rainy morning. East wind. Bursts of sunshine.

Very busy all morning paying monthly rolls of mechanics &c. and miscellaneous matters.

Call from Mr. Bosworth to employ me as architect on a dwelling house he proposes to erect in Fourth Dist.[18]...

May 3   70° 72° 72°

Beautiful weather. East wind. In the morning, rains, very heavy, at midday. Clouds and sunshine in afternoon....

All the family came to the Custom House at 11, and I took them down to the "Mint" which we had barely time to go over when the rain set in, and they had to make the best of their way home.

Went over Mr. Reid's house, which has been renewed since the fire and is now nearly finished.[19]...

May 4   70° 71° 73°

Pleasant breezy morning. East wind....

At 5 Mr. Bosworth called by appointment and I went with him to see his property on Washington Avenue. Settled the details of the house &c. and agreed to terms for Plans and superintendence. The house to be finished by the first of November....

[18] Abel Ware Bosworth (ca. 1816-1885) was a wholesale and retail ice dealer. His residence on Washington Avenue between Magazine and Camp streets is the most important of Wharton's designs. Known as the Bosworth-Hammond house, it is still standing at 1126 Washington Avenue. *Daily Picayune*, Oct. 12, 1885; NOCD 1859.

[19] James M. Reid's two-story frame house at 88 St. Charles, between Thalia and Melpomene, was rebuilt by Alphonso H. Kerr and John L. Albright at a cost of $2,000. The rear part and upper story of the house had been destroyed in a fire on January 19, 1859. A. T. Wood was the architect for the original house built in 1852. *Daily Picayune*, Jan. 20, 1859; NONA, James Graham, Feb. 1, 1859.

Abel Ware Bosworth residence, Richard Koch, photographer, between 1940 and 1950 (1980.220), gift of Boyd Cruise.

May 9   68° 70° 70°

Clouds and sunshine. Wind due south. Weather clearing up, and wind changing to West. Showery, however, in the afternoon....

Very pleasant gentlemen's dinner party at Mr. Low's to meet Capt. Gibson the East Indian traveller. Mrs. Low & her sister Mrs. Brown. Drs. Bein, Benedict & Slocum, Capt. Gibson, Messrs. Dix, Low, Brown & myself.[20] Many interesting anecdotes of Eastern adventure, and detailed accounts of the Malaysian, Polynesian and Australasian groups &c. &c. Described the curious "Bomarang" shaped thus and the splendid purple blossoms of the "Rafflesia Arnoldi" of the Islands of Java and Sumatra, the flowers about 36 inches in diameter. Story of his imprisonment by the Dutch Colonial Government at Batavia, on trifling pretexts. His hair breadth escapes on the Brazilian Coast, too, in one of his voyages in a small vessel of his own fitted out for private cruising &c. &c.

The dinner, claret, and champagne were of the most tempting excellence, and it was quite dark when the company "dissolved."

[20] Dr. Richard Bein lived at 271 Magazine; Dr. N. B. Benedict lived on Camp Street at the corner of Race. NOCD 1856.

May 15   74° 78° 80°

Sunday. Lovely weather. East wind, dry and dusty.

Revd. Dr. Howard preached an exquisite sermon from John 14. 23. "If a man love me, he will keep my words: and my Father will love him, and we will come unto him, and make our abode with him." He said more in a short half hour, than most of our droning preachers compress into half a year. All the pews were well filled.

The Fire Bells rung out violently while we were at Church. After dinner I went to the spot and found the large sugar refinery of A. Thompson on 2nd. Street near Annunciation, covering nearly a square, entirely reduced to ashes.

May 16   76° 80° 82°

Hot, dry & dusty. East wind.

Framing commenced at Mr. Low's.

Hostilities commenced in Europe.[21] Lago Maggiore, Lago Guarda, Lago Como, will soon be dyed with human gore, and the Isola Bella, and a thousand spots of poetic and artistic fame will draw new interest from the now opening Contest of nations.

After dinner Mr. Bosworth called by appointment and we went together to his property on Washington Avenue, measured up the Buildings now on it, determined the grade &c. &c. Then went to see the improvements going on in different parts of the District &c. and returned home at sunset.

May 20   77° 80° 81°

Pleasant sunshine. Fine breeze from the Eastward.

Very weak today.

Called at Mr. Bosworth's on my way to the Office and took the pencil studies of my design for his house. All completely considered and figured. They agreed with his views and he wished to retain them for close examination until this evening.

Very busy at the Office until near 3.

Mr. Bosworth called at 5 with the drawings, after having carefully examined them with his partner and says they meet his views exactly. He desires no change whatever so I shall go on with the set at once.

We went together to examine different flagging, on the yard of Nicholson & Co. and he agrees with me that machine faced North River is the best. Drawing Plans after tea until 11.

May 24   76° 80° 83°

Beautiful summer weather, East wind. Very hot in the middle of the day.

At Mr. Low's work morning & evening. Writing specifications after dinner, and until 10 P.M.

There is so much detail about a nice dwelling house, and every [thing] has to be considered so carefully, that I find it pretty hard work to do it at night, this hot weather, and under the sting of a thousand musquitoes. Why don't the people bring their orders along in winter? Drawings & specifications need cool weather; I don't care how hot it is when the building time comes.

May 31   79° 81° 84°

Hot, dry and dusty. South East wind.

Up very early writing specifications &c.

Inspected Mr. Low's work before breakfast.

Very busy at the Custom House. Paid Officer's Pay roll for the month. Received Capt. Duncan's papers & keys, as his works are all turned over to Major Beauregard's Superintendence today, and all the business details to me. Capt. Smith (his clerk) will turn over his Desk and Books to me tomorrow, so that I shall have my hands very full indeed, to commence double work on the 1st. June. The new works turned over, are the New Marine Hospital, repairs of U.S. Branch Mint, building U.S. Warehouses at Quarantine Station, Boarding station at Pass a l'Outre, but the Hospital & Warehouses only in active operation.[22] Fortunately the change involves additional pay....

June 29   80° 82° 80°

Fine sunny morning. South East wind.

The City Council made the annual election of a new School Board to serve for the next 12 months. 6 members of the old Board are dropped including Mr. J. M. Reid. I am re-elected....

[21] In 1859 Emperor Napoleon III provided French aid to the kingdom of Sardinia in its effort to drive Austria from northern Italy. The battles of Magenta and Solferino proved so costly that the French signed a separate armistice, but the Sardinians fought on, reuniting Italy in 1861.

[22] On February 10, 1859, the Treasury Department advertised for proposals for constructing warehouses at the Quarantine Station sixty miles below New Orleans. The bids were to be received in Washington and opened April 1. Pass à l'Outre is one of the eastern passes of the Mississippi River.

Quarantine Station by Alfred R. Waud, between 1866 and 1871 (1965.62).

July 7   81° 81° 82°

…Emily came at 2 to the Office having determined to go the next trip of the "Vicksburg" to Natchez on a long promised visit to the Thornhill's. She & Tommy, Mrs. Ladd & Ellen will go. I shall have to stay and attend to business and keep house.…

July 13   82° 83° 83°

Fine and clear. Cool West wind. Cloudy in the afternoon.

Much harrassed at the Office by the errors and confusion in which the accounts of the Marine Hospital were left by the former management.[23] Extra claims of Contractors &c.…

July 14   82° 84° 84°

Pleasant sunny morning. South East wind. Hot and oppressive thro' the day.…

Home at 2 P.M. to prepare for the steamer at 5.

After dinner McManus came for the trunks and we followed in time to get things comfortably settled before the Boat started which was punctually at the time. Tommy was enchanted with the novelty of the thing, and they started under the most favorable auspices with bright sunshine and every thing comfortable.…

For the first time all alone since we were married. Em. has left every thing in the best order, and a good willing servant to look after things.

July 26   83° 86° 88°

Fine sunny weather. West wind. Very hot indeed at midday. The thermometers in town exposed to street radiation, tho' in the shade, reached 96° at 3 P.M.

Today, I have had my Cistern thoroughly cleansed, and a good new top, so that the first rain will give me very fine water. I have also had the River water turned on my Hydrant.

August 2   83° 85° 86°

Hot sunshine, South wind.

Paid off Mechanics & Laborers of N Custom House, between $3000 & $4000, prepared and sent off Estimates of Funds for August for both works, and also reports of operations for both during July, &c. &c. and home to dinner at 3.

At the Library after dinner; approved the monthly Bills &c. &c.

August 13   83° 84° 83°

Fine sunny morning: South East wind. Clouds rose at 9. Heavy tropical rains, with thunder and lightening from 1 to 2, somewhat deranging my operations at home, as I expected to complete the outside painting today. However in spite of it, all damage was repaired, and the whole work complete before 6 P.M.

I then "fixed" the flower borders and Theresa reddened the pavements and front banquette so that every thing looks new and sweet for Sunday.[24] And my labors in preparing & repairing the house &c. &c. are brought to a close.…

August 16   81° 80° 82°

Rains & thunder thro' the night. Sunny morning with West wind, but overcast again at 8, with heavy showers thro' the morning but brightened up about 1 P.M.

Arranged every thing at the Office; took my stateroom on the "Charmer" and returned home to pack the last of my things and an early dinner.

Boat moved off punctually at 5, but few passengers. One of the handsomest and largest boats on the river, entirely new, well commanded, and every thing under the best management, with all modern improvements and luxuries.…

August 17

The weather <u>is</u> lovely. A sweet summer breeze, pure and fresh, blowing all the time. Soft, lazy summer clouds floating over the blue, and the banks on either side of gemmy green melting into the clear pearl tints, far far away.

---

[23] The contract for the Marine Hospital was awarded to the Trenton Locomotive Machine Manufacturing Co., which gave the masonry contract to Joseph Moorehouse. NONA, Hilary B. Cenas, May 16, 1857.

[24] Sidewalks (banquettes) were sometimes coated with red brick dust to give them a new appearance.

Natchez Under-the-Hill, Mississippi, Alfred R. Waud, delineator, 1874 (1974.25.30.151).

Six long years since 1853 have I been pent up in the stifling air of town. And now the River breeze plays around me once more, and I feel "myself again". I left town with a severe head ache, pains in every limb, and languid action in every part of my machinery. It is all gone now.

Red River landing at 12 and at 6½ the high cliffs of Natchez were before us, bathed in a flood of crimson sunset, which blazed back from the windows along the water's edge like the mouths of so many furnaces. At 7 we touched the wharf. Mr. Richard Thornhill was standing there waiting for the Boat. I ordered a carriage and we drove immediately to Mr. David Stanton's (the Elms) where, as good luck would have it, my family & Mr. & Mrs. Thornhill, happened on the gallery to give me a warm reception, tho' they had not expected the "Packet" until a much later hour.[25] The evening slipped thro' our fingers like magic, and "nature's sweet restorer" closed the scene.

[25] The Whartons were staying in Natchez at the Elms, the residence of Anna E. and David Stanton. Located at 215 South Pine Street, the Elms was begun about 1805 and enlarged in 1859. The billiard room, added in 1857, was moved across the street to 804 Washington Street in the 1870s.

August 21

Sunday. Up at 6 enjoying the fresh air of the gardens before breakfast. Clear blue overhead.

Carriage at the front at 11. Mr. Richard, Nannie & I went to the Episcopal Church.[26]…

The Church neat, comfortable, well finished. Light and air in sufficient quantity, all in good taste, solid and durable. Exterior the Hexastyle Doric of the Theseion, with plain square bell tower in the rear; all colored with delicate Portland stone tint, a favorite tinge in Natchez, and vastly more beautiful than the clumsy brown ochres of New Orleans.…

[26] Trinity Episcopal Church, erected in 1822 and remodeled with a Greek temple-type portico in the 1830s, is located on Commerce at the corner of Washington Street in Natchez.

The Natchez *docked at Algiers, Jay Dearborn Edwards, photographer, between 1857 and 1860 (1982.32.16); Thomas P. Leathers, captain of the* Natchez, *1871 (1974.25.27.238).*

August 24

Up and in the saddle at 6 with Ellen; we rode 8 or 10 miles before breakfast, on the Woodville road....

This alas! is our last day. After breakfast a Cigar, and then preparing for New Orleans.

Preparations complete, billiards before dinner, and at 4 our Trunks &c. were dispatched to the steamer "Natchez".[27] The two carriages drove up to the door, and then leave-taking, tears, and hearty good wishes, at which the whole retinue of servants assisted, then down to the boat where we parted with our excellent host Mr. Thomas Thornhill....

The Boat is less encrusted with ornament than the "Charmer" but liberally supplied with every comfort, and every luxury that a traveller could sigh for. Smooth, gliding rapid motion, no jar. Tables epicurean, separate as usual now. Mr. Thornhill will, of course, share ours during the trip. Capt. Leathers, an experienced and now wealthy navigator, and every department complete....

[27] The steamboat *Natchez* was one of seven boats of the same name operated by Captain Thomas P. Leathers, a Mississippi River captain who built an elegant mansion in New Orleans at Carondelet and Josephine in 1859; Henry Thiberge was the architect and William K. Day, the builder.

August 25

Up at 5 breathing the pure crystal air of morning! Bayou Sara at 6 (half way, 150 miles) woods & river bathed in golden sunrise. A cup of coffee to take off the aguish edge of the early morning. Sugar now succeeds to cotton, and tops the shores in long, level lines of living green, great stretches of ancient forest in between, and snow white cranes meditating at the water's brink, or sailing lazily across the woodland. Tommy & I walked the upper deck, drawing in the fresh morning air, while the rest were dressing for breakfast at 7, which was, as usual, an appetizing display of abundance, and good cookery.

Baton Rouge & its Castellated Capitol &c. &c. at 8½.[28] At 9 to 10 we all sat in the lofty Pilot house, watching the changing Panorama. Vast sugar Estates, large mansions, half hid in groves of fine trees and flowering shrubs; sugar houses with their great square chimneys and long rows of neat, white washed "Quarters", all glistening under a burning sun, but a glorious breeze coursing thro' the Boat. At 20 miles below Baton Rouge the Pilot pointed out to us the wreck of the ill fated "Princess" lying on the bank, with the "Bell

[28] The Louisiana State Capitol was built in 1852 in the Gothic Revival style. James H. Dakin was the architect.

Facade of old capitol building, Baton Rouge, rebuilt after the Civil War, Stuart M. Lynn, photographer, 1945 (1979.326.88), gift of Stuart M. Lynn.

St. Mary's Assumption Church, ca. 1915 (1981.350.263).

Boat" by her side, still engaged in rescuing objects of value. The Natchez was the first boat to reach her after the explosion, and her cabin floor was quickly covered with 70 victims suffering every imaginable degree of agony, 16 of whom died before they reached Natchez.

At 11 lunch. Fine water melon from the ice box on the guards at our staterooms, excellent dinner at 2, then a pleasant breezy afternoon at the bow. Plantation after plantation. Carrolton at 6, and the Levee, (safely moored) at 6½. Off with baggage on a car, and ourselves in a carriage, and in 10 minutes we were at home again; after a visit of rare enjoyment, and not a single incident to recall with other than the liveliest pleasure.

September 12   83° 84° at 3 88° at 4 88°

Very fine and clear. Warm sunshine East wind.

The Public Schools of the First Dist. reopen today....

All the school houses of the First Dist. have been thoroughly repaired, painted, and whitewashed during the vacation, and supplied with large new cisterns, altogether at an aggregate cost of $7000. They present a most attractive appearance, large and airy, clean & commodious. The new "Madison" is a very handsome well arranged building. Altogether I doubt whether any city in the United States can show more complete arrangements for popular education, or an abler corps of Teachers....

September 24   76° 76½° 78°

Cool air from the East: sunny sky. Very hot sun at mid day....

At the Office busy in arranging records of the works &c. Invited Mr. Roy to go with me to the New Opera House, now hastening to completion.[29] Went over it, and were sorry to remark the usual effect of hasty building, evidences of unequal subsidence, bad brickwork, immense mortar joints, cracks every where, and the construction, tho' bad, was no worse than the design & details of exterior, which are simply abominable.

October 6   76° 78° 78°

Dry, clear, & dusty: North East wind....

Long and interesting meeting of the Directors Pub. S. at the City Hall this evening, full reports, and much miscellaneous business. I offered a resolution to appoint a Committee of Conference for the purpose of enquiring into the present course of instruction as overtaxing many of our pupils with a very undue amount of labor in so enervating a climate, and devise proper modes of relief, by extending the course time, or otherwise. Adopted unanimously and placed in the care of the Committees on High Schools and Teachers.

October 10   72° 73° 75°

Cold North wind, clear sky, dry & very dusty....

Got off my Quarterly Report of New Custom House to the Treasury Department, & home to dinner at 3. After dinner took Tommy to see the fine new Catholic Church in Josephine Street.[30] It towered up grandly against the broad moon. It is a fine piece of brickwork.

October 11   71° 73° 74°

Dry & very dusty. East wind.

The 4th. District suffers severely for want of water, but we are fortunate in having the Hydrant, which leaves our cistern still half full of the purest & best.

[29] The French Opera House at the corner of Bourbon and Toulouse streets was built by Gallier and Esterbrook, architects, in 1859. The building burned in 1919. NONA, Adolph Boudousquié, Apr. 19, 1859.

[30] St. Mary's Assumption at Constance and Josephine streets, a large, impressive brick church in the German Baroque style, was built for the German Catholics (1858-1860).

French Opera House, Vieux Carré Survey, Historic New Orleans Collection.

At the Office completed my report for the New Marine Hospital for the Quarter ending Sept 30. Long and interesting conversation with Mr. [J. G.] Parham Superintendent of Public Schools in 4th. Distt. I sent in my resignation as Director of the 1st. Dist. this morning to the two Boards of the Common Council which meet this evening. I am impelled to it by the steady opposition of my wife from the first, and the recent accumulation of duties in my official position, three important Government works being now in charge of the Office, New Custom House, New Marine Hospital, and Quarantine Warehouse.

October 17   76° 80° 81°

Damp and foggy, mild air from the South East. Cleared off with hot sunshine in the afternoon.

Every time I go down town I meet gentlemen who express their deep regret at my resignation from the School Board. I can only refer them to the oft repeated aphorism that every man's place can be supplied.

October 23   67° 69° 70°

Sunday. Clouds & sunshine. Cool North East wind....

A disastrous fire occurred in the night destroying our fine new market and every building from the drug store of Dr. Hastings, corner of Felicity Street, up to Josephine Street, every store round the market, and Mr. A. B. Cammack's elegant mansion, on Josephine.[31] The destruction was complete and embraced an average width of two to three squares. I dressed at half past two in the morning and spent an hour at the fire then returned home and went to bed again.

October 24   66° 69° 69°

Light clouds & pleasant sunshine. North East wind.

The loss by fire last night amounted to $500.000. I took Tommy to see the ruins before going down to the Office, and condole with friends who were sufferers. Dr. Wood among the rest, who just a year

ago was called in to attend Tommy in his severe attack of "Yellow Fever".[32] How glad I am that he is so well now!

October 26   69° 73° 74°

Fine and sunny. North East wind....

At 2 went to the High School by invitation to hear the paper of the "intermediate course" read. Dr. Lindsay & Mr. Rogers were there. The paper contained some beautifully expressed remarks on my retiring from the Board, and the feeling expressed on all sides was so kind and cordial, and the general regret evidently so sincere that I responded to it at the close of the exercises in a few acknowledgments, and assurances of the interest I should continue to feel in the progress of that fine Institution. They all seem to feel that they have suffered a great loss, which really took me by surprise, as I am not conscious of doing any thing more than taking a kind & friendly interest in their success, but the Principal & Teachers say they don't want my place supplied, but to remain vacant for me.

November 6   64° 67° 68°

Sunday. Clouding up and preparing for rain. North East wind. Cleared off at 11 A.M.

Dr. Duncan has resigned the Pastorate of the Bapt. church, and Dr. Howard received the appointment. He enters upon his charge today. My family, however, do not desire to attend the church any longer so I gave up my pew last Monday.

Today we all remained at home making it literally a day of rest.

November 7   65° 68° 69°

Warm, clear, and parching dry. North East wind.

General Election day.[33] Went to the Polls & voted early. Then went down to the Custom House, where I found a letter from the Engineer in Chief raising my Salary to $2.400.00 per annum. Answered Major Bowman's dispatch of 5th. and a very complimentary communication from the Girl's High School on my

[31] After being destroyed by fire in 1858, the Magazine Market was rebuilt at a cost of $27,200. At its first meeting after the 1859 fire, the city council authorized city surveyor Louis Pilié to undertake the immediate rebuilding of the market. *Daily Delta*, Oct. 25, 1859; *Daily Crescent*, Sept. 12, 1859. After the fire, Samuel Hastings erected a row of eleven brick buildings on Magazine and St. Mary, across from the market, known as Hastings Row.

[32] After the fire, Dr. William B. Wood erected a row of twelve brick buildings at the corner of Josephine and Magazine known as Dr. Wood's Row.

[33] In the election of November 7, 1859, Thomas Overton Moore (1804-1876) of Rapides Parish was elected governor of Louisiana, defeating the Whig candidate, Thomas J. Wells. Before serving as governor (1860-1864), Moore had been a member of the state legislature (1847-1860). *DLB.*

resignation of Directorship. Visit from Mr. Low on church matters &c. &c.

November 8   67° 68° 69°

Cool dry and sunny. East wind. Clouding up for rain.

Answered Major Bowman's letter & thanked the Department for my increase of salary. Each Secretary of the Treasury since I became a Government Officer, has raised my salary during his term of Office, and each by the same amount per annum....

The Election just over is a complete defeat of the Democratic & Independent movement. The American Ticket is elected, but only 7000 votes were polled, about ½ the registered Voters....

November 14   49° 50° 53°

Bitter cold: with north west wind: every thing parched up with drought, and overlaid with dust. Ice formed out of town night before last, and, I doubt not, last night too.

The fire yesterday morning in the 4th. Dist. was terrible.[34] 9 squares totally destroyed, 83 dwellings, producing great suffering, and an aggregate value $100.000 reduced to ashes....

November 15   48° 53° 54°

Plentiful white frost sprinkled over every thing at sunrise, with North West wind. Dry mild and sunny during the day with immense dust.

Mr. Reid & I went to St. Joseph's church and examined the mode of hanging sash referred to by Mr. Low for the proposed repairs in the Baptist church.[35] Disapprove of it entirely and reported accordingly, together with the proper mode of conducting the repairs....

Another heavy fire in the night in 4th. District.[36] Got up at 3 and spent an hour on the spot.

---

[34] The fire started on Chippewa Street, between Harmony and Pleasant. *Daily Delta*, Nov. 15, 1859.

[35] St. Joseph's Church on Tulane Avenue, opposite Charity Hospital, was erected in 1847-1849 in the Gothic style. T. E. Giraud was the architect. Later known as St. Catherine of Siena, the church was demolished in 1966.

[36] Nine squares were burned in the area of Pleasant, Tchoupitoulas, Ninth, and Chippewa. The loss was estimated at $95,000. *Daily Delta*, Nov. 15, 1859.

St. Joseph's Church, James Wells Champney, delineator, Scribner's Monthly, *December 1873 (1974.25.7.71i).*

November 17   58° 62° 64°

Rain at last in fine refreshing showers from the South East. No more dust or empty cisterns. Showers thro' the day until 10 P.M.

Wild ducks are now in fine season and perfectly delicious. I bought a brace yesterday, and again today, that were simply superb, and at the cheap rate of 75¢ & 80¢ a pair.

November 19   55° 59° 59°

Fine and sunny. West wind....

Visited New Opera House with Messrs. Roy & Thiel. Interior ornamentation chaste, simple & tasteful; far better than the construction, which has been too hasty. The work is now nearly complete.

November 28   71° 73° 74°

Cloudy and warm. South East wind....

Tommy says quite good things at times. The other day at dinner, Mamma, said he, when people grow up their mothers ain't their mothers any longer, are they? Why certainly, why not? Because I thought they <u>always</u> turned to <u>Grandmothers</u>. Many months ago he was watching his mother wreathing her hair with beautiful orange bloom (by the way, she needs not the "foreign aid of ornament"). "O! Ma," he said, "How sweet that is! You just look as if Pa was dead, and you were going to be married over again"....

November 29   68° 68° 70°

Rain in the night: cloudy and drizzling this morning, with North wind.

At the Church before breakfast.

Letter from Major Bowman which led me to decline the Department increase of my pay to $2400....

November 30   70° 72° 73°

Damp and foggy. North East wind. Warm and unhealthy weather....

This day closes the summer & fall of 1859. The absorbing summer topic in New Orleans — health — has been easily disposed of. But few cases of the "special institution" — yellow fever — have been recorded and the last official report shewed but 2 deaths by that disease....

December 6   66° 70° 71°

Damp & foggy. Warm South East wind. Hot bursts of sunshine....

Major Beauregard transmitted my application to be relieved from my additional duties to the Treasury Department, with a most handsome & eulogistic letter to the Secretary of the Treasury, on the value & fidelity of my services &c. &c....

December 8   34° 38° 41°

Severely cold all night. Ice on the pools this morning ³/₄ inch thick, heavy icicles from the cistern drip. Bright sunshine, North wind.

Tommy and I had a good slide on the square opposite. The ice did not melt in the shade during the day. I understand the thermometer during the night stood at 25°. Mine at the Custom House shews a somewhat higher temperature than in exposed situations being enclosed by heavy walls, still, however, open to the free play of the still atmosphere.

December 9   38° 40° 43°

Still severely cold: ice formed in the night tho' not quite so thick as the night previous. Wind due North: sky perfectly clear.

Pleasant half hour at the Boy's High School, with the young men of the "Society of Natural Science". Inspected their cabinet, and made a contribution of beautiful specimens of marble highly polished &c. &c. Met Mr. Shields, Chairman of the Committee on School House and suggested a handsome cabinet with glass doors &c. and as the Society is a growing one I gave them for a motto "viresque adquirit eundo" A[e]neid. Lib 4 line 175.[37]

Finished a drawing &c. &c. to complete the Contract of W. B. Whitehead Esqr. on a/s of the firm of Wharton and Reid as we are now fully associated as equal partners in all architectural business outside of our Government Offices.

December 12   46° 50° 52°

Mild & pleasant: sunny sky. North wind.

In the evening met Mrs. Bartlett who invited me in to see her night school at the "Washington" which is in fine order and well lighted with gas &c.[38]

December 13   48° 52° 54°

Fine and pleasant: warm sunshine: North West wind.

The suit of Costa v. Whitehead is at length decided by Judge Eggleston on the basis of the report rendered by me & Mr. Reid, in favor of the plaintiff.

[37] Thomas H. Shields was a member of the first district school board. NOCD 1860. Trans.: It gains strength with the passage of time.

[38] Mrs. J. B. Bartlett was principal of the Franklin School. NOCD 1859.

December 16 52° 53° 55°

Rains and gloomy clouds, mild air, East wind. Heavy rains until midday. Sun broke out at 2 P.M. and wind changed to North West. Quite cool again.

Last night we heard an awful clanging of fire bells when we were all in bed, but I little supposed that I was at all interested. This morning, however, when I got down to the New Custom House I found that the temporary wooden offices occupied by the Time keeper, and the assistant Architect had taken fire from the stove pipe passing thro' the shed roof. These wooden buildings were entirely consumed. My money safe which was in one of them was exposed to intense heat. On opening it, I found the papers Pay rolls and a bank Bill but slightly touched. The gold and silver coin were so much discolored that I sent them down to the Branch Mint and the Officer politely replaced the amount with bran new pieces of $20 $10 and $5 denominations and half dollars. The loss and repairs will not exceed $3000. Of course the regular office routine was somewhat unhinged by the accident, and it was quite late when I got home again. One of the firemen was unfortunately injured by falling down in the discharge of duty.

December 22 39° 40° 42°

Sharp frost in the night. Wind due north. Cold & cloudy. A few flakes of snow fell about 11 A.M.

Letter from the Dept. granting my request to be relieved from duty on the New Marine Hospital & Quarantine Warehouse. After the 1st. Jany. my duties will be restricted to the Custom House with the same pay as heretofore according to my application, but not one word of compensation for my seven month's hard service on the accounts &c. of those additional works which I consider as an indignity, for which I must & will have reparation. No former Secretary of the Treasury would have treated me so: but Howell Cobb is a "mere politician" and I doubt much whether he is capable of appreciating an officer who performs real and valuable services to the Government.

December 24 40° 44° 46°

Heavy frost in the night. Cold and bracing today: pure air from the North West, bright sunny sky.

Answered the Letter of the Secretary of the Treasury relieving me from Extra duty, thanking him for the same, and asking for a moderate compensation for my services while so employed.

Christmas eve was celebrated at home in a general display of presents at the supper table. Numerically Tommy's outshone all the rest and yielded him unbounded delight. My handsome "dressing-gown", however, was something to admire and talk about....

December 28 64° 66° 68°

Foggy, mild & damp: South E. wind.

After dinner spent some time at the church with Mr. Reid.

After tea finished my pencil drawing of the "Elms" at Natchez.[39] It makes a very sweet picture, and, when framed, I intend it as a New Year's present to Mrs. Thornhill.

December 30 58° 58° 58°

Wind has gone over to the North West. The air is cold again & the sky covered with clouds....

I have made a good arrangement today by which my income from the Government Office will after the 1st. Proxo. be increased from $2100 per ann. to $2700. This with my other resources will "about do."

December 31 48° 49° 48°

Heavy rains & high wind from the N. East thro' the night. Dark and gloomy today with continued storm. Partially clear[?] in the afternoon with a severe wind from the North West....

Paid off the hands at the New Custom House instead of deferring it as usual until the 2nd or 3rd of the ensuing month in order to give the poor fellows a chance to disburse freely on their New Year's dinner &c. a courtesy which 84 good, trusty, mechanics and workmen seemed fully to estimate....

"We bring our years to an end as a tale that is told" but the "annual story" is after all a long and pleasant one....

---

[39] Wharton's sketch of the Elms still hangs in the house, now the residence of Mrs. Alma Kellogg Carpenter.

1860

January 1   38° 40° 40°

Sunday. The New Year opens with a "nipping and an eager air." The North West "wind bites shrewdly". Dun sky.

Calm Sabbath rest, disturbed only by the "feux de joie" [bonfires, here apparently misused to mean fireworks] of untamed youth who cannot dissever the celebration of the "New Year" from the destruction of "powder".

Enjoyed the day quietly at home.

January 2   36° 38° 41°

Bitter cold night, with heavy ice for this latitude. Cold north wind today, relieved by clear sunshine and bright blue sky.

Banks and places of business all open, so that much of the visiting was thrown upon the latter part of the day and evening, and many omitted it altogether. However, there was quite enough activity among "callers" to make a very pleasant day of it....

January 6   46° 48° 48°

Cloudy & threatening. N. East wind....

Thro' the politeness of the Renshaws we were supplied with Tickets to the Concert of the "Classic Music Society."[1] Emily, Mrs. Ladd and I went. The elegant concert room at "Odd Fellow's Hall" was quite filled, about 40 performers. The instrumentation was simply "perfect". The "French horns" and "double Bass" were managed with exquisite delicacy and <u>power</u>....

January 7   54° 54° 56°

Clouds and sunshine.

Approved another "advance" on Mr. Seymour's work at the church which was immediately cashed by Mr. Low.[2] They both met me at the church at 5 P.M. together with the Agent for the "Fire alarm Telegraph", and we settled details about the further operations, applying the "Wires" to the large Tower Bell &c. &c. Benson commenced on refitting & repairing the glass work &c. with 3 hands today.

[1] The Classical Music Society, founded in 1855, performed a series of six concerts a year at Odd Fellows Hall. Robert C. Reinders, *End of an Era: New Orleans, 1850–1860* (New Orleans, 1964), 188.

[2] George Seymour, builder, First near Bacchus (now Danneel). NOCD 1859.

January 10   60° 66° 66°

Rainy weather. East wind. Warm and unpleasant.

I have closed my Quarterly papers for New Custom House to January 1. 1860, showing

Total disbursements from the first	$2.819.548.66
Value of materials on hand.	145.066.68
Amt gone into the work	$2.674.481.98

January 12   65° 62° 62°

Damp & foggy. South East wind: quite warm. Wind changing to North West and growing colder.

Met Mr. Reid at the church and consulted about the final completion of the work roof &c. We agree not to take down the present roof, as it will not cost less than $10.000 or $12.000, but to ornament, and grain it &c. &c.[3]

January 18   48° 50° 54°

Cool air from the North West: cloudy.

Turned out exceedingly fine at noon, which I am rejoiced at as Tommy is going to a "juvenile party" this evening at Mr. R. B. Sumner's. It is expected that all will be "en costume" and 200 invitations are out. Tommy will go in a handsome Highland dress, and calculates upon a world of pleasure. I want him to have all the "sunshine" he can as the "shadows" will come soon & thick enough....

At 8 took Tommy & Ellen and left them at the "party"....

At 11½ went back to Mr. Sumner's for the young ones, found them in the flood tide of happiness, and no signs whatever of "breaking up" soon; so I went in amongst them and met several friends Messrs. Renshaw, Kearney &c. &c. and ladies that I knew enjoying the tableau. It was indeed extremely beautiful. The costumes were rich and tasteful, and a handsomer group of children up to 15 or 16 it would be hard to find. Tommy's beautiful highland dress was the object of universal admiration and became him wonderfully. Indeed taking it as a whole it was the most perfect in the room. The three Renshaw's were richly draped. Harry in full robes as an Oxford student, Jimmy in Continental uniform, and little Willy as a Sailor. All carried out in perfection and there were costumes in character, and out of character, but all rich & many very

costly, and all set off by bright fresh pretty faces, and lithe, elastic forms. And we "thinking" ones concluded that these juvenile displays were vastly more interesting appropriate and elegant than similar gatherings among older folks, where the gravity of maturer life is compromised for gaudy harlequinry and hollow mockery.

About 12 a general move was made for home and Mr. Renshaw kindly urged our taking seats in his carriage, but it was nearly one before we were quietly seated over the fireside talking over the doings of a very agreeable evening.

January 20   48° 54° 56°

Beautiful morning! West wind.

On my way to the Office called at Mrs. Renshaw's who sent for me to consult on the preparations necessary for a handsome party to construct a temporary supper room on the grass plot....

January 24   56° 62° 63°

Fine and sunny. South wind.

Mortified at slow progress in all my building operations but mechanics here are a difficult class to control. What I have on hand now is mere child's play yet I find it as hard to complete anything as to execute a new temple of "Karnac"....

January 27   54° 54° 52°

Cold North West wind. Sunny sky.

Called on Mr. Tisdale at the Office of the Gas Co. and requested his assistance to obtain for me the Superintendcy of the works made vacant by the recent death of Col. [W. S.] Campbell.[4] The appointment will not be made immediately, but our interview was of the most satisfactory character, and as far as he can make them available I feel certain that I shall have his good Offices....

February 1   44½° 46° 48°

Great change in the night, rain first and then a cold stormy North West wind, which still blows fresh this morning but the clouds are

[3] Wharton may be referring to interior surfaces of the open-truss roof of the Coliseum Place Baptist Church.

[4] Nathan O. J. Tisdale (b. ca. 1815), treasurer of the New Orleans Gas Light Company, and his wife, Marie L. McRea Tisdale, were the parents of Eugene Francis (ca. 1842-1860) and Victor (b. ca. 1844). The Tisdales lived on Magazine Street below Edward. U.S. Census, La., Jefferson Parish, 1850; NOCD 1853, 1857; *Daily Delta*, Apr. 8, 1860.

Dr. George W. Campbell residence, photoprint courtesy Samuel Wilson, Jr.

parting, and letting the sunshine thro', but it is bitter cold and I suffer much from my inflamed eye.

I believe our work at the Church is successful. I can trace no leakage after the driving rains of last night.

Very busy at the Office on the monthly Papers for all three works, then on my way home encountered all the family on Camp Street shopping. Tommy and I walked up together leaving the rest to finish their purchases &c. &c.

In the evening Emily and I went to the third Concert of the "Classic Music Society." It was a superb affair even more so than the last, 54 Performers and the vast Hall quite filled with the best "taste and intelligence" of the city. The Prima Donna of the "Orleans" executed two fine pieces, the first from "Der Freyschutz" with the "Orchestral" accompaniment, which far exceeded the latter, supported only by the Piano. The minuetto in Mozart's Jupiter, 4th. symphony was delicious, and the Overture of Masaniello (La Muette di Portici) was perfectly splendid; and received with the usual "rapturous applause."

February 2   42° 45° 49°

Splendid weather after a very cold night. North wind.

My inflamed eye is so much better this morning that I verily believe bathing it last night in a "flood of light" was far better than a lotion of lead water or arnica....

February 3   46° 50° 53°

North wind. Fog in the early morning, after white frost in the night. Cleared off very fine indeed.

Called at the Franklin School on my way to the Office.

My eye is entirely well and I went thro' the business of the morning "swimmingly". The evening was lovely, brilliant moonlight and mild. I took them all down to see the Bunyan Tableaux.[5] Tommy was deeply interested as I have already gone over the greater part of "Pilgrim's Progress" with him, and the "Panorama" was to him full of beauties where a practised eye could only see defect.

February 6   58° 58° 58°

Violent rains and vivid lightening, roaring thunder and soaking deluge all the livelong night. This morning dark and unsettled with

[5] The tableaux illustrating John Bunyan's *Pilgrim's Progress* was on exhibit at Armory Hall. *Daily Delta*, Feb. 1, 1860.

North East wind, and showers at intervals.

Fortyfying myself with a cup of strong coffee I sallied out to inspect the church, with some misgivings, I confess, after the furious gale of the night, but to my surprise and pleasure I found the whole work storm proof, and but a few drops of water had forced themselves thro' the sash & roof, which the glazier and tinman can easily remedy for the future and I notified them accordingly. Our work on this church thus proves a perfect triumph.

February 16   60° 63° 66°

Beautiful weather. Wind due north....

Returning to the Office the Major and I went over Dr. Campbell's elegant new mansion at the corner of Julia and St. Charles.[6]

February 19   57° 58° 60°

Sunday. Very clear and sunny. Cold bracing North wind.

Spent half an hour with Mr. Todd in the Church after breakfast.[7] All prepared as it was for the services of the day, it looked as sweet fresh and comfortable as if the whole were quite new, and the handsome new carpetting, cushions and windowblinds give a fine finish to the works on which we have been engaged for the last two months, and which now they are completed seem to give entire satisfaction....

February 20   56° 60° 61°

Lovely weather. North East wind. Clouding up in middle of the day, wind changing to due East, and threatening rain.

From 10 to 1 attended the closing exercises of the Term at the Girl's High school, and distribution of Diplomas to the Graduating class of 26 excellent Scholars whose progress I have had an opportunity to mark thro' the severest studies of the course.

When I went to the Office, it was 10 to 1 that I could not be absent from 10 to 1 but there being no important letters by Mail, I went. The room was decorated beautifully, and filled to overflowing. On invitation of the President I took my wonted seat on the Platform among the Directors. The talented Dr. Palmer, who has attended the examinations of the last week regularly, was on the Platform with us, and a deeply attentive auditor to the beautiful compositions read by members of the class, the songs, in between, well sung by the whole school....

The "Valedictory" which followed was happily conceived and well read by one of the best pupils in the class, and the company separated with the honest conviction that it was the most interesting exhibition of the kind they had ever attended. After dinner examined the plasterwork in the upper stories of the "Seamen's Home" with a view to pointing up &c., the wood framing having by this time reached its ultimate bearing. The brick walls do not seem to have settled at all, and the whole work is exceeding substantial and comfortable. I met the Pres[iden]t. J. W. Stanton Esq. this morning, and he desired me to make the examination as he thinks this a good time to do the work. The roof is as good as the first day, and the contact of (No. 12) Zinc with the Valley gutters (of 12 lb. Copper) seems to have been attended with no bad effect, tho' now on 2 years and 4 months. Major Beauregard feared galvanic corrosion.

February 21   64° 67° 62°

Damp and cloudy: wind due East. Violent storm of wind and rain from 12 to 1 with fall of thermo' from 67° to 64°. Trees uprooted dwellings & public buildings flooded &c. &c.

The work on the Baptist Church stood the gale extremely well. Some little water came in but almost entirely thro' the zinc roof which it will be impossible to make completely tight. Nothing but an inside ceiling will do.

Reported on the necessary repairs of St. Paul's amounting to $1100.00 including our Bill of $100 for Superintendence. Mr. Tisdale called on me at the Office, and we had a long and serious interview in regard to the Superintendency &c. &c.

After dinner examined the effect of the gale on St. Paul's church and found it leaking shockingly, especially in the Tower. After tea took them all, including Tommy, down to Lafayette Square to see the grand illuminated procession of the "mistic Krewe of Komus" on their way to their annual "Mardi gras" Ball at the "Varieties".[8]

---

[6] George W. Campbell's house was designed and built by Lewis E. Reynolds at a cost of $40,000. During the Civil War, it was used as Federal headquarters. The house was demolished in 1965. NONA, Theodore O. Stark, May 31, 1859; *Daily Crescent*, Sept. 12, 1859.

[7] J. P. Todd of Todd and Co., carpet merchants, at 120 Canal St. NOCD 1858.

[8] The Mistick Krewe of Comus, a Mardi Gras organization still in existence, was founded in 1857. The parade was followed by an elaborate ball at the Varieties Theater. *Daily Delta*, Feb. 22, 1860.

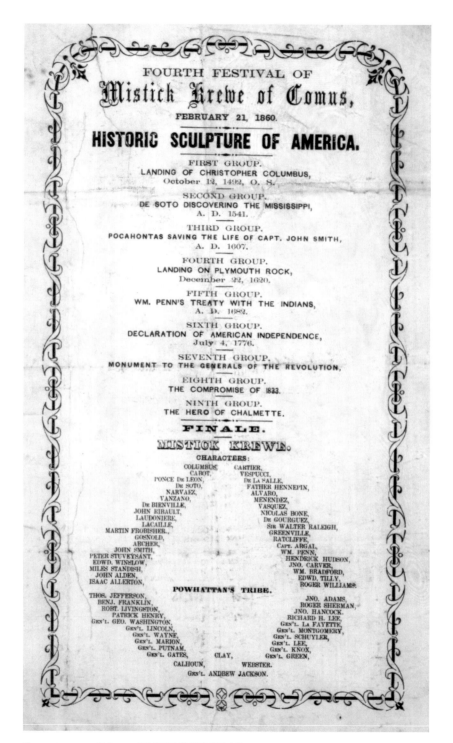

Comus program, February 21, 1860 (1958.102.15).

An earlier Comus parade, 1858 (1974.25.19.1), with a different theme, but showing the lively effect of a torchlit parade.

February 22   61° 64° 68°

Very beautiful weather after the tornado. Gentle breeze from the South West.

The works at the Custom House suspended in honor of Washington's Birthday.

The tornado of yesterday destroyed at least five lives, besides a large amount of valuable property.

Went to the Office and walked over the works with the brother in law of our Marble Contractor, Mr. Moss, from Rhode Island. Received and answered letter from Mr. Sumner, stating that the "Memorial" had been fully signed by the "Chamber of Commerce" and duly forwarded to Mr. Slidell our Senator in Washington. Then met my engagement with Mr. Tisdale at 12, at the Gas Office. Went with him to the Gas works and examined everything, the working of the entire machinery &c. &c. and spent two hours at least with Mr. Tisdale, talking over the prospects of eventual Superintendency &c. &c. In the evening went down to the Library and back &c. &c.

February 23   58° 60° 62°

Bright and clear: cool North wind....

After dinner went to the Library and got a fine article on the subject of "Gas" which I am studying out as carefully as if I were sure of that appointment. I shall prepare myself for it in every detail, and if I don't get it, the information acquired will be of use to me.

March 2   60° 64° 66°

Fine spring weather: North East wind. Hot in the middle of the day.

Very busy paying off mechanics & laborers at the New Custom House. Got thro' at 1, right to a cent.

Beautiful present from Messrs. Learned & Fisher of New York, per J. Stroud, of polished specimens of the exquisite marble formed by incrustation on the Boilers of steamer "Cahawba" after being in use 4 years and 5 months.[9] Pleasant walk up to dinner with Mr. Robt. Marsh and presented him with one of the specimens, exquisitely cut and polished. Brought home for Emily another slab, larger and cut with great taste, and highly polished surfaces.

If it could be produced in sufficient quantity it would make the most beautiful mantles and other ornaments that have ever been manufactured.

March 3   62° 65° 68°

Beautiful weather warm and sunny. East wind.

Finished my Reports of February for the 3 works then joined Tommy and Ellen at the Amphitheatre where the "Marsh children" were performing Cinderella to a crowded house, as usual; of the humanities two thirds at least were under 15 and enjoyed it with, I will venture to say, ten times the relish that older folks feel.[10]

March 4   64° 66° 69°

Sunday. Lovely spring weather, warm and genial. South East wind.

Emily Tommy and I at the "Steel Chapel" in the morning. Plain, good, Methodist sermon but altogether too long 1 hour and 5 minutes.

After dinner long walk thro' the 4th. District, and pleasant call at the Hathaway's and Tisdale's. Eugene improving a little.

March 6   66° 70° 73°

Warm and sunny. South East wind.

Very busy at the Office on Estimates & getting off reports for the three works. Visit from Adolphus Hamilton to say that he had made a full explanation to Bishop Polk of my wishes in regard to the projected Southern University, and the Bishop's views coincide with his own and mine.[11] So far, so good. I must follow it up with a personal interview....

March 7   70° 74° 76°

Beautiful spring weather. South West wind.

Long conversation with Mr. Tisdale. Introduction to Mr. Phoenix Wood, President of the Gas works, &c. &c.[12] Mr. Tisdale will keep me advised of the proper steps to take when the Directors determine to appoint a Superintendent....

---

[9] John Stroud & Co.'s marble warehouses were at 146 Common Street and at the corner of St. Charles and Girod. NOCD 1860.

[10] The performance was at Spalding and Rogers Amphitheater.

[11] Wharton sought the appointment as architect for the proposed Episcopal University of the South at Sewanee, Tennessee.

[12] Phoenix N. Wood, financier James Robb's close associate, was president of Robb's bank and of his gas works.

Bird's-eye view of the fourth district of New Orleans from the fire tower on Washington Avenue, Jay Dearborn Edwards, photographer, between 1857 and 1860 (1982.32.9), showing Camp and Fourth streets. Wharton frequently took walks in this area, now known as the Garden District. This photograph shows the empty lots, wooden fences, unpaved streets, and newly planted trees of the neighborhood; several churches may be seen on the horizon, including St. Patrick's Catholic, Trinity Episcopal, and Coliseum Place Baptist. Houses pictured which still stand, although many have been considerably altered, include 1206 Third, 2427 Camp, 1239 First, and 1410 Jackson.

Masonic Hall, 1874 (1951.41.60).

March 9   60° 61° 63°

...In the evening took all hands to see the Panorama at Masonic Hall, consisting of a long series of "Bible Scenes" from the Creation to the period of Solomon.[13] As a painting it was of a vastly better than the "Bunyan Tableaux". Some of the skies, middle distances and mountain ranges were really very beautiful. Some of the tropical vegetation, too, carefully painted, chiefly a variety of fine Palms. "Jacob's Dream" was expressed with great brilliance, but the human figures throughout were badly drawn and coloured as usual. The whole thing, however, was quite interesting and seemed to produce a deep impression on the audience of spectators, who were numerous, and no doubt little able or disposed to be critical. We had, however, to be <u>auditors</u>, too, for the proprietor accompanied it with a "running commentary" in a high nasal key. Dr. Palmer & others that we knew were there, and we all, especially Tommy derived much pleasure from it. Moonlight, and sweet odors of orange bloom in going home.

March 10   60° 62° 65°

Cold dry dusty. Clear sky, wind due North.

The "Memorial" to Congress to obtain a full appropriation for the New Custom Ho. was returned today with the signatures of all the "<u>solid</u> <u>men</u>" around. I immediately enclosed it, with a note from Major Beauregard, to the Hon. M. Taylor, M.C. from Louisiana, with a request to present and back it up with his influence.[14] I do not think we shall fail of an appropriation this year after the efforts that have been made. It requires about $800.000 to finish the work, which can easily be accomplished in 3 years if Congress will supply the funds as called for. After dinner took Tommy down to the Library and Mr. Kerr selected a book of stories for him, which interested him very much indeed when I read the first one to him after tea.

[13] J. Insco Williams's Bible panorama was on exhibit at the Masonic Hall. The Masonic Hall, located at St. Charles and Perdido streets, was designed by James Gallier in 1845 as the Commercial Exchange. In 1853, the building was sold to the Grand Lodge of Louisiana. It was demolished in 1891. *Daily Delta*, Mar. 9, 1860.

[14] Miles Taylor (1805-1873) was a planter, attorney, and congressman (1855-1861). *DLB.*

March 14   54° 58° 60°

Fine, dry and very dusty. East wind....

Met my appointment with Bishop Polk at 6 and sat with him in his study until near 10, discussing the proposed University. He showed me among other things a book of water colour drawings of the scenery from different points of the "domain". It is on the plateau of the Cumberland mountains, 1000 feet above the valley of Tennessee and 2000 above tide water. Waterfalls of the greatest beauty, rich woodlands, warm tinted, moss hung Sandstone rocks, and splendid views over the distant country.

March 22   60° 66° 69°

Fine and sunny. East wind.

Worked off much detail business at the Office very satisfactorily and dispatched the voluminous documents to head quarters. At the "Home" after dinner. A dozen hands at work on plastering and woodwork. Every thing going on very well indeed. After tea finished up the Plans and specifications for Col. W. B. Whitehead, but I dread this night work. It is trying beyond measure on eyes & brain after the regular day.

March 23   65° 69° 70°

Soft balmy air from the South East: clear sky.

Tommy came down to the Office at 11 and whilst I went on with my morning's work I gave him one of my desks, and he spent a couple of hours in copying the endorsements of our blank forms. His first clerical effort and he did it remarkably well too. Then I took him over the work to the top most stone of the mountain of marble, then to "Maurice's" for the usual supply of good things then home in the omnibus to dinner.

At the Sailor's Home after dinner. Our large force are getting along admirably with that work.

March 27   56° 58° 59°

Cold dry North East wind: light clouds.

Emily's Birthday, she is now twenty five, and professes to feel like a "Saurian" or some other such relic of a former world.

Major Beauregard is very ill yet. Note from him this morning. He has appointed Messrs. Reid, Roy & myself to constitute a board to examine claims of the Contractors of the New Marine Hospital for unsettled extras amounting to near $20.000. We met at 10 A.M. and adjourned at 3. Mr. Van Cleve the president of the Company, and Mr. Houdayer their agent having been invited to be present. We succeeding in deciding but two points and shall go to work again at 11. tomorrow....

April 8   75° 77° 78½°

Sunday. Very warm and cloudy South wind.

My marketing this morning was exceedingly nice, young lamb, chicken &c. &c. but very expensive, $2.20 for what usually costs me $1.75. Last evening I received a note from Mr. Tisdale saying that poor Eugene expired at 3 P.M. We went to the funeral this morning. It was attended by quite a large number of friends and after the usual services at the house we all went out to the Cemetery of the 4th. District, and saw the body deposited in the tomb. The ceremonies were conducted by the chaplain of Bishop Polk, the Rev. Mr. Hawley.[15]...

April 10   76° 80° 80°

Clouds floating across the sky: South wind. Very debilitating weather.

Pleasant letter from sister Emily. Went back to the Office after dinner to finish up my writing.

A stereoscopist named "Thompson" from Niagara brought a series of 36 large views of the "Falls" &c. in winter and summer, the most superb things I ever saw. The pillars of ice and frosted stalactites sparkle as only ice can in the clear sunshine.

April 12   74° 74° 78°

Dry and dusty as ever. North West wind.

Works at the Custom House suspended in honor of the "monumental inauguration".[16]

[15] The cemetery of the Fourth District was Lafayette Cemetery I on Washington Avenue, between Prytania and Coliseum. Fletcher J. Hawley became rector of Trinity Church when Bishop Polk resigned in 1860. He served until 1862. Carter and Carter, *So Great A Good*, 122.

[16] A ceremony was held on April 12 celebrating the inauguration of the statue of Henry Clay on Canal Street. *Daily Delta*, Apr. 12, 1860.

Lafayette Cemetery I, A. Wittemann, photographer, ca. 1892 (1971.14.30). On the left are wall vaults along Washington Avenue; family tombs are on the right.

At 10 Emily Tommy & I, Ellen & Josey went by arrangement to Mr. G. B. Young's office on Camp Street, where we met several friends, and had a perfect & detailed view of the immense procession of 3 miles long as it defiled slowly by, its splendid banners of rich coloured silk, filling the long avenue with kaleidoscopic tints of incomparable beauty. Thence we passed to the New Custom House where we found the Major in his office and after resting awhile in mine, went up to the top of the building. There were quite a number of people assembled on the South West angle of the exterior scaffold, where seats had been arranged and an awning spread for the occasion. Here we had a superb view of the whole ceremony, up the long densely crowded avenue of Canal Street, the glittering costumes, and the unveiling of the statue. At 2½ the masses began to disperse, and after spending half an hour in looking at those beautiful stereoscop[ic] views of "Niagara" which had been left by Mr. Thompson for our inspection, we again mingled in the crowd, and got seated, by strange good fortune, in the Prytania Street omnibus, without a moment's detention, and home to dinner.

In the [evening?] walked down again and examined the statue. It is colossal over 12 feet high finely designed & well cast, the granite pedestal too is beautiful but bears no proportion whatever to the mass of the figure, it is too scant in every dimension and at least 25 feet too low....

April 14   72° 75° 76°

Damp & cloudy inclining to rain: East wind.

Pleasant visit at the Normal School. At the Office sent off my Quarterly Returns for the 1st. Quarter of 1860, and in spite of the constant interruptions of the last month, caused by the complicated investigation into the Marine Hospital accounts I have got all the business of the three works fairly finished up to date. That is, the current business. The Contractor's claims for account of "Marine Hospital" is still undergoing examination and I carry home with me at dinner time 16 pages of closely written matter, with illustrative drawings, to "lick into shape" and prepare for the "jealous" eye of the Department.

April 17   77° 78° 72°

This is my birthday, but the inexorable demands of business, and changing a servant at home, will prevent our marking it with anything unusual beyond receiving beautiful presents from Emily & Tommy....

April 18   73° 74° 77°

Still cloudy and unsettled, the wind inclining to South West. Cleared up at noon, warm and sunny.

Mr. McConnell & Revd. Chas. Goodrich called upon us at the Office to make arrangements about repairing "St. Paul's."[17] We will meet them at the Church at 5 this evening. Met them at the time appointed and found a fine $4000 organ going up, but we stopped the work at once, finding the gallery too weak, and shall have to go to work immediately to support it from below. After tea writing up Marine Hospital report on Claims &c. &c.

April 19   76° 77° 78°

Warm South West wind: light clouds.

Met Messrs. Reid & Baird at St. Paul's on the way to the Office, and pointed out the necessary work to the latter.[18]

Finished the heavy series of papers &c. relating to the Claims of the Contractors against the New Marine Hospital, &c. &c. amounting to upwards of $23.000.00. After dinner saw Revd. Dr. Goodrich & Mr. Sloo, in regard to the work required at the Church and received the Bids of Messrs. Baird and Ringé (that is, the proposals of each) and told them to meet me at 10 tomorrow at my Office.[19]

After tea, Emily being tired I took Tommy to the Fair of the "Orphan's Home" at "Odd Fellow's Hall", very full indeed and had a very pleasant time until 10½ when we rode home.

Met Mr. McConnell at the fair, and took him aside explained what had passed between me, Mr. Goodrich & Mr. Sloo. Read the Bids to him, and the one accepted, Mr. Baird's, being the lowest, he accepted officially as Treasurer of the Church and signed at a side table. We then mingled with the full crowd three fourth's of whom I was acquainted with more or less, and Tommy enjoyed the evening immensely, with his purchases, Ice cream & strawberries &c. &c.

[17] Charles Goodrich had been rector of St. Paul's Episcopal Church since 1839 when the first church was built. The repairs were to be made to the second church erected on the same site in 1853. Duncan, *Diocese of Louisiana*, 83.

[18] Thomas Baird, a builder, lived on St. Mary Street, near Annunciation. NOCD 1859.

[19] Thomas Sloo, Jr., agent and later president of the Sun Mutual Insurance Co., was one of two members who represented St. Paul's Church in the Diocesan Convention of 1839. Jean Ringé, a carpenter, lived on Galvez Street, near Dumaine. NOCD 1859.

Inauguration of the statue of Henry Clay on Canal Street, engraving with the addition of crowds and a platform from a photograph taken from the roof of the Custom House, Jay Dearborn Edwards, photographer, 1860 (1959.159.7), gift of Harold Schilke and Boyd Cruise.

Henry Clay Statue, Frank Leslie's Illustrated Newspaper, *May 5, 1860 (1974.25.24.99), Canal Street at Royal, with Christ Church in the background at right.*

April 20   76° 78° 79³/₄°

Hot and sunny, floating clouds. South wind.

Called on Revd. C. Goodrich in going to the Office, to explain to him the arrangements I had made.

At 10 Messrs. Baird & Ringé called at the Office & I read the Bids to them, accepting Mr. Baird's & directing him to go to work, as instructed in detail, without delay....

At the Church again after dinner, with Revd. C. Goodrich and Mr. McConnell. We are using the two Hydraulic Jack screws of the New Custom House to raise the front Plate of the Organ Gallery which has deflected nearly two inches in the middle, by the pressures from time to time imposed upon it.

April 21   76° 77° 78°

Pleasant spring weather. South wind.

At St. Paul's at 8¹/₂. Work going on well the front of gallery raised by the screws to the full height, and the shoring complete. At the Office, New Marine Hospital business "ad nauseam." We are all sick and tired of the ill conceived and worse conducted project. All the valuable time of our Office is consumed in turning over the charred bones, withered skeletons, and refuse ashes of the defunct "Duncan administration" consisting of claims brought by the Harpy Contractors for alleged "extra work" ordered by said sapient administration, beyond the regular stipulations of the Contract, and reaching by this time the handsome figure of about $25.000, all in small detail accounts, made up of an infinite amount of minute items referring to transactions and correspondance, orders &c. spread over a space of four years....

April 28   65° 68° 70°

Clear sunshine, dry and very dusty: cold North East wind: very hot sunshine in the middle of the day.

At St. Paul's both in going to the Office and returning. Pleasant walk down with Mr. Robt. Marsh, after spending a short time in listening to the charming tones of the new Organ, which I got Mr. Mills to shew off to us; it is one of Henry Erben's fine instruments and will cost $4000.[20]

[20] Henry Erben (1800-1884), noted New York organ builder, furnished organs for several New Orleans churches, including the Presbyterian Church (1824, later Dr. Clapp's "Strangers Church"), St. Patrick's Church (1843), and the First Presbyterian Church (1857), as well as St. Paul's.

Paid off the Officer's at the different works, and got thro' a rush of miscellaneous business.

Strawberries are becoming quite an institution here. Twice a week hundreds of boxes come by the railroad to the different Grocers &c. Mr. Marsh & I sent each 3 Boxes home to our families for their special amusement and admixture with ice cream &c. &c.

After dinner went to the Church again, met Messrs. Goodrich & McConnell. Our Iron columns both in basement, and under Organ Gallery are set complete, and the scaffolding removed. All firm & solid, and in good proportion.

April 30   67° 69° 72°

Dry and dusty: clear sunshine, South West wind. Very warm at noon: real autumn weather. Dangerous to the unacclimated, and painful to all, producing a sense of weariness, debility and pain in the muscular system, nerves &c. &c. &c....

The tones of the new Organ (now finished) are very fine, and rich in variety, it has 33 stops. The "clarabella" "Dulciano" and "clarionet" are singularly smooth and mellow, and the open and stop Diapasons fill the Church with a grand volume of harmony....

May 6   72° 74° 76°

Sunday: fine, sunny sky. South East wind.

Last evening our Irish cook asked to go out; said she would certainly be back at 9, left her clothes &c. &c. and that is the last we have seen of her. So the house this morning is in another perplexity for the 199th. time from the same cause. Tommy & I, however, went to market and carried the basket, bought a "beautiful" dinner, and Tommy thought it excellent fun. I have kept house for 12 years and never before had to carry the market basket, but the demon of misrule seems to have taken entire possession of the Irish menials, they demand $15 a month, and then do just as they please, go or stay, work or play, "a piacere".[21] During the morning she returned, said that her friends had lost a child by measles, and forced her to stay to the "wake" and "burial" was very penitent &c. &c. so Emily forgave her, and she went to work again.

Morning teaching Tommy, writing, a walk &c. &c.

[21] Trans.: at their pleasure.

May 7   74° 76° 78°

Hot, dry & dusty. South East wind.

At St. Paul's on my way to the Office. At 1 Messrs. Robt. Marsh, Trea[surer] Tisdale and I went by agreement to see the portrait of Mr. P. N. Wood at the rooms of Mr. Healey, Artist.[22]

The likeness was a decided hit, so, too, of several other portraits in the studio, of familiar faces. The style also superior to anything we have yet had in New Orleans....

May 10   66½° 70° 74°

Cold North West wind: clear sunny sky. Brilliant atmosphere.

Met Mr. Sloo at the Church at 9. He is delighted with our work, and I had a pleasant walk down with him, talking over details &c. &c. He agrees with me that the additional support that I propose by connecting the 2 large Iron Columns of the Nave with the Gallery front, by Iron [1" tie?] rods, flattened against, and screwed into the shafts, must be introduced, in spite of the "Treasurer's" opposition. At the church after dinner, and at 8 P.M. our grand Sacred Concert came off with great success, and an ample audience.[23] I took all hands including Tommy and Miss Josey Cook. About 50 vocalists, and many very fine, well trained voices. The choruses were decidedly capital, and the noble organ rolled the finest volume of harmony thro' the Gothic aisles. Our Gallery extension is a vast improvement both as to convenience and artistic effect, and the loveliness of the night added a finishing charm to an evening of great pleasure.

May 12   72° 75° 76°

Very fine indeed: West wind. Sky of the purest sapphire but very hot in the sun.

At the church at 8½. Then at 11 sent Mr. Grey from the Office to bring Tommy down in the omnibus and take him to the "Panopticon of India" for the second time.[24] It was quite a pretty entertainment, well attended, and Tommy enjoyed it hugely,

John Slidell, 1858, after Mathew B. Brady, photographer (1974.25.27.401).

applauding most vociferously when a good point was in review. Mr. Roy had his children, too; and altogether it was a decidedly pleasant time. Returned to the Office at 2, then closed up, took Tommy to Maurice's for good things then rode home to dinner.

At the Church after dinner; scaffolding and all cleared away, and every thing snug and nice for Sunday's services.

May 28   80° 83° 85°

Hot and dry. West wind.

Very busy at the Office.

Major Beauregard quietly announced to me the fact that this evening he will be married to Miss Deslondes, a sister in law of our Senator John Slidell.[25] This affair has been going on for sometime and its "denouement" will give universal satisfaction to all cognizant parties.

Marine Hospital papers after dinner.

---

22 George Peter Alexander Healy (1813-1894), a well-known portrait and historical painter, painted a large number of portraits during intermittent stays in New Orleans in 1860 and 1861. The Historic New Orleans Collection owns a portrait of James Robb that has been attributed to Healy (1988.43). Healy may have resided at the St. Charles Hotel. *ENOA.*

23 The concert was at St. Paul's Church. *Daily Delta,* May 10, 1860.

24 D. C. Larue's panopticon of the war in India and the Sepoy Rebellion was exhibited at Armory Hall. *Daily Delta,* May 10, 1860.

25 Caroline Deslonde (1830-1864) was the daughter of André Deslonde, a St. James Parish sugar planter, and Henriette Rosine Chastant. A sister Mathilde was married to John Slidell, and another sister Henriette was married to R. W. Adams. Keyes, *Madame Castel's Lodger,* 240; *DLB.*

May 29   81° 84° 85°

Very hot, dry & dusty. South West wind.

Quiet day at the Office and left early for home, the heat being most oppressive. Went over Christ's Church with Mr. Reid. We at once resolved that it is still by far the most beautiful, and best built church in the City, and is kept in most perfect condition. It was my first effort in architecture, about 15 years ago; I made the drawings chiefly at Holly Springs, and Mr. James Gallier Senior took the Contract and executed the work with some changes agreed to by the Contracting parties.

After dinner on Marine Hospital papers.

May 31   79° 82° 83°

Fine & exceedingly agreeable after the rains of yesterday. Gentle West wind. Very hot at midday....

Major Beauregard back at the Office today. His wedding on the 28th. was a strictly family affair, confined exclusively to close connections. The respective families are so widely known that any other arrangement would have amounted to a "mass meeting"....

June 1   80° 83° 83°

Very hot indeed, dry and oppressive.

Got up early and went to market. At the Office closing up accounts of the 3 works for May.

Clouds gathered at 3 and gusts of wind indicated a storm as I returned home in the omnibus to dinner. In the evening I took Ellen & Josey Cook to the annual Exhibition of Miss Hull's School at Lyceum Hall, full room and hot as a furnace, exercises long but interesting, and music very creditable. A beautiful ballad by Miss Dora Renshaw (by invitation) being a former Graduate, and overture of "La Muette di Portici", on 8 Pianos. Closing by Distribution of prizes & Diplomas, and a long, dull speech from a young gentleman which excited little attention, but smoothed down our pillows for a snug night's rest.

June 3   84° 85° 86°

Sunday. Very beautiful weather but very hot, with South West wind.

Thirty years ago, and on just such a morning as this, I and my family entered the charming Bay of New York. That was a day of

intense enjoyment, and I recall it each year, as time rolls on, with profound emotion. The unmingled happiness of that day seemed to pencil out a future of joy and success which has thus far, with but few drawbacks, been amply fulfilled.

I went to market early, and my purchases will make a dinner table worthy of the anniversary, as the Hotel cards say, consisting of the "best the market affords", and that in New Orleans is something in the month of June. Such tomatoes, egg plants, artichokes, cucumbers & vegetables of lesser note, meats & poultry &c.

In the morning at home, reading to Tommy "Bunyan" and those passages in my "Journal" referring to our arrival in New York in 1830, with the illustrations &c. Then writing until near dinner time. Walk in the evening after the heat.

June 12   84° 86° 88°

Hot, dry and dusty. South West wind, to North West, and in returning at 3 to dinner in the omnibus, it was almost beyond endurance, the heat suffocating. Rain is much needed. None yet this month.

After dinner we all went up in the Magazine Street omnibus and enjoyed the delicious breeze on the River bank at Freeport.[26]

June 30   80° 84° 84°

Fine and sunny. Wind south. Heat intense in the sun but pleasant in shade.

Very busy indeed at the Office winding up the month's business &c. &c.

The failure of our appropriation Bill of $300.000, passed by the Senate, but killed in the House, reduces us to a very scant available Balance, and we are now awaiting instructions from the Department as to the disposition we shall make of it, and of ourselves too! as some removals must inevitably be made, and not unlikely an early suspension of the entire work [will] result from this fatal and vindictive action of the House.

---

[26] The borough of Freeport, incorporated in 1846 and dissolved in 1850, included what later became Jefferson City, as well as Hurstville and Bloomingdale. Freeport extended from Toledano Street to the Bloomingdale line above State Street. Wharton is probably referring to the Hurstville-Bloomingdale area. *New Orleans Architecture*, 7:27-28.

July 8   83° 89° 93°

Sunday. Cool & pleasant when I went to market at 7 with South West wind, but the sunshine for some days past has been inordinately severe after 9 A.M. and while we have no yellow fever to record, the cases of "coup de soleil" [sunstroke] yesterday at a large fire up town were no less than 8![27] The firemen chiefly were attacked with it. Today the heat is again most oppressive, and not a solitary cloud to mitigate the fiery rigor of the afternoon sun....

July 11   85° 90° 92°

Hot and dry, West wind. Fearfully hot at midday with a dense smoky atmosphere and myriads of musquitoes.

The Department writes today that $20.000 has been appropriated by Congress for the fitting up of half the Post Office Department, and $5000 for the preservation of the rest of the work, but none for its continuance, and orders all operations to be stopped when those objects are accomplished.

Answered said immortal document after dinner preparatory to additions and further "hot shot" from the Major.

July 12   86° 89° 92°

Heat worse than ever, with the same saucy sunshine & the same distressing dry west wind, blowing over a noisome swamp.

Our assistant architect's poor little boy died in the night, and one of our stout stone cutters expired of sun stroke last evening. The list of deaths from this cause is assuming a frightful importance.

Today the Major issued a "special order" to all officers & employees on the N. Custom House announcing that in consequence of the failure of Congress to appropriate for the Continuance of the work, and of orders from the Treasury Department, he would be compelled to dispense with their services at the end of the present month. I and Mr. Roy, however, will be retained, at least until the Completion of the work on the Post Office &c. &c. in October. Post prandial operations consisted of the preparation of a complete reply to the Department letter of the 5th. after full discussion with the Major this morning. He proposed sending a copy of it, with his reflections thereon, to Mr. John Slidell, our friendly Senator, that he may hold an interview over it with the Secretary of the Treasury, and see what can be done.

[27] The fire was at St. Andrew and New Levee streets. *Daily Picayune*, July 9, 1860.

At twilight a sudden storm of wind rain, thunder and lightening sprung up from the East, and cooled the atmosphere down to a pleasant temperature.

July 14   83° 86° 89°

Wind round to South West again, dry and hot. Very hot. Hotter than ever, sickly feeling heat, damp, steamy, fiery: human life, if retained, is hardly worth the trouble of preservation....

July 17   84° 88½° 88°

Hot & clear, North East wind.

The Board of Health reports the first case of "yellow fever" during the past week, and an immense amount of miscellaneous fatality, 300 in all. A pretty heavy list for 1 week, 80 odd of sunstroke & apoplexy. Sent off Quarterly Returns for the 2nd. Qr. of 1860 to Treasury Department.

Total expenditure on the work to June 30. 1860. $2.909.047.06....

July 19   82° 89° 90°

Hot & dry: South East wind. Very hot at noon in the sun but pleasant in the shade.

When I got down to the Office I found a heavy fire raging in the block opposite the Canal & New Levee Street corner of the New Custom House.[28] The streets were crowded and the flame was driven by the wind directly upon our Granite walls, but by a judicious use of our fire apparatus and the exertions of our entire force the Granite remained uninjured, tho' the fire raged for two hours, from 7½ to 9½ A.M. and completely destroyed two 4 story stores. Went down after dinner to see the ruins &c. &c.

July 23   84½° 88° 91°

Fine & sunny: South East wind....

At 7 went to the City Hall and met the New School Board. They welcomed me back to their Council room most heartily, and we sat till 9½ P.M. The chief business being the organization of the Board

[28] The fire was in Henry Goldman's drugstore at the corner of Canal and Levee streets. *Daily Picayune*, July 20, 1860.

and appointment of the Standing Committees: I am again Chairman of Lyceum & Library, and on three other Committees.

July 25 85° 90° 92°

Hot & sultry: heavy threatening clouds: North West wind. Cleared off at 10 A.M. and the sun shone forth as savagely as ever.

I have addressed a letter to Mr. J. M. Reid discontinuing our connection as architects: the experience of the past year has proved to me beyond a doubt that I can do far better single-handed. Received an important letter from the Treasury Department, a copy of which I at once enclosed to Major Beauregard at Pascagoula, with comments. It reverses the order of July 5 to suspend operations at the New Custom House, deferring the proposed suspension until further notice from the Department, which means that the letter of July 11 (to which this is a reply) has done its work handsomely, and will yield a full return for the thought the Major & I expended on it....

August 10 85° 89° 86°

Sunny morning: North East wind. Clouds rising, and fine cooling showers at midday.

Pleasant letter from Bishop Polk, inviting me to furnish Plans &c. for the "Southern University", in accordance with the published proposals to architects.[29] He sends me, moreover, a sketch shewing the general ideas of the Committee, which sketch closely corresponds with the general distribution we agreed upon together in a long conversation on the subject last winter. The Plans have to be sent in by the 1st. October. The prospects for me are very favorable.

August 11 82° 85° 78°

Heavy rains in the night with high wind, from the East. Dark and showery this morning: rains at intervals. Storm of wind and rain at 2 to 3 P.M. Got very wet in returning home to dinner notwithstanding the assistance afforded by the omnibus. Storm in the afternoon....

After dinner the wind increased to a gale, and the rain fell in fitful dashes. The storm increased up to about midnight when it subsided, and the morning opened with brilliant sunshine.[30]...

[29] An invitation to architects to submit designs for the central building of the University of the South at Sewanee, Tennessee, appeared in the *Daily Picayune* August 7-12, 1860.

[30] A hurricane, described as a great gale, struck the area on the fourth anniversary of the disastrous storm that destroyed Last Island in 1856. *Daily Picayune*, Aug. 14, 1860.

August 13 81° 84° 86°

Beautiful weather. Cool north East wind.

Letter from Major Beauregard, and answered by Mail.

Accounts from different points on the Lake, River and Gulf Coast came in fearfully; the effects of the gale on the 11th. were terrific. At Proctorville the whole country is submerged and about 40 lives lost. Mr. Reid came up from "Quarantine" and reported the slate roof of our New Warehouse greatly damaged by the gale, and all the materials collected there for the new wharf, amounting in value to near $3000, entirely washed and blown away....

August 16 82° 89° 88°

Fine, clear and dry: East wind....

Fort keeper from Fort St. Phillip came up and reports all the outworks, levees &c. washed away in the late hurricane; and the water making a clean breach over the entire site....

August 22 82° 88° 86°

Light clouds: South East wind.

Having matured my notes, sketches and general designs for my "University Building" I took them all down to the Office today with my instruments &c. and made a commencement on the complete set of drawings on Antiquarian paper. I have got a large table, Drawing boards, and all other conveniences in the Architects Office of the New Custom House, and have made today good progress.

At the Library &c. in the evening.

September 17 74° 81° 83°

Cool and pleasant: bright sun: N. East wind.

Attended the wedding of Miss Emma Layet at 10 A.M. at the Baronne Street Chapel, with Emily Tommy & the rest, who met me at the time appointed.[31] Very pleasant affair. The marriage Party started at 12 for Mobile.

Very busy at the Office; finished my elevation of "University" and home to dinner at 4 P.M.

Took tea at Mr. Paul Cook's then returned home and finished my

[31] Emma Layet (d. 1871) and Joseph Touart of Mobile were married at Jesuit Church on Baronne St. between Canal and Common. *Sunday Delta*, Sept. 23, 1860; *Daily Picayune*, Apr. 21, 1871.

copy for the Printer of the "University Specifications", and a long stupid letter about that detestable Quarantine Warehouse to go to the Treasury Department tomorrow. Worked thus until near midnight. Deaths during last [week] were 160 and only 1 of yellow Fever.

September 22   67° 78° 79°

Cool dry & sunny: North East wind.

I went to a fire last night which proves to have been a most disastrous calamity.[32] Many persons were killed or crushed & injured by the falling of walls. I was shocked this morning to learn that among the killed was John J. Roy, the son of our Assistant Architect at the New Custom House, and a most estimable young man of about 21 years old. In going to the fire I met one of the sufferers being carried off on a litter, but had no idea of the extent of the calamity until this morning when I went to the Office. Another fire this morning destroyed a whole side of a square on Apollo Street. I went to it before breakfast.

My Plans are going on rapidly to completion.

Wrote to Bishop Polk to say that I should leave with my Plans for the University grounds on Friday next.[33]

September 28   79° 86° 89°

Fine and clear: East wind.

Very busy indeed preparing to go away. Visits from Mr. Grimshaw & others to see my Plans; strong letter from Mr. Grimshaw to Bishop Elliot, and from Mr. T. A. Adams to Bishop Polk. Left home for the Jackson Railroad at 7½ P.M. and at 8 got fairly under way for the mountain, with comfortable Sleeping Car fine moonlight &c. &c.[34]

[32] The fire began in Karstendiek & Co.'s four-story liquor warehouse on Tchoupitoulas Street between Lafayette and Girod. Exploding alcohol caused the collapse of the brick walls, killing 14 people including John Roy, Jr., aged 23. *Daily Picayune*, Sept. 22, 23, 1860.

[33] The University Archives at Sewanee contain considerable information about this competition, including a master's thesis by Daniel Randle.

[34] Bishop Stephen Elliott of Georgia joined Bishop Polk in raising funds for the new University of the South at Sewanee, Tennessee, and with Bishop Polk laid its cornerstone on October 10, 1860. Carter and Carter, *So Great A Good*, 122. Wharton's account of the ceremonies appeared in the *Daily Picayune* on Oct. 23, 1860. Wharton suspended his journal during the trip to Sewanee and on his return to New Orleans on October 22, entered the daily record of weather conditions during his absence. Two letters, dated October 1 and October 8, 1860, from Wharton to his wife while he was in Tennessee are in the University Archives at Sewanee.

October 22   70° 72° 68°

Dry: North wind.

Arrived this morning per steamer "Charmer" after three weeks of varied & most exciting incident, but too kaleidoscopic by far for record, suffice it that my visit to University Place has been in the main highly satisfactory and I am delighted to be at home again.

October 23   62° 78° 76°

Fine and sunny. North West wind. Very dry and dusty.

Active operations at the Custom House dispatching business that has accumulated in my late absence.

Pleasant letter from Francis D. Lee, Architect, Charleston, S.C. one of the competitors in the recent struggle for architectship of the University.[35] His fine Roman design, my Grecian, and Anderson's Gothic were the three that came under the final consideration of the Board, and the premium was awarded to the Gothic on the ground of style only.[36] I have every assurance that when it comes to the appointment of an architect, I shall receive the commission; in the meantime Mr. Anderson is distinctly informed that he is not appointed architect, tho' his Gothic design has received the premium. The Clergy all go firmly for the monastic sombreness &c. &c....

The appointment of Architect has yet to be made and I have every assurance that can reasonably be required that it is mine. We had a delightful time on the mountain, and were most hospitably entertained. The air was pure and bracing. The maximum thermometer 75°. The minimum thermometer 28°....

October 24   63° 80° 78°

Fine and clear, very dusty: West wind.

Very busy at the Office.

The Picayune published my letter this morning descriptive of the Ceremonies on Sewanee Mountain on the 10th. Strange enough, the Editor in his prefatory makes me a clergyman; do I look like it?...

[35] The works of Francis D. Lee (1826-1885) include the remodeling of the Unitarian Church interior (1852-1854) and the design for St. Luke's Church (1859), both in Charleston. After the Civil War, Lee practiced in St. Louis, Missouri. Beatrice St. Julien Ravenel, *Architects of Charleston* (Charleston, 1945), 219-28.

[36] Charles Frederick Anderson, the author of *American Villa Architecture* (1860), practiced in Washington and New York. D. F. Francis, *Architects in Practice, New York City, 1840-1900* (New York, 1879), 11.

October 29   63° 72° 75°

Damp and misty, North West wind. Cleared off at noon....

After tea took all hands with the Bryants' &c. (a round dozen) to the corner of Canal & Camp to hear the "Breckenridge oration" of Mr. Yancey.[37] Lovely moonlight, pleasant time generally.

October 31   71° 73° 74°

Damp & cloudy indicating rain. East wind. Light showers thro' the morning.

Visited Girl's High School and Library on my way to the Office; Very busy at the Office until 3½ P.M.

Could not get thro' at the Office but had to take my work home to write at night. My prospects for hard work increase, as the Major insists upon discharging the Time Keeper who is my assistant; and at the same time proposes to increase the force so as to use up the Funds available at the earliest period, say two months; I told him that I disagreed with him on this policy entirely but it is of little use to talk to an army Officer when he takes a set. I wish myself most heartily out of Government employ, mismanaged, as it now is, and am ready to turn to any thing else that will be moderately remunerative. And so ends the month; with poor prospects, but strong energies.

November 4   63° 70° 70°

Sunday. Pleasant sunny weather: East wind.

Reading to Tommy and walk in the morning. Then they all went to Church and I like a heathen stayed at home....

Mr. G. B. Young came in the evening & invited us to his house to see the great "Bell" procession tomorrow.[38]...

[37] Edwin K. Bryant (1818-1886) of E. K. Bryant & Co., proprietors of the Orleans Cotton Press, lived on Terpsichore near Coliseum. He and his wife, Martha (1820-1887), were the parents of Laura (b. ca. 1843), Josephine (b. ca. 1846), Frank (b. ca. 1849), and Ella (1851-1858). Also in the household were Victor Bryant (1837-1858) and Josephine Bryant (b. ca. 1835), probably siblings or cousins of E. K. Bryant. Historic Cemetery Survey, Historic New Orleans Collection; U.S. Census, La., Orleans Parish, 1850; NOCD 1860. William Lowndes Yancey (1814-1863) was a member of the Alabama delegation to the Democratic National Convention in Charleston in 1860 and a leader in the secession movement. He served in the Confederate senate from 1862 to 1863. Yancey spoke at a political meeting urging support for John C. Breckinridge for president. *DAB*; *Daily Picayune*, Oct. 30, 1860.

[38] The candidates in the 1860 presidential election were Abraham Lincoln, Stephen A. Douglas, John C. Breckinridge, and John Bell. Bell supporters held a procession the night before the election. *Daily Picayune*, Nov. 6, 1860.

November 5   —   62° 76° 74°

Fine & pleasant. East wind.

At the improvement of J. J. Wright's Store on my way to the Office, then very busy until 3 P.M.[39] Tommy went to School today. After tea we went to Mr. Young's who had everything very pleasant for us, and we enjoyed the view of the great "Bell procession" from his gallery. It was the longest I ever saw. Filing by at good marching pace for near two hours, and filling St. Charles Street with a blaze of lights and glowing colors; Tommy was in his glory. Then champagne and cake, then home to bed.

November 6   68° 78° 74°

Fine and clear. East wind.

Went to the Polls right after breakfast, but too crowded to squeeze in; so hastened down to business, called at the work on Wright's store, and opened my books, then up again in the omnibus at 10½ when, as I expected, the Polls were pretty clear, and I had no detention in voting; then home for a short time, then down town in the omnibus....

Little doing at the Office, the Election absorbs every one's attention, and every thing goes on decently and in order. Returned home to dinner early at 2 P.M.

November 7   68° 76° 77°

Fine and sunny, East wind.

The City polled 10.500 votes yesterday of which Bell got over 5000. Douglass & Breck[in]ridge the rest. A very quiet and orderly election day.

November 16   65° 68° 68°

Rains in the night, clearing off this morning, wind from the South West. Very bright and sunny at midday and thro' the afternoon.

The Postmaster has commenced moving today into the new apartments we have prepared for him in the New Custom House.

[39] Dr. John Wright, was a pharmacist and co-owner of John Wright & Co., pharmaceutical agents, on Chartres St. NOCD 1859.

November 19   64° 74° 76°

Fine and clear: West wind.

Busy times round the Custom House on the removal of the Post Office. A fluent and resilient wave of people all the time, and the South West angle of the building the centre of attraction. Major Beauregard has been appointed by the President to the Superintendency of West Point. Shewed me his "Special order" to that effect this morning.

November 24   44° 50° 51°

Cold and clear: North East wind. Ice at night.

Very busy at the Custom House closing up accounts &c. for the Post Office. Serious failures of heavy commercial houses have occurred during the week, Fellowes & Co. for 4.000.000.[40] Others will go soon; all due to the present panic in politics and finance.

In the evening took Tommy and Ellen to the Circus at the St. Charles Theatre.[41] It is beautifully appointed every way; and the performances are the best of their kind we have ever had in New Orleans, and the audience very large and orderly.

December 2   54° 64° 62°

Beautiful quiet Sunday morning, North wind: cool and bracing: changed to East.

Walked after breakfast to see the new church of "Calvary" just finished for the Revd. Mr. Fulton (Episcopalian). It is perfectly plain, of wood, but comfortable and rational for a congregation of small means; it is on Prytanea Street near Sixth.[42] I am more and more opposed to rearing expensive churches, encumbered with debt. And above all, weak, flimsy false Gothic; full of architectural "lies", and badly drawn ornament; deficient in light, comfort, tightness and durability, and yet costing much more than a handsome well finished Greek or Italian structure of the same capacity, owing to the fact that

in Gothic there is at least 30% loss in useless mass alone; and the boasted "dim religious light" resolves itself into mere "groping in the dark". I should like to know where in the world light diffuses itself in more golden showers than thro' the "Nave" & "choir" of "York Minster", the finest Gothic extant. For Ecclesiastical purposes there is nothing in the entire range of human art so perfect, so impressive, so sublime as true Gothic, as executed in British Cathedrals, and Parochial Churches of the 13th, 14th, & 15th Centuries. But heaven preserve us from the base, and expensive imitations in brick and plaster which are now the "clerical mania" of the United States. Genuine Gothic can only be executed with full effect in cut stone....

December 5   40° 48° 47°

Bitter cold night with frost. Cold North west wind today, and clear sky....

Dangerous fire at 9 in the store of Hall, Rodd & Co. within 100 yards of the Northwest angle of the New Custom House and a strong wind blowing directly over our building, but the fire was confined by the steam fire engine to the building in which it originated, and in an hour all was subdued without the least injury to our works; all our force, however, were on the alert; about one hundred men, and the hose and hydrants, Cisterns &c. all ready for action in case of danger to our Granite Front, which is liable to injury from cracking and scaling on exposure to intense heat.[43]...

December 6   40° 56° 56°

Frost in the night. Fine & bracing today: clear sky: North West wind.

Pleasant walk with W. O. Rogers to the Madison School, and much gratified by an hour's examination of the progress of pupils in the Principal's Department. It is a fine School and I regret that its far-off locality from the haunts of business prevents my visiting it often, being, for the Quarter, on the Committee of that School.

My appointment as Secretary of the Draining Commission of the 1st. Dist. has been confirmed.[44]...

[40] The firm C. Fellowes & Co., cotton factors and commission merchants, was located at 149 Common Street. NOCD 1861.

[41] Nixon's Royal Circus. *Daily Picayune*, Nov. 24, 1860.

[42] Rev. John Fulton was an assistant rector at Trinity Church from 1857 to 1858. In 1860, he became pastor of Calvary Church (Episcopal) which was erected in 1860 at the corner of Prytania and Conery streets. In 1885, Calvary Church merged with St. John's Church and rented its Prytania Street building to Christ Church while the new Christ Church at St. Charles Avenue and Sixth Street was being erected. Duncan, *Diocese of Louisiana*, 206, 247.

[43] The fire was in a three-story brick store on Customhouse (now Iberville) between Levee (now Decatur) and Chartres, the upper part of which was occupied by Hall & Rodd, commission merchants, and the ground floor by a lager beer saloon. The building was entirely destroyed. *Daily Picayune*, Dec. 6, 1860.

[44] The Board of Commissioners for Leveeing, Draining, and Reclaiming Swamp Lands in the parishes of Orleans and Jefferson, First District, Isaac G. Seymour, president. NOCD 1859.

December 8   60° 70° 72°

Warm and cloudy: South West wind.

Ellen & Tommy came down at 1 P.M. to the office and I took them to see the Hippopotamus which is a fine well kept specimen about 2 years old and weighing about 800 Pounds.[45] The aquaria of indigenous fish were very beautiful, and contained quite a large variety from our neighbouring Lakes and Bayous, all floating in pure water and surrounded by seashells, and corals. The specimens in Zoology, Ornithology and Herpetology, tho' not numerous, were finely chosen and creditable to the Taxidermist.

December 12   48° 60° 59°

Fine & sunny: cold North wind. Very pleasant in the middle of the day.

News from the North indicates a gradual return to "common sense" on the part of the canting, hypocritical, "Black Republican" party. The anti-slavery agitation should now be set at rest for ever.

December 18   63° 69° 67°

This is the Ninth Anniversary of our Wedding day, and a cheerful sunshine smiles upon it, with a soft elastic air from the Eastward. Wind rose during the morning, and rain set in about 2 P.M. Got home dry, however, at 3.

After dinner notwithstanding the showers, I took Tommy to see the interior of the New German Cathc. Cathedral which looked well and impressive under the subdued light of evening.[46]

December 21   56° 73° 72°

Fine and clear. North West wind, to West.

Very busy at the Office, on detail business due to Major Beauregard's resignation.

Human nature is a sad complication of inconsistencies. The news of the dissolution of the Union reached us today and as much jubilation and gun firing was expended on that "event" as on the original consolidation of said Union less than a Century ago.[47]

December 24   56° 70° 69°

Cool East wind: light clouds in the afternoon clouding up with wind from South East.

Paying off monthly rolls &c. at the Office. At 12 Emily came down and we went together to call upon Mrs. Beauregard, the Major's bride, on Esplanade Street.[48] Very pleasant visit. Her manner is quite fascinating and Emily was charmed with her; returning to the Office found Ellen & Tommy, got thro' some business, then took them to buy Christmas presents and sent them home in the omnibus; returned to the Office and finished up the business of the day at 3.

Pleasant Christmas; display of presents, nice supper &c. Tommy delighted with his "fire hat" books &c. and noisier than usual having invested extensively in fire crackers, and "detonators".

December 25   56° 63° 62°

Christmas Day. Works at the Custom House suspended as usual. Cheerful sunshine, light clouds: cool North wind.

Pleasant walk in the morning, and Christmas salutations from many friends. Very different, here, from the bleak Christmas at the north; gardens full of the brightest roses; narcissus, and amaryllides, and half the trees still in leaf. In Mrs. Low's garden the orange coloured flowers of the "shrub flax" are perfectly exquisite.

December 30   43° 42° 41°

Sunday. Rain all night, and again this morning: very gloomy, with cold North East wind.

Dispatches from all parts of the country look very warlike; but newspaper information has, of late, become so unreliable that I attach little importance to them. . . .

[45] The hippopotamus, on view at Spalding and Rogers Amphitheatre, came from the Royal Zoological Gardens, London. *Daily Picayune*, Nov. 4, 1860.

[46] St. Mary's Assumption at Constance and Josephine was a parish church, not a cathedral.

[47] South Carolina, the first of the southern states to withdraw from the Union, seceded on December 20, 1860. On December 22, the *Daily Delta* reported a general endorsement of South Carolina's action.

[48] This house, now incorporated into the Italian Union Hall at 1020 Esplanade, was built by James Gallier, architect, for William Nott in 1835. In 1851 the house was acquired by Senator John Slidell who gave it to Caroline Deslonde, his sister-in-law, when she married P. G. T. Beauregard. NONA, H. B. Cenas, Nov. 21, 1835; *New Orleans Architecture*, vol. 5, eds. Mary Louise Christovich, Sally K. Evans, and Roulhac Toledano, *The Esplanade Ridge* (Gretna, La., 1977), 51.

Interior of St. Mary's Assumption Church, 1915 (1981.350.264).

1861

January 2   46° 50° 53°

Cloudy and damp: cold North East wind. Cleared off pleasant in the afternoon.

Mr. Hatch, the Collector, kindly sent a letter today to the Secretary of the Treasury recommending me most strongly as the Successor of Major Beauregard on the New Custom House and New Marine Hospital. At 5 I met the members of the 1st. Dist. Draining Commission, and took my seat as Secretary of the Board; the meetings are held in the Supts' Office, New Custom House, and the gentlemen being thoroughly well acquainted with business, we dispatched our evening's work in less than 2 hours.

January 7   64° 69° 74°

Rain in the night. Dark warm and damp this morning with South East wind, and the sun breaking out at intervals warm and summerlike. Wind changed to South West.

Major Beauregard formally turned over to me today the Superintendence of the New Custom House, and the New Marine Hospital; which was duly communicated to the Treasury Department, and to the Collector of the Port, Mr. F. H. Hatch, who expressed the highest Satisfaction at the arrangement. The Major leaves for West Point tomorrow.

Left the Office at 2 and went to the Polls to vote for members of the Convention to be held Jany 23 at Baton Rouge to determine the attitude of Louisiana in the present crisis.

January 8   58° 63° 66°

Dense fog, with South West wind.

The vote yesterday was in favor of the candidates who advocate the withdrawal of this State from the Union and then the construction of a Southern Confederacy....

January 9   62° 73° 72°

Wet and foggy: South West wind. Cleared off warm and pleasant at noon, but still threatening clouds.

Major Beauregard got off this morning at 7 in the Jackson R.R. Cars.

The Superintendency of the Custom House comes very naturally, and pleasantly to me; it is now 7 years since I occupied that post, and as I am the only person left on the work who commenced it

I sincerely hope that, in spite of our political troubles, it will be finished under my direction. This is, with me, an object of ambition: as it will be, when complete, the finest <u>commercial</u> structure in the world.

January 14   69° 78° 75°

Warm, with light clouds: South wind. Very unhealthy weather.

Very busy at the Office trying to keep the operations at the Custom House in unbroken progress until the wounds that afflict the country are healed or a permanent settlement of the "questio vexata" determined upon.

January 15   71° 63° 59°

Dark, stormy & very rainy with South wind, changing to West and growing gradually colder.

Received my Commission this morning from the Secretary of the Treasury as Superintendent of the Construction of the New Custom House, at a per diem of $8.00 to take effect on the 8th. Jany 1861. Answered by Mail accepting the appointment....

January 16   48° 64° 60°

Cold and clear: West wind. Very pleasant weather.

Addressed a strong remonstrance to the Secretary of the Treasury representing the bad effects on our hands, and creditors of the New Custom House, arising from the delay in remitting the draft called for of Ten thousand dollars; and enclosed a semi-official letter to S. M. Clark Esqr. Engineer in Charge of Treasury Buildings, asking him as a personal favor to support my application in behalf of our suffering Mechanics Laborers and other claimants. The original Estimate was sent by my predecessor Major Beauregard, and has since been urgently called for by the Collector without effect; I now deem it my duty, in assuming control, to make the above appeal....

SKETCH OF THE HISTORY OF THE NEW CUSTOM HOUSE NEW ORLEANS LA.

January 17

Pursuant to an act of Congress and an appropriation for construction of a Custom House in New Orleans, La. the following Commissioners were appointed by the Hone. R. J. Walker Secretary of the Treasury in the Year 1847 viz. W. M. Gwin, Denis Prieur, and Alcée LeBranch; with power to call for Plans Proposals for Contracts &c.

On the 22nd. day of November 1847 the Plan of A. T. Wood archt. was adopted by the Secretary of the Treasury and the works were commenced on the 23rd. day of October 1848. They have since been carried on under the Superintendence successively of Col. W. Turnbull, Topographical Engineers, T. K. Wharton and Major G. T. Beauregard Corps of Engineers. The latter having recently been appointed Superintendent of the Military academy at West Point, the works have been recommitted by the Hone. Secretary of the Treasury to the Superintendence of Mr. T. K. Wharton, who is assisted by Mr. John Roy archt. who has acted in that Capacity for the last 6 years with the highest ability.

The Plan of the Building is a Trapezium: the longest point on Canal street being 334 feet and the shortest on Custom House street 251' 6". The Exterior linear dimensions are about 1200 feet and the superficial Area 87.333 feet all to be included under one roof.

The height is 85 feet on the Front divided into 4 stories: and the Collector's or Marble room in the centre is to be 140 feet high.

The exterior is all faced with Granite Ashlar backed with brick. The centre room for the collector is of white Marble and the entire structure is essentially fire proof being composed of stone and brick in the exterior and party walls and the floors of Iron Beams and Girders combined with segmental arches of brick laid in cement. The windows doors and Trimmings thereto are also Iron. The roof will be of the same material.

The Exterior walls are now complete up to the Granite Entablature which is now ready to ship and only awaiting an order to that effect, which will be given when a suitable appropriation is made for that object.

The Interior walls are nearly ready for the Iron roof which has already been partly rolled out by the Contractor, and is lying on his hands subject to order, based, as in the case of the Granite upon a suitable appropriation: and it is distinctly to be understood that an early completion of this part of the work (the roof is of imperative necessity for the preservation of the interior structure: for, without this roof every shower of rain and the corrosive atmosphere penetrate to nearly all parts of the work, which the sunshine only reaches it in occasional gleams. Hence the work of disintegration and destruction goes on rapidly in such a climate as this, especially in the immense and costly system of iron work extending throughout the edifice; all of which would be forever arrested by the speedy Construction of the contemplated Roof.

The settlement of the building in a soil like this is comparatively trifling; two feet were allowed for it in the Original Plan, but such is the strength of the Foundation that the allowance has not yet been reached and is not likely to be, as the yearly subsidence is now reduced to about an inch and constantly diminishing.

Part of the building is finished and occupied; being covered by temporary roofing.

On the 5th. of August 1856 the whole of New Levee Front and a part of Canal and Custom House Street front, were turned over to the Government for the Revenue Service; together with a large amount of accommodation for storage. On the 18th. Novr. 1860 one half of the apartments destined for the Post Office on old Levee Front was temporarily completed and turned over to the Post Master and is now occupied by him and his force.

All these important accommodations tho' inferior to the apartments that will, on the completion of the Structure, be assigned to the different Officers, yet are far more commodious than those heretofore occupied by the Collector F. H. Hatch Esqr. and the Post Master Dr. Riddell and at a great saving of Rent.

There are also finished offices within the building assigned to the Light House and War Department and occupied by Officers in these two Branches of Public Service.

The Building when completed will be the most Capacious, Carefully Constructed, and best arranged Commercial Structure in the United States.

The amount of appropriations from Congress and derived from sales up to January 1st. 1861 has been	$2.982.992.16
The amount expended in cash or Certified Voucher due to same date	$2.958.783.15
of which there is on hand valuable material such as Marble, Granite, Iron &c. paid for but not set in the Building worth about	$ 800.000.00

The amount estimated for its Completion as per statement of Major Beauregard dated Decr. 16th. 1860 is as follows viz. Full Estimate	$1.585.341.90
Reduced Estimate leaving out work that may be dispensed with not impairing the utility or strength of the work	$1.065.043.21
Or say an Amount allowed for four years of	$ 250.000.00

It may however, be finished if desirable in less time, and it cannot be too urgently enforced that an early Completion of the Contemplated Roof is essential to the salvation of the vast amount of Costly and best Class workmanship already executed, and it must be added, the health of the Occupants distributed in the finished portions of the work.

T. K. Wharton
Superintendent

Supt's Office
New Custom House
New Orleans. Jany. 17. 1861

———

SKETCH OF THE HISTORY OF THE U.S. NEW MARINE HOSPITAL NEW ORLEANS LA.

The U.S. Marine Hospital is situated on Common Street, on a square bounded by Common, Broad, Gravier and White Streets about 2 miles from the River Mississippi.

The Building is of Iron Veneering to represent Stone Ashlars, and intended originally to have been backed in with Pise: that is common soil dried and rammed in so as to form a solid mass; that being found difficult in execution: recourse was had to "adobes" or unburnt pressed brick: this also proved a failure, and the Iron fronts are now finally filled in with common brick of the usual quality.

The square of ground upon which the Building stands, contains an area of abo[u]t 220.575 superficial feet well filled in to the depth of about 4 feet.

The building itself stands upon an area of about 51.000 superficial feet and its foundations are laid on piles driven deep into the soft soil. It consists of a Centre portion and two wings; the latter being two stories in height, the former three, the first being 15 feet high, the second 17' 6" and the third 15 feet. The Centre is surmounted by a Dome somewhat low in proportion and the two wings also with the same Dome finish, but not of as great altitude.

The whole is roofed in complete, but as the appropriations for the work are nearly exhausted it has been closed up and placed in care of a Watchman by Order of the Treasury Department subject to the control of the Superintendent of the New Custom House.

The work was commenced under a Contract with the Trenton Locomotive Machine Company in the year 1856 and has been superintended respectively by Capt. G. W. Smith Capt. J. K. Duncan and Major Beauregard.

The appropriations for the Construction
have Amounted $484.659.20
and for Contingent Expenses $ 24.800.00
The Total amount of the Contract
for Construction with Extras allowed
is, up to August 1. 1860 $426.814.54
The Amount remaining to be
appropriated for Completion   47.087.74
Total amount expended on Contract $379.726.80

The difference between this amount and Total appropriations has been nearly consumed by expenses of grading site Contingencies, and minor Contracts.

T. K. Wharton
Engineer in Charge

Superintendent's Office,
New Custom House,
New Orleans Jany. 17. 1861.

SKETCH OF THE HISTORY OF
U.S. QUARANTINE WAREHOUSE
NEAR NEW ORLEANS LA.

This work is situated on the bank of the Mississippi River 60 miles below the City of New Orleans La. On a strip of ground measuring 350 feet front on the River and running back 40 Acres between parallel lines.

It was recommenced under an appropriation by Congress of $50.000.00 in December 1859, and completed and accepted by Major G. T. Beauregard U.S.A. (the Superintendent) on the 31st. day of May 1860. The Contract was awarded to B. T. Colby of Lynn Mass. who executed it to the satisfaction of the Government.

The Building is of brick almost entirely fire proof, the roof truss and certain trimmings only being of wood. The floors are composed of wrought Iron Beams, and brick segmental arches. It is two stories high, each 12 feet in the clear, and the 1st. floor [?] feet above the ground line; the River front is 190 feet long, the whole superficial Area is about 6980 sup. feet

The plan is rectangular thus

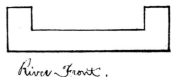

with proper ramps and graded embankments
The amount of the Contract of B. T. Colby complete was
$31.984.00
The Contract for the wharf built in front by J. Davis
$4.500.00

The Balance of the appropriation has been nearly consumed by the minor Contracts for building two additional rooms for the Keeper, Coping walls, cleaning and fencing the site and Contingencies. The work was transformed by the Superintendent to the charge of the Collector of this Port by order of the Treasury Dept. On the 15th. day of October 1860.

T. K. Wharton

New Custom House,
Supt. New Custom Ho.
New Orleans, Jany. 18. 1861

January 25   42° 42° 40°

Dark rainy morning, rain, rain, rain: cold North East wind. Rained all morning.

My Books just completed shew the expenses of the New Custom House up to January 1. 1861 to have amounted to $2.958.783.15

A large amount of material included in the above is still unset in the work, and I have ordered a statement and valuation to be made forthwith. Made up my accounts at the Custom House today to shew in full all liabilities, and the amount required to carry on the works provisionally at an uniform rate, until existing difficulties can be adjusted among the States, say 5 or 6 months; the latter amount I find to be $4000, per month. The present liabilities due amount to about $8.000.

January 26   39° 47° 49°

Cold and grey: North West wind.
Wrote to Gridley J. F. Bryant in Boston.
The "Ordinance of Secession" of Louisiana was passed at 12½ P.M. and announced to the City by the Simultaneous ringing of the Fire Alarm Telegraphs, and the booming of cannon....

January 28   43° 60° 60°

White frost at night. Fine and sunny: North West wind. Very fine indeed at midday, perfectly lovely after the rains of the preceding fortnight.
Every thing financially, politically, and socially, is resolved into an aggregate of utter incertitude; I, therefore, have no record to make, no opinion! but simply fill my daily round of duty as Constructional Officer in charge of important Federal works — the New Custom House and New Marine Hospital.

January 30   54° 66° 69°

Fine & clear: West wind. Very warm at midday.
Last evening Emily & Tommy, Mrs. Ladd & I went to hear the Swiss Bell Ringers at Armory Hall; it was a delicious musical treat — different from any kind of music I ever heard before except the intensely beautiful chimes of the churches in Manchester, England, at abt. 9 O'clock on Sunday morning, which I used to listen to with the sensitive and delighted ear of boyhood.
Things look dark today at the New Custom House, I fear that I shall have to Suspend operations.

January 31   56° 68° 64°

Light clouds: South East wind. Rain in the afternoon.
This morning I went thro' the painful official duty of suspending the works at the New Custom owing to the failure of the Department in Washington to send funds for the payment of hands & other claims due; I summoned the hands (50 in number) at one

O'clock, and plainly & clearly explained to them all the facts, and my duty under the regulations of the Department; I then addressed the Hone. Secretary of the Treasury informing him of my action and the causes that led to it; and then in common with all other Officers tendered my resignation to the Federal Govt. in consequence of the ordinance of the State Convention, which requires Officers under Federal orders to resign subject to speedy recommission by the State authority. This is by far the most delicate and painful tissue of official duties I ever went thro', and I breathe more freely now that they are so far accomplished. I scarcely slept last night at all in anticipation of the suffering that would inure to the hands by suspending work at this time.

February 1   72° 75° 74°

Warm and moist: South wind. Cleared off at noon.
Visit from Dr. J. B. Wilkinson member of the Convention of the State to gather important information in regard to works under my Superintendence, and to obtain my credentials of Office to see what steps will be necessary to be pursued in order to the Continuance of my functions under the State authority.[1]
By arrangement I waited upon him at the Convention in Lyceum Hall at 3 and he informed me that the Committee had decided that the "Ordinance of Convention" retained me in Office without the formality of taking oath as in the case of the Collector of the Port &c. &c.
Very busy in routine business at the Office closing up for January, and for the now expired Dynasty &c. &c.

February 4   40° 54° 52°

Bright and sunny: cold North wind.
Very busy in trying to get a Settlement with the new authorities in favor of the hands, and claims against N. Custom Ho. up to Jany. 31. 1861. Made out full Estimates, and waited upon Govr. Moore of Louisiana, with Mr. Hatch, the Collector, who introduced me to him &c. I hope to get a warrant for payment of dues in a few days. In the meantime I am worked almost to death and did not sleep, except in snatches, all last night; I counted every clock from 9 P.M. to 7 A.M....

---

[1] Joseph Biddle Wilkinson, the son of General James Wilkinson, owned Pointe Celeste Plantation in Plaquemines Parish. P. A. Champomier, *Statement of the Sugar Crop Made in Louisiana, 1852-1853* (New Orleans, 1853), 22.

February 5   41° 58° 60°

White frost in the night. Fine & clear: North West wind.

Driven almost to death this morning with accumulated business; the Collector informed me this morning that Governor Moore had no power to warrant for my Estimate of liabilities on the New Custom House, say $11.500, and that the Subject had been placed in the hands of the Finance Committee, with whom he requested <u>me</u> to treat. I immediately took the papers, hastened to the Convention, and spent two hours with the different members & chairman of the Finance Committee, and other influential members; explaining carefully all details, and begging that they would bring the subject to an early issue as the pay of our Mechanics & Laborers for December & January is now wholly dependent upon their action....

February 6   48° 58° 61°

Fine and clear. North East wind.

Met the Committee of Finance on the Custom House business at 9½ and explained the whole subject, earnestly entreating them to pass, after examination, the back Payrolls of Mechanics and Laborers. I then went to the office and prepared and recorded a full Estimate including <u>all</u> liabilities up to Jany 31. 1861. on completed Payrolls and Vouchers, and then went back to the Convention, and presented them, now fully made up and explained, for immediate action, which I trust will be Successful, as I have worked very hard for it....

February 8   50° 66° 68°

Fine and sunny: West wind.

Deeply engaged all morning with the Finance Committee of the Convention, and the Collector &c. to have my relief Bill for the New Custom House of $10.192.82 passed today. I drew up the resolutions myself & expect they will pass. Letters from Treasury Department placing me in charge of all the Civil Government works at this Port, and also a pleasant private letter from S. M. Clark, Engineer in Charge at Washington full of cordial good feeling.

February 9   60° 65° 70°

Fine & sunny: light clouds: South East wind. Wind rose at noon, with clouds of dust, and a heavy sky indicating rain at hand....

Letter from Col. Beauregard, at New York; two hours after he himself was at my Office. My letter has been <u>5 days</u> longer on the way than he! No infrequent event in these troublous times of tempest, and political storms. His letter explained the political intrigue at Washington by which he was ordered back from West Point to this Station. At his request I enclosed the letter to Judge Walker of the Delta, and J. G. Seymour (a copy) of the Bulletin; not for publication but to place the facts at the disposal of those gentlemen. The Colonel then sat down in my office, and wrote his resignation of his Commission in the U.S. Corps of Engineers, to be mailed this evening; he read it to me, and also his farewell letter to General Totten, the Chief Engineer. In my notes to the above Editors I mentioned this fact also....

February 11   58° 70° 70°

Fine and clear: South West wind.

Wrote an earnest appeal to the Convention to provide for the protection of the valuable works at the New Custom House, until the New Government shall be enabled to make suitable arrangements for their Completion. I presented it in Convention at 12 O'clock to the President; I have done my duty; represented the facts, and accompanied them with an Estimate of Ten thousand dollars to cover the objects embraced in my letter. It is for the Convention now to act and assume the responsibility.

My "relief Bill" for the Mechanics, Laborers, and other claimants against the work up to Jany 31. 1861. amounting to $10.192.82 was reported on favorably today by the Finance Committee, and made the Special order of the day at 12 M. tomorrow....

February 12   59° 68° 69°

Fine & sunny: West wind....

My draft for $10.000 for the Service of the works during January, arrived, sure enough, yesterday, as stated in "Clark's private letter to me" but Collector Hatch, the Disbursing Agent, sent it immediately back to Washington; had it come when due, on the 21st. Jany. all the trouble about paying hands and other claims against the New Custom House, would have been spared.

February 13   60° 71° 71°

Bright & clear in the morning with East wind which rose to a strong breeze by 4 P.M. bringing over heavy clouds, and sprinkling rain.

At 11 I went to the Office of the Convention's Secretary at the City Hall, and read the Ordinance for the payment of Custom House claims; it was passed in the very words in which I wrote it, except the substitution of the words "President of the Convention" instead of "Governor." I immediately waited upon the President (ExGovernor Alexr. Mouton) at the St. Louis, and before I left him he gave me his warrant on the State Depository for the whole amount $10.192.82. and also gave me my appointment, under the second Resolve of the ordinance continuing me in office as Superintendent of the New Custom House and other Public Works; at $8 per diem.[2] Thus my unremitting labors on this Bill are not only rewarded by the ability to pay the poor men their 2 months wages, and other claims; but I am myself retained in a lucrative and responsable office.

In the evening I went to the City Hall again, and obtained all my papers and Vouchers relating to the Bill.

My Second Bill of Ten thousand Dollars for continuing the work was presented too late for final action but will be taken up on the reassembling of the Convention on the 4th. of March.

February 14   57° 65° 64°

Bright and sunny. West wind.

On reaching the office I presented my draft of $10.192.82 to the Collector, who told me that I could immediately draw the gold and silver; I, at once, drew $4229.95 with which I paid off the Mechanics & Laborers for Decr. and January; much to their surprise and delight as great suffering has already been felt by them for want of the money. This is the proudest and happiest day of my life; 150 poor human being made happy solely thro' my Successful energy....

February 16   48° 58° 56°

Heavy showers, and high wind in the night. Lovely weather today with bracing North West wind.

I was sworn in this morning under the State Ordinance, as Superintendent of the New Custom House and other Public Works.

Very busy in settling up outstanding claims under the Provisions of the Ordinance.

March 2   66° 78° 76°

Fine and sunny. Wind E. South East. Very warm at midday. Clouding up at 4 P.M.

Finished up the Foundation Plan and 1st. & 2nd. Story Plan of Mr. Cook's house, and went thro' all the business of the Office as usual getting home to dinner at 4 P.M.[3]

A Dispatch from Washington announces the acceptance of Coll. Beauregard's resignation from the U.S. Army, and another, from Montgomery, of his confirmation as Brigadier General under the Southern Confederacy.

After dinner went to Mr. P. Cook's and took with me the Specifications of his house, left them for his examination & approval.

March 7   54° 65° 66°

Bright and sunny: East wind....

Lincoln's Inaugural is still the theme, and gives great dissatisfaction and uneasiness at the South....

March 18   52° 52° 52°

Very rainy: North East wind. Very raw and unpleasant, decidedly aguish.

Very pleasant private letter from S. M. Clark, Esqr. Engineer in charge of Public Buildings in Washington, dated 11th Inst. full of kind feeling; he says in conclusion,

"I do not yet despair of seeing our Southern brethren back into the fold on just and equitable terms, if so, I trust you will again be one of my parish."

---

[2] Alexandre Mouton (1804-1885), president of the Louisiana secession convention, was a U.S. senator from 1837 to 1842 and governor of Louisiana from 1842 to 1846. *DLB.*

[3] Wharton designed a splendid mansion for Paul Cook on St. Charles between Joseph and Arabella. NONA, W. L. Poole, Apr. 7, 1860.

Interior of St. Alphonsus Church, Robert S. Brantley and Jan White Brantley, photographers, ©1992.

March 29

71° 80½° 78°

Warm & cloudy: South wind: cleared off hot at 10 A.M. Showery at 1½ P.M.

At 9 went in the cars with Mr. P. Cook by appointment to his Square of ground at Rickerville; I determined the lines of his new house, and carefully examined the property with reference to all conveniences and ornament: gardens, greenhouse, stables &c.[4] It is a noble square, very high & dry. About 250 x 500 and beautiful[ly] planted with choice fruit trees, vegetables &c. already. Mr. Cook owns in addition 5 contiguous squares. We returned to town in the 11 O'clock Train; and being Good Friday and no business doing at the Custom House, I returned home and went to work on my "Cotton Press" Plans, and made good progress.

March 31

72° 82° 78°

Sunday. A very lovely day with bland South East wind.

After breakfast reading to Tommy; then a walk, and looked in at the two great Catholic Churches, St. Alphonse, and the German Cathedral; crowded with worshippers, today being Easter Sunday; then returned home, and spent the morning in writing while the rest went to Church....

April 9

66° 75° 79°

Bright clear sunshine: West wind. Very hot at midday.

Opened the 4 bids for Mr. Cook's house. They ranged from $18.500 to $19.950. Mr. Keating's being the lowest, was accepted.[5] Mr. Cook being present at the opening of Proposals....

[4] Paul Cook's property was actually in Hurstville, not in the adjacent Rickerville.

[5] James Keating, carpenter, St. Mary near Nayades (now St. Charles). NOCD 1859.

April 14   70° 80° 78°

Sunday. Fine spring weather: South West wind. Weather perfectly charming.

General Beauregard covered himself with honor yesterday by the capture of Fort Sumpter; the first victory! And that, of the Confederate States of the South; fortunately, too, as stated in the Dispatches; without loss of life. It is hoped that one or two other victories on our part will convince the madmen of the North that their system of aggression must be abandoned. Fort Pickens at Pensacola, will probably be reduced next by General Bragg; in the meantime a salute of 100 guns was fired yesterday, opposite the Cathedral of St. Louis, in welcome of the "first success."[6]

April 16   62° 69° 70°

Fine and clear: North West wind. Bracing bouoyant weather....

Messrs. Cook, Keating, Pride and Bailey at my Office on business, and Mr. Grimshaw on the defences of the Bars of the Mississippi to keep out hostile fleets....

April 17   64° 75° 78°

My forty seventh Birthday.

A most lovely day, with bracing air from the North West: and warm at midday.

I cannot help feeling a natural movement of pride in thinking over my present position in my profession as Architect, at a comparatively early period of life; I am in entire charge of all the Government works (civil) in and around New Orleans; and have the confidence of both Governments; the old not having yet accepted my resignation tendered in January; and the new Secretary of the Confederate Treasury responding to my letters by return of mail, and approving of all my acts.

My private business, too, is in good progress, and in spite of the political disquietude of the country, my personal and home interests are more strongly fortified than ever — by success — but I have worked, and studied hard for it....

April 18   68° 79° 81°

Fine and sunny: wind South West.

Referring to my Books, I have received as compensation from the Government since my first appointment $24.000.00....

Virginia seceded this morning and 100 guns in honor of the event were fired near the Custom House at 2.

Letter from Col. Hebert asking for additional facilities for construction of Gun carriages; granted them at once and advised the Secretary of the Treasury of my action.[7]

Visit from Major Chase who cordially approves of my arrangements to make New Orleans the Gibraltar of the South, and wrote in my office to adjutant General Cooper to that effect.[8]

Visit from the newly appointed Confederate Judge [E. Warren?] Moise and shewed him my Plans, which I am now maturing, to prepare accomodations for the Confederate Courts after the Artillery operations are completed; and he was very much pleased with the distribution, together with the handsome provisions I have made for the present accomodations of his offices and my own "private office" which I have, for the present assigned to him.

April 20   66° 75° 74°

Wind North East: very clear and sunny. Hot at midday, and the wind veering to the Eastward.

Made my final arrangements with Mr. Tirrel for the Press and gave the Plans to J. K. Collins for his Estimate.[9] All the Estimates to

[6] As southern states seceded and a Confederate government was formed in 1860-1861, federal buildings, such as forts, post offices, and the New Orleans Custom House, were seized by southern authorities. Forts Sumter and Pickens, strategically situated to protect the harbors of Charleston and Pensacola respectively, remained in Union hands. General Beauregard commanded the Confederate forces which fired the first shots of the Civil War on April 12, 1861, at Fort Sumter; the Union garrison surrendered on April 14, and the fort remained a Confederate stronghold throughout the war. Fort Pickens, meanwhile, was successfully reinforced and played an important role in Union naval operations along the Gulf Coast. Braxton Bragg (1817-1876), a sugar planter in Lafourche Parish, Louisiana, volunteered for service in the Confederate army at the outbreak of the war. After his promotion to the rank of general, Bragg succeeded P. G. T. Beauregard in command of the Army of Tennessee. *Biographical Dictionary of the Confederacy* (hereafter *BDC*).

[7] Probably Louis Hébert (1820-1901), chief engineer for the State of Louisiana (1855-1859) and an officer in the Louisiana militia (1847-1861). *DLB*.

[8] Samuel Cooper (1798-1876) was adjutant general of the U.S. Army from 1852 to March 1861 when he resigned to join the Confederate army. During the Civil War he served as adjutant and inspector general and was named a full general in May 1861. *BDC*.

[9] John K. Collins, a builder at 341 Carondelet St., built several houses designed by the architect Henry Howard and an addition to the New Orleans School of Medicine for which Howard and Diettel were the architects. NOCD 1861; NONA, S. Magner, June 14, 1856, J. Graham, May 27, Sept. 14, 1857.

Silver service presented to Francis H. Hatch, collector of the port of New Orleans. Neal Alford Company, auction catalogue, November 5, 1988.

be sent in by the 1st. May. The Steamer "Star of the West" with Federal troops on board has been captured by our forces and is lying under the guns of Fort St. Philip. Virginia, Maryland, Kentucky and Tennessee are presenting an unbroken front against Northern aggression.

April 24   74° 81° 83°

Fine & warm: South wind. Very hot at midday.

Everything going on well at the office, and all business public and private still in the very best progress notwithstanding the excitement produced by the Civil War.

My engagement[s] are now a severe tax on my "corporeity" but too interesting and too profitable to admit of a "relax."

Emily Mrs. Ladd and I at Odd Fellow's Hall to hear Mozart's Grand 12th Mass — very fine & very full splendid evening.

May 4   74° 78° 80°

Warm and cloudy: wind due East in the morning: South West in the afternoon.

General Beauregard writes to his brother Armand, from Charleston (29th. Ulto) that he will be in Montgomery in a few days under orders....

Preparing Plans and Estimates for completion of "Confederate Courts" in New Custom House and roofing parts of the work under an appropriation by our Southern Congress of $25.000....

May 12   82° 87° 85°

Sunday. Hot & sunny: South wind.

At 11 went to the presentation of a splendid silver service, to the Collector F. H. Hatch Esq. which we Government Officers have been getting up for him entirely without his knowledge so as to give him an agreeable surprise.[10] It was a pleasant occasion & the Collector responded to the presentation in a beautiful speech, about 100 gentlemen being present and an elegant collation prepared. The

[10] This elegant silver service was sold for $60,000 at auction on November 5, 1988, at Neal Alford Company. It is illustrated in the catalogue for that auction with the information that it was crafted by New Orleans silversmiths Bernard Terfloth and Christopher Christian Kuchler and had been in the Hatch family since the presentation. Neal Alford Company auction catalogue, November 5, 1988, no. 138.

Camp Walker, Marie Adrien Persac, delineator, Pessou & Simon, lithographer, 1861 (1974.25.9.147).

reason why Sunday was selected was that the pressing duties of the week prevent the Officers of the Customs from engaging in a festive occasion like the present. The large salver of solid silver is enriched with a beautiful chased copy of the first perspective drawing I made for the New Custom House in 1848, and thus connects me artistically, as well as in the capacity of a strong friend of the Collector, with the event of the day; the silver work is exquisite, and the whole thing was done in fine taste, and with the greatest satisfaction to all....

May 14 78° 83° 82°

Cloudy with South East wind: and very warm.

Very much debilitated by the hot weather, and severe tax on brain and energy; but I try to do the best I can in my responsible offices, and hope it will not all be thrown away; home to dinner at 3 P.M.

At 5 Mrs. Thornhill came in her carriage, with Ellen & took Emily & me to see the breaking up of Camp Walker; we had a charming drive; her horses are high bred; we took tea with the Thornhills.[11]

May 20 84° 90° 94°

Clear & hot: South wind. Very hot indeed at midday....

My office was crowded this morning with the officers, captains, mates &c. collected together by the Capture of 6 Prizes. Judge Moise took his seat, and the proper lawyers were in attendance.

At the new building after dinner.

May 22 70° 80° 82°

Cloudy & cold wind from North East. Very hot and sunny at midday....

The prizes come in quick, today a ship from Boston, the Abellino, with 800 Tons of Ice, just what we want.

11 Either the Thomas or John Thornhills. John Thornhill (b. 1818) of the firm of Thornhill & Co., a prominent commission merchant and cotton factor, lived across Coliseum Square from Wharton. An unverified attribution credits Wharton as the architect of the house, still standing at 1420 Euterpe. *New Orleans Architecture*, 1:126. Camp Walker, originally named Camp Metairie, was established at Metairie Ridge in 1861. The camp was abandoned because it proved to be unhealthy. John Smith Kendall, *History of New Orleans*, 3 vols. (Chicago, 1922), 1:240.

May 23 76° 81° 84°

Fine & clear. North East wind....

Today at the office a dispatch was handed to me by Judge Moise, requiring me to provide him with a Court Room in the Building for immediate occupancy. I went with the Judge to select the apartment, say a room of 40 ft. by 27'3¾" and in twenty minutes commenced the work, to be turned over ready for use in 10 days, then addressed the Hone. Secretary of the Treasury, stating what I had done, and asking his approval. It anticipates part of my project of operations under the recent appropriation by Congress, and combines well with the provision I have nearly completed for the Marshal. By the by, just as I left my Office a list of 12 U.S. ships came in all seized under the Law; at this rate the old Federal attack upon the South will cost them at the North frightfully, but they have made their bed, selecting the thorns without the roses.

May 27 78° 90° 92°

Fine & sunny. Wind South. Very hot at noon.

Letter from General Beauregard at Charleston May 22. Still engaged on the Harbor works and no reference whatever to a change of command.

Very busy at the Office in providing for the Confederate Courts.

The Blockade at the mouth of the River has been commenced by the War Steamer Brooklyn! We must take her....

May 28 80° 86° 90°

Hot & dry: North East wind.

Answered General Beauregard's letter. Received from him this morning by Adam's Express 2 Pieces of the Flag staff that was shot down by our balls at Fort Sumpter, to be presented to Major Numa Augustin of the Orleans Guards, and Capt. J. W. Thomas of the Beauregard Rifles.[12] I immediately dispatched the orderly with the pieces (15 feet long, 4" x 4") to the officers, with a presentation letter. At 1 P.M. Major Augustin & M. Bienvenu waited on me at my office to thank me for my letter & invite me in person to the presentation of colors to take place on the 2nd. June, when the Flag piece will receive due honors....

May 30 80° 90° 92°

Very hot & dry: wind South East. Dreadfully hot and dusty at midday....

Conversation with Pierre Soulé & Coll. Augustin referring to the defences of Louisiana against the savage hordes of the North.

Advancing rapidly with the Court Room for the Confederate Court.

June 2 80° 88° 88°

Sunday. Fine and clear: South wind.

Went to the Custom House at 10 to look after my new Court room, and found everything in good forwardness to open Court at 10 tomorrow. I am sorry to have my hands employed on Sunday but in these war times there is no help for it.

At 11 went to M. Leprêtre's, corner of Orleans & Dauphine, to the presentation of the Flag prepared for the Guard d'Orleans, the staff being part of the Fort Sumpter staff sent me by General Beauregard.[13] It was a magnificent affair. The Battalion numbered 500 in the best accoutrements & discipline, and composed of the most opulent family representatives in the 2nd. District. The noble mansion of M. Leprêtre was crowded with ladies, chiefly French: & the collation and wines &c. &c. of the most careful selection.

June 11 82° 88° 87°

Hot & sunny: East wind. Very hot at midday....

Every body seems to think that I can do every thing, for I am daily invited to perform the most impossible achievements in trying to get men into positions, both civil & military; to say nothing of the applications to patronize gunboats to destroy the Northern blockading squadron &c. &c....

June 12 82° 92° 90°

Hot sunshine: East wind. Hotter than ever at noon.

Very busy all morning on Public works and also examining Marble Mantles, and determining pattern of Iron Veranda for Mr. Cook's house....

---

[12] Adams & Harnden's Joint Express Company, serving New York, Mobile, St. Louis, Louisville, Chicago, Cincinnati, Cairo, and Memphis, was located at 96 Camp Street, New Orleans. NOCD 1859.

[13] This unusual three-story and basement house was erected in 1836 for Dr. Joseph Coulon Gardette, a dentist; Frederick Roy was the builder. The cast-iron galleries were added about 1850 by Jean Baptiste Le Prêtre, a planter who purchased the house in 1839 and owned it until 1878.

Le Prêtre Mansion, 1920s (1993.129.15), gift of Rose C. Radford.

June 13   84° 92° 90°

Hot with light clouds: N. East wind.

Fast Day appointed by Congress.

No work at Custom House.

Went at 9 to see the Tirrel Cotton Press which he has confided to his builder (Mr. Jamison) without Superintendence; the work, so far, is decidedly bad, and fully accounts for Mr. Jamison's objections to my superintendence; while it deprives me of the opportunity to claim the work as Architect; I should be ashamed of it, as it departs in essential features from my Plans and specifications.[14] Mr. Jamison has foolishly deprived himself of good, paying works which will be denied him. I shall always reject his name as a bidder, and did so the other night in the School Board for a Normal School at abt. $30.000.

June 24   88° 93° 92°

Hot & dry: West wind. Very hot at midday....

Called upon Mr. Frank Williams, who received his telegram in time to take his wife to the funeral of Judge Huling at Amite City; I received mine too late, by some inadvertence in the Telegraph Office; I went to his office at the Bank of New Orleans (He is its President, and married a niece of Mrs. Huling).[15] He says the Judge was severely injured by the accident, so much so that he was entirely unconscious, and suffered no pain, tho' he lived two hours after the event. He spoke once in reply to a question if he were in pain, and he said No. One leg was cut off, his skull fractured and ribs broken. He had been, as usual, to get his newspapers, with some friends and lingered behind, in his absent way, just as the train advanced; he stepped to the Platform, but too late! The Train struck him, and he is now no more! My poor, kind hearted old father in law....

June 25   85° 91° 82°

Hot and dry: West wind, with clouds rising: heavy shower at noon: wind changed to South East with thunder, and dark clouds....

Distributed the 30 pieces of Fort Sumpter Flag staff, as directed by the General, and sent the remaining pieces to Mrs. Beauregard with a note....

[14] Samuel Jamison, a prominent builder, was with the firm Jamison and McIntosh, bricklayers, at 250 Baronne; his residence was at 248 Baronne. Richard Terrell's cotton press building was in the square bounded by Orange, St. Thomas, Richard, and Pacanier. NOCD 1859; NONA, Theodore Guyol, May 8, 1861.

[15] Judge Frederick W. Huling was run over by the Jackson train near Amite. *Daily Picayune*, June 23, 1861.

June 27   83° 91° 87°

Pleasant weather: North West wind. Changed to East and very hot in the sun.

At the office every thing as usual but less pressure as the new officials of the Confederate Courts begin to understand their position; I am responsible only to the Hone. Secretary of the Treasury, and whatever I can do to add to the convenience of Government officers accommodated within the walls of an unfinished building I do with pleasure but much of it must necessarily be rather of favor on my part than of right on theirs....

June 28   84° 95° 84°

Hot & dry: South East wind. Very hot at midday with light clouds....

Very busy all morning receiving Estimates for different details of my works, paying off for the month of June, and answering requisitions from the War Department.

At the Custom House 150 officers are notified that they will be no longer required after the 30th. Inst. owing to the existing blockade of the Port....

June 29   83° 91° 92°

Hot & dry: South East wind. Dreadfully hot at noon.

Very busy all morning at the office.

Wrote to Mr. Paul Cook enclosing Mr. Keating's proposals to erect an observatory and finish the Attic, for $1225, which I find quite reasonable.

Great preparations going on in my workshops for a vigorous attack upon the enemy at Ship Island and the Balize; but details necessarily kept from the Press &c. &c.

After took Tommy in the Cars to the Bayou St. Jean, and had a very pleasant trip, brought home superb peaches &c. &c.

June 30   86° 92° 94°

Sunday. Hot & dry: South wind.

Read to Tommy an hour after breakfast. Pleasant walk until 11 then reading at home in the shade while the rest went to church; after the constant work and anxiety of the week, in these times of war and invasion, I do think that I am entirely justified in resting quietly at home on Sunday, rather than waste my attention on a ministry that has in numerous instances at the North become a party to the troubles that now afflict the country.

After dinner visited Dr. Ames and examined his house now in erection.[16]

Closed the month on the cool front gallery with Tommy and a cigar.

July 1   86° 93° 88°

Hot & dry: South wind. Very hot at noon. Last night was the hottest I ever felt in New Orleans....

The new Confederate War Steamer "Sumpter" passed the Blockade, and went to sea last evening; she will [combine?], in Lake Borgne, with important preparations, now in process at the New Custom House & War Offices for Ship Island, and for general defence of the Gulf Coast.[17]...

July 4   76° 85° 86°

Damp & cloudy: North East wind.

85th. Anniversary of American Independence. Works on Custom House suspended.

Took Tommy at 10 A.M. to Camp Lewis in the Cars.[18] Visited Col. Numa Augustin in his Marquée, and partook of his liberal hospitalities; then took the next train to Carrolton and enjoyed the attentions &c. of W. P. Duncan, the Superintendent of the Road, returning to the City in the 1 O'clock train.[19]

In the evening Tommy and I took the Cars and mingled with masses attending the Picnic for the Military, at the City Park and Bayou St. John, and enjoyed ourselves as well as we could in a crowd until 9½ P.M. The grand old groves of oak, and the Sunset on the Bayou were alone worth the trip.

[16] Dr. Ed Ames lived at 362 Camp Street from 1859 to 1861. By 1866 he had moved to 350 Camp between Erato and Thalia (now 1216 Camp), a two-story brick house with a cast-iron balcony. NOCD, 1859-1861, 1866; *New Orleans Architecture*, 1:116.

[17] The ocean-going steamer *Habana* was purchased by the Confederate navy and converted into the warship and sea-raider *Sumter*, commanded by Raphael Semmes. Charles L. Dufour, *The Night the War Was Lost* (Garden City, N.Y., 1960), 61.

[18] Camp Lewis was laid out in Greenville, above the city, just below Carrollton. Dufour, *The Night the War Was Lost*, 117.

[19] William P. Duncan was superintendent and chief engineer of the Carrollton Railroad. NOCD 1861.

July 6   82° 79° 80°

Clouds rising: South East wind. Showers in the middle of the day....

Met Mr. Keating & Mr. Baird on business of my works; and arranged details of the Observatory and Attic for Mr. Cook's house; the Observatory will have a floor, within Balustrade, of 25 feet by 12 ft. and command the most beautiful view in the vicinity of New Orleans....

July 8   85° 95° 87°

Hot & dry: South East wind. Clouds rose at midday, and at 2 P.M. it became very dark with vivid lightening, and loud thunder: & light rain.

Ship Island is being rapidly fortified and will soon present a bold front; much heavy tackle, iron blocks &c. went off from my Tool house for that object at the request of the commanding officer and I am only too happy to promote so important a service.

After dinner went up with Mr. Keating to Mr. Cook's house; found Mr. Cook there. Shocked to find that a sad accident had happened at the house during the brief thunderstorm at 2 P.M. The fluid [flash?] entered the house, and instantly killed two fine negroes (slaters) and threw down & stupified the Framer, and five other white men, all of whom, however, recovered. The Coroner was summoned, and the inquest and verdict, according to the facts, rendered in our presence; the bodies were severely burned and presented a ghastly spectacle. One large chimney and part of a gable were demolished, and thirteen window frames shivered to splinters. The loss falls on the Builder.

July 9   85° 90° 94°

Hot & dry: South wind: rising clouds.

Wrote to the Secretary of the Treasury calling for an appropriation of $5000. to fit up the great Entrance to the Confederate Courts, and a Newspaper Department. Spent an hour with Mr. Keating and Mr. Church the builder & bricklayer at Mr. Cook's devising modes to overcome the injuries of yesterday's storm &c. &c. Commenced the roof work at the Custom Ho. Contract for which I approved today say 5750 Feet Square. In the evening Mr. Keating and I examined the new house and found that the injuries of the other day can be thoroughly repaired at a small cost.

Ship Island under Federal occupation and the approaches to New Orleans, 1862 (1974.25.9.247i–iv).

July 11   80° 90° 89°

Fine & pleasant after the rain. North wind.

Tommy went down with me to the Office, and we had a general good time together until 2 when we rode home in the Cars to dinner; his being with me in my Office is very pleasant to me, and, as he is very self-reliant, in no way impedes my business, and he derives much instruction from the valuable mechanical operations going on in the workshops under my charge, as he is very observant; he also attended Judge Moise's Admiralty Court this morning, now held in my building, and watched the proceedings with deep interest.

After dinner went to the new house. Repairs & general work going rapidly forward; Mr. Gunstenhauser (the framer) who was so seriously stunned by the lightening has recovered, and resumed work on the Building.

July 15   83° 94° 92°

Hot & dry: North wind.

Very busy at the office on Contract work &c. and numerous visitors to see 6 splendid Brass Guns 24 and 12 Pounders we have just received from Richmond.

Emily, Tommy & I went at 4 P.M. to the Sumners' to see the funeral Cortège of Col. Dreux, lately killed in Virginia.[20] The Soldiery made a fine appearance to the number of about 5000.

July 16   84° 91° 94°

Hot & dry: East wind. Very hot in the middle of the day.

Wrote to the Honorable Secretary of the Treasury asking his approval of my recent action in furnishing machinery for the fortification of Ship Island, and Fort Livingston.[21]…

July 19   83° 92° 88°

Damp and cloudy: West wind: very hot and clear at midday.

Very exciting & gratifying news of victory by Genl. Beauregard's forces over the Barbaric hordes of the North.[22]…

July 28   85° 90° 90°

Sunday. Very hot and dry: wind from the South East.

Reading to Tommy, and walk in the morning; fine air, and passing clouds, every object, and especially the lovely gardens, looking jocund and jubilant, as if in celebration of the recent and forthcoming victories of our young Confederacy. The impudent "Lincoln blockade" is acting in our favor by keeping out yellow fever, and stimulating our heretofore dormant industry and self reliance, every necessary and luxury of life are as abundant as ever, and in but few particulars are prices advanced; fruits are more amply supplied than ever; the finest peaches, nectarines, grapes, melons, pears and apples load our fruit stands. The only delicacies which the "Blockade" withdraws from us are "Pompano," "Red Snapper" & "Grouper," which can be caught only in the deep waters of the Gulf. But we can readily dispense with them for one Season, in view of the happiness & prosperity that will inure to the South from the establishment of her Nationality.

August 1   84° 91° 83°

Hot and dry: North wind.

Last evening I attended a special Committee at the City Hall at 6 P.M. to examine a case of alleged disloyalty of one of our Teachers, Dr. Morse; the charge was brought by General Grivot but after a close scrutiny we believe the General has been too hasty.[23]…

August 3   84° 93° 83°

Hot & dry: South East wind.

Took Tommy & left him at the Library to spend the morning; Charles brought him to the office at 1, and when I got thro' we took

[20] Charles Didier Dreux (1832-1861), an attorney and soldier, was the first Confederate officer killed in action. His body lay in state at City Hall before the funeral. In 1922, a monument was erected to him on the Jefferson Davis Parkway neutral ground at Canal Street. *DLB*; *Daily Picayune*, July 14, 1861.

[21] Ship Island is off the coast of Ocean Springs, Mississippi. Fort Livingston is in Jefferson Parish on Grande Terre Island. Powell A. Casey, *Encyclopedia of Forts, Posts, Named Camps, and Other Military Installations in Louisiana, 1700-1981* (Baton Rouge, 1983), 107.

[22] Beauregard commanded troops guarding a vital railroad junction at Manassas, Virginia; they repulsed the first Union attempt to take it on July 18, 1861. While Union troops scouted the area, Beauregard was reinforced by General Joseph E. Johnston. The first battle of Manassas on July 21 was a major victory for the Confederacy.

[23] Maurice Grivot was an attorney and adjutant general of Louisiana. NOCD 1859.

the Cars for home to dinner; he had a nice morning; and drove the Car himself which he often does as he is a favorite with the drivers & takes the reins whenever he chooses.

Heavy Storm of wind, rain, thunder and lightening at 3 to 4 with change of wind to North West.

August 16   79° 82° 83°

Very threatening sky: North East wind. Cleared off at 10 A.M.

Crowded with visitors and strangers at the office to see the models of gun Boats & steamers for naval objects, brass Howitzers, 8 inch Columbiads &c. which now adorn the Building, with the usual routine of examining the work under Contract, making Vouchers for payment &c. &c.…

August 28   81° 85° 82°

Fine & sunny: South East wind. Showers set in at 10½ A.M.

I have had the piece of Fort Sumter Flag Staff sent me by General Beauregard, elegantly turned into a cane, stained, polished, and mounted with heavy silver and engraved on the mounting as follows.

General Beauregard to T. K. Wharton
Fort Sumter Flag staff
April 13.th. 1861.…

September 5   80° 81° 84°

Clear sunshine: S. East wind. Rain set in at 11½ A.M. Showers and gleams of sunshine during the day.

Wrote to General Polk, commanding Second Division of Confederate army, to say that I had received authority from the Treasury Department to deliver to him the Iron wire, for Telegraph connections, now stored in the New Custom House; I have on hand 100 miles, and have anticipated the approval of the Department by delivering 10 miles on the 28th. Ulto. to the General's Special Agent.…

September 7   80° 84° 78°

Light clouds: South West wind. Heavy clouds at 11. And rain at 2 P.M.

Letter from Governor Moore of Louisiana asking me to retain the Telegraph wire (say 90 miles) in my possession until he can confer with the Department and have the permission given to

General Leonidas Polk, as per my letter of yesterday, either modified or countermanded. Mr. Hatch, the Collector, wrote & transmitted the Dispatch.…

September 9   81° 89° 78°

Sunny morning: East wind. Heavy rains set in at noon & continued for some hours.

Received a pleasant letter from General Beauregard, dated, Manassas Va Sept. 1. He expects an early conflict with the Northern foe.

Answered by Mail. Received also Order No. 1034 from Governor Moore requiring me as Supt. of Public Works to deliver for the State Service 70 miles Telegraphic wire in my possession at the New Custom House; turned it over thro' my Engineer and telegraphed accordingly to the Hone. Secretary of the Treasury, & wrote to General L. Polk, Commanding 2nd. Division C. S. Army on important business; heavy military work for a <u>Civil</u> officer.

After dinner went to see the Governor and had a satisfactory interview relative to his requisition.

September 24   76° 80° 84°

Mild air from the North: clear sky: hot sun at noon.

Very unwell with a Severe cold: and very busy at the office in trying to meet the necessities of the many Government officers, now quartered, and seeking to be quartered on the works under my charge.

At the house at 5 with the ladies & gentlemen of the Cook family, who were all greatly pleased; it is now nearly finished and is a spacious, charming mansion, no display but elegant & solid.

September 30   69° 83° 78°

Fine and clear: North East wind. Hot at noon.

Mailed my Report of the Works under my charge for September, with a letter, to the Honorable Secretary of the Treasury; also addressed him relative to balance of appropriations for completion of Conf[ed]erate Courts, and other important business connected with the Same.

The heavy obstructing chains have been laid successfully across the River just below Forts Jackson & Fort St. Philip: our Defenses are improving daily.…

October 2   77° 86° 84°

Damp and cloudy: East wind. Turned out warm and sunny in the middle of the day.

The War Department, by Telegraphic Dispatch, desires the use of part of the Old Marine Hospital as a Powder Mill, and a room in the New Marine Hospital for the temporary storage of a quantity of powder, just arrived; of course there can be no objection to so important a measure, and I had an interview with the Governor of the State on the Subject at 10½ A.M.

All the morning buried down with business, both Public and private: Judge Moise wants to open his new Court two weeks before the prescribed time, and I have given the necessary orders & directions (too complaisant in me by half!). Mr. Cook called in regard to his marble mantles, stables &c. &c. and I gave him such information &c. as he required: the whole work will soon be ready for occupancy, and seems to give great satisfaction to Mr. Cook, and his large family, which is gratifying; as I have tried my best to please them.

After dinner I [took] the 5 O'clock train for Mr. Cook's place, with Tommy.

October 8   69° 80° 76°

Bright sunshine: cold North East wind: hot sun at midday....

There is a good deal of unnecessary alarm spreading throughout the city in uninformed quarters, growing out of the occupation of the passes at the mouth of the River by Federal War Vessels....

October 10   75° 88° 85°

Fine and sunny: North East wind. Very hot at midday....

Went down to the Levee at 12½ to see the Gun Boat "Manassas" start on her destructive mission: she steamed down the river with fine speed: all her Iron Casing was prepared in my work shops.[24]...

October 12   64° 75° 72°

Cold bracing wind from North East: bright sunshine: very warm at midday.

Heavy firing at the Balize, the smoke of the broadsides was visible from the top of the New Custom House at 1½ P.M. Commodore Hollins will doubtless distinguish himself.[25]

Very busy in my office until 2. on miscellaneous Government work.

At the house with Tommy after dinner. Splendid naval victory by Commodore Hollins over the Federal fleet of 8 ships at the Balize: the Preble sunk, and the rest driven ashore: the joy here is intense: an extra out at 5 P.M.

October 13   70° 78° 79°

Sunday: Fine & clear: North West wind: at noon very warm in the sun: and musquitoes very bad.

Went to the Custom House at 11 in the hope of seeing Commodore Hollins and the naval officers in command, who arrived last night: their offices were not open so I sent my card, with congratulations, to Commodore Hollins by his Orderly; in the meantime had an interview with Judge Moise, who had just left the Governor, and it is certain that the whole Federal Squadron is beached at the mouth of the River after suffering immense damage!...

October 14   70° 79° 76°

Fine and sunny: North wind. Very warm in the sun at noon with light haze: musquitoes very bad.

Pleasant interview with Commodore Hollins and congratulations on his signal triumph at the Passes.

Visited the C. S. Steamers, Tuscarven and McCrea, both uninjured by the enemy's shot & shells: saw the captured yawl, lying on the Levee, with tremendous holes driven thro' her sides, and one thwart destroyed by our shot: the Manassas gun boat will be in order immediately and the bold war game will be renewed: the Floating Batteries also, with large armaments, destined for the Mouth of the River will soon be in service.

Mr. Cook called at my office and signed the Papers for the Stable Buildings; at $3500: at 5 P.M. went up to the house: the marble mantles are being set, and the family beginning to move in.

[24] The *Manassas*, originally a steam tug, had been converted into a powerful ironclad ram. In the successful attack on Union blockaders at the Head of Passes, she became the first American ironclad to see action, predating the famous duel between the *Monitor* and the *Virginia* (formerly the *Merrimac*). She was destroyed the following year by the Union fleet attacking New Orleans.

[25] George N. Hollins (1799-1878), a commander in the Confederate navy, was in charge of the naval station at New Orleans and later commanded all Confederate naval forces on the Mississipppi River. *BDC*.

The ironclad ram Manassas *with battle damage, 1862 (1978.224.2); the* Manassas *in action on the Mississippi River, 1862 (1974.25.9.44).*

Mortar boats (floating batteries), Alexander Simplot, delineator, 1862 (1974.25.9.259iii). These are Union boats but are similar to the Confederate floating battery constructed in New Orleans for the defense of the Mississippi.

October 19   65° 69° 68°

Still rainy, with West wind: clouds and sunshine: showers at 3 P.M.

Letter from the Hone. Secretary of the Treasury dated 15th. Inst. approving of my action in delivering material to Genl. Twiggs (95 Coils of Iron Wire) for War purposes. The New Custom House is a mine of wealth to the New War Department, and I, by the blessing of Providence, am the miner. I am overwhelmed with applications to use my influence with the new officer in command of the Military defences of Louisiana (Major General M. Lovell) for appointments on his staff & otherwise.[26]

October 26   70° 80° 75°

Pleasant weather: East wind. Clouds & sunshine and very warm at noon.

Visited the Floating Battery and found it rapidly perfecting her

[26] Mansfield Lovell (1822-1884), a West Point graduate and engineer, was appointed major general in the Confederate army on October 7, 1861, and assigned to command at New Orleans. *DLB.*

armaments &c. The chassis & carriages for the Columbiad & Parrot guns are being constructed in my shops and will soon be ready. She and her consort will be amply sufficient to keep every Lincolnite War ship out of our River.

October 30   64° 70° 68°

Fine weather: cool North East wind. Very warm at noon.

Attended auction sales for Pianos &c. but in spite of the times &c. the prices realized were large; Second rate pianos brought $325. Did not buy; of course!! Approved Bill of Extra work on Mr. Cook's house to the amount of $1517.10.

November 6   63° 69° 74°

Fine weather: South wind: early River fog: very hot, in the sun at noon. Very busy on the Courts &c. &c.

Fixing & furnishing house for the winter, and making every thing pleasant in spite of the imbecile but arrogant Northern foe, whom I have learned to contemn more intensely than the meanest reptile that crawls on earth's surface....

November 16   64° 66° 70°

Fine and sunny: East wind: very hot at noon.

Busy at the office as usual.

Emily & Tommy came to the office at 2 P.M. for shopping and other objects.

I took Tommy on board of the Floating Battery, now nearly ready for action, much to his delight. Its appointments are splendid, and no Federal ship can pass it when in place, which will be in a few days.

After dinner took Tommy to see the review of 10.000 splendid troops all drawn up in line from the river to the suburbs on the South Side of Canal Street: these form but one fourth of the effective force for the defence of this City, notwithstanding the vast numbers who have been assigned to Virginia.[27]

November 20   74° 74½° 76°

Fine & clear: clouds rising at 7 A.M. South East wind: showers set in at 8 A.M.

Read President Davis' Message before breakfast: it is a noble production![28] Not a word too many, not a word too few, and explains the true state of the country in few words as perfectly as if he had written an entire work, as voluminous and as elegant as Bossuet's "Histoire Universelle."[29] I complimented his father in Law this morning (Col. Howell) in the connection which exists between him and a man who is in every respect to our Southern Confederacy what Washington was to the first Federal Government.[30] The day was marked by frequent showers and bursts of hot sunshine.

November 23   50° 59° 56°

Fine & clear: cold North wind. Very warm sunshine at 1 P.M.

Works at the Custom House suspended, and also all business in town, to gain the day for a grand military display of all our City troops on Canal Street.[31]

I took Emily and Tommy down at 10 and we had splendid views of the pageant from the various commanding points of my huge structure, none better than from my own offices, fronting on Canal Str. on the second floor: both very spacious with good warm fires &c. &c. I had a double guard at the great entrance all day to keep out the "oi polloi" but accommodated large parties of friends, including Judge McCaleb & family; Judge Beverly's friends, the Cook family, the Dimitrys; the Mayoress of Carollton, Mrs. Purcell, with friends; "Dorothea" of the "Crescent" cum multis aliis."[32]

It was near dark when we threaded thro' the crowded streets home to dinner: not the least possible chance to ride. No less than 28.000 to 30.000 fine and well appointed troops passed in review under my windows: it was a noble and inspiring scene, and doubtless reassured the hearts of thousands of both sexes who crowded the wide galleries, in the resources and security of our beautiful City against the barbarians of the North. The day was lovely in the extreme, and one that will be remembered as an epoch in the history of New Orleans; it must also be borne in mind that, in addition to the above large force, there are 12.000 New Orleans troops now in active Service at distant, besides a respectable numerical quota doing valuable service on the water.

November 24   53° 61° 64°

Sunday. Very lovely weather, cool West wind. Changing to North West at 12 M.

Reading to Tommy after a late breakfast at 9 from different works, among the rest a short abstract of the life and sufferings of Christ, closing with that beautiful passage.

"Io sono la vita, la verita, la via;
nessuno va al Padre se non per me."[33]

Then a walk to the market for exercise, and to see if the foe were starving us out yet according to their programme. Nothing left but the choicest meats & fish; new potatoes, eggplants white & purple, green peas, okra, all the common vegetables, with fine tomatoes poultry & game, crabs &c. all in profusion, altho' so much later in the day than market hours, and all at old fashioned not <u>war</u>! prices! Not likely to be starved out yet awhile! or ever by so contemptible a foe!!

---

[27] There was a parade and review of the First Brigade under Col. Charbonnet. *Bee*, Nov. 16, 1861.

[28] Jefferson Davis's message to the Confederate Congress was delivered at Richmond on November 19, 1861. It was published in the *Daily True Delta* on November 20.

[29] Jacques Benigne Bossuet, *Discours sur l'histoire universelle*.

[30] William Burr Howell was the father of Varina Howell, wife of Jefferson Davis. *DLB*

[31] The Louisiana Militia was reviewed by Thomas O. Moore, governor and commander-in-chief. *Bee*, Nov. 19, 1861.

[32] Alexander Dimitry (1805-1883), an educator and public official, was postmaster general of the Confederacy. His wife was Mary Powell Mills. *DLB*. Samuel Pursell (d. 1867) was mayor of Carrollton from 1861 to 1863 and from 1866 to 1867. Wilton P. Ledet, "The History of the City of Carrollton," *Louisiana Historical Quarterly* 21(January 1938):35-36. Trans.: with many others.

[33] Slightly misquoted. John 14:6. I am the way, the truth, and the life. No one comes to the Father but through me.

In the meantime Julia went <u>as usual</u> to market at 7 A.M. and we shall have <u>as usual</u> a most appetizing dinner, with a bottle of good wine to dissolve it and aid assimilation, digestion &c. &c. &c. It seems rather odd to write of the details of "la table" but my maxim is that what is done <u>regularly</u> three times a day <u>ought</u> to be done <u>well</u> and enjoyed! I am no "<u>gourmand</u>" but I do live carefully and well and desire that all my family should do likewise, at least they have the opportunity.

November 26   62° 70° 71°

Beautiful weather: mild West wind.

Every indication favors the belief that England and the other great European Powers will be glad to welcome our Southern Confederacy into the family of nations....

At 10 A.M. for the rest of the day, weather variable, with dazzling sunshine and threatening clouds: until near sunset when it became exceedingly pleasant and I took Tommy to see the effects of a terrible explosion, that occurred yesterday, of the locomotive "Mississippi" at the Depot near Tivoli Circle.[34] The glass in the windows for some distance around was shattered, and we found large fragments of the Iron lying at different points within about 200 yards of the Scene of accident; strange to say only one man was killed, and two scalded, altho' in so populous a locality....

November 30   62° 66° 68°

Heavy showers in the night with change of wind to North East. Quite cool this morning, fires very necessary. Hot sunshine at midday.

Very busy closing up accounts for the month making Vouchers &c. &c.

Em. & Tommy came to the office at 12 and I took them to "Loeffler's" to select the Gas fixtures, as I am having the gas introduced into my house.

Company to dinner at 4 P.M. Miss Emma Palmer & Miss Clara Sumner.

The month closes very pleasantly: every interest under my charge is in a high degree prosperous: the Confederate Courts are finished, occupied and give great satisfaction. Mr. Cook's beautiful mansion is also finished and fully occupied, except the Carriage house addition which is in good progress: the Military Defences of Louisiana are almost perfect, and every day adds to their strength; my "little cottage," the New Custom House, is a mine of wealth for that <u>all</u>

absorbing object, and in spite of the menacing attitude of the North, and their terrible denunciations of us "rebels" we treat their flippant threats, their promises to annihilate us! to subjugate us! their men? their money? all that belongs to them? if <u>anything</u>; with supreme derision and contempt.

December 2   75° 76° 74°

Warm & cloudy: South West wind. Sudden showers and wind rising. Dark storm clouds at 1 P.M. and rain at 2....

In the afternoon took Tommy to "Leed's Foundry" and examined the whole of that fine Establishment, now in full blast in preparing large numbers of the very best brass cannon and any quantity of shot and shells for our State defences.

December 7   72° 73° 72°

Warm & threatening rain: South East wind: cloudy all the morning and very pleasant air.

Wrote to General Leonidas Polk introducing my good friend Dr. N. B. Benedict. Took a carriage at 11 and bestowed therein my wife, Tommy, Mrs. Ladd, and Ellen, & myself & proceeded to the Fortifications, 6 miles below the City: they are admirably constructed & extend from the river to the swamp, occupying the site of the famous Battle field of Jany. 8. 1815.[35] Tommy collected mementoes of that event on the field: which is now covered within the fortifications with the Tents and Soldiery of two regiments, while the naval force of some twenty vessels adds an assurance of further security to the City. The gardens, orange orchards, and plantations exhibited a perfect gushing tide of almost tropical luxuriance, and the drive was quite delicious; the temperature, tho' warm, being reduced by friendly clouds, and the roads in excellent order: we got home to dinner at 2½ P.M....

December 11   64° 72° 75°

Fine & sunny: South East wind. Very hot at noon in the sun....

This evening we lit the gas chandelieurs, and all the burners were clear & very pure in light: it is an immense improvement over our former Astrals, Carcel & Coal Oil Lamps, Candles &c. and makes our rooms ten times more cheerful & attractive.

---

[34] The Carrollton railroad locomotive burst its boiler on Nayades Street (now St. Charles) near Clio, just outside the depot yard. *Bee*, Nov. 26, 1861.

[35] The fortifications below the city were erected at Chalmette where the Battle of New Orleans had been fought. *Bee*, July 15, 1861.

Fort John Morgan, 1862 (1974.25.9.239i).

December 18   60° 68° 70°

This is the 10th. Anniversary of our wedding day: & the weather, as usual, lovely with soft warm air stealing over us from the eastward, and my morning Journals full of glorious news, England (sensible to the last) spurns with indignation the northern insult offerred to her Flag by the Capture of our Confederate Commissioners (Slidell & Mason) sailing for England on the English Mail Steamer Trent, from the "neutral" Port of Havana.[36] Immense mass meeting[s] were held in London and Liverpool demanding the Government of Great Britain to require immediate and complete reparation from the power in Washington, and the return of the Commissioners to England.

[36] In October 1861 John Slidell and James Murray Mason (1798-1871), former senator from Virginia, were appointed Confederate diplomatic commissioners to France and England. Sailing from the neutral port of Havana aboard the British packet ship *Trent*, they were forcibly removed by American naval forces and imprisoned in Boston. British protests against this breach of international law led to an official apology and release of the prisoners, who reached their destinations in January 1862. Despite some initial encouragement, neither France nor England recognized the Confederacy as a nation.

At 11 the Carriage was at the door and I took all the family to visit the new fortifications above Carrolton, say 8 miles from town — a charming drive, among gardens and orange groves laden with fruit, and beautiful flowers, & fine river & land views all sparkling under a pure warm sunshine.[37] The works are well constructed, of great extent, and with a dozen guns of the heaviest metal, 4 already on the Pintles & prepared for action. The 18th. Regiment were greatly pleased with the files of last week's papers which we have saved for them, and took with us. The excursion was delightful; Tommy rode on the box and enjoyed it extensively, and we were home again in time for a handsome three O'clock dinner.

December 22   64° 67° 70°

Sunday: Fine and sunny, wind from the East: overclouded, however, at 9 A.M. and rain set in about 10.

Walk with Tommy after breakfast.

[37] Fort John Morgan (later Camp Parapet) was on the river in the vicinity of what is now Causeway Boulevard. An old powder magazine is still standing and has been restored by Jefferson Parish.

Emily is quite lucky this year in the way of presents, notwithstanding the "pressure" supposed to "arise"! from the Blockade? Last evening Mr. Keen kindly brought up (himself) a handsome chair for her, carefully upholstered for that object and certainly not worth less than $40 or $50. Other beautiful and costly tributes have also flowed into her reservoirs. I have carefully drawn in colors, lead pencil and sepia a variety of small pictures of scenery &c. associated with historical events and localities of deep interest which I have had handsomely bound, to add to Emily's treasures, this, however, is a modest and unassuming tribute, wholly artistic in character, and, unlike gems from the Indies such as sapphires, rubies, amethysts, and opals, are wholly without marketable & quotable value....

December 25 53° 66° 67°

Christmas day. Works at the Custom House suspended as usual.

The weather is perfectly charming, with a mild easterly breeze, and a rise in the thermometer at 7, since the same hour yesterday, of 10 degrees.

When I awoke at 5 the Cathedral bells were pealing a loud and joyous Christmas welcome, very sweet, and very English: silvery as Manchester Bells.[38]

Last night we had our Christmas tree of evergreens hung with fruits and decorated with a host of beautiful and costly presents; silver, jewels, books, drawings, bijouterie of different kind, and a set of Tools for Tommy, of the best manufacture, which I got my head carpenter to select for me; and sharpened carefully before he sent them home. The money value was between $200 and $300 paid in cash which during the existence of war may look a good round sum for a family of modest pretensions, but when there is such great stagnation in the world of trade I think it a duty in those who have a few spare dollars to disburse freely.

Tommy had his Christmas edition of his paper richly illuminated with designs drawn & colored by himself, for which, of course, I had to pay in solid silver notwithstanding the present specie suspension.

At 11 I went to the Custom House and assisted at the presentation of a splendid silk Flag to the "Smith Artillery" of which I am an honorary member.[39]...

Our Christmas Turkey, with oysters, and other collaterals dissolved from the table at 3; like the "baseless fabric of a vision" and left scarce a "wreck behind" and the remainder of even[in]g passed as pleasantly as the most fastidious taste could desire.

December 29 56° 68° 70°

Sunday. Fine and clear: wind north.

Exactly at midnight we were aroused by a terrific explosion which shook the house and effectually shook off our slumber; I got up, put on my wrapper, and went to the front door where I discovered at once from the great wreaths of smoke rolling up from the direction of the River, and the strong fumes of sulphur, that it was the Old Marine Hospital, being used for the manufacture of powder by the firm of "Hobart & Forster" under the auspices of the Government, which relieved for the time Mr. Hatch (the Collector) & myself as joint custodians: my papers this morning verify my decision; the Hospital is totally destroyed.[40] And it is an important loss, not only as the Building was large & handsome, but because Powder is, at this time, one of our elements of strength against the Northern foe....

[38] Probably the bells of St. Patrick's Church, which served as a procathedral.

[39] Smith's Artillery was named for Major Martin L. Smith (1819-1866) who was commissioned a major in the Confederate corps of engineers and was promoted to major general in 1862. During the Civil War, Smith was in charge of the river defenses for New Orleans and Vicksburg, and served as chief engineer for the Army of Northern Virginia and for the Army of Tennessee. The captain was John Roy. *BDC.*

[40] Hobart & Foster, commission merchants, 46 St. Charles. NOCD 1861. The *Daily True Delta* reported that "at twelve o'clock last night one of the state powder mills, that at the old United States Marine Hospital at Gretna, blew up with a report that shook the whole city to its foundation stones.... It must have been the diabolical work of some incarnate fiend." *Daily True Delta*, Dec. 29, 1861.

January 1 60° 72° 70°

The New Year opens delightfully with a gentle air from the East, and a Southern sunny sky: a light shower fell at 11 but the sun again shone out and the rest of the day was very pleasant.

I wrote letters to the Department &c. in my office until 12 and then sallied out to make my customary New Year's Calls, which this year's difficulties, growing out of the war, made none the less joyous, and the usual beautiful preparations met me in every house, in some actual splendor....

January 2 68° 73° 68°

Light fog: East wind: sunshine at noon: rain at 1 P.M. then variable thro' the afternoon....

My two month's leave of absence from the School Board having expired, I attended the regular meeting this evening from 7 to 9 and was most cordially greeted by all members: the debates were of unusual and grave interest, and elicited many excellent speeches in which I bore my part in my usual off-hand, and, I trust, not ineffectual manner.[1]

January 7 54° 55° 54°

...Wrote to the Secretary of the Treasury recommending the taking down of the great Central Derrick of the New Custom House as its decay renders it useless for construction, and dangerous to the works....

January 18 70° 72° 76°

Damp and foggy: East wind. Cleared off at noon, very warm.

Writing at the office very closely, then went on board of the Confederate gun boats Livingston, Jackson & McCrea, examined their guns, quarters &c.[2] Found every thing in fine order. Heavy guns, fine chassis & carriages, careful traverses and healthy looking crews with whom I conversed socially, without form, & returned to dinner at 4.

[1] At the meeting of the First District School Board it was suggested that an appeal for funds be made to parents and the public if the city council was unable to finance the schools because of the war. *Daily Delta*, Jan. 4, 1862.

[2] The *Livingston*, the *Jackson*, and the *MacRea* were part of Commodore Hollins's "mosquito fleet" that had attacked the federal blockaders in October 1861. Dufour, *The Night the War Was Lost*, 61, 75, 105.

1862

January 20   70° 76° 78°

Damp & cloudy. South West wind. Turned out hot and sunny at 9 A.M.

Correspondance with Commodore Hollins, relative to Plate Iron for Navy objects, which I turned over to him subject to the approval of the Hone. Secretary of the Treasury, and his receipt for the same.

February 3   62° 72° 76°

Fine weather, East wind to South West, hot sun at noon.

Efforts are being made, in political circles, I regret to say, to supplant officers of tried reputation: I trust they will make no attack upon me, because, altho' on principle, a man of peace, yet when principle, professional reputation, and the interests of my own family are at stake, I can & will fight and bid defiance to all political cormorants.

February 6   68° 75° 76°

Clouds and sunshine: wind South. Light showers in the middle of the day.

Wrote my Report of Lyceum and Library, and Washington School.

Wrote to the Honorable Secretary of the Treasury relative to a sale of our old Lime which I have just disposed of for $100 Cash which is a large price, as the lime has been slaked for seven years, and is to a great extent air slaked, in bulk not more than 150 Barrels, with waste and expense of removal. It was bought in 1855 by the Custom House for $1.49 per Bbl. I ask the Secretary what I shall do with the inuring Funds....

February 14   65° 55° 52°

Storm of wind, rain, thunder and lightening from 2 A.M. to 9 A.M. Wind North West.

Letter from the Hone. Secretary of the Treasury. Very unsatisfactory: Funds are getting very low in the Treasury Department.

February 15   42° 40° 40°

Cold rains, & gloomy clouds. North wind. Rain, rain all day!

War news encouraging to our side and sadly depressing to the Vandals of the North; the sooner they give up the unequal contest the better for them. The war <u>injures</u> us, it will <u>destroy</u> them.

February 27   60° 68° 74°

Fine & clear: light air from N. East. Hot sun at noon.

Wrote to the Secretary of the Treasury enclosing receipt for 126.000 Pounds of Cast Iron which I have transferred to the War Department from the New Custom House stores for the benefit of the Defenses of Louisiana....

March 10   68° 69° 70°

Fine & clear: warm South wind.

Yesterday at noon the city was suddenly shocked by two terrible explosions, within a few seconds of each other; our house quivered as with an earthquake, and Tommy actually fell down. It turns out to have been the two Powder Mills erected in the rear of the Old Marine Hospital, which was destroyed by the same cause on the 29th. Decr. 1861. I deeply regret to add that 5 operatives were instantly blown to atoms: & the Soldier on duty is supposed to be fatally wounded. The mills contained 3000 Pounds of Powder....

March 15   50° 53° 56°

Cold West wind: clear sky.

Martial Law is declared today by General Lovell. It will have a happy effect, and free the City from disloyal persons....

March 21   50° 59° 60°

Cold West wind: clear sky. Hot at noon: splendid sunshine.

Renewed my Oath of allegiance to the South at 9 A.M. an immense crowd attending, all ready in the ardor of their patriotism to stand firm and defend the great interests of the South.

After dinner took Tommy to Leed's Foundry and examined a large number of splendid brass cannon in process of completion.

March 22   46° 58° 58°

Clouds and sunshine: cold North West wind. Hot at noon....

Took Tommy at 5 O'clock over to Gretna in the fine new Ferry Boat.[3]

---

[3] The east bank landing of the Gretna ferry was at Louisiana Avenue in what was then Jefferson City. Gretna, established in 1836 on the west bank of the Mississippi, has been the parish seat of Jefferson Parish since 1884.

Ferry landing, New Orleans, Jay Dearborn Edwards, photographer, between 1857 and 1860 (1982.167.9).

We had a most delightful ramble among meadows of clover covered with flowers, a beautiful bouquet of which we culled....

March 23   46° at 7 A.M. 49° at 9 A.M. 56° 54°

Sunday. Clear sky: West wind.

Went to market with Tommy before breakfast, bought fine fish, veal and Vegetables, but the War has advanced all prices, choice Beef &c. 25 cents per lb. small chickens One dollar each & so on.

March 30   67° 78° 80°

Sunday. Dense fog. South Wind.

Went to market with the Servant at 7, got fine fish, Veal, vegetables &c. but found prices still ruling high notwithstanding the Martial law Tariff, established by Genl. Lovell.

Clouds and fog rolled off at 10 A.M. and the sun brightened every object; roses, amaryllides, geraniums, Verbenas, Oxalides, Mignonette, Violets and all the "Milles fleurs" for which our gardens are now so marked with loveliness.

Visited the encampment on the Square at Race Street, and was received by the officers with their characteristic cordiality and "overflowing" hospitality, and again in the evening with Tommy to see the dress Parade.[4] Hundreds of ladies present: hospitality as usual.

April 4   70° 82° 80°

Fine & pleasant: wind South West. Hot sun at noon....

In the evening visited Camp Railey, and then attended a drill of a fine Company on Coliseum Square: at the close of the drill I addressed the company for about 10 minutes, under the pure starlight.[5]

April 6   74° at 8 A.M. 75° at 9 A.M. 82° at 12. M. 84° at 4 A.M.

Sunday. Pleasant spring weather. South West wind. Very hot sunshine at noon.

Visited Camp Westmore, and the Army offices after breakfast: then spent some time in my Office at the New Custom House, writing an

Garden Flowers, Syngenesia &c. &c. drawn hastily, but from Nature.

important letter to the Honorable Secretary of the Treasury.[6] Every one at Church when I got home except my naughty self; but what can I do? when a savage and demoniac war is waged against us at our very doors by the immaculate and supremely pious!! puritans of New England, and the refined? and polished!! powers of the North. Pleasant walk with Emily &

---

[4] The camp on Race Street occupied Annunciation Square, a few blocks from Wharton's residence.

[5] Camp Railey was one of several temporary Confederate camps established in and around New Orleans.

[6] Fort Westmore was named for Samuel M. Westmore (1806-1896), adjutant general of Louisiana (1853-1854) and brother of Dr. Preston Moore, surgeon general of the Confederacy. *DLB.*

Tommy after dinner among the beautiful flower gardens of the 4th. District. Visited its Cematary, and I made a drawing of the fine marble tomb of our friends the "Bryants" the young survivors of the family we found gathered around it.[7]

April 12   65° 75° 76°

Fine and sunny this morning, with South West wind, changing to North West.

Wrote to Mr. F. H. Hatch, the Collector, saying that I had removed all the Government Records, Drawings, & Property from the Office formerly occupied by Genl. Beauregard; and more recently assigned by me to Judge Möise, for the use of the Naval Officer, Lieut. Freeman, who is charged with the important service of making drawings for Gunboats to defend our River. The Lieutt. and the Collector waited on me at 1 P.M. and I delivered the key to the Naval Officer Freeman.

April 15   75° 81° 80°

Light clouds: East wind, to South East.

The attack has been commenced by the Federal Gunboats on Forts Jackson & St. Phillip but thus far without serious injury to us, as I learned from the officers at the War Department at 2 P.M.[8] Their object appearing to be the reduction of our Forts by distant shelling, rather than by direct assault, but I think we will disconcert them with our Ironclad Rams & Fire Boats.

April 16   76° 82° 79°

Mild and pleasant. Light clouds. Wind South East.

Last evening a splendid dress Parade of the Confederate & Louisiana Guards took place on the fine Square opposite our house: it was attended, as usual, with a vast concourse of ladies. The line of Soldiery extended the entire length of the Square, say about 1000 feet, and under the admirable discipline of their able general officer, Col. Gerault, maneuvered with skill and precision.

It is with deep sorrow that I note the deaths in recent actions of some of our noblest & most valiant officers and privates, especially at Shiloh, where the Northern foe lost not less than 20.000 men. Very many of the lost on our side I knew well....

April 17   74° 82° 80°

This is the 48th. anniversary of my Birthday.

"Time is winging us away to our eternal home"

Pleasant weather: wind South East. Very hot sunshine at noon.

Every thing right at the office.

Paid General Beauregard's Taxes and my own for 1861.

Shotting and shelling going on with vigor on Forts Jackson & St. Phillip without any perceptible effect: we hold our fire, and they, with their 13 inch guns & mortars, ranging two miles, trying to strike our Barbette, Casemate, & Breastheight guns to dismount them: yet I have not heard that they have struck once; owing to the impetus given by such heavy charges at two miles, throwing the balls and shells in a parabolic curve <u>over</u> the Forts into the swamp beyond, and I do not think their immense Armada dare approach much nearer for fear of red hot shot from our 200 heavy guns.

Splendid dress Parade at 5 P.M. on Coliseum Square opposite to us.

My Birthday is also signally [enhanced?] by a complete Victory over the Northern Foe by our brave Confederates in the Peninsula.[9]

April 18   75° 76° 77°

Good Friday. Pleasant weather. Wind South East. Rain at noon.

The works at the Custom House for Military and Naval Service go on as usual: owing to the exigencies of war. Spent several hours at the Office in writing letters &c. and returned in the Cars early. By the way those cars are becoming an intensified nuisance rather than a convenience, for at the cheap rate of 5 Cents they are overwhelmed with all the "Oi polloi" of the City and environs....

---

[7] The E. K. Bryant tomb in Lafayette Cemetery I, a plastered brick structure with corner pilasters and a heavy pediment, is on the center cross aisle near Prytania Street. Ella Bryant, the youngest child in the family, and Victor Bryant both died in 1858 and are buried in this tomb. Historic Cemetery Survey.

[8] The attack of the Federal fleet on Fort Jackson and Fort St. Philip, beginning with days of artillery shelling by mortar boats, is covered in detail in Chester G. Hearn's *The Capture of New Orleans, 1862* (Baton Rouge, 1995).

[9] Wharton's reference to a Confederate victory would seem to be mistaken. In the war in the Peninsula of Virginia, Union troops won a small victory on April 16 preparatory to their march on Yorktown. New Orleans newspapers did, however, carry a lengthy account of the battle of Shiloh (not in Virginia, but in Tennessee) which mistakenly implied a Confederate victory. *Daily Picayune*, Apr. 17, 1862.

Union fleet entering the Mississippi at the beginning of the campaign to capture New Orleans, 1862 (1978.205).

Union fleet passing Forts St. Philip and Jackson, April 24, 1862, Currier & Ives, publisher (1972.25), with the Manassas *in the foreground. Having passed the forts and disabled Confederate ships, the fleet had a clear path up the river to New Orleans.*

April 20   63° 60° 56°

Sunday. Light clouds after rain in the night. Wind South West to N. West.

Went to market at 6½ and for the first time in my life carried the basket myself as it is Easter Sunday and my Cook, being an Irish Catholic must of course be permitted to attend the early services of "ill mumbled mass," muttered by stupid Priests in equally stupid monkish Latin, not a word of which she understands and not a word of which a classic Scholar would wish to understand.

Heaven preserve me
From such Latinity.

Visited Camp Railey in the evening and received the usual hospitable welcome from the officers in command.

April 21   50° 62° 64°

Cold dry & clear: West wind. Hot sunshine at noon.

The 13 inch shells of our foe still continue to pour around our Forts, but thus far without serious injury to us but heavy loss to them.

April 24   65° 77° 80°

Fine and clear: cool West wind. Hot at noon.

Great excitement in town on the news of some Federal gunboats having passed the Forts. Silly nonsense!

Cotton-laden vessels set afire by Confederates as the Union fleet approached New Orleans, April 25, 1862 (1974.25.9.239 vi); Broadside by John T. Monroe, mayor of New Orleans, April 25, 1862 (86-2219-RL).

April 25   70° 74° 77°

Fine & clear, Wind South West. Light clouds rising.

Last night the Cotton in New Orleans was burned: Sugar & molasses destroyed, and today we hear that the enemies' gunboats are only 9 miles below the city: and that our city authorities will capitulate....

The gunboats of the enemy reached the City this evening & Tommy & I inspected.

April 26   65° 65° 70°

Fine & clear. Wind South West. Changing suddenly to North East. Went to the office as usual.

From the top of the Custom House I had a clear view of 5 Federal War ships: all of which left at 4 P.M.

Pleasant visit to Mrs. General Beauregard: made several speeches to our men &c.

April 27   65° 75° 74°

Sunday. Fine weather. Wind North changing from S.W. & N.E.

Went to the Custom House to see that all was right there, as in these dangerous times I shall adhere to my post of duty to the last.

TO THE PEOPLE
OF
NEW ORLEANS.

Mayoralty of New Orleans,
CITY HALL, April 25th, 1862.

After an obstinate and heroic defence by our troops on the river, there appears to be imminent danger that the insolent enemy will succeed in capturing your city. The forts have not fallen; they have not succumbed even beneath the terrors of a bombardment unparalleled in the history of warfare. Their defenders have done all that becomes men fighting for their homes, their country and their liberty; but in spite of their efforts, the ships of the enemy have been able to avoid them, and now threaten the city. In view of this contingency, I call on you to be calm, to meet the enemy, not with submissiveness nor with indecent alacrity; but if the military authorities are unable longer to defend you, to await with hope and confidence the inevitable moment when the valor of your sons and of your fellow-countrymen will achieve your deliverance. I shall remain among you, to protect you and your property, so far as my power or authority as Chief Magistrate can avail.

JOHN T. MONROE,
MAYOR.

Union ships anchored in the Mississippi River at New Orleans with cotton bales burning along the levees, April 25, 1862 (1953.61), gift of Harold Schilke and Boyd Cruise.

Landing of Union officers in New Orleans to demand the surrender of the city, William Waud, delineator, 1862 (1958.43.20i).

April 28   68° 76° 78°

Fine & clear. East wind.

At the Custom House as usual, and at the City Hall twice to meet a called assembly of the 1st. Dist. Draining Commission, but to my surprise no member was there: the Hall was surrounded by a tumultuous mass infuriated by the appearance of seven gunboats of the Federal fleet opposite the City, and their demand for the surrender of the City.

April 29   70° 79° 80°

Fine & clear. East wind.

At the office as usual, and at the City Hall to hear the speech of the Hon[orabl]e. Pierre Soulé.[10]

April 30   70° 74° 76°

Fine & clear: East wind. Rain at noon.

The month closes with the deplorable fact that our City has been abandoned by the Governor, Genl. Lovell and all his forces, and all our Government officers. We are now in the hands of Federal troops, with large fleets of square rigged ships and gunboats in the River.

Mayor Monroe has behaved most nobly throughout.[11]

May 1   70° 76° 75°

Fine weather: north wind.

I went to the Custom House as usual but as it has been taken possession of by the Federal officers with a large fleet of War steamers to sustain them I could transact no business, and the sudden north wind has enfeebled me sadly.

[10] When martial law was declared in New Orleans on March 14, 1862, Soulé was appointed provost marshal for the third district. On April 29 Soulé wrote a letter for Mayor Monroe's signature regarding Farragut's threat to bombard the city. Dufour, *The Night the War Was Lost*, 312-13.

[11] John T. Monroe (1822-1871), a native of Virginia, was mayor of New Orleans when the city fell to Federal forces in the Civil War. Deposed and imprisoned in 1862 by General Benjamin Butler, Monroe was reelected mayor in 1866 and deposed a year later by General Philip Sheridan. *DLB.*

Scene in New Orleans – the 26th Mass. Vol., Col. Farr, practicing street firing in Carondelet Street, between 1862 and 1865 (1974.25.9.4).

May 2   66° 70° 79°

Fine & clear. Wind North West.

Took Tommy to the Custom House to look at the U.S. Troops now quartered there about 1000.

My orderlies came to my house with Pay rolls &c. for Lyceum & Library, and to receive my notices for the Draining Company.

May 3   68° 74° 80°

Fine and clear: wind due West. Changed to South: very warm.

Went to the Custom House & the City Hall and found both occupied by large bodies of Federal troops, to whom I had nothing to say.

May 4   70° 74° 80°

Sunday. Fine & clear: South wind.

The river is pouring over the Levees, and running thro' the streets in torrents, quite a cleanser.

May 6   68° 76° 79°

Fine & clear: cool North wind.

The City is now in full occupation by Federal troops under the command of Major General Butler.[12]

Went down town in the Cars as usual but all the rumors I find afloat relating to the war require official confirmation.

Beauregard is too prudent to dispatch or write at this juncture; and it may be too busy on the field of battle.

[12] Benjamin F. Butler (1818-1893), a Massachusetts politician, was appointed major general by Abraham Lincoln on May 16, 1861. While in command of Federal troops occupying New Orleans, Butler was called by southerners "Spoons Butler" for alleged corruption and "Beast Butler" because of his General Order No. 28, which ordered that any woman treating U.S. troops with disrespect would be considered "a woman of the town plying her avocation." He was replaced in command by General Nathaniel P. Banks in December 1862. *DLB.*

The New Orleans Custom House occupied by Union troops, John R. Hamilton, delineator, 1863 (1958.43.12).

Had a friendly & pleasant interview with our noble Mayor Monroe, by accident, however, today as I met him in Canal Street, returning from an interview with Major Genl. Butler, the particulars of which he desired me not to speak of, and consequently do not record.

At 5½ met the Draining Board in regular monthly meeting and sat in careful discussion on our affairs until 8 P.M. We still meet in our office at the City Hall that building having been vacated by the Federal troops.

May 7   68° 70° 80°

Fine and clear: wind North East.

Wrote my minutes of the Draining Board & sent notices for meeting on 10.

[End of Journal]

Thomas K. Wharton died May 24, 1862.

Index

Page numbers in bold indicate identifying note; italics refer to illustrations.

Cooper, Ann, 48n75
Cooper, Peter, **146n34**, 169
Cooper, Samuel, 248, **248n8**
Cooper Union, **146n34**
Cornelle, Mrs. M. F. R. L., 34, **34n52**
Costa, Marie M., 193n10
Costa v. Whitehead, 193, **193n10**, 214
Cottage plantation, 84n28
Cotton bales, *13*, 272, *272, 273, plates 5, 7, 12, 14*
Cotton presses, 38, *38*, 39, 42, *43*, 200, 200n16, n17, *201*, 253
Cox, Elijah, 120n26, 126
Crevasses: Bell crevasse, *157*, 157, *158*, 159, **159n16**, 160, *162*, 163; Labranche crevasse, 161, 161n21, 163, 169; McCarty crevasse, 161, 161n22
Crimean War, **14n15**, 23, 60, 104, 104n51, 110n8
Cronan, Denis, 115n19, 190
Cronan v. Peters, **115n19**, 120
Crossman, Abdil D., 110n7, 112, **112n9**
Crozier, Robert, 174, **174n39**
Cude, John, 148n44
Custom House: accidents at, 199; accounting for, 8, 43, 44, 59, 62, 120, 133, 144, 172, 180, 192, 206, 210, 217, 222, 227, 233, 245; and appraisers, 104; appropriations for, 72, 123, 144, 169, 200, 224, 232, 241, 242, 249; arches in, 31, 32, 62, 64, 70, 80; article by Wharton for *DeBow's Review*, 190, 190n5; brickwork at, 8, 10, 17, 22, 24, 25, 26, 26n34, 32, 32n44, 39, 43, 72, 80, 178; chimneys of, 165, 166; and cholera, 55; and Confederacy, xv, xvii, xviii-xix, 245-246, 248n6, 249, 251, 253, 254, 260, 266; descriptions of, 72-73, 241-242; design disputes, xv, 9n9, 17n19; and federal courts, 41, 41n60, 72; and fires, 108, 108n2, 143, 143n28, 215, 233, 237; foundation of, xvi, 161, 162, 163, 175; gutters of, 165; history of, 241-242; illustrations of, *6, 11, 15, plate 7*; ironwork for, 32, 32n42, 69, 70, 80, 104; and lawsuits, 115, 115n19, 120; layoff of workers, 233, 253; and lightning, 144; marble hall, 108, 108n1, *109*, 110n3, 116, *116*, 117, 125; masonry work at, 24, 25, 70; mismanagement of, 236; north wall of, 157, 160; occupation by U.S. troops, 166, 168-169, 275-276, *276*; operations dictated by secretary of the treasury, 5; and post office department, 233, 242; revenue department as tenants of, 120, 242; roof work at, 59, 64, 163, 241-242; salary reductions at, 139; scaffolding around, 100; settlement of, 147, 242; and sheet piling, 63; and slow progress on Custom House, 41n61; stonework on, 10, 10n13, 25, 38, 39, 44, 45, 52, 53, 56-57, 58, 64, 72, 80, 103-105, 176, 177; suspension of funding for, 148, 150, 232; suspension of work at, 4, 48, 62, 175, 199, 222, 225, 244, 261, 264; taking down central derrick of, 265; Wharton as architect of, 48-49; Wharton as superintendent of, xviii-xix, 240-241, 246; Wharton's drawings of (including construction details), xv, *31, 32, 44, 53, 56, 57, 63, 69, 70, 73, 76, 77, 81, 87, 90, 94, 100*, 125; and white marble, 45; and wire rope, 53; and yellow fever, 44, 47, 183, 185
Cyrrhestes, Andronicus, tower of, 73, **73n15**; as Tower of the Winds, 73n15

Da Silva, Jean, 136, **136n8**, 137, 145

Daguerreotypes, 80, 115, 143
Dakin, Charles B., 76n21
Dakin, James H., xvi, 9n9, 14n18, 40n57, 76n21, 77n23, 208n28
Davis, Jefferson, 261, 261n28
Davis, Varina Howell, 261n30
Day, James Ingersoll, 77, **77n23**, 117
Day, Sarah Armitage, **77n23**
Day, William K.: and Brown residence, 175, 175n40, 185, 187-188; and commercial property, 140; and Harris house, 140n21, 153; and Harrison house, 146; and Leathers house, 208n27; and Seamen's Home, 137, **137n11**, 138, 147; and yellow fever, 176
De Haas, Mauritz F. H.: Farragut's fleet passing the forts below New Orleans, *plate 21*
De la Ronde, Louise, 26n37
De Pouilly, Jacques Nicholas Bussière, 17n20, **26n36**, 64n4, 126n36
Deacon, William, 185, **185n62**
Defrasse, Auguste, 108, 110, **110n3**, 116, 124, 125
Delacroix, Cyril, 181, 181n51
Delagrave (tenor), 140, 140n20
Delassize (L. T.) brickyard, 196, **196n12**
Democratic Party, 104, **104n50**
Deslonde, Adrian, 176
Deslonde, André, 176, **231n25**
Deslonde, Edward, 176, **176n42**
Devries, 19
Dimitry, Alexander, 261, **261n32**
Disciples of Christ. *See* Christian Church
Diseases: cholera, xiii, 33, 34n51, 38, 42n63, 44, 55, 59, 84; heart disease, 99; and immigrants, 120; malaria, 90; pulmonary consumption, 36; theories of origin of, 57-58; typhoid, 179; Wharton's theories on, 88. *See also* yellow fever
Dix, Mr., 203
Dodd, Daniel, 80
Dolbear, Clotilde, **22n26**
Dolbear, Rufus, 22, **22n26**
Domestic servants, 24, 42, 65, 206, 230, 271
Donati's comet, 179, *179*, 181-182, *181, 182*
Douglas, Stephen A., 236, 236n38
Dreux, Charles Didier, 256, **256n20**
Dryades Church, **115n14**
Ducatel, Amédée, 184, **184n56**
Duhamel, Clement, 155, **155n9**
Duncan, Mrs., 97
Duncan, A., 199
Duncan, Johnson Kelly, 123, **123n33**, 136, 165, 165n25, 204, 243
Duncan, The Rev. William Cecil: and church spire, 88; and repair of Coliseum Place Baptist Church, 77; residence of, **65n6**; resignation of, 212; sermons of, 65, 70, 89, 145, 159, 166; visits with Wharton, 74, 97, 128
Duncan, William P., 254, **254n19**

Wharton, Henry, 34
Wharton, Jane Brooks, 34n51
Wharton, Maria Huling, xv, **9n6**, 34, 36
Wharton, Marianne. See Gillette, Marianne Wharton
Wharton, Robert John, 34, **34n51**
Wharton, Thomas Kelah: architectural apprenticeship of, xiii, 33-34; biography of, xiii-xix; birth of, xiii; birthdays of, 139, 227, 248, 269; burial of, xix; and business travel, 235; Catholicism, views on, 17, 17n20, 24, 51, 95, 97, 99, 271; childhood and youth of, xiii, 32-33, 232; and Christ Church, xv, xviii, 34, *35*, 36, 36n53, 110, 232; church attendance of, 4, 55, 80, 88, 140, 144, 212, 254; court appearances of, 40; death of first wife, xv; as debt free, 8; and design disputes on Custom House, 17n19; drawings by, *xii, 30, 31, 32, 35, 39, 44, 53, 56, 57, 63, 69, 70, 73, 76, 77, 81, 82, 83, 85, 86, 87, 89, 91, 94, 96, 98, 100, 106, 179, 181, 182, 203, 268*; drinking problems of, xix; earnings of, 21, 80, 87, 117, 118, 144, 212, 214, 215, 241, 248; education of, 32-33; father's remarriage, 34; first architectural design of, xiv; at Flushing Institute, xiv, 33-34; in Fourth District, 269; health of, 1n1, 4, 10, 14, 16-17, 69, 107, 138, 143, 144, 176, 185, 207, 218, 257; immigration of, 32-33; Irish, view on 42, 45n69, 60, 230, 271; journal of, *plate 1*; at Louisiana militia review, 261; marriages of, xv, xvi, 1n2, 34, 36; mother's death, xiv, 33; on school board, 171-176, 185, 204, 210, 212, 233-234, 265; sketch of the Elms (Natchez), 215n39; as painter, xiv; reporting the temperature, xviii; resignations of, 212, 244, 248; at St. Paul's College, xiv, 34; at St. Thomas Hall, xiv, 34; at Seamen's Home, 139-140, 145, 148; siblings of, 34; and slow progress on Custom House, 41n61; as superintendent of Custom House, xviii, 240-241, 246, 247, 250, 253; and Swiss bell ringers, 244; teaching positions of, xiv; and University at Holly Springs, Miss., xiv-xv, 34; and University of the South at Sewanee, 222, 222n11, 225, 234, 235, 235n34; vacations of, xvii, 1, 1n1, 206-208, 210; writings of, 41, 100, 128, 128n41, 190, 190n5. *See also* specific buildings
Wharton, Thomas Prescott: at art exhibits, 152, 153; and Bell crevasse viewing, 160, 163; birth of, xvi, 2n5, 36; birthday of, 145; career of, xix; childhood entertainment, 84, 188; Christmas celebrations of, 59, 107, 129, 215, 264; church attendance of, 55, 89, 144, 202, 222; at *Cinderella*, 222; at circus, 133, 193, 237; and Clay monument, 227; at concerts, 231; and daguerreotypes, 80, 143; death of, 2n5; and explosion of Marine Hospital, 266; and explosion of *Virginia* steamboat, 174; and family outings, 25, 44-45, 97, 102, 110, 117, 202, 238, 254, 268; on ferry, 266; on floating battery, 261; in French Quarter, 154; at funerals, 256; health of, 93, 144, 182, 183; inspecting Union gunboats, 272; at Leeds & Co., 262, 266; at library, 178, 224, 256; literacy of, 14, 181, 230; at Lower Cotton Press, 200; and Mardi Gras, 154, 196, 219; at market, 143, 187, 268; marriage of, xix, 2n5; at mayor's receptions, 190; on mother, 214; at museum, 136; and New Year's jubilee, 61; at orphan's home fair, 227; at panopticon exhibits, 231; and panoramas, 224; parties attended, 140, 217; relationship with father, 115, 117, 146, 150, 210, 247, 253, 254, 256, 258, 261, 264; and stereoscopes, 155; teething of, 32; and Thanksgiving Day, 187; tools for, 188, 264; visit to Natchez, 206; visits to Custom House, 58, 110, 145, 152, 157, 161, 225, 256, 261, 262, 275;

weaning of, 10; and weddings, 234; and yellow fever, 182, 183, 185, 212
Wharton house: description of, xvi, **1n3**; furniture for, 51; gas chandeliers in, 263; illustrations of, *xxviii, plates 3, 9*; improvements of, 22, 40, 146; initial occupation of, xvi; leasing of, 47, 80, 124; rental price, 4, 47; repairs to, 47, 117; roofing of, 49; sale of, 17, 117
Wheeler, J. F., 139, **139n17**, 185
Whig Party, 104n50
White, Mr., 124, 126
White, Thomas L. (bookseller), 188, **188n65**; advertisement, *188*
Whitehead, W. B., 154, **154n8**, 156, 163, 193, 193n10, 214, 225; and warehouse of , 156, 171, 172
Whitney, J. H., 48
Wilkinson, Joseph Biddle, 244, **244n1**
Williams, Frank, 253
Williamson, Nathaniel, 148n44
Wing, Frederick, 174, **174n39**, 176, 177
Winter, J. L., 74, **74n18**
Wood, Alexander Thompson: and Custom House, xv, 9n9, **48n73**, 73, 241; death of, 48, 48n76; discharged from Custom House project, xvi; and Florance House Hotel, 131n1; marriages of, xvii, 48n73; and New Orleans Architects Company, 49n77; and Reid house, 133, 202n19; Wharton hired by, xvi
Wood, Phoenix N., 222, **222n12**, 231
Wood, Thompson Mallory, 48n73
Wood, William B., 182, **182n55**, 212, 212n32
Wray (James) house, *plate 9*
Wright, John, xvii, 236, **236n39**; Wright (John) & Co., 236, 236n39
Wright's, Miss Sophie B., Home Institute, 192n6

Yancey, William Lowndes, 236, **236n37**
Yellow fever: and black vomit, 84, 84n26, 177; and blockade of Mississippi River, 256; in Cuba, 41, 84; at Custom House, 44, 47, 183, 185; epidemic of 1837, 42n64; epidemic of 1853, xvii, 2, *2*, 2n6, *41*, 57, 58, *58*, 58n93, 103, 116; epidemic of 1854, 51; epidemic of 1855, 103; epidemic of 1858, 175, 176; and frost, 52; illustrations of, *174, 177*; and immigrants, 88, 102, 120; mortality rates for, 38, 38n55, 41, 48, 59, 97, 102, 103, 104, 146, 171, 174, 176, 177, 178, 179-180, 182, 183, 184, 185, 214, 235; mosquitoes and, 51n81; and Pass Christian, 102, 102n45; and quarantine, 23, 145; and sanitary conditions, 10n11, 48, 58n93; statistics on, 38, 38n55, 47, 49, 233; theories of origin of, 57-58; traced to shipping, 88
Young , Ammi Burnham, 9, **9n4**, 17n19, 136n7, 137, 138
Young, George B., Jr., 4, **4n12**, 164, 227, 236